Praise for *The Idea of America*

"Gordon S. Wood is more than an American historian. He is almost an American institution. Of all the many teachers and writers of history in this republic, few are held in such high esteem. . . . The strength of Wood's scholarship derives from qualities of caution, balance, and restraint that are uniquely his own."

—David Hackett Fischer, *The New York Times Book Review*

"Mr. Wood is our premier student of the Founding era. He has been writing history for about a half-century, roughly a fifth of the days since the origin of the republic. He has scrupulously avoided appropriating his subject for modern-day political purposes and instead tried to understand it on its own terms and as a whole. Historians will of course bring to their study certain questions and concerns of their own time—no one can or should avoid this—but the greatest historians are those, like Mr. Wood, who do not make our criteria of importance the main theme. . . . It is Mr. Wood's most 'personal' work, providing us, along with much fine history, glimpses into the thinker and the man."   —*The Wall Street Journal*

"Exceptional . . . This is a remarkable study of the key chapter of American history and its ongoing influence on American character."

—*Publishers Weekly* (starred review)

"Wood . . . has long been recognized as one of the preeminent historians of the era of the American Revolution. In this series of cogent, beautifully written essays, Wood repeats some of his familiar themes, but they are well worth revisiting."   —*Booklist* (starred review)

"[*The Idea of America*] represent[s] the incredible range of this eminent scholar's contributions to the historiography of the Revolutionary era. . . . Intellectually expansive and elegantly woven, Wood's writings are the closest thing we have to an elegant mediation between today's readers and the founding generation. Required reading for Revolutionary War enthusiasts on all levels."   —*Library Journal*

PENGUIN BOOKS

THE IDEA OF AMERICA

Gordon S. Wood is the Alva O. Way University Professor Emeritus at Brown University. His 1969 book, *The Creation of the American Republic, 1776–1787*, received the Bancroft and John H. Dunning prizes and was nominated for the National Book Award. His 1992 book, *The Radicalism of the American Revolution*, won the Pulitzer Prize and the Emerson Prize. His 2009 book, *Empire of Liberty: A History of the Early Republic, 1789–1815*, won the New-York Historical Society Prize in American History. In 2011 Wood was awarded a National Humanities Medal by President Obama. Wood contributes regularly to the *New Republic* and the *New York Review of Books*.

THE IDEA OF AMERICA

Reflections on the Birth of the United States

GORDON S. WOOD

PENGUIN BOOKS

PENGUIN BOOKS

Published by the Penguin Group

Penguin Group (USA) Inc., 375 Hudson Street, New York, New York 10014, U.S.A. • Penguin Group (Canada), 90 Eglinton Avenue East, Suite 700, Toronto, Ontario, Canada M4P 2Y3 (a division of Pearson Penguin Canada Inc.) • Penguin Books Ltd, 80 Strand, London WC2R 0RL, England • Penguin Ireland, 25 St. Stephen's Green, Dublin 2, Ireland (a division of Penguin Books Ltd) • Penguin Books Australia Ltd, 250 Camberwell Road, Camberwell, Victoria 3124, Australia (a division of Pearson Australia Group Pty Ltd) • Penguin Books India Pvt Ltd, 11 Community Centre, Panchsheel Park, New Delhi – 110 017, India • Penguin Group (NZ), 67 Apollo Drive, Rosedale, Auckland 0632, New Zealand (a division of Pearson New Zealand Ltd) • Penguin Books (South Africa) (Pty) Ltd, 24 Sturdee Avenue, Rosebank, Johannesburg 2196, South Africa

Penguin Books Ltd, Registered Offices: 80 Strand, London WC2R 0RL, England

First published in the United States of America by The Penguin Press,
a member of Penguin Group (USA) Inc. 2011
Published in Penguin Books 2012

5   7   9   10   8   6

THE LIBRARY OF CONGRESS HAS CATALOGED THE HARDCOVER EDITION AS FOLLOWS:
Wood, Gordon S.
The idea of America : reflections on the birth of the United States / Gordon S. Wood.
p. cm.
Includes bibliographical references and index.
ISBN 978-1-59420-290-2 (hc.)
ISBN 978-0-14-312124-4 (pbk.)
1. United States—History—Revolution, 1775–1783—Influence.   2. United States—Politics and government—1775–1783.   3. United States—Politics and government—1783–1809.   4. United States. Constitution.   5. Democracy—United States.   6. Republicanism—United States.   I. Title.
E302.1.W77 2011
973.3—dc22   2010045829

Printed in the United States of America
Designed by Marysarah Quinn

To my friends and colleagues
at Brown University

CONTENTS

THE IDEA OF AMERICA

INTRODUCTION

WELL OVER A HALF CENTURY ago Isaiah Berlin published a little book entitled *The Hedgehog and the Fox: An Essay on Tolstoy's View of History*. He borrowed his title from a line among the fragments of the Greek poet Archilochus which says, "The fox knows many things, but the hedgehog knows one big thing." Berlin interpreted the words broadly and found in them one of the deepest differences that divide writers and thinkers and perhaps even human beings in general. On one side of this chasm, wrote Berlin, were the foxes, "who pursue many ends, often unrelated and even contradictory, connected, if at all, only in some de facto way, for psychological or physiological cause, related by no moral or aesthetic principle." On the other side were the hedgehogs, "who relate everything to a single central vision, one system less or more coherent or articulate, in terms of which they understand, think and feel—a single, universal, organizing principle in terms of which alone all that they are and say has significance."

So in this scheme of things Berlin labels Dante as a hedgehog and Shakespeare as a fox. "Plato, Lucretius, Pascal, Hegel, Dostoevsky, Nietzsche, Ibsen, Proust are, in varying degrees, hedgehogs; Herodotus, Aristotle, Montaigne, Erasmus, Molière, Goethe, Pushkin, Balzac, Joyce are foxes."[1]

Although Berlin was interested mainly in placing great writers into one or another of these two categories, one might do the same with more mundane historians. There are historians who work on many different subjects, jumping from topic to topic as their various interests lead them. I have a remarkable colleague who began with a study of Congress in the 1930s, and followed that by an analysis of the impact of the New Deal on the states. Then, after he had written an impressive biography of an important politician of the 1940s and early 1950s, he wrote an extraordinary book on America's struggle with poverty in the twentieth century. This work was followed by a fascinating history of cancer in modern American culture, which in turn was succeeded by an examination of an important Supreme Court decision of the 1950s. At the same time, this colleague was writing a huge narrative account of twentieth-century America and a prize-winning book on the decades in America following World War II. Even now he is on to brand-new subjects in modern America.

This colleague of mine is a fox and a superb one. He knows many things and is interested in many things. He even once said to me as he was casting about for a new subject to write about that if I had any ideas for him to please let him know.

By contrast, as a historian I fear I am a simple hedgehog. Throughout my career I have been most interested in the American Revolution and the political, social, and cultural changes that it engendered. Of course, I have taught university lecture courses that ranged from Columbus to the Jacksonian era and have led seminars on various topics. But nearly all of my publications have dealt with the American Revolution and its consequences. In addition to several books on the Revolution and its leaders, I have published a number of articles on the Revolutionary era, some of which are collected in this book.

My preoccupation with the Revolution comes from my belief that it is the most important event in American history, bar none. Not only did the Revolution legally create the United States, but it infused into our culture all of our highest aspirations and noblest values. Our beliefs in liberty, equality, constitutionalism, and the well-being of ordinary people came out of the Revolutionary era. So too did our idea that we Americans are a special people with a special destiny to lead the world toward liberty and democracy. The Revolution, in short, gave birth to whatever sense of nationhood and national purpose we Americans have had.

Establishing their nationhood was not easy for the Revolutionaries, as my essay on "The American Enlightenment" in this volume attempts to show. Americans knew that they were not yet a nation, at least not a nation in the European sense of the term. Since the identity of the United States as a nation remains unusually fluid and elusive, we Americans have had to look back repeatedly to the Revolution and the Founding (as we call it) in order to know who we are. We go back to the Revolution and the values and institutions that came out of it in order to refresh and reaffirm our nationhood. That for me is why the Revolutionary era remains so significant.

ALTHOUGH I HAVE BEEN WORKING on the Revolutionary era for my entire career, I don't now conceive of it in the same way as I did a half century ago. Like most other graduate students in the country in the early 1960s, I was trained to think of early American history as the period from the initial settlements in the seventeenth century to the establishment of the Constitution in 1787–1788. Specializing in the several decades following 1789 meant that one was not a colonial-Revolutionary historian but an early national historian. One specialized either in the colonial-Revolutionary period or in the early decades of the national period, but not in both. If colonial-Revolutionary historians did happen to spill over into the 1790s, they tended to see those years as the culmination of what had gone on before—the eighteenth century and the Revolution.

Early national historians who began their teaching and research on the 1790s not only rarely looked back to the colonial or Revolutionary periods but generally tended to look ahead to the Civil War or to the urbanization and industrialization that essentially occurred after the 1820s. So they often treated the period between 1789 and the 1820s as a prelude to what was really important to them in the nineteenth century. Consequently, graduate students in the 1960s who wished to study the early decades of the nation's history were apt to fall between two specializations of the historical profession. Colonial-Revolutionary historians knew the period only as an epilogue; early national historians knew it only as a prologue. Neither group saw it in its own right.

Thus I began my teaching in the 1960s thinking of myself as exclusively a colonial-Revolutionary historian. I taught a two-semester course, with one semester dealing with the colonial period up to 1760 and a second dealing with the Revolutionary period from 1760 to 1788. But since my university had no history course covering the period from 1789 to the age of Jackson, I began to feel obliged to offer such a course. The experience in the 1970s of organizing a course on this period was eye-opening and ultimately very rewarding.

When I first began exploring the period, I was surprised by the nature of the historical scholarship on these decades following the creation of the Constitution. It didn't seem to treat the period as seriously as I had expected; indeed, as historian James H. Broussard, who founded the Society for the History of the Early American Republic (SHEAR) in the late 1970s and almost single-handedly revived interest in the period, once pointed out, it was "often treated almost as a backwater of historical scholarship."[2] There were, of course, many good books and articles, especially biographies of the great men and the not-so-great men of the Revolutionary era. Mammoth editing projects promising to publish virtually everything written to and by each of the major Founders had been launched and were well along. Some works of scholarship—for example, a study of racial attitudes of early white Americans and an analysis of the Massachusetts Federalists—were truly outstanding, but they remained isolated and unconnected to any overall interpretation of the period.[3] Despite publications like these, the early decades of America's history seemed to lack what Broussard called an "organizing theme." All kinds of labels and books flew about, but, as Broussard lamented, the problem was "how to group them together in a meaningful whole."[4]

In the early 1960s the origins of political parties had attracted some scholarly interest, but they did little to invigorate the period. Political scientists and political sociologists like William Nisbet Chambers and Seymour Martin Lipset were not really interested in the history of the 1790s per se but instead in the conditions out of which political structures and political parties were created. They wanted to form generalizations about politics that were applicable to their present. Thus the United States became the "first new nation" and the conflict between the Federalists and the Jeffersonian Republicans became the "first party system"—object lessons for the newly developing and ex-colonial nations of the 1950s and 1960s.[5] Consequently, these political scientists were not always sensitive to the differentness of the past, and in their works they often left readers with a very unhistorical and anachronistic view of America's political parties in the 1790s.

All in all, the lack of any comprehensive synthesis of the period seemed to have given the decades of early national history a reputation for dreariness and insignificance. It seemed to be the most boring part of American history to study and teach.[6]

This was baffling to me. After all, the decades between 1789 and the 1820s seemed to have an immediate and palpable importance for all Americans. Not only was the period dominated by some of the greatest and most heroic figures in American history (Washington, Hamilton, Adams, Madison, Jefferson, and Marshall), but during these decades Americans established their political institutions—the presidency, the Congress, the Supreme Court—and created both political parties and modern democratic politics. Indeed, so much of political significance occurred in this period of the early Republic that the historians' neglect of it was puzzling.

After much pondering, I concluded that historians themselves had created the problem. The so-called consensus interpretation of American history that dominated what has been called the "golden age" of historical writing in the 1950s and early 1960s was responsible for the diminished respect accorded the period of the early Republic.[7] In fact, those historians who had written in the aftermath of World War II had effectively destroyed the dominant synthesis of the period created in the first half of the twentieth century and had not put anything else in its place.

During the first half of the twentieth century the Progressive generation of historians—those professional historians whose assumptions about reality came out of the Progressive era at the beginning of the twentieth century—not only had an overarching scheme for understanding the early Republic, but also had a special fascination for this period. Although the Progressive historians offered a framework for understanding all of American history, it was the period of the early Republic— from the Revolution to the age of Jackson—that particularly interested them. All the giants among them—Carl Becker, Charles Beard, Arthur Schlesinger Sr., Vernon Parrington—tackled problems in this period and felt most at home in this period. Even Frederick Jackson Turner thought his "frontier thesis" had a special applicability to the half century following the Revolution. The early Republic seemed to be the natural arena for demonstrating the truth of the Progressive historians' interpretation of American history.[8]

These historians tended to see American history as full of conflicts, especially conflicts between a populist majority, usually agrarian, and a narrow aristocratic or business minority. According to these historians, the Revolution and the early Republic were essentially characterized by the seesawing struggle between these two groups. The aristocratic and merchant interests of the 1760s lost control of the resistance movement to more popular and radical elements who moved America into revolution. By the 1780s, however, the conservative and mercantile interests had reasserted themselves to the point where they were able to write the new federal Constitution of 1787. Charles Beard's provocative book *An Economic Interpretation of the Constitution* (1913) became the linchpin of this Progressive interpretation. These historians saw the 1790s as a continuation of the struggle between the commercial interests led by Alexander Hamilton and the popular agrarian and artisanal forces led by Thomas Jefferson.

With Jefferson's election in 1800, the popular agrarian majorities finally came into their own. The next two or three decades saw the relentless emergence of the "common man" in American history. The last remnants of the colonial ancien régime were cast aside or destroyed. The churches were disestablished, the suffrage gates were opened, and the clamoring populace rushed to the polls and overthrew the commercial aristocracy, at least outside the South. The entire struggle climaxed with the election of Andrew Jackson, marking the completion of the unfinished business of the Revolution.

It was a powerful interpretative framework. It accommodated a wide variety of facts, and it was simple enough to be applied by hosts of student disciples. No wonder that some of the best and most durable monographs on the period, particularly the histories of states, have been written by followers of the Progressive historians. All had similar titles and themes, and all described political developments in terms of "from aristocracy to democracy."[9]

This Progressive paradigm dominated historical writing about America's past during the first half of the twentieth century. But in the years following World War II, this interpretative framework was assaulted from a hundred different directions and dismantled by a thousand different monographs. Book after book, article after article in the 1950s and 1960s ate away at every aspect of the Progressive explanation of America's past. In this rich and flourishing period of American history writing, often labeled the era of "consensus" history, the Progressive interpretation that had featured social conflicts in America's past was replaced by one that emphasized the similarity and like-mindedness of all Americans. This destruction of the Progressive interpretation affected all aspects and all eras of American history, but it affected the period of the early Republic the most.

The 1950s and 1960s assault on the Progressive understanding of the early Republic took the form of denying the extent of change that had taken place in the period. Colonial America, it appeared from a number of consensus studies, was not an ancien régime after all. Since roughly 60 percent of adult white males in the colonial period could legally vote, the high suffrage barriers that the Progressive historians had posited turned out to be not so high after all. The churches in the eighteenth century were already weak and did not much need disestablishment. The aristocracy that existed was hardly an aristocracy by European standards and scarcely required elimination. All in all, colonial Americans did not have much to revolt against; their revolution seemed to be essentially a mental shift, an intellectual adjustment to what had already taken place over the previous century or more. The Americans were born free and equal and thus, as Tocqueville had written, did not have to become so. The American Revolution therefore became a peculiarly conservative affair, an endorsement and realization, not a transformation, of the society.[10]

As early American historians were reinterpreting the colonial period, other historians were reevaluating the Jacksonian era. Not only did it now appear that the Jacksonians had less unfinished business to deal with than historians used to think, but Jacksonian society seemed less egalitarian and less democratic than earlier historians had believed. The distribution of wealth in the 1820s and 1830s was more unequal than it had been earlier in the century; indeed, some studies showed that the distribution of wealth after the Revolution was more unequal than in the colonial period. Some historians even suggested that the age of Jackson ought to be called "the era of the uncommon man."[11]

Thus it seemed that no democratic Jacksonian revolution had occurred after all. It was hard to see much difference between the Democratic and Whig parties. As historians Richard Hofstadter and Bray Hammond emphasized, both parties were composed of men on the make; certainly they did not stand for coherent social classes in conflict.[12] Nearly everyone in the North, at least, seemed to belong to the middle class. America was liberal and individualistic to its toes, and, according to Louis Hartz, whose 1955 book *The Liberal Tradition in America* epitomized the so-called consensus interpretation of the post–World War II decades, it had been so from the very beginning of its history.[13]

These attacks on the Progressive paradigm affected all periods of America's past, but they especially ravaged the period between the

Revolution and the age of Jackson, for the Progressive interpretation really had its heart and soul in these decades of the early Republic. If the Progressive interpretation was true anywhere, the Progressive historians believed, it was true there in the early Republic. This, after all, was the time when the conservative European-like aristocratic forces were supposed to have been finally shattered, when American democracy was first established, and when modern American liberalism was born.

But if this were not truly the case, if Revolutionary Americans were in fact already free and equal and did not have to experience a democratic revolution, then what significance could this period of the early Republic have? According to the findings of the consensus historians of the 1950s and 1960s, the period was not formative after all. The Progressive historians had been wrong about it; and with the collapse of their interpretative framework, the period of the early Republic on which they had rested so much of their case sank into insignificance.

By the time I began putting my course on the early Republic together in the 1970s, there were some tentative efforts to reinvigorate the period and to see it whole. Some historians tried to apply the social science concept of "modernization" to the period. But, as often happens, historians began using the concept just as it was going out of fashion among social scientists. Thus the effort died aborning, and much of the scholarship of the period remained diffuse and unconnected, without compelling significance.[14]

One of the problems faced in the 1970s by historians who were trying to deal with the period of the early Republic was the overriding dominance of politics and the presence of so many heroic political figures, such as Washington, Hamilton, and Jefferson. By writing so many biographies of these great men and thus describing the early Republic mainly in terms of the actions of great individual political leaders, historians tended to fragment our understanding of the period. Moreover, political events and political institutions in general tended to overwhelm the period and prevent historians who wished to write about other things from having much breathing room. With the establishment of America's political institutions, a major rebellion, crises of various sorts, crucial elections, the beginnings of judicial review, the use of economic sanctions as an alternative to war, and a war itself, the period is full of what might be called headline events. Indeed, there is probably no period of American history that has more of these headline events concerning politics and diplomacy than the early Republic.[15]

Unfortunately, the new generation of historians coming of age in the late 1960s and early 1970s did not want to write about great headline political events. The social and cultural history they were interested in tended to deal with impersonal long-term developments. Such new history might involve changing demographic patterns over several generations or shifting attitudes toward childhood or death. The early Republic was probably the period of American history least receptive to treatment by these new social and cultural historians. Its extraordinary number of major political and diplomatic happenings tended to inhibit social and cultural studies that sought to sweep through decades and ignore prominent individuals and national elections in favor of statistical aggregates and long-term mentalities. Unlike the colonial period, when there were no presidents and congressional elections and very few headline events, the early Republic seemed to be an unattractive place for the new social and cultural history.

Yet in the end it was the new social and cultural historians themselves who helped revive interest in the early Republic. It was they who first began conceiving of the Revolutionary era in the most comprehensive manner and began knitting together the two periods that hitherto had been separated from one another: the colonial-Revolutionary era and the early Republic. In the late 1970s and the 1980s they wrote increasing numbers of broad social and cultural histories that ranged in time from the middle or last quarter of the eighteenth century to the early decades of the nineteenth century. These included impressive works on women and the family, the emerging professions, the decline of apprenticeship, the rise of statistics, the creation of common schools, the spread of alcohol drinking, the transformation of artisans, the emergence of capitalism, the change in urban mobs, the experience of the native Indians, the development of slavery and antislavery, and the emergence of the postal system. New studies of law were less interested in the decisions of the Marshall Court and more concerned with the long-term relationship between law and society. Indeed, even the most seemingly insignificant subjects—log construction in Ohio from 1750 to 1840, for example—were worthy of histories as long as they covered a long enough period of time.[16]

Not only did these social and cultural historians, together with the formation of SHEAR and the *Journal of the Early Republic*, help turn the early Republic into one of the most exciting and vibrant fields of American history writing, but they created new ways of dating developments—such as from 1750 to 1820, or 1780 to 1840—that ignored or transcended the traditional periodization that had used prominent political events to separate one era from another.[17] Within these new and broader perspectives, the Revolution, when it was mentioned at all, became merely a political event expressive of wide-ranging social and cultural changes that took longer than a decade to work out. I came to believe that this new periodization marked a radical and rewarding change in American historiography.

It certainly had a powerful effect on my understanding of early America, and I began to think of the Revolution in new ways—not as a political event that could be confined to the period between 1763 and 1787 but one with great social and cultural significance that ran from at least the middle of the eighteenth century to the early decades of the nineteenth.

When I began studying and teaching both the colonial era and the early Republic up to the Jacksonian era, I was increasingly struck by how different the two periods were from one another politically, socially, and culturally. I became convinced that more had changed between 1760 and 1820 than the "consensus" historians of the 1950s had allowed. I began to suspect that the old Progressive historians had been more right than not in their interpretation of the Revolution and its consequences. Colonial society appeared to me much more of an ancien régime than the "consensus" historians had thought. It was certainly not quite the ancien régime that the Progressives had described—of rigid classes, legally restricted voting, and rich, exploitative merchants—but it was not the liberal, egalitarian, democratic society of Tocqueville's America either.

Colonial society seemed to me to be hierarchical and patriarchal, a society generally organized vertically, not horizontally, and tied together by kinship and patron-client relations. Some of this traditional, hierarchical, small-scale eighteenth-century world survived the Revolution, but not much, at least not in the North. Many of the new social and cultural studies of the 1970s and 1980s, especially those having to do with economic developments, tended to stress the fundamental differences between the old aristocratic pre-Revolutionary society and the new bumptious popular commercial society that emerged in the nineteenth century. Studies of mid-eighteenth-century farm families in New England suggested their almost medieval-like practices and outlooks; they were portrayed as patriarchal communities concerned with patrimony and kin and resembling nothing like the brash capitalistic world of the early Republic. America, it seemed, was not born liberal after all, but became so in the decades following the Revolution.[18]

With this new understanding in hand, I tried to express these changes that had taken place between the mid-eighteenth century and the early decades of the nineteenth century. In effect, I hoped to create a more refined, more complicated, and more nuanced version of the old Progressive interpretation of the Revolution and the early Republic. I sought to recover the social conflict that had taken place—not quite the conflict the Progressive historians had emphasized, but a social conflict nonetheless. My theme became essentially the same as the Progressive historians' theme: the change from aristocracy to democracy.

By seeking to write a more subtle version of the Progressive historians' interpretation of the Revolution and early Republic, I hoped to improve upon that interpretation in two important respects. First, I wanted to emphasize the importance of ideas in the historical process—something the Progressive historians, in their preoccupation with economic and other underlying interests, had tended to belittle. And second, I wanted to avoid the partiality that plagued their histories, a partiality that was prompted by the need to find antecedents for the divisions of their own time.

As I point out in the opening essay, "Rhetoric and Reality in the American Revolution," the Progressive historians generally had considered ideas to be manipulated entities, rationalizations or propaganda, mere epiphenomenal coverings for the underlying and determinative social reality. I thought they were wrong to conceive of ideas in this way. Without denying the importance of the underlying social reality, I wanted in my own work to write history that gave a proper place to the significance of ideas and to escape from the polarities that have plagued the historical profession. As historian Daniel T. Rodgers has reminded us, many of the debates historians have with one another have long been "reflexively dualistic: ideas versus behavior; rhetoric versus 'the concrete realities of life'; propaganda and mystification on the one hand, the real stuff on the other."[19] I wanted to avoid these false dichotomies and see events like the Revolution or the making of the Constitution from both sides, both the intellectual and the social—in other words, to see events whole.

Although I have most often written about ideas, I have never assumed that ideas were the driving force explaining social change. As I tried to make clear in my "Rhetoric and Reality" essay of 1966, I have never believed that any event as momentous as the Revolution could be explained solely by the ideas of the participants. Ideas are important, but they ought never be set in opposition to economic interests as "causes" of human action. In fact, I do not believe that ideas "cause" human behavior. I am with David Hume in holding that passions, not reason, are the ruling element in all human action. T. H. Breen, in a recent book on the Revolution, has rightly emphasized this point. Of course, he writes, the American Revolutionaries had ideas. "But these were ideas driven by immediate passions; they were amplified through fear, fury, and resentment."[20]

There are always forces larger than reason driving events, and I have indicated as much many times in my writings. I had a section on "Whig

Resentment" in my first book, *The Creation of the American Republic, 1776–1787*, and in my subsequent work I have always emphasized the underlying importance of structural forces—demographic, economic, and social changes—in accounting for the various expressions of ideas, including the periodic eruptions of religious enthusiasm.

In much of my work I have concentrated on ideas simply because I find them more interesting to write about than economic behavior and not because I believe they are a more important cause of events. As I suggested in my essay "Interests and Disinterestedness in the Making of the Constitution," for example, economic interests of various sorts may have been crucially important in creating the Constitution.

Explaining human behavior is complicated, and the notion of "cause" is not very helpful. In fact, as I try to indicate in my essay entitled "Conspiracy and the Paranoid Style," I think it is difficult, if not impossible, to apply the physical notion of "cause" to human action. Ideas do not "cause" people to act. Even if they did, historians would never be able to prove it; all they could do is multiply their citations of the documents in which ideas were expressed and stress their conviction that the historical participants were really sincere when they said they acted out of principles of republicanism or the public good. But hard-nosed realists like the twentieth-century historians Charles Beard and Sir Lewis Namier will simply smile knowingly at the naivety of those who would make ideas the cause of behavior and inform them of how little they know about the "real" world of human experience. Indeed, all that we have learned about the psychology and sociology of human behavior during the past century suggests that the realists are right and that the simple-minded notion that people's professed beliefs—"no taxation without representation" or "devotion to our country"—are the motives for their behavior will never be persuasive. The tough-minded realists will always tell us otherwise, will tell us, in Namier's words, that "what matters most is the underlying emotions, the music, to which ideas are a mere libretto, often of a very inferior quality."[21]

Such realists or materialists—that is, the Progressive historians—may be right that ideas do not "cause" behavior, but it does not follow that ideas are unimportant and have little or no effect on behavior, or that they can be treated as just one "factor" that now and then comes into play in human experience. Otherwise we would not spend so much time and energy arguing about ideas. I think it is possible to concede the realist or materialist position—that passions and interests lie behind all our behavior—without deprecating the role of ideas. Even if ideas are not the underlying motives for our actions, they are constant accompaniments of our actions. There is no behavior without ideas, without language. Ideas and language give meaning to our actions, and there is almost nothing that we humans do to which we do not attribute meaning. These meanings constitute our ideas, our beliefs, our ideology, and collectively our culture. As we have learned from both "the linguistic turn" and "the cultural turn" over the past several decades, our minds are essential to the ordering of our experience.

Elite and popular thinking are of a piece in this ordering of our experience. One of the great contributions that the so-called cultural turn has made to recent historiography has been to bring high intellectual life, the so-called classic texts, down to the level of the general culture. It turns out that when we thoroughly contextualize the thinking or the texts of the likes of Locke, Montesquieu, or James Madison, we find that they were expressing ideas that grew out of and had great resonance in the culture of their time and place. Others were saying similar things but not as elegantly, not as pointedly, not as persuasively as they were. If they were not products of their society and culture and speaking directly to that society and culture, they, like Giambattista Vico earlier in the eighteenth century, would have been ignored, not listened to. Elite thinkers, in other words, are only refined extensions of other more popular thinkers in the culture, and, like ordinary thinkers, they have to be understood in relation to the context—the cultural and social circumstances—of their time.

Culture and society are not really separate entities. Because human behavior is of a piece with the meanings or ideas we give to it, our ideas do not exist apart from social circumstances or some more real world of economic behavior. Hence it is foolish to try to divide up historical explanations for events such as the Revolution or the making of the Constitution into "ideological" or "economic" schools. Ideas are essential to our experience. They are the means by which we perceive, understand, rationalize, judge, and manipulate our actions. The meanings that we give to our actions form the structure of our social world. Ideas or meanings make social behavior not just comprehensible but possible. We really cannot act unless we make our actions meaningful, unless we can find words that justify, legitimate, or explain our actions.

Of course, we are not free at any moment to give whatever meaning we wish to our behavior. This is where the Progressive historians went wrong. Ideas are not the easily manipulated entities they thought they were; ideas are not mere propaganda. We cannot simply create new words or a new language to justify and explain our actions. The words we use, the meanings we give to our behavior, are public ones, and they are defined and limited by the conventions and the available normative language of the culture of the time. Since democracy, for example, is highly valued in our society, we often try to label some controversial action we wish to engage in as "democratic." But if we are unable to convince most people of our attributed meaning, then those who oppose our action or behavior as undemocratic win the intellectual debate, and we are inhibited in behaving in an undemocratic manner.

It is in this sense that culture—the collection of meanings available to us—both limits and creates behavior. It does so by forcing us to describe our actions in its terms. The definitions and meanings that we seek to give to our behavior cannot be bizarre or arbitrary; they have to be to some extent acceptable to the culture, to be part of the culture. Our actions thus are meaningful only publicly, only with respect to an inherited system of conventions and values. What is "liberal" or "tyrannical," "democratic" or "aristocratic," is determined by this cultural structure of meanings.

Our intellectual life is made up of struggles over getting people to accept different meanings of our experiences—in effect, trying to change the culture. The stakes are always high because actions that we cannot make meaningful—cannot conceive of, rationalize, legitimate, or persuade other people to accept—we in some sense cannot undertake. What is permissible culturally affects what is permissible socially or politically, so that although ideas may not be the motives for behavior (underlying interests and passions are the real motives), ideas do affect and limit behavior. They are not mere superstructure or epiphenomena.[22]

Indeed, once a new idea is expressed and becomes reasonably acceptable to many people, it can spawn new and sometimes unexpected behavior. When Alexander Hamilton, in *The Federalist* No. 78, suggested that judges were as much agents of the people as were the members of the state legislatures (a point developed in this collection of essays), he was only trying to find a novel justification for the judicial review of legislation. But others soon picked up Hamilton's suggestion and began running with it. Before long some polemicists were arguing that if the judges were in fact a kind of representative of the people, then maybe the people ought to elect them. And sure enough this began to happen in the Jacksonian era; today, as I indicate in my essay on American constitutionalism, some thirty-nine states elect their judges in one way or another. This was a development that Hamilton could never have imagined and would have been appalled by, yet he helped to produce it. In our efforts to make new behavior meaningful, we create all sorts of unanticipated consequences.

This is certainly what happened with the arguments of the Federalists in 1787–1788. They were faced with the difficult task of justifying their new and strong national government in the face of both deeply rooted American fears of far-removed central power and the traditional theory that held that republics had to be small in size and homogeneous in character. Their opponents in the debate, the Anti-Federalists (the very name foisted on them suggests the polemical effectiveness of the Federalists), thought that the Constitution was an aristocratic and undemocratic document designed to limit certain popular pressures on government. They had considerable evidence to support their position; they had, in other words, many inherited meanings drawn from past Whig experience in the British Empire that made distant centralized power dangerous, and they made a persuasive case that the Constitution was a consolidated and an elitist threat to popular liberty.

If the Federalists were to combat these arguments and convince people that the new expanded federal government was thoroughly republican and not a threat to liberty, they would have to find new meanings for old words and somehow not repudiate the Americans' long-existing Whig experience with power and liberty. In the debates over ratification of the Constitution, they were extraordinarily successful in exploiting the old idea of separation of powers in new ways and in giving a novel twist to the conventional meaning of sovereignty by locating it in the people. Yet by using the popular and democratic rhetoric that had emerged in the polemics of the previous decade to justify the aristocratic and expanded republic created by the Constitution, the Federalists created consequences they never intended. Their concessions to popular sovereignty and their many new democratic ideas were now on the table to be taken up and used by others in new ways. The Anti-Federalists may have lost the battle over the Constitution, but during the subsequent generation they essentially won the war over the character of the new nation.

When confronted with this 1787–1788 debate over the "aristocratic" and "democratic" nature of the Constitution, historians are not supposed to decide which was more "correct" or more "true." The historians' task, rather, is to explain the reasons for these contrasting meanings and why each side should have attempted to give to the Constitution the meanings it did. There was not in 1787–1788 one "correct" or "true" meaning of the Constitution. The Constitution meant whatever the Federalists or the Anti-Federalists could convince the country to accept. That is why the debate over the Constitution was so important.

I wish we could avoid the polarization of interpretations—setting those that are "ideological" against those that are "economic"—that seems to afflict the historical profession and instead try to explain events of the past in their entirety, from the top down as well as from the bottom up. Of course, the past is so complicated that there will always be disagreement over historians' varying perceptions of it. Despite the fact that we collectively know much more now about the origins of the Revolution and the writing of the Constitution than Charles Beard and the other Progressive historians ever did, no single historian can know everything; thus the debates over our various historical explanations for the Founding or any other great event in our past will never cease.

IN ADDITION TO EMPHASIZING the importance of ideas in past behavior, I wanted my revisionist interpretation of the Progressive approach to the Revolution and the early Republic to avoid what I took to be the partisanship and one-sidedness of their interpretation. The partiality of the Progressive historians came out of their experience at the beginning of the twentieth century. Disgusted with the way the big corporations and the robber barons were exploiting the farmers and working people of their own time, they were naturally biased against Alexander Hamilton and the Federalists, whom they assumed were the progenitors of this despicable business world. They thus made Jefferson their hero; he was the one who led all the ordinary working people of the Democratic-Republican Party against those whom the popular historian of the 1920s Claude G. Bowers called "the rich, the powerful, and their retainers" in whose "drawing room were heard the sentiments of Chambers of Commerce—in glorification of materialism."[23] Unfortunately, too much of our history writing tends to take sides in this gross manner, crudely reading back into the past the issues of the present.

We have a somewhat different present now from that of a century ago. Class struggles against the rich and powerful still preoccupy many scholars, but in many cases their anticapitalist concerns have been supplanted by issues of race and gender. This in turn has transformed many historians' perspectives on the early Republic. They still see a contest between Federalists and Republicans, but their bias has shifted. Because Jefferson and the other Southern leaders of the Republican Party were slaveholders, many present-day scholars have switched sides in accord with the political and cultural needs of our own time. Much as most historians continue to dislike businessmen and the commercial classes, they dislike slaveholders and racists more.

Since most of the Federalists were Northerners and opposed to slavery, their status has dramatically risen in the eyes of present-day scholars.[24] In today's society, where many scholars see an illiberal and narrow-minded populism running rampant, the elitism of the Federalists doesn't seem all that bad. The Federalists might have been aristocrats, but, as some recent historians contend, at least they "were significantly more receptive than the Jeffersonians to the inclusion of women in the political process." Indeed, the Federalists' "conservative elitism" appears to present a "kinder face" on issues of gender and race than the Jeffersonian Democratic-Republicans do. "Federalists encouraged the migration of women to the West, believing that the presence of families there would counter the wildness of the frontiersmen. They called for fair treatment of Indians and tried to prohibit the spread of slavery into the region. The defeat of the Federalist vision by the new democratic order," these historians conclude, "spelled a diminished status for women, Indians, and Africans." Perhaps most damaging for the reputation of the Jeffersonian Republicans in our own time was their promotion of minimal government, which some scholars believe was motivated mainly by the need to protect slavery. By contrast, the Federalists were "committed to the idea that government was necessary to protect the weak."[25]

So it has gone, each generation of historians finding in the era of the Revolution and early Republic whatever fits its particular political and cultural needs. This is perhaps understandable but nonetheless lamentable. Because the present is so strong and can easily overwhelm and distort interpretations of the past, we historians have to constantly guard against it. Of course, historians live in the present, and they cannot and should not ignore it in their forays into the past; historians are not antiquarians who wallow in the past for its own sake. Indeed, historical reconstruction is only possible because historians have different perspectives from those of the past about whom they write. The present is important in stimulating historical inquiry and the questions historians ask of the past. "There is always," writes the eminent historian Bernard Bailyn, "a need to extract from the past some kind of bearing on contemporary problems, some message, commentary, or instruction to the writer's age, and to see reflected in the past familiar aspects of the present." But without "critical control," says Bailyn, this need "generates an obvious kind of presentism, which at worst becomes indoctrination by historical example."[26]

In many recent studies of the era of the Revolution and the early Republic, this "critical control" has not always been what it should have been. Our present preoccupation with race and gender has sometimes tended to misrepresent the period in much the same way that Charles Beard's Progressive generation misrepresented the period with their preoccupation with the common people against the business interests. One would think that the exaggerations of Progressive historiography (which most historians now recognize as such) would make present-day historians wary of making the same mistake—of reading their present so heavy-handedly into their interpretations of the past. It is one thing for the present to provoke questions about the past; it is quite another when it shapes and controls what historians find there.[27]

I don't believe that historians should take sides with the contestants of the past, whether Anti-Federalists versus Federalists or Republicans versus Federalists. The responsibility of the historian, it seems to me, is not to decide who in the past was right or who was wrong but to explain why the different contestants thought and behaved as they did.

Once we transcend this sort of partisan view of the past, once we realize that people in the past did not know their future any more than we know ours, and once we try to understand their behavior in their terms and not ours, then we will acquire a much more detached historical perspective. We can then come to appreciate more fully, for example, just how many illusions the generation of Founders lived with. Many of them hated political parties and tried to avoid them, and yet parties arose. Many of them thought their society in time would become more like Europe's, and yet it did not, at least not during the first half of the nineteenth century. Many also believed that slavery would sooner or later die a natural death—that it would simply wither away. They could not have been more wrong. Many of them also thought that the West could be settled in an orderly fashion, in a manner that could protect Indian culture and keep the native peoples west of the Appalachians from disappearing as they believed they had in New England.

They had many illusions about the future, as I suggest in my essay "Illusions of Power in the Awkward Era of Federalism." As late as 1822 Thomas Jefferson thought that "there is not a *young man* now living in the United States who will not die a Unitarian."[28] A Unitarian! What could he have been thinking? And this at a time when the evangelical Methodists and Baptists were growing by leaps and bounds.

If Jefferson, as smart and as well-read as he was, had illusions about the future, there is not much hope for the rest of us avoiding illusions about our future. But that is precisely the point of studying history. Before we become arrogant and condescending toward these people in the past, we should realize that we too live with illusions, only we don't know what they are. Perhaps every generation lives with illusions, different ones for each generation. And that is how history moves from one generation to another, exploding the previous generation's illusions and conjuring up its own.

If we approach the past in this way, we become more aware of just how much people then were victims as well as drivers of the historical process. We come to realize that those in the past were restricted by forces that they did not understand nor were even aware of—forces such as demographic movements, economic developments, or large-scale cultural patterns. The drama, indeed the tragedy, of history comes from our understanding of the tension that existed between the conscious wills and intentions of the participants in the past and the underlying conditions that constrained their actions and shaped their future. If the study of history teaches anything, it teaches us the limitations of life. It ought to produce prudence and humility.

PART I

THE *American Revolution*

CHAPTER ONE

RHETORIC *and* REALITY
in the AMERICAN REVOLUTION

*I*F ANY CATCHPHRASE IS TO characterize the work being done on the American Revolution by this generation of historians, it will probably be "the American Revolution considered as an intellectual movement."[1] For we now seem to be fully involved in a phase of writing about the Revolution in which the thought of the Revolutionaries, rather than their social and economic interests, has become the major focus of research and analysis. This recent emphasis on ideas is not, of course, new, and indeed right from the beginning it has characterized almost all our attempts to understand the Revolution. The ideas of a period which Samuel Eliot Morison and Harold Laski once described as, next to the English revolutionary decades of the seventeenth century, the most fruitful era in the history of Western political thought could never be completely ignored in any phase of our history writing.[2]

It has not been simply the inherent importance of the Revolutionary ideas, those "great principles of freedom,"[3] that has continually attracted the attention of historians. It has been rather the unusual nature of the Revolution and the constant need to explain what on the face of it seems inexplicable that has compelled almost all interpreters of the Revolution, including the participants themselves, to stress its predominantly intellectual character and hence its uniqueness among Western revolutions. Within the context of Revolutionary historiography, the one great effort to disparage the significance of ideas in the Revolution—an effort which dominated our history writing in the first half of the twentieth century—becomes something of an anomaly, a temporary aberration into a deterministic social and economic explanation from which we have been retreating for the past two decades. Since roughly the end of World War II we have witnessed a resumed and increasingly heightened insistence on the primary significance of conscious beliefs, and particularly of constitutional principles, in explaining what once again has become the unique character of the American Revolution. In the hands of idealist-minded historians, the thought and principles of the Americans have consequently come to repossess that explanative force which the previous generation of materialist-minded historians had tried to locate in the social structure.

Indeed, our renewed insistence on the importance of ideas in explaining the Revolution has now attained a level of fullness and sophistication never before achieved, with the consequence that the economic and social approach of the previous generation of behaviorist historians has never seemed more anomalous and irrelevant than it does at present. Yet paradoxically it may be that this preoccupation with the explanatory power of the Revolutionary ideas has become so intensive and so refined, assumed such a character, that the apparently discredited social and economic approach of an earlier generation has at the same time never seemed more attractive and relevant. In other words, we may be approaching a crucial juncture in our writing about the Revolution where idealism and behaviorism meet.

IT WAS THE REVOLUTIONARIES THEMSELVES who first described the peculiar character of what they had been involved in. The Revolution, as those who took stock at the end of three decades of revolutionary activity noted, was not "one of those events which strikes the public eye in the subversions of laws which have usually attended the revolutions of governments." Because it did not seem to have been a typical revolution, the sources of its force and its momentum appeared strangely unaccountable. "In other revolutions, the sword has been drawn by the arm of offended freedom, under an oppression that threatened the vital powers of society."[4] But this seemed hardly true of the American Revolution. There was none of the legendary tyranny that had so often driven desperate peoples into revolution. The Americans were not an oppressed people; they had no crushing imperial shackles to throw off. In fact, the Americans knew they were probably freer and less burdened with cumbersome feudal and monarchical restraints than any part of mankind in the eighteenth century. To its victims, the Tories, the Revolution was truly incomprehensible. Never in history, said Daniel Leonard, had there been so much rebellion with so "little real cause." It was, wrote Peter Oliver, "the most wanton and unnatural rebellion that ever existed."[5] The Americans' response was out of all proportion to the stimuli. The objective social reality scarcely seemed capable of explaining a revolution.

Yet no American doubted that there had been a revolution. How then was it to be justified and explained? If the American Revolution, lacking "those mad, tumultuous actions which disgraced many of the great revolutions of antiquity," was not a typical revolution, what kind of revolution was it? If the origin of the American Revolution lay not in the usual passions and interests of men, wherein did it lay? Those Americans who looked back at what they had been through could only marvel at the rationality and moderation, "supported by the energies of well weighed choice," involved in their separation from Britain, a revolution remarkably "without violence or convulsion."[6] It seemed to be peculiarly an affair of the mind. Even two such dissimilar sorts of Whigs as Thomas Paine and John Adams both came to see the Revolution they had done so much to bring about as especially involved with ideas, resulting from "a mental examination," a change in "the minds and hearts of the people."[7] The Americans were fortunate in being born at a time when the principles of government and freedom were better known than at any time in history. The Americans had learned "how to define the rights of nature—how to search into, to distinguish, and to comprehend, the principles of physical, moral, religious, and civil liberty," how, in short, to discover and resist the forces of tyranny before they could be applied. Never before in history had a people achieved "a revolution by reasoning" alone.[8]

The Americans, "born the heirs of freedom,"[9] revolted not to create but to maintain their freedom. American society had developed differently from that of the Old World. From the time of the first settlements in the seventeenth century, wrote Samuel Williams in 1794, "every thing tended to produce, and to establish the spirit of freedom." While the speculative philosophers of Europe were laboriously searching their minds in an effort to decide the first principles of liberty, the Americans had come to experience vividly that liberty in their everyday lives. The American Revolution, said Williams, joined together these enlightened ideas with America's experience. The Revolution was thus essentially intellectual and declaratory: it "explained the business to the world, and served to confirm what nature and society had before produced." "All was the result of reason. . . ."[10] The Revolution had taken place not in a succession of eruptions that had crumbled the existing social structure, but in a succession of new thoughts and new ideas that had vindicated that social structure.

The same logic that drove the participants to view the Revolution as peculiarly intellectual also compelled Moses Coit Tyler, writing at the end of the nineteenth century, to describe the American Revolution as "preeminently a revolution caused by ideas, and pivoted on ideas." That ideas played a part in all revolutions Tyler readily admitted. But in most revolutions, like that of the French, ideas had been perceived and acted upon only when the social reality had caught up with them, only when the ideas had been given meaning and force by long-experienced "real evils." The American Revolution, said Tyler, had been different: it was directed "not against tyranny inflicted, but only against tyranny anticipated." The Americans revolted not out of actual suffering but out of reasoned principle. "Hence, more than with most other epochs of revolutionary strife, our epoch of revolutionary strife was a strife of ideas:

a long warfare of political logic; a succession of annual campaigns in which the marshalling of arguments not only preceded the marshalling of armies, but often exceeded them in impression upon the final result."[11]

IT IS IN THIS HISTORIOGRAPHICAL context developed by the end of the nineteenth century, this constant and at times extravagant emphasis on the idealism of the Revolution, that the true radical quality of the Progressive generation's interpretation of the Revolution becomes so vividly apparent. For the work of these Progressive historians was grounded in a social and economic explanation of the Revolutionary era that explicitly rejected the causal importance of ideas. These historians could scarcely have avoided the general intellectual climate of the first part of the twentieth century, which regarded ideas as suspect. By absorbing the diffused thinking of Marx and Freud and the assumptions of behaviorist psychology, men had come to conceive of ideas as ideologies or rationalizations, as masks obscuring the underlying interests and drives that actually determined social behavior. For too long, it seemed, philosophers had reified thought, detaching ideas from the material conditions that produced them and investing them with an independent will that was somehow alone responsible for the determination of events.[12] As Charles Beard pointed out in his introduction to the 1935 edition of *An Economic Interpretation of the Constitution*, previous historians of the Constitution had assumed that ideas were "entities, particularities, or forces, apparently independent of all earthly considerations coming under the head of 'economic.'" It was Beard's aim, as it was the aim of many of his contemporaries, to bring into historical consideration "those realistic features of economic conflict, stress, and strain" which previous interpreters of the Revolution had largely ignored.[13] The product of this aim was a generation or more of historical writing about the Revolutionary period (of which Beard's was but the most famous expression) that sought to explain the Revolution and the formation of the Constitution in terms of socioeconomic relationships and interests rather than in terms of ideas.[14]

Curiously, the consequence of this reversal of historical approaches was not the destruction of the old-fashioned conception of the nature of ideas. As Marx had said, he intended only to put Hegel's head in its rightful place; he had no desire to cut it off. Ideas as rationalization, as ideology, remained—still distinct entities set in opposition to interests, now, however, lacking any deep causal significance, becoming merely a covering superstructure for the underlying and determinative social reality. Ideas therefore could still be the subject of historical investigation as long as one kept them in their proper place, interesting no doubt in their own right but not actually counting for much in the movement of events.

Even someone as interested in ideas as Carl Becker never seriously considered them to be in any way determinants of what happened. Ideas fascinated Becker, but it was as superstructure that he enjoyed examining them, their consistency, their logic, their clarity, the way men formed and played with them. In his *Declaration of Independence: A Study in the History of Political Ideas*, the political theory of the Americans takes on an unreal and even fatuous quality. It was as if ideas were merely refined tools to be used by the colonists in the most adroit manner possible. The entire Declaration of Independence, said Becker, was calculated for effect, designed primarily "to convince a candid world that the colonies had a moral and legal right to separate from Great Britain." The severe indictment of the king did not spring from unfathomable passions but was contrived, conjured up, to justify a rebellion whose sources lay elsewhere. Men to Becker were never the victims of their thought, but always the masters of it. Ideas were a kind of legal brief. "Thus step by step, from 1764 to 1776, the colonists modified their theory to suit their needs."[15] The assumptions behind Becker's 1909 behaviorist work on New York politics in the Revolution and his 1922 study of the political ideas in the Declaration of Independence were more alike than they at first might appear.

Bringing to their studies of the Revolution similar assumptions about the nature of ideas, some of Becker's contemporaries went on to expose starkly the implications of those assumptions. When the entire body of Revolutionary thinking was examined, these historians could not avoid being struck by its generally bombastic and overwrought quality. The ideas expressed seemed so inflated, such obvious exaggerations of reality, that they could scarcely be taken seriously. The Tories were all "wretched hirelings, and execrable parricides"; George III, the "tyrant of the earth," a "monster in human form"; the British soldiers, "a mercenary, licentious rabble of banditti," intending to "tear the bowels and vitals of their brave but peaceable fellow subjects, and *to wash the ground with a profusion of innocent blood*."[16] Such extravagant language, it seemed, could be nothing but calculated deception, at best an obvious distortion of fact, designed to incite and mold a revolutionary fervor. "The stigmatizing of British policy as 'tyranny,' 'oppression' and 'slavery,'" wrote Arthur M. Schlesinger, the dean of the Progressive historians, "had little or no objective reality, at least prior to the Intolerable Acts, but ceaseless repetition of the charge kept emotions at fever pitch."[17]

Indeed, so grandiose, so overdrawn, it seemed, were the ideas that the historians were necessarily led to ask not whether such ideas were valid but why men should have expressed them. It was not the content of such ideas but the function that was really interesting. The Revolutionary rhetoric, the profusion of sermons, pamphlets, and articles in the patriotic cause, could best be examined as propaganda, that is, as a concerted and self-conscious effort by agitators to manipulate and shape public opinion. Because of the Progressive historians' view of the Revolution as the movement of class minorities bent on promoting particular social and economic interests, the conception of propaganda was crucial to their explanation of what seemed to be a revolutionary consensus. Through the use of ideas in provoking hatred and influencing opinion and creating at least "an appearance of unity," the influence of a minority of agitators was out of all proportion to their number. The Revolution thus became a display of extraordinary skillfulness in the manipulation of public opinion. In fact, wrote Schlesinger, "no disaffected element in history has ever risen more splendidly to the occasion."[18]

Ideas thus became, as it were, parcels of thought to be distributed and used where they would do the most good. This propaganda was not, of course, necessarily false, but it was always capable of manipulation. "Whether the suggestions are to be true or false, whether the activities are to be open or concealed," wrote Philip Davidson, "are matters for the propagandist to decide." Apparently ideas could be turned on or off at will, and men controlled their rhetoric in a way they could not control their interests. Whatever the importance of propaganda, its connection with social reality was tenuous. Since ideas were so self-consciously manageable, the Whigs were not actually expressing anything meaningful about themselves but were rather feigning and exaggerating for effect. What the Americans said could not be taken at face value but must be considered as a rhetorical disguise for some hidden interest. The expression of even the classic and well-defined natural rights philosophy became, in Davidson's view, "the propagandist's rationalization of his desire to protect his vested interests."[19]

With this conception of ideas as weapons shrewdly used by designing propagandists, it was inevitable that the thought of the Revolutionaries should have been denigrated. The Revolutionaries became by implication hypocritical demagogues, "adroitly tailoring their arguments to changing conditions." Their political thinking appeared to possess neither consistency nor significance. "At best," said Schlesinger in an early summary of his interpretation, "an exposition of the political theories of the antiparliamentary party is an account of their retreat from one strategic position to another." So the Whigs moved, it was strongly suggested, easily if not frivolously from a defense of charter rights to the rights of Englishmen, and finally to the rights of man, as each position was exposed and became untenable. In short, concluded Schlesinger, the Revolution could never be understood if it were regarded "as a great forensic controversy over abstract governmental rights."[20]

IT IS ESSENTIALLY ON THIS point of intellectual consistency that Edmund S. Morgan has fastened for the past decade and a half in an attempt to bring down the entire interpretive framework of the socioeconomic argument. If it could be shown that the thinking of the Revolutionaries was not inconsistent after all, that the Whigs did not actually skip from one constitutional notion to the next, then the imputation of Whig frivolity and hypocrisy would lose its force. This was a central intention of Morgan's study of the political thought surrounding the Stamp Act. As Morgan himself has noted and others have repeated, "In the last analysis the significance of the Stamp Act crisis lies in the emergence, not of leaders and methods and organizations, but of well-defined constitutional principles." As early as 1765 the Whigs "laid down the line on which Americans stood until they cut their connections with England. Consistently from 1765 to 1776 they denied the authority of Parliament to tax them externally or internally; consistently they affirmed their willingness to submit to whatever legislation Parliament should enact for the supervision of the empire as a whole."[21] In other words, from the beginning they consistently denied Parliament's right to tax them, but at the same time they consistently affirmed Parliament's right to regulate their trade. This consistency thus becomes, as one scholar's survey of the current interpretation puts it, "an indication of American devotion to principle."[22]

It seemed clear once again after Morgan's study that the Americans were more sincerely attached to constitutional principles than the behaviorist historians had supposed, and that their ideas could not be viewed as simply manipulated propaganda. Consequently the cogency of the Progressive historians' interpretation was weakened if not unhinged. And as the evidence against viewing the Revolution as rooted in internal class conflict continued to mount from various directions, it appeared more and more comprehensible to accept the old-fashioned notion that the Revolution was after all the consequence of "a great forensic controversy over abstract governmental rights." There was, it seemed, no deprived and depressed populace yearning for a participation in politics that had long been denied; no coherent merchant class victimizing a mass of insolvent debtors; no seething discontent with the British mercantile system; no privileged aristocracy, protected by law, anxiously and insecurely holding power against a clamoring democracy. There was, in short, no internal class upheaval in the Revolution.[23]

If the Revolution was not to become virtually incomprehensible, it must have been the result of what the American Whigs always contended it was—a dispute between Mother Country and colonies over constitutional liberties. By concentrating on the immediate events of the decade leading up to independence, the historians of the 1950s have necessarily fled from the economic and social determinism of the Progressive historians. And by emphasizing the consistency and devotion with which Americans held their constitutional beliefs, they have once again focused on what seems to be the extraordinary intellectuality of the American Revolution and hence its uniqueness among Western revolutions. This interpretation, which, as Jack P. Greene notes, "may appropriately be styled neo-whig," has turned the Revolution into a rationally conservative movement, involving mainly a constitutional defense of existing political liberties against the abrupt and unexpected provocations of the British government after 1760. "The issue then, according to the neo-whigs, was no more and no less than separation from Britain and the preservation of American liberty." The Revolution has therefore become "more political, legalistic, and constitutional than social or economic." Indeed, some of the neo-Whig historians have implied not just that social and economic conditions were less important in bringing on the Revolution than we once thought, but rather that the social situation in the colonies had little or nothing to do with causing the Revolution. The Whig statements of principle iterated in numerous declarations appear to be the only causal residue after all the supposedly deeper social and economic causes have been washed away. As one scholar who has recently investigated and carefully dismissed the potential social and economic issues in pre-Revolutionary Virginia has concluded, "What remains as the fundamental issue in the coming of the Revolution, then, is nothing more than the contest over constitutional rights."[24]

In a different way, Bernard Bailyn in a recent article has clarified and reinforced this revived idealistic interpretation of the Revolution. The accumulative influence of much of the latest historical writing on the character of eighteenth-century American society has led Bailyn to the same insight expressed by Samuel Williams in 1794. What made the Revolution truly revolutionary was not the wholesale disruption of social groups and political institutions, for compared to other revolutions such disruption was slight; rather it was the fundamental alteration in the Americans' structure of values, the way they looked at themselves and their institutions. Bailyn has seized on this basic intellectual shift as a means of explaining the apparent contradiction between the seriousness with which the Americans took their Revolutionary ideas and the absence of radical social and institutional change. The Revolution, argues Bailyn, was not so much the transformation as the realization of American society.

The Americans had been gradually and unwittingly preparing themselves for such a mental revolution since they first came to the New World in the seventeenth century. The substantive changes in American society had taken place in the course of the previous century, slowly, often imperceptibly, as a series of small piecemeal deviations from what was regarded by most Englishmen as the accepted orthodoxy in society, state, and religion. What the Revolution marked, so to speak, was the point when the Americans suddenly blinked and saw their society, its changes, its differences, in a new perspective. Their deviation from European standards, their lack of an established church and a titled aristocracy, their apparent rusticity and general equality now became desirable, even necessary, elements in the maintenance of their society and politics. The comprehending and justifying, the endowing with high moral purpose, of these confusing and disturbing social and political divergences, Bailyn concludes, was the American Revolution.[25]

Bailyn's more recent investigation of the rich pamphlet literature of the decades before independence has filled out and refined his idealist interpretation, confirming him in his "rather old-fashioned view that the American Revolution was above all else an ideological-constitutional struggle and not primarily a controversy between social groups undertaken to force changes in the organization of society." While Bailyn's book-length introduction to the first of a multivolumed edition of Revolutionary pamphlets makes no effort to stress the conservative character of the Revolution and indeed emphasizes (in contrast to the earlier article) its radicalism and the dynamic and transforming rather than the rationalizing and declarative quality of Whig thought, it nevertheless represents the culmination of the idealist approach to the history of the Revolution. For "above all else," argues Bailyn, it was the Americans' worldview, the peculiar bundle of notions and beliefs they put together during the imperial debate, "that in the end propelled them into Revolution." Through his study of the Whig pamphlets Bailyn became convinced "that the fear of a comprehensive conspiracy against liberty throughout the English-speaking world—a conspiracy believed to have been nourished in corruption, and of which, it was felt, oppression in America was only the most immediately visible part—lay at the heart of the Revolutionary movement." No one of the various acts and measures of the British government after 1763 could by itself have provoked the extreme and violent response of the American Whigs. But when linked together they formed in the minds of the Americans, imbued with a particular historical understanding of what constituted tyranny, an extensive and frightening program designed to enslave the New World. The Revolution becomes comprehensible only when the mental framework, the Whig worldview into which the Americans fitted the events of the 1760s and 1770s, is known. "It is the development of this view to the point of overwhelming persuasiveness to the majority of American leaders and the meaning this view gave to the events of the time, and not simply an accumulation of grievances," writes Bailyn, "that explains the origins of the American Revolution."[26]

It now seems evident from Bailyn's analysis that it was the Americans' peculiar conception of reality more than anything else that convinced them that tyranny was afoot and that they must fight if their liberty was to survive. By an empathic understanding of a wide range of American thinking Bailyn has been able to offer us a most persuasive argument for the importance of ideas in bringing on the Revolution. Not since Tyler has the intellectual character of the Revolution received such emphasis and never before has it been set out so cogently and completely. It would seem that the idealist explanation of the Revolution has nowhere else to go.[27]

. . .

LABELING THE RECENT historical interpretations of the Revolution as "neo-Whig" is indeed appropriate, for, as Page Smith has pointed out, "After a century and a half of progress in historical scholarship, in research techniques, in tools and methods, we have found our way to the interpretation held, substantially, by those historians who themselves participated in, or lived through the era of, the Revolution." By describing the Revolution as a conservative, principled defense of American freedom against the provocations of the English government, the neo-Whig historians have come full circle to the position of the Revolutionaries themselves and to the interpretation of the first generation of historians.[28] Indeed, as a consequence of this historical atavism, praise for the contemporary or early historians has become increasingly common.

But to say that "the Whig interpretation of the American Revolution may not be as dead as some historians would have us believe" is perhaps less to commend the work of David Ramsay and George Bancroft than to indict the approach of recent historians.[29] However necessary and rewarding the neo-Whig histories have been, they present us with only a partial perspective on the Revolution. The neo-Whig interpretation is intrinsically polemical; however subtly presented, it aims to justify the Revolution. It therefore cannot accommodate a totally different, an opposing, perspective, a Tory view of the Revolution. It is for this reason that the recent publication of Peter Oliver's "Origin and Progress of the American Rebellion" is of major significance, for it offers us—"by attacking the hallowed traditions of the revolution, challenging the motives of the founding fathers, and depicting revolution as passion, plotting, and violence"—an explanation of what happened quite different from what we have been recently accustomed to.[30] Oliver's vivid portrait of the Revolutionaries, with his accent on their vicious emotions and interests, seriously disturbs the present Whiggish interpretation of the Revolution. It is not that Oliver's description of, say, John Adams as madly ambitious and consumingly resentful is any more correct than Adams's own description of himself as a virtuous and patriotic defender of liberty against tyranny. Both interpretations of Adams are in a sense right, but neither can comprehend the other because each is preoccupied with seemingly contradictory sets of motives. Indeed, it is really these two interpretations that have divided historians of the Revolution ever since.

Any intellectually satisfying explanation of the Revolution must encompass the Tory perspective as well as the Whig, for if we are compelled to take sides and choose between opposing motives—unconscious or avowed, passion or principle, greed or liberty—we will be endlessly caught up in the polemics of the participants themselves. We must, in other words, eventually dissolve the distinction between conscious and unconscious motives, between the Revolutionaries' stated intentions and their supposedly hidden needs and desires, a dissolution that involves somehow relating beliefs and ideas to the social world in which they operate. If we are to understand the causes of the Revolution, we must therefore ultimately transcend this problem of motivation. But this we can never do as long as we attempt to explain the Revolution mainly in terms of the intentions of the participants. It is not that men's motives are unimportant; they indeed make events, including revolutions. But the purposes of men, especially in a revolution, are so numerous, so varied, and so contradictory that their complex interaction produces results that no one intended or could even foresee. It is this interaction and these results that recent historians are referring to when they speak so disparagingly of those "underlying determinants" and "impersonal and inexorable forces" bringing on the Revolution. Historical explanation which does not account for these "forces," which, in other words, relies simply on understanding the conscious intentions of the actors, will thus be limited. This preoccupation with men's purposes was what restricted the perspectives of the contemporaneous Whig and Tory interpretations, and it is still the weakness of the neo-Whig histories, and indeed of any interpretation which attempts to explain the events of the Revolution by discovering the calculations from which individuals supposed themselves to have acted.

No explanation of the American Revolution in terms of the intentions and designs of particular individuals could have been more crudely put than that offered by the Revolutionaries themselves. American Whigs, like men of the eighteenth century generally, were fascinated with what seemed to the age to be the newly appreciated problem of human motivation and causation in the affairs of the world. In the decade before independence, the Americans sought endlessly to discover the supposed calculations and purposes of individuals or groups that lay behind the otherwise incomprehensible rush of events. More than anything else, perhaps, it was this obsession with motives that led to the prevalence in the eighteenth century of beliefs in conspiracies to account for the confusing happenings in which men found themselves caught up. Bailyn has suggested that this common fear of conspiracy was "deeply rooted in the political awareness of eighteenth-century Britons, involved in the very structure of their political life"; it "reflected so clearly the realities of life in an age in which monarchical autocracy flourished, [and] in which the stability and freedom of England's 'mixed' constitution was a recent and remarkable achievement."[31]

Yet it might also be argued that the tendency to see conspiracy behind what happened reflected as well the very enlightenment of the age. To attribute events to the designs and purposes of human agents seemed after all to be an enlightened advance over older beliefs in blind chance, providence, or God's interventions. It was rational and scientific, a product of both the popularization of politics and the secularization of knowledge. It was obvious to Americans that the series of events in the years after 1763, those "unheard of intolerable calamities, spring not of the dust, come not causeless." "Ought not the PEOPLE therefore," asked John Dickinson, "to watch? to observe facts? to search into causes? to investigate designs?"[32] And these causes and designs could be traced to individuals in high places, to ministers, to royal governors, and their lackeys. The belief in conspiracy grew naturally out of the enlightened need to find the human purposes behind the multitude of phenomena, to find the causes for what happened in the social world just as the natural scientist was discovering the causes for what happened in the physical world.[33] It was a necessary consequence of the search for connections and patterns in events. The various acts of the British government, the Americans knew, should not be "regarded according to the simple force of each, but as parts of a system of oppression."[34] The Whigs' intense search for the human purposes behind events was in fact an example of the beginnings of modern history.

In attempting to rebut those interpretations disparaging the colonists' cause, the present neo-Whig historians have been drawn into writing as partisans of the Revolutionaries. And they have thus found themselves entangled in the same kind of explanation used by the original antagonists, an explanation, despite obvious refinements, still involved with the discovery of motives and its corollary, the assessing of a personal sort of responsibility for what happened. While most of the neo-Whig historians have not gone so far as to see conspiracy in British actions (although some have come close),[35] they have tended to point up the blundering and stupidity of British officials in contrast to "the breadth of vision" that moved the Americans. If George III was in a position of central responsibility in the British government, as English historians have recently said, then, according to Edmund S. Morgan, "he must bear most of the praise or blame for the series of measures that alienated and lost the colonies, and it is hard to see how there can be much praise." By seeking "to define issues, fix responsibilities," and thereby to shift the "burden of proof" onto those who say the Americans were narrow and selfish and the empire was basically just and beneficent, the neo-Whigs have attempted to redress what they felt was an unfair neo-Tory bias of previous explanations of the Revolution;[36] they have not, however, challenged the terms of the argument. They are still obsessed with why men said they acted and with who was right and who was wrong. Viewing the history of the Revolution in this judicatory manner has therefore restricted the issues over which historians have disagreed to those of motivation and responsibility, the very issues with which the participants themselves were concerned.

The neo-Whig "conviction that the colonists' attachment to principle was genuine"[37] has undoubtedly been refreshing, and indeed necessary, given the Tory slant of earlier twentieth-century interpretations. It now seems clearer that the Progressive historians, with their naive and crude reflex conception of human behavior, had too long treated the ideas of the Revolution superficially if not superciliously. Psychologists and sociologists are now willing to grant a more determining role to beliefs, particularly in revolutionary situations. It is now accepted that men act not simply in response to some kind of objective reality but to the meaning they give to that reality. Since men's beliefs are as much a part of the given stimuli as the objective environment, the beliefs must be understood and taken seriously if men's behavior is to be fully explained. The American Revolutionary ideas were more than cooked-up pieces of thought served by an aggressive and interested minority to a gullible and unsuspecting populace. The concept of propaganda permitted the Progressive historians to account for the presence of ideas, but it prevented them from recognizing ideas as an important determinant of the Americans' behavior. The weight attributed to ideas and constitutional principles by the neo-Whig historians was thus an essential corrective to the propagandist studies.

Yet in its laudable effort to resurrect the importance of ideas in historical explanation, much of the writing of the neo-Whigs has tended to return to the simple nineteenth-century intellectualist assumption that history is the consequence of a rational calculation of ends and means, that what happened was what was consciously desired and planned. By supposing "that individual actions and immediate issues are more important than underlying determinants in explaining particular events," by emphasizing conscious and articulated motives, the neo-Whig historians have selected and presented that evidence which is most directly and clearly expressive of the intentions of the Whigs—that is, the most well-defined, the most constitutional, the most reasonable of the Whig beliefs, those found in their public documents, their several declarations of grievances and causes. It is not surprising that for the neo-Whigs the history of the American Revolution should be more than anything else "the history of the Americans' search for principles."[38] Not only, then, did nothing in the Americans' economic and social structure really determine their behavior, but the colonists in fact acted from the most rational and calculated of motives: they fought, as they said they would, simply to defend their ancient liberties against British provocation.

By implying that certain declared rational purposes are by themselves an adequate explanation for the Americans' revolt—in other words, that the Revolution was really nothing more than a contest over constitutional principles—the neo-Whig historians have not only threatened to deny what we have learned of human psychology in the twentieth century, but they have also in fact failed to exploit fully the terms of their own idealist approach by not taking into account all of what the Americans believed and said. Whatever the deficiencies and misunderstandings of the role of ideas in human behavior present in the propagandist studies of the 1930s, these studies did for the first time attempt to deal with the entirety and complexity of American Revolutionary thought—to explain not only all the well-reasoned notions of law and liberty that were so familiar but, more important, all the irrational and hysterical beliefs that had been so long neglected. Indeed, it was the patent absurdity and implausibility of much of what the Americans said that lent credence and persuasiveness to their mistrustful approach to the ideas. Once this exaggerated and fanatical rhetoric was uncovered by the Progressive historians, it should not have subsequently been ignored—no matter how much it may have impugned the reasonableness of the American response. No widely expressed ideas can be dismissed out of hand by the historian.

In his recent analysis of Revolutionary thinking, Bernard Bailyn has avoided the neo-Whig tendency to distort the historical reconstruction of the American mind. By comprehending "the assumptions, beliefs, and ideas that lay behind the manifest events of the time," Bailyn has attempted to get inside the Whigs' mind, and to experience vicariously all of what they thought and felt, both their rational constitutional beliefs and their hysterical and emotional ideas as well. The inflammatory phrases—"slavery," "corruption," "conspiracy"—that most historians had either ignored or readily dismissed as propaganda took on a new significance for Bailyn. He came "to suspect that they meant something very real to both the writers and their readers: that there were real fears, real anxieties, a sense of real danger behind these phrases, and not merely the desire to influence by rhetoric and propaganda the inert minds of an otherwise passive populace."[39] No part of American thinking, Bailyn suggests—not the widespread belief in a ministerial conspiracy, not the hostile and vicious indictments of individuals, not the fear of corruption and the hope for regeneration, not any of the violent seemingly absurd distortions and falsifications of what we now believe to be true, in short, none of the frenzied rhetoric—can be safely ignored by the historian seeking to understand the causes of the Revolution.

Bailyn's study, however, represents something other than a more complete and uncorrupted version of the common idealist interpretations of the Revolution. By viewing from the "interior" the Revolutionary pamphlets, which were "to an unusual degree, *explanatory*," revealing "not merely positions taken but the reasons why positions were taken," Bailyn like any idealist historian has sought to discover the motives the participants themselves gave for their actions, to reenact their thinking at crucial moments, and thereby to recapture some of the "unpredictable reality" of the Revolution.[40] But for Bailyn the very unpredictability of the reality he has disclosed has undermined the idealist obsession with explaining why, in the participants' own estimation, they acted as they did. Ideas emerge as more than explanatory devices, as more than indicators of motives. They become as well objects for analysis in and for themselves, historical events in their own right to be treated as other historical events are treated. Although Bailyn has examined the Revolutionary ideas subjectively from the inside, he has also analyzed them objectively from the outside. Thus, in addition to a contemporary Whig perspective, he presents us with a retrospective view of the ideas—their complexity, their development, and their consequences—that the actual participants did not have. In effect his essay represents what has been called "a Namierism of the history of ideas,"[41] a structural analysis of thought that suggests a conclusion about the movement of history not very different from Sir Lewis Namier's, where history becomes something "started in ridiculous beginnings, while small men did things both infinitely smaller and infinitely greater than they knew."[42]

In his *England in the Age of the American Revolution*, Namier attacked the Whig tendency to overrate "the importance of the conscious will and purpose in individuals." Above all he urged us "to ascertain and recognize the deeper irrelevancies and incoherence of human actions, which are not so much directed by reason, as invested by it *ex post facto* with the appearances of logic and rationality," to discover the unpredictable reality, where men's motives and intentions were lost in the accumulation and momentum of interacting events. The whole force of Namier's approach tended to squeeze the intellectual content out of what men did. Ideas setting forth principles and purposes for action, said Namier, did not count for much in the movement of history.[43]

In his study of the Revolutionary ideas, Bailyn has come to an opposite conclusion: ideas counted for a great deal, not only being responsible for the Revolution but also for transforming the character of American society. Yet in his hands ideas lose that static quality they have commonly had for the Whig historians, the simple statements of intention that so exasperated Namier. For Bailyn the ideas of the Revolutionaries take on an elusive and unmanageable quality, a dynamic self-intensifying character that transcended the intentions and desires of any of the historical participants. By emphasizing how the thought of the colonists was "strangely reshaped, turned in unfamiliar directions," by describing how the Americans "indeliberately, half-knowingly" groped toward "conclusions they could not themselves clearly perceive," by demonstrating how new beliefs and hence new actions were the responses not to desire but to the logic of developing situations, Bailyn has wrested the explanation of the Revolution out of the realm of motivation in which the neo-Whig historians had confined it.

With this kind of approach to ideas, the degree of consistency and devotion to principles become less important, and indeed the major issues of motivation and responsibility over which historians have disagreed become largely irrelevant. Action becomes not the product of rational and conscious calculation but of dimly perceived and rapidly changing thoughts and situations, "where the familiar meaning of ideas and words faded away into confusion, and leaders felt themselves peering into a haze, seeking to bring shifting conceptions somehow into focus." Men become more the victims than the manipulators of their ideas, as their thought unfolds in ways few anticipated, "rapid, irreversible, and irresistible," creating new problems, new considerations, new ideas, which have their own unforeseen implications. In this kind of atmosphere the Revolution, not at first desired by the Americans, takes on something of an inevitable character, moving through a process of escalation into levels few had intended or perceived. It no longer makes sense to assign motives or responsibility to particular individuals for the totality of what happened. Men were involved in a complicated web of phenomena, ideas, and situations from which in retrospect escape seems impossible.[44]

By seeking to uncover the motives of the Americans expressed in the Revolutionary pamphlets, Bailyn has ended by demonstrating the autonomy of ideas as phenomena, where the ideas operate, as it were, over the heads of the participants, taking them in directions no one could have foreseen. His discussion of Revolutionary thought thus represents a move back to a deterministic approach to the Revolution, a determinism, however, which is different from that which the neo-Whig historians have so recently and self-consciously abandoned. Yet while the suggested determinism is thoroughly idealist—indeed, never before has the force of ideas in bringing on the Revolution been so emphatically put—its implications are not. By helping to purge our writing about the Revolution of its concentration on constitutional principles and its stifling judicial-like preoccupation with motivation and responsibility, the study serves to open the way for new questions and new appraisals. In fact, it is out of the very completeness of his idealist interpretation, out of his exposition of the extraordinary nature—the very dynamism and emotionalism—of the Americans' thought that we have the evidence for an entirely different, a behaviorist, perspective on the causes of the American Revolution. Bailyn's book-length introduction to his edition of Revolutionary pamphlets is therefore not only a point of fulfillment for the idealist approach to the Revolution, it is also a point of departure for a new look at the social sources of the Revolution.

IT SEEMS CLEAR that historians of eighteenth-century America and the Revolution cannot ignore the force of ideas in history to the extent that Namier and his students have done in their investigations of eighteenth-century English politics. This is not to say, however, that the Namier approach to English politics has been crucially limiting and distorting. Rather it may suggest that the Namier denigration of ideas and principles is inapplicable for American politics because the American social situation in which ideas operated was very different from that of eighteenth-century England. It may be that ideas are less meaningful to a people in a socially stable situation. Only when ideas have become stereotyped reflexes do evasion and hypocrisy and the Namier mistrust of what men believe become significant. Only in a relatively settled society does ideology become a kind of habit, a bundle of widely shared and instinctive conventions, offering ready-made explanations for men who are not being compelled to ask any serious questions. Conversely, it is perhaps only in a relatively unsettled, disordered society, where the questions come faster than men's answers, that ideas become truly vital and creative.[45]

Paradoxically it may be the very vitality of the Americans' ideas, then, that suggests the need to examine the circumstances in which they flourished. Since ideas and beliefs are ways of perceiving and explaining the world, the nature of the ideas expressed is determined as much by the character of the world being confronted as by the internal development of inherited and borrowed conceptions. Out of the multitude of inherited and transmitted ideas available in the eighteenth century, Americans selected and emphasized those which seemed to make meaningful what was happening to them. In the colonists' use of classical literature, for example, "their detailed knowledge and engaged interest covered only one era and one small group of writers": Plutarch, Livy, Cicero, Sallust, and

Tacitus—those who "had hated and feared the trends of their own time, and in their writing had contrasted the present with a better past, which they endowed with qualities absent from their own, corrupt era."[46] There was always, in Max Weber's term, some sort of elective affinity between the Americans' interests and their beliefs, and without that affinity their ideas would not have possessed the peculiar character and persuasiveness they did. Only the most revolutionary social needs and circumstances could have sustained such revolutionary ideas.[47]

When the ideas of the Americans are examined comprehensively, when all of the Whig rhetoric, irrational as well as rational, is taken into account, one cannot but be struck by the predominant characteristics of fear and frenzy, the exaggerations and the enthusiasm, the general sense of social corruption and disorder out of which would be born a new world of benevolence and harmony where Americans would become the "eminent examples of every divine and social virtue."[48] As Bailyn and the propaganda studies have amply shown, there is simply too much fanatical and millennial thinking even by the best minds that must be explained before we can characterize the Americans' ideas as peculiarly rational and legalistic and thus view the Revolution as merely a conservative defense of constitutional liberties. To isolate refined and nicely reasoned arguments from the writings of John Adams and Jefferson is not only to disregard the more inflamed expressions of the rest of the Whigs but also to overlook the enthusiastic extravagance—the paranoiac obsession with a diabolical crown conspiracy and the dream of a restored Saxon era—in the thinking of Adams and Jefferson themselves.

The ideas of the Americans seem, in fact, to form what can only be called a revolutionary syndrome. If we were to confine ourselves to examining the Revolutionary rhetoric alone, apart from what happened politically or socially, it would be virtually impossible to distinguish the American Revolution from any other revolution in modern Western history. In the kinds of ideas expressed, the American Revolution is remarkably similar to the seventeenth-century Puritan Revolution and to the eighteenth-century French Revolution: the same general disgust with a chaotic and corrupt world, the same anxious and angry bombast, the same excited fears of conspiracies by depraved men, the same utopian hopes for the construction of a new and virtuous order.[49] It was not that this syndrome of ideas was simply transmitted from one generation or from one people to another. It was rather perhaps that similar, though hardly identical, social situations called forth within the limitations of inherited and available conceptions similar modes of expression. Although we need to know much more about the sociology of revolutions and collective movements, it does seem possible that particular patterns of thought, particular forms of expression, correspond to certain basic social experiences. There may be, in other words, typical modes of expression, typical kinds of beliefs and values, characterizing a revolutionary situation, at least within roughly similar Western societies. Indeed, the types of ideas manifested may be the best way of identifying a collective movement as a revolution. As one student of revolutions writes, "It is on the basis of a knowledge of men's beliefs that we can distinguish their behavior from riot, rebellion or insanity."[50]

It is thus the very nature of the Americans' rhetoric—its obsession with corruption and disorder, its hostile and conspiratorial outlook, and its millennial vision of a regenerated society—that reveals, as nothing else apparently can, the American Revolution as a true revolution with its sources lying deep in the social structure. For this kind of frenzied rhetoric could spring only from the most severe sorts of social strain. The grandiose and feverish language of the Americans was indeed the natural, even the inevitable, expression of a people caught up in a revolutionary situation, deeply alienated from the existing sources of authority and vehemently involved in a basic reconstruction of their political and social order. The hysteria of the Americans' thinking was but a measure of the intensity of their revolutionary passions. Undoubtedly the growing American alienation from British authority contributed greatly to this revolutionary situation. Yet the very weakness of the British imperial system and the accumulating ferocity of American antagonism to it suggests that other sources of social strain were being fed into the revolutionary movement. It may be that the Progressive historians, in their preoccupation with internal social problems, were more right than we have recently been willing to grant. It would be repeating their mistake, however, to expect this internal social strain necessarily to take the form of coherent class conflict or overt social disruption. The sources of revolutionary social stress may have been much more subtle but no less severe.

Of all of the colonies in the mid-eighteenth century, Virginia seems the most settled, the most lacking in obvious social tensions. Therefore, as it has been recently argued, since conspicuous social issues were nonexistent, the only plausible remaining explanation for the Virginians' energetic and almost unanimous commitment to the Revolution must have been their devotion to constitutional principles.[51] Yet it may be that we have been looking for the wrong kinds of social issues, for organized conflicts, for conscious divisions, within the society. It seems clear that Virginia's difficulties were not the consequence of any obvious sectional or class antagonism, Tidewater versus Piedmont, aristocratic planters versus yeoman farmers. There was apparently no discontent with the political system that went deep into the social structure. But there does seem to have been something of a social crisis within the ruling group itself, which intensely aggravated the Virginians' antagonism to the imperial system. Contrary to the impression of confidence and stability that the Virginia planters have historically acquired, they seemed to have been in very uneasy circumstances in the years before the Revolution. The signs of the eventual nineteenth-century decline of the Virginia gentry were, in other words, already felt if not readily apparent.

The planters' ability to command the acquiescence of the people seems extraordinary compared to the unstable politics of the other colonies. But in the years before independence there were signs of increasing anxiety among the gentry over their representative role. The ambiguities in the relationship between the burgesses and their constituents erupted into open debate in the 1750s. And men began voicing more and more concern over the mounting costs of elections and growing corruption in the soliciting of votes, especially by "those who have neither natural nor acquired parts to recommend them."[52] By the late sixties and early seventies the newspapers were filled with warnings against electoral influence, bribery, and vote seeking. The freeholders were stridently urged to "strike at the Root of this growing Evil; be influenced by Merit alone," and avoid electing "obscure and inferior persons."[53] It was as if ignoble ambition and demagoguery, one bitter pamphlet remarked, were a "Daemon lately come among us to disturb the peace and harmony, which had so long subsisted in this place."[54] In this context, Robert Munford's famous play *The Candidates*, written in 1770, does not so much confirm the planters' confidence as it betrays their uneasiness with electoral developments in the colony, "when coxcombs and jockies can impose themselves upon it for men of learning." Although disinterested virtue eventually wins out, Munford's satire reveals the kinds of threats the established planters faced from ambitious knaves and blockheads who were turning representatives into slaves of the people.[55]

By the eve of the Revolution, the planters were voicing a growing sense of impending ruin, whose sources seemed in the minds of many to be linked more and more with the corrupting British connection and the Scottish factors but for others frighteningly rooted in "our Pride, our Luxury, and Idleness."[56] The public and private writings of Virginians became obsessed with "corruption," "virtue," and "luxury." The increasing defections from the Church of England, even among ministers and vestrymen, and the remarkable growth of dissent in the years before the Revolution, "so much complained of in many parts of the colony," further suggests some sort of social stress. The strange religious conversions of Robert Carter may represent only the most dramatic example of what was taking place less frenziedly elsewhere among the gentry.[57] By the middle of the eighteenth century it was evident that many of the planters were living on the edge of bankruptcy, seriously overextended and spending beyond their means in an almost frantic effort to fulfill the aristocratic image they had created of themselves.[58] Perhaps the importance of the Robinson affair in the 1760s lies not in any constitutional changes that resulted but in the shattering effect the disclosures had on that virtuous image.[59] Some of the planters expressed openly their fears for the future, seeing the products of their lives being destroyed in the reckless gambling and drinking of their heirs, who, as Landon Carter put it, "play away and play it all away."[60]

The Revolution in Virginia, "produced by the wantonness of the Gentleman," as one planter suggested,[61] undoubtedly gained much of its force from this social crisis within the gentry. Certainly more was expected from the Revolution than simply a break from British imperialism, and it was not any crude avoidance of British debts.[62] The Revolutionary reforms, like the abolition of entail and primogeniture, may have signified something other than mere symbolic legal adjustments to an existing reality. In addition to being an attempt to make the older Tidewater plantations more economically competitive with lands farther west, the reforms may have represented a real effort to redirect what was believed to be a dangerous tendency in social and family development within the ruling gentry. The Virginians were not after all aristocrats who could afford having their entailed families' estates in the hands of weak or ineffectual eldest sons. Entail, as the preamble to the 1776 act abolishing it stated, had often done "injury to the morals of youth by rendering them independent of, and disobedient to, their parents."[63] There was too much likelihood, as the Nelson family sadly demonstrated, that a single wayward generation would virtually wipe out what had been so painstakingly built.[64] George Mason bespoke the anxieties of many Virginians when he warned the Philadelphia Convention in 1787 that "our own Children will in a short time be among the general mass."[65]

Precisely how the strains within Virginia society contributed to the creation of a revolutionary situation and in what way the planters expected independence and republicanism to alleviate their problems, of course, need to be fully explored. It seems clear, however, from the very nature of the ideas expressed that the sources of the Revolution in Virginia were much more subtle and complicated than a simple antagonism to the British government. Constitutional principles alone do not explain the Virginians' almost unanimous determination to revolt. And if the

Revolution in the seemingly stable colony of Virginia possessed internal social roots, it is to be expected that the other colonies were experiencing their own forms of social strain that in a like manner sought mitigation through revolution and republicanism.

It is through the Whigs' ideas, then, that we may be led back to take up where the Progressive historians left off in their investigation of the internal social sources of the Revolution. By working through the ideas— by reading them imaginatively and relating them to the objective social world they both reflected and confronted—we may be able to eliminate the unrewarding distinction between conscious and unconscious motives, and eventually thereby to combine a Whig with a Tory (an idealist with a behaviorist) interpretation. For the ideas, the rhetoric, of the Americans was never obscuring but remarkably revealing of their deepest interests and passions. What they expressed may not have been for the most part factually true, but it was always psychologically true. In this sense their rhetoric was never detached from the social and political reality; and indeed it becomes the best entry into an understanding of that reality. Their repeated overstatements of reality, their incessant talk of "tyranny" when there seems to have been no real oppression, their obsession with "virtue," "luxury," and "corruption," their devotion to "liberty" and "equality"—all these notions were neither manipulated propaganda nor borrowed empty abstractions, but ideas with real personal and social significance for those who used them. Propaganda could never move men to revolution. No popular leader, as John Adams put it, has ever been able "to persuade a large people, for any length of time together, to think themselves wronged, injured, and oppressed unless they really were, and saw and felt it to be so."[66] The ideas had relevance; the sense of oppression and injury, although often displaced onto the imperial system, was nonetheless real. It was indeed the meaningfulness of the connection between what the Americans said and what they felt that gave the ideas their propulsive force and their overwhelming persuasiveness.

It is precisely the remarkable revolutionary character of the Americans' ideas now being revealed by historians that best indicates that something profoundly unsettling was going on in the society, that raises the question, as it did for the Progressive historians, why the Americans should have expressed such thoughts. With their crude conception of propaganda, the Progressive historians at least attempted to grapple with the problem. Since we cannot regard the ideas of the Revolutionaries as simply propaganda, the question still remains to be answered. "When 'ideas' in full cry drive past," wrote Arthur F. Bentley in his classic behavioral study *The Process of Government*, "the thing to do with them is to accept them as an indication that something is happening; and then search carefully to find out what it really is they stand for, what the factors of the social life are that are expressing themselves through the ideas."[67] Precisely because they sought to understand both the Revolutionary ideas and American society, the behaviorist historians of the Progressive generation, for all of their crude conceptualizations, their obsession with "class" and hidden economic interests, and their treatment of ideas as propaganda, have still offered us an explanation of the Revolutionary era so powerful and so comprehensive that no purely intellectual interpretation will ever replace it.

AFTERWORD TO CHAPTER I

If the tendency of subsequent scholarship is any indication, this 1966 article—my first publication in early American history—seems to have had very little influence on the historical profession. Much of the scholarship on the Revolution during the several decades following its publication ignored the "reality" of American society and instead concentrated very heavily on the "rhetoric" of the Revolution, which was by and large equated with something called "republicanism." I suppose my book *The Creation of the American Republic, 1776–1787* (1969) contributed its share to the so-called republican synthesis that emerged in the 1970s and 1980s to become something of a monster that threatened to devour us all. My article, however, was supposed to tame the monster before it was unleashed.

When I wrote the "Rhetoric and Reality" piece, I had already essentially completed my *Creation of the American Republic*, even though the book was published several years later. In that book I never intended to argue that the Revolution was fundamentally an "ideological" movement, or that the Revolution could be explained solely in "ideological" terms. Indeed, as I have pointed out in the introduction to this collection, I have never thought that one could explain anything fully by referring only to the beliefs of people. In writing the article I was well aware of the powerful implications of Bernard Bailyn's introduction to his *Pamphlets of the American Revolution*, which had just been published in 1965 and which would eventually become *The Ideological Origins of the American Revolution* (1967). As shatteringly important as I knew Bailyn's work to be, I nevertheless thought it tried to explain the Revolution too much in terms of the professed beliefs of the participants. Thus I wrote the "Rhetoric and Reality" article as a corrective to the idealist tendency I saw in the neo-Whig historical literature of the 1950s and early 1960s that I believed had climaxed with Bailyn's stunning work. Without denying in any way the significance of ideas (after all, I had just completed a book on the political thought of the Revolution), I simply tried to urge historians not to get too carried away with exclusively intellectual explanations of the Revolution. If we were ultimately to see the Revolution whole—from both the top and from the bottom—then, I suggested, we had to examine its social sources as well.

The problem with such a suggestion was that it too easily reinforced the traditional assumptions of neo-Progressive social history, which, as I indicated in my introduction, tended to create polarities of ideas versus behavior, rhetoric versus reality. Despite my perverse and misguided title, I wrote my article as a protest against just such dualities, against such sharp separations of ideas from social circumstances. I wanted to acknowledge the importance of both ideas and underlying psychological and social determinants in shaping human behavior and yet avoid returning to the crude neo-Progressive polarities of the past made famous by such historians as Charles Beard. In parts of my *Creation of the American Republic*, I tried to do just that, which is probably why so many historians could not decide what school of historical interpretation that book put me in.

Although cultural history of one sort or another has seized the day during the past generation (even the Marxists now write only cultural history), several historians have explicitly attempted to explore the linkages between culture and society that I suggested existed in the relatively stable colony of Virginia. Rhys Isaac, in his *Transformation of Virginia*, T. H. Breen in his *Tobacco Culture*, Richard R. Beeman in his study of Lunenburg County, and Jack P. Greene in several articles have all sought to relate social developments in Virginia to the ideology of the Revolution.[1]

Although these works are very different, they are imaginative examples of what might be done. History that recognizes the importance of both culture and society and both consciousness and underlying social and material circumstances is ultimately the kind of history we need to write.

CHAPTER TWO

The LEGACY of ROME
in the AMERICAN REVOLUTION

THE LATE EIGHTEENTH CENTURY in the Atlantic world has been called "the age of the democratic revolution." It might better be called "the age of the republican revolution." For it was republicanism and republican principles, not democracy, that brought down the ancient monarchies.[1]

It was an astonishing moment in Western history, and we are living with its effects still. Monarchies that had existed for centuries were suddenly overthrown and replaced by new republican governments. Since republican governments have become so natural and normal for most of the world in the early twenty-first century, it is hard to recover the surprisingly novel and radical character of those eighteenth-century republican revolutions. In the eighteenth century, monarchy was still the standard for most people, and, as events in our own time demonstrate, there was always something to be said for large and diverse countries being ruled from the top by a single authority. Monarchy had history on its side; the kings of Europe had spent centuries consolidating their authority over unruly nobles and disparate peoples. The Bible endorsed kingship. Had not the ancient Israelites proclaimed that "we will have a king over us; that we . . . may be like all the nations"?[2]

Since most people in the Atlantic world and elsewhere had lived with kings for all of their recorded histories, why in the late eighteenth century should these kings have been so suddenly overthrown by republican revolutions? Why, as John Adams wondered in 1776, should "[i]dolatry to Monarchs, and servility to Aristocratical Pride [be] so totally eradicated from so many minds in so short a Time"?[3] If change were inevitable, why should republicanism have been chosen as the alternative to the ancien régimes? There were political and constitutional changes short of establishing republics that could have been tried. Hereditary lines could have been shifted; new kings could have been set upon the thrones. After all, the English in their Glorious Revolution in 1688–1689 and in their constitutional adjustment in 1714 had not abolished monarchy; they merely had found new heirs to the crown and placed some new limits on their king. Besides, during the seventeenth century the English had already tried a brief experiment in republicanism, and it had ended in disaster and dictatorship. Why would anyone want to try such an experiment again? The tiny self-proclaimed republics that did exist in eighteenth-century Europe—the Swiss cantons, the Italian city-states, and the Dutch provinces—were in various stages of confusion and decay and were very unlikely models for the large and populous countries of the Western world. Why would any state—either the sprawling provinces of British North America or the conglomeration that constituted the ancien régime of France—want to emulate them?

Amidst this monarchy-dominated culture, however, there was one republican model that did seem worth emulating—one republic that had achieved in glory and fame all that any people anywhere could ever hope for. And that republic was ancient Rome. While the eighteenth century was not much interested in the past, antiquity was the exception; no modern era has ever invested so much in the classical past. And although all the ancient republics—Athens, Sparta, Thebes—were familiar to educated people in the eighteenth century (their names had "grown trite by repetition," said one American), none was more familiar than that of Rome. People could not hear enough about it. "It was impossible," said

Montesquieu, "to be tired of as agreeable a subject as ancient Rome." There was nothing startling about Edward Gibbon's choice of subject for his great history. "Rome," he wrote in his *Autobiography*, "is familiar to the schoolboy and the statesman." To be educated in the eighteenth century was to know about Rome; Latin, as John Locke had said, was still regarded as "absolutely necessary to a gentleman."[4]

If any one cultural source lay behind the republican revolutions of the eighteenth century, it was ancient Rome—republican Rome—and the values that flowed from its history. It was ancient Rome's legacy that helped to make the late eighteenth century's apparently sudden transition to republicanism possible. If the eighteenth-century Enlightenment was, as Peter Gay has called it, "the rise of modern paganism," then classical republicanism was its creed.[5] To be enlightened was to be interested in antiquity, and to be interested in antiquity was to be interested in republicanism. Certainly classical antiquity could offer meaningful messages for monarchy too, but there is no doubt that the thrust of what the ancient world, and particularly Rome, had to say to the eighteenth century was latently and at times manifestly republican.

If the Enlightenment was to discover the sources of a flourishing society and human happiness, it was important to learn what lay behind the ascendency of republican Rome and its eventual decline and fall. The French and American revolutionaries' view of the ancient past was therefore very selective, focusing on the moral and social basis of politics and on social degeneracy and corruption. Since the eighteenth century believed that "similar causes will forever operate like effects in the political, moral, and physical world," the history of antiquity inevitably became a kind of laboratory in which autopsies of the dead republics, especially Rome, would lead to a science of political sickness and health—"political pathology," one American called it—matching the medical science of the natural world.[6]

It was the writings of the golden age of Latin literature that fascinated the eighteenth-century Enlightenment, preoccupied as it was with cyclical history and the decline and fall of the Roman republic. These

Roman writings of the Enlightenment spanned the two centuries from the breakdown of the republic in the middle of the first century B.C. to the reign of Marcus Aurelius in the middle of the second century A.D. Together with the Greek Plutarch, the Roman authors of this literature— Cicero, Sallust, Livy, Virgil, Tacitus—set forth republican ideals and values about politics and society that have had a powerful and lasting effect on Western culture. Writing at a time when the greatest days of the Roman republic were crumbling or were already gone, these Latin writers contrasted the growing corruption, luxury, and disorder they saw about them with an imagined earlier republican world of ordered simplicity and Arcadian virtue and sought to explain why the republic had withered and decayed.[7]

These classical ideals and values were revived and refurbished by the Italian Renaissance—becoming what has been variously called "civic humanism" or "classical republicanism"—and were carried into early modern Europe and made available in the seventeenth and eighteenth centuries to wider and deeper strata of the population, which rarely possessed an original or unglossed antiquity; they often saw a refracted image of the vanished republic, saw the classical past and classical values as Machiavelli and the Renaissance had passed them on. While some in the English-speaking world did own and read the ancient authors in Latin, most generally preferred translations, popularizations, and secondary surveys such as Thomas Gordon's *Sallust* and *Tacitus*, Basil Kennett's *Roman Antiquities*, Walter Moyle's dabblings in antiquity, Charles Rollin's popular histories, Thomas Blackwell's *Memoirs of the Court of Augustus*, Oliver Goldsmith's history of Rome, and Edward Wortley Montagu's *Reflections on the Rise and Fall of the Antient Republicks*. By the eighteenth century, monarchical culture in Europe and particularly in Great Britain was thoroughly infused with these republican writings and their classical values and to that extent at least was already republicanized.[8]

The source of monarchy's destruction and replacement by republicanism in the late eighteenth century was already present several generations earlier. Consequently, monarchy was not supplanted by republicanism all at once—not in 1776 with the Declaration of Independence, not in 1789 with the calling of the Estates General, not even in 1792–1793 with the National Convention's proclamation of the republic and the execution of Louis XVI. The change came before these events, and slowly. Classical republican values ate away at monarchy—corroding it, gradually, steadily—for much of the eighteenth century. Republicanism seeped everywhere in the eighteenth-century Atlantic world, eroding monarchical society from within, wearing away all the traditional supports of kingship, ultimately desacralizing monarchy in France and America to the point where, as David Hume observed, "the mere name of king commands little respect; and to talk of a king as God's vice-regent upon earth, or to give him any of these magnificent titles which formerly dazzled mankind, would but excite laughter in everyone."[9]

Of course, the French and English subscribed to these classical republican values with varying degrees of intensity, and the term "republican" remained pejorative, something to hang on the head of an opponent in order to damage his credibility, if not his loyalty to the crown. Nevertheless, what is remarkable is the extent to which the thinking of the educated eighteenth-century French and English on both sides of the Atlantic was republicanized in substance, if not in name. It is true that many thinkers, such as Montesquieu, Mably, and Rousseau, despite their admiration for ancient Rome, conceded that a country like France was too large to become a republic. But some, like Mme. Roland, actually confessed that reading Plutarch "had disposed me to become a republican; he had aroused in me that force and pride which give republicanism its character, and he had inspired in me a veritable enthusiasm for the public virtues and for liberty."[10] Although most others were reluctant to admit to being republican, some responded as did the editor of the *South Carolina Gazette*, Peter Timothy, in 1749 when he was denounced as a republican for publishing *Cato's Letters*: he was not a "Republican . . . ," Timothy said, "unless Virtue and Truth be Republican."[11]

These classical ideals, this vision of what James Thomson in his Whig poem "Liberty" called "old virtuous Rome," thus became the best means by which the disgruntled French and dissatisfied Britons on both sides of the Atlantic could voice their objections to the luxury, selfishness, and corruption of the monarchical world in which they lived.¹² Although the intellectuals and critics who invoked republican principles and classical values were opposed to the practices and values of the dominant monarchical world, few of them actually intended to foment revolution and overthrow monarchy. They sought to reform and revitalize their society and to enlighten and improve monarchical rule, not cut off the heads of kings. These critics and many others—including good, loyal colonial subjects of His Britannic Majesty—used republicanism of classical antiquity merely as a counterculture to monarchy. Though rarely cited specifically by name, classical republicanism represented all those beliefs and values that confronted and criticized the abuses of the eighteenth-century monarchical world.

Monarchical and republican values therefore existed side by side in the culture, and many good monarchists, including many good English Tories, adopted what were in substance if not in name republican ideals and principles without realizing the long-run political implications of what they were doing. Although they seldom mentioned the term, educated people of varying political persuasions celebrated classical republicanism for its spirit, its morality, its freedom, its sense of friendship and duty, and its georgic vision of the good society. Classical republicanism as a set of values, an explanation of history, and a form of life was much too pervasive, comprehensive, and involved with being liberal and enlightened to be seen as subversive or as antimonarchical.

Instead of being some thin eddy that ran only on the edges of British or European culture, this classical republicanism thus became an important current in its own right that blended and mingled with the monarchical mainstream and influenced its color, tone, and direction. Eighteenth-century republicanism did not so much displace monarchy as transform it. At times it became virtually indistinguishable from monarchy. Certainly it came to stand for something other than a set of political institutions based on popular election. In fact, republicanism was not to be reduced to a mere form of government at all; instead it was what Franco Venturi has called "a form of life," classical ideals and values that were entirely compatible with monarchical institutions. Republicanism "was separated from the historical forms it had taken in the past, and became increasingly an ideal which could exist in a monarchy."[13]

This republicanism rooted in the Latin writings of ancient Rome was thus never a besieged underground ideology, confined to cellar meetings and marginal intellectuals. On the contrary: kings themselves participated in the cult of antiquity. While reading a passage from Livy's Roman history to the artist Benjamin West, George III suggested to West that he paint *The Departure of Regulus* (1767) as an example of self-sacrificial patriotism. The archbishop of York likewise requested a classical painting from West, drawing on a passage from Tacitus. There were no more enthusiastic promoters of classical republicanism than many members of the English and French nobility, who were presumably closest to monarchy and whose privileges depended upon it. All those French nobles who in 1785 flocked to the Paris salon to ooh and aah over Jacques-Louis David's severe classical painting *The Oath of the Horatii* had no idea they were contributing to the weakening of monarchy and their own demise. Likewise, all those aristocratic sponsors of the 1730 edition of James Thomson's Virgilian-derived georgic poem "The Seasons"—including the queen, ten dukes, thirty-one earls and countesses, and a larger number of the lesser peerage and their sons and daughters—little sensed that their celebration of agricultural simplicity and rural virtue was contributing to the erosion of the monarchical values that made their dominance possible. When even hereditary aristocrats, "disclaiming as it were [their] birthright, and putting [themselves] upon the foot of a Roman," could subscribe enthusiastically to the view voiced by Conyers Middleton in his *Life of Cicero* (1741) that "no man, howsoever born, could arrive at any dignity, who did not win it by his personal merit," then we know something of the power of these republican sentiments in the culture. "Radical chic" was not an invention of the twentieth century.[14]

No culture in the Western world was more republicanized than that of

England and its North American colonies. The literature of the first half of the eighteenth century in the English-speaking world—both belles lettres and political polemics—was a literature of social criticism, and this social criticism was steeped in classical republican values. Most English writers of the period—whether Tory satirists like Pope and Swift or radical Whig publicists like John Trenchard and Thomas Gordon—expressed a deep and bitter hostility to the great social, economic, and political changes taking place in England during the decades following the Glorious Revolution of 1688. The rise of banks, trading companies, and stock markets, plus the emergence of new moneyed men, the increasing public debt, and the corruption of politics all threatened traditional values and led opposition poets and polemicists alike to set classical models and morality against the spreading luxury and commercialization. They knew from the experience of ancient Rome that the same energy that produced a country's rise eventually caused an excess of wealth and luxury that in turn led to its inevitable fall.[15]

Classical republican Rome, like some South Sea tribes for twentieth-century anthropologists, became the means by which the enlightened eighteenth-century English could distance themselves from their own society and criticize it. Gibbon admired Juvenal because the Roman satirist refused to surrender his republican ideals in the face of monarchical realities. He had, said Gibbon, "the soul of a republican" and was "the sworn enemy of tyranny." Thus Dr. Johnson found that the best way to condemn the corruption of eighteenth-century London was to imitate Juvenal's third satire on Nero's Rome.[16]

So pervasive, so dominant was this literature of social criticism that it is difficult to find anything substantial that stood against it. All the great eighteenth-century British writers spoke in republican tones. The long administration of Sir Robert Walpole (1722–1742) eventually united in intellectual opposition all of what William Pulteney called "the gay, the polite and witty Part of the World"; and that opposition, whether from the Tory John Gay in *The Beggar's Opera* or the Whig James Thomson in his poem "Liberty," inevitably drew on classical republican values to voice its love of freedom and its antagonism to corruption. Hume in 1742 thought that more than half of what had been written during the previous twenty years had been devoted to satirizing the machinations of Walpole, the figure who seemed most responsible for what ailed Britain. One administration defender in 1731 concluded that, simply for the sake of getting at Walpole, "the whole nation hath been abused, Corruption and Degeneracy universally charged." All the country-opposition citations to Roman writers were moral strictures against a polluted court, and as such they were often unwitting celebrations of republican values. Consequently, it is virtually impossible to separate the country-opposition tradition, which included radical Whigs and estranged Tories, from this republican heritage of antiquity, so intertwined were they.

Although some Englishmen in the late seventeenth century had found in the age of Augustus a model of restored stability where the arts were allowed to flourish, most after 1688—even aristocrats close to the court—criticized Augustus and looked to the Roman republic for values and inspiration. Cicero and Cato, not Augustus, were the Romans to be admired. To Voltaire, Augustus was "*ce poltron qui osa exiler Ovide*" ("this coward who dared to exile Ovid"). For Jefferson, Augustus was always that "parricide scoundrel." Augustus, Montesquieu said, had led the Romans "gently into slavery," and most Englishmen agreed. Augustus became a code word for tyrant, and as such he was attacked by nearly everyone except royal absolutists. The Tories, thinking of George I, called Augustus a despot, but the court Whigs and all defenders of the Hanoverian settlement, thinking of the Stuarts, did likewise.

From 1688 on, the need for the government to defend the Whig settlement and to attack the Stuart pretensions to the crown meant that a quasirepublican, antiroyalist bias was necessarily built into the official center of English culture. During Walpole's era, both court and country writers alike condemned Augustus as an imperial dictator, the murderer of Cicero, and the destroyer of the republic. If Virgil and Horace were tainted by their too-close association with, in Gibbon's words, "the crafty tyrant," then it had to be argued, as Thomas Blackwell and Thomas Sheridan did, that these great Augustan poets were really republican in spirit, that their talent had actually been formed under the republican era that preceded Augustus's monarchical takeover.

From Addison to Dr. Johnson, English intellectuals expressed their admiration for Tacitus's anti-Augustan, prorepublican view of Roman history. Tacitus remained for Jefferson "the first writer in the world without a single exception." Thomas Gordon originally dedicated his edition of *Tacitus* to Walpole, his patron, but the work so fully expressed a republican antagonism toward Augustus ("the best of his Government was but the sunshine of Tyranny") that it was celebrated by English commonwealthmen as well. David Hume thought that even the Tories had been so long obliged to talk "in the republican stile" that they had at length "embraced the sentiments as well as the language of their adversaries."[17]

These appeals to antiquity made anything other than a classical conception of leadership difficult to justify. All political leaders were measured by the ancient republicans:

> You then whose Judgment the right Course wou'd steer,
> Know well each ANCIENT's proper Character,
> His Fable, Subject, Scope in ev'ry Page,
> Religion, Country, Genius, of his Age.[18]

SO ALEXANDER POPE TOLD HIS countrymen, and nearly every gentleman agreed. It was almost always classical standards—Catonic and Ciceronian standards—that British opposition writers invoked to judge the ragged world of eighteenth-century politics. They all placed the character of classical republicanism—integrity, virtue, and disinterestedness—at the center of public life.[19]

Although these classical republican ideals were set within a monarchical framework, they nonetheless established the foundations not only for liberal arts education and for political debate in the English-speaking world but also for what a good society ought to be. The writings of classical antiquity thus provided more than scholarly embellishment and window dressing for educated Britons on both sides of the Atlantic; they were in fact the principal source of their public morality and values. All political morality was classical morality; people could not read enough about Cato and Cicero. Every lawyer aspired to be another Cicero, and Cato—well, there was no ancient hero like him. Addison's play *Cato* was one of the most popular in the English-speaking world; Thomas Gray even declared it to be a better model for English tragedy than anything by Shakespeare.[20] In America the play went through at least eight editions before 1800. George Washington saw it over and over and incorporated its lines into his correspondence; he learned from it what it was to be a stoical classical hero and an uncorrupt public leader.

The classical past helped to form much of eighteenth-century political theory in the English-speaking world—from the ideal of balanced government to the conception of virtuous citizenship. According to the antique republican tradition, man was by nature a political being, a citizen who achieved his greatest moral fulfillment by participating in a self-governing republic. Public or political liberty—or what we now call positive liberty—meant participation in government. And this political liberty in turn provided the means by which the personal liberty and private rights of the individual—what we today call negative liberty—were protected. In this classical republican tradition, our modern distinction between positive and negative liberties was not yet clearly perceived, and the two forms of liberty were still often seen as one.[21]

Of course, the English did not need ancient Rome to tell them about liberty—at least, not about negative liberty. An acute sense of their liberties and rights, expressed and reinforced by their common law, had been a central part of their culture from time immemorial—from before the Norman conquest and, some said, from before the Roman invasion. Yet however little the classical republican conception of liberty may have affected English law and culture on the home island, it did have important effects on some of the North American colonists. To the extent that colonial Americans' thinking about liberty was affected by the classical past and made positive and republicanized, so was liberty made compatible with the maintenance of slavery. The ancient Romans, after all, had seen no inconsistency between their love of liberty and their practice of slavery; indeed, the labor of their slaves was what made possible their liberty— that is, their independence and their participation in government. All of this made the slaveholding Southern planters of America extraordinarily receptive to classical republicanism.

This kind of positive liberty was realized when the citizens were virtuous—that is, willing to sacrifice their private interests for the sake of the community, including serving in public office without pecuniary rewards. This virtue could be found only in a republic of equal, active, and independent citizens. To be completely virtuous citizens, men—never women, because it was assumed they were never independent—had to be free from dependence, and from the petty interests of the marketplace. Any loss of independence and virtue was corruption.

The virtue that classical republicanism encouraged was public virtue. Private virtues such as prudence, frugality, and industry were important but, said Hume, they only made men "serviceable to themselves, and enable them to promote their own interest"; they were not "such as make them perform their part in society." Public virtue was the sacrifice of private desires and interests for the public interest. It was devotion to the commonweal. All men of genius and leisure, all gentlemen, had an obligation to serve the state. "Let not your love of philosophical amusements have more than its due weight with you," Benjamin Franklin admonished the New York royal official Cadwallader Colden in 1750. Public service was far more important than science. In fact, said Franklin, even "the finest" of Newton's "Discoveries" could not have excused his neglect of serving the commonwealth if the public had needed him.[22]

The power of the ancient Roman republic had flowed from the freedom of its citizens to govern themselves. But as Rome's fate showed, republics required a high degree of civic virtue and disinterestedness among their citizens, and thus they were very fragile polities, extremely liable to corruption. Republics demanded far more morally from their citizens than monarchies did of their subjects. In monarchies each man's desire to do what was right in his own eyes could be restrained by fear or force, by patronage or honor. In republics, however, each man somehow had to be persuaded to sacrifice his personal desires, his luxuries, for the sake of the public good. Monarchies could tolerate great degrees of self-interestedness, private gratification, and corruption among their subjects. After all, they were based on dependence and subservience and had all sorts of adhesives and connections besides virtue to hold their societies together. Monarchies relied on blood, family, kinship, patronage, and—ultimately—fear, as one loyalist clergyman in western Massachusetts tried to make clear to several of his neighbors who were thinking of taking up arms against their king in 1775. Do not do it, the cleric warned. "The king can send a company of horse through the country and take off every head; and in less than six weeks you will be glad to labor a week for sheep's head and pluck."[23] But republics could never resort to such force. In their purest form they had no adhesives, no bonds holding themselves together, except their citizens' voluntary patriotism and willingness to obey public authority. Without virtue and self-sacrifice, republics would fall apart.

One did not have to be a professed republican or a radical Whig, however, to believe in virtue and the other classical values that accompanied it. Virtue, along with the concept of honor, lay at the heart of all prescriptions for political leadership in the eighteenth-century English-speaking world.

If virtue was based on liberty and independence, then it followed that only autonomous individuals free from any ties of interest and paid by no master were qualified to be citizens. Jefferson and many other republican idealists hoped that all ordinary yeoman farmers who owned their own land and who depended for their subsistence only "on their own soil and industry" and not "on the casualties and caprice of customers" would be independent and free enough of pecuniary temptations and market-place interests to be virtuous.[24]

Others, however, questioned the capacity of most ordinary people to rise above self-interest, particularly those who were dependent on "the casualties and caprice of customers." No doubt Cicero and other ancients believed that everyone was born to seek what was morally right, and that this heritage reinforced the moral sense philosophy of the eighteenth century that formed a basis for the eventual emergence of democracy. Indeed, Jefferson's famous aphorism about a ploughman knowing right from wrong better than a professor can be traced through Trenchard and Gordon's "Cato" back to Cicero.[25] Yet Cicero and classical republicanism scarcely celebrated the democratic mass of ordinary people. The classical republican heritage assumed that common people and others involved in the marketplace would be usually overwhelmed by their interests and would thus be incapable of disinterestedness. Of course, these common people were not to be the leaders of the society. Although republicanism, compared to monarchy, rested on a magnanimous view of common people, it retained a traditional classical patrician bias in regard to office-holding. Many good Whigs and republicans believed that important public offices, including even membership of grand juries, ought to be filled only with "the better sort because they are less liable to temptations, less fearful of the frowns of power, may reasonably be supposed of more improved capacities than those of an inferior station." As ancients from Aristotle to Cicero had pointed out, people who had occupations, who needed to engage in the market, who worked with their hands, who were without a liberal education could scarcely possess the enlightenment and disinterestedness to stand above the haggling of the marketplace and act as impartial umpires.[26]

Classical republicanism was naturally suspicious of the marketplace, of commerce and business. Of course, commerce as the handmaiden of agriculture was considered benign and in the eighteenth century was even applauded as a source of peace and prosperity among nations. Still, classical republicanism was mistrustful of merchants as political leaders. Despite the fact that they moved agricultural goods abroad and brought great wealth into the country, merchants were thought to put their own interests ahead of those of their country and thus seemed incapable of disinterestedness.

Since merchants and mechanics and others who worked for a living were generally unqualified for disinterested public office, the responsibility rested on those leisured gentry whose income came to them, as Adam Smith and Francis Hutcheson said, without much exertion.[27]

If public service were to be truly disinterested, the officeholder ought to serve without salary—in accord with what Jefferson called "the Roman principle." "In a virtuous government," he said, ". . . public offices are, what they should be, burthens to those appointed to them, which it would be wrong to decline, though foreseen to bring with them intense labor, and great private loss." Public employment contributes "neither to advantage nor happiness. It is but honorable exile from one's family and affairs." For these reasons Washington refused a salary as commander in chief and attempted to refuse his salary as president. And for these same reasons Benjamin Franklin at the Philadelphia Convention proposed that all members of the executive branch of the new federal government receive no fees or salaries.[28]

Leaders were not to be modern professional politicians but ideally aristocratic farmers who temporarily assumed the burdens of office out of patriotic obligation. In ancient Rome, wrote James Wilson, magistrates and army officers were always gentlemen farmers, always willing to step down "from the elevation of office" and, like Washington in 1783, resume "with contentment and with pleasure, the peaceful labours of a rural and independent life." These Horatian and Virgilian notions of agriculture as a sacred activity were central to eighteenth-century English culture; Addison described Virgil's *Georgics* as "the most complete, elaborate, and finished piece of all antiquity." Many gentlemen on both sides of the Atlantic sought to establish country houses where they could escape from the trials and tribulations of the world. The wealthy Virginia planter Landon Carter named his plantation Sabine Hall after Horace's rural retreat "Sabine vale" located in the hills behind Rome.[29]

But classical agrarianism was not seen simply as Horatian retirement. It was celebrated as well for being a Virgilian source of virtue and social health. Indeed, the georgic vision of moral and social happiness flowing from the simple life of field and plow was shared equally by Southern planters and New England Federalists. Jefferson's praise of the yeoman farmer and the georgic writings of Connecticut poets such as Timothy Dwight and David Humphreys are virtually unintelligible except within this classical republican tradition.[30] How else but in the context of this classical heritage can we make sense of John Dickinson's pose in 1767 as a "Pennsylvania Farmer"? Dickinson was in fact a wealthy Philadelphia lawyer very much involved in city business, yet at the outset he had to assure his readers of his disinterestedness by informing them that he was a farmer "contented" and "undisturbed by worldly hopes or fears," living not off participation in the market but off "a little money at interest."[31] How else can we explain the fervor with which New England Revolutionary War officers in the 1780s set out to establish landed estates in the wilds of the newly acquired territory of Ohio in emulation of those military veterans described by Gibbon who settled in the provinces conquered by Rome? Well into the early decades of the new American Republic's history, establishing a seat in the country and experimenting georgic style with new agricultural products remained a consuming passion, especially among the New England gentry.[32]

The American Revolutionaries exploited all of these classical ideas in their creation of the United States. Many of them saw the new country as a rebirth of the ancient Roman republic. They established mixed constitutions in emulation of ancient Rome and re-created the Roman conception of citizenship open to everyone in the world. For Alexander Hamilton, Rome had been "the nurse of freedom." For John Adams, it had "formed the noblest people and the greatest power that has ever existed."[33] The Revolutionaries hoped to realize what England, according to its critics, had been unable to realize—the antique republican values of the good society, free of contention, selfishness, and luxury. The American leaders went to extraordinary lengths to fulfill classical ideals and to create suitable classical settings and personae. On the banks of a tiny tributary of the Potomac (called Goose Creek and renamed the Tiber) they laid out grandiose plans for a spacious and magnificent classical capital for their new Rome. Like David Humphreys, they believed the Revolution represented a recovery of antique virtue:

> What Rome, once virtuous, saw, this gives us now—
> Heroes and statesmen, awful from the plough.[34]

Joseph Warren actually wore a toga while delivering the Boston Massacre oration in 1775. Joseph Hawley, in a supreme act of Catonian denial, resolved never to accept any promotion, office, or emolument under any government. Patrick Henry's "Give me liberty or give me death" echoed the cry of Cato in Addison's play: "Gods, can a Roman senate long debate / Which of the two to choose, slavery or death!" Likewise, Nathan Hale's dying words, "I only regret that I have but one life to give for my country," resembled Cato's "What a pity is it / That we can die but once to serve our country." John Adams, like Brissot de Warville, idolized Cicero and yearned to have his own Ciceronian moment in which talent alone would count as it had in Roman times. Samuel Adams's virtue was legendary, and he became known as "one of Plutarch's men." And George Washington became the perfect Cincinnatus, the Roman patriot who returned to his farm after his victories in war.[35]

It was a neoclassical age and it was a neoclassical revolution the Americans undertook. They hoped to make their new republic a worthy place—a Columbia, the poets called it—where, in the words of Ezra Stiles, the enlightened president of Yale, "all the arts may be transported from Europe and Asia and flourish . . . with an augmented lustre." Of course, the Americans realized, as Benjamin Rush said, that the arts "flourish chiefly in wealthy and luxurious countries" and were symptoms of social decay. To the end of his life, John Adams, despite his sensuous attraction to the arts, remained convinced, as he told his wife in 1778 in a letter from France, "that the more elegance, the less virtue, in all times and countries." Buildings, paintings, sculpture, music, gardens, and furniture—however rich, magnificent, and splendid—were simply "bagatelles introduced by time and luxury in change for the great qualities and hardy, manly virtues of the human heart."[36] If Americans were to exceed Europe in dignity, grandeur, and taste, they would somehow have to create a republican art that avoided the vices of overrefinement and luxury.

The solution lay in the taut rationality of republican classicism. Classicism allowed artistic expression without fostering corruption and social decay; it froze time and defied change. Classicism offered a set of values that emphasized, as the commissioners who were charged with supervising the construction of public buildings in Washington, D.C., put it in 1793, "a grandeur of conception, a Republican simplicity, and that true elegance of proportion, which correspond to a tempered freedom excluding Frivolity, the food of little minds."[37] Such a neoclassical art was not an original art in any modern sense, but it was never intended to be. The Americans' aim in their literature, painting, and architecture of the 1780s and 1790s was to give a new and fresh republican spirit to old forms, to isolate and exhibit in their art the eternal and universal principles of reason and nature that the ancients had expressed long ago. Poets in the wilds of the New York frontier thus saw nothing incongruous in invoking comparisons with Virgil or Horace. And Joel Barlow could believe that his epic of America, *The Columbiad*, precisely because of its high moral and republican message, could exceed in grandeur even Homer's *Iliad*.

Jefferson was completely taken with neoclassicism. Although in the 1780s he momentarily accepted the Benjamin West–inspired fashionableness of having Houdon's statue of Washington done in contemporary dress, several decades later his true feelings came out: he was more than happy that Canova's statue of Washington was done in a Roman toga. "Every person of taste in Europe" preferred the Roman costume, he said. "Our boots and regimentals have a very puny effect." Jefferson was contemptuous and even ashamed of the "gothic" Georgian architecture of his native Virginia, and he sought in Monticello to build a house that would do justice to those Palladian villas that harked back to Roman antiquity. In the 1780s he badgered his Virginia colleagues into erecting as the new state capitol in Richmond a magnificent copy of the Maison Carrée, a Roman temple in Nîmes from the first century A.D., because he wanted an

American public building that would be a model for the people's "study and imitation" and "an object and proof of national good taste." The Maison Carrée was a building, he said, that "has pleased universally for near 2,000 years." Almost single-handedly he became responsible for making America's public buildings resemble Roman temples.[38]

The cultural relics of these revolutionary classical dreams are with America still: in the names of cities and towns like Rome, Syracuse, and Troy; in the designation of political institutions like senates and capitols; in the profusion of unread georgic poems like Timothy Dwight's "Greenfield Hill"; in the political symbols like the goddess Liberty, the numerous Latin mottos, and the Great Seal of the United States with its Roman eagle, its phrases *novus ordo seclorum* and *annuit coeptis* from Virgil's *Georgics* and *Eclogues*, and its Roman numerals, MDCCLXXVI, for greater dignity; and of course in the endless proliferation of Roman temples. But the spirit that inspired these things—the meaning these institutions, artifacts, and symbols had for the revolutionaries—has been lost, and it was being lost even as they were being created.

The American leaders may have begun their Revolution trying to recover an idealized and vanished Roman republic, but they soon realized that they had unleashed forces that were carrying them and their society much further than they had anticipated. Instead of becoming a new and grand incarnation of ancient Rome, a land of virtuous and contented farmers, America within decades of the Declaration of Independence had become a sprawling, materialistic, and licentious popular democracy unlike any state that had ever existed. Buying and selling were celebrated as never before, and the antique meaning of virtue was transformed. Ordinary people who knew no Latin and had few qualms about disinterestedness began asserting themselves with new vigor in the economy and in politics. Far from sacrificing their private desires for the good of the whole, Americans of the early Republic came to see that the individual's pursuit of wealth or happiness (the two were now interchangeable) was not only inevitable but justifiable as the only proper basis for a free state.

In the rapid transformation to democracy in the decades following the Revolution, ancient Rome lost much of its meaning for Americans. The transformation began early, often initially taking the form of attacks on the relevance of learning Latin or Greek in school. These democratic assaults on republican values, like the earlier ones on monarchical values, were undertaken by people who had little idea of the ultimate consequences of their actions. Benjamin Rush, for example, had contended that the study of Greek and Latin was "improper in a peculiar manner in the United States" because it tended to confine education to only a few, when in fact republicanism required everyone to be educated. Within a few years, however, Rush became alarmed that too many ordinary people were going to college and lowering the standards of civilization. But it was too late to stop the spread of this bumptious and bustling democracy.[39]

By the 1820s American society had left the georgic dreams of quiet farms and settled husbandmen far behind. Classical Rome was now thought to be too stolid and imitative to express the restlessness and vulgar originality of this new democratic America. Ancient Greece, said Edward Everett, was a better model. Ancient Greece, Homer's Greece, was tumultuous, wild, and free, said Everett, "free to licentiousness, free to madness."[40] For most Americans the great legacy of ancient Rome was gone.

AFTERWORD TO CHAPTER 2

This piece was presented as a lecture several times, including at a conference held in Rome in October 2008 sponsored by the Robert H. Smith International Center for Jefferson Studies at Monticello. In the course of reading and listening to the other papers at that conference, I concluded that some of our historical debates over the influence of the classics on the Founders were misplaced.

No doubt the classical world was an important part of the political memory of the Founders. We might even say that the relationship between the Founders and the classical past was similar to our present relationship to the Founders. Just as we use the Founders, such as Jefferson and Washington, to get our bearings and reaffirm our beliefs and reinvigorate our institutions, so too did the Founders use antiquity, especially republican antiquity, to help shape their values and justify their institutions. It was a memory bank that they drew on to make sense of their experience. Today this classical memory bank—those sets of ancient meanings—no longer exists for most Americans.

My distinguished mentor Bernard Bailyn once wrote that the classics played a minor role in the thought of the Founders. Antiquity, he said, was mere "window dressing" to the ideas of the Revolutionaries. It was "illustrative, not determinative" of their thought—not determinative, he says, in the way their radical Whig ideology was. The classics "contributed a vivid vocabulary but not the logic or grammar of thought, a universally respected personification but not the source of political and social beliefs. They heightened the colonists' sensitivity to ideas and attitudes otherwise derived."[1]

One of many discussions at the Rome conference focused on Bailyn's provocative remarks. The question I raised is the following: are the ideas of one era ever *determinative* of the thought of another? I don't think so. I don't believe ideas of an earlier period ever *determine* the ideas of a later period. What really *determines* thought are the events of the participants' present, their immediate interests and emotional needs, their present experience. Reality presses in upon us, and we look to bodies of ideas, or sets of meanings, to make sense of that reality, to explain, justify, or condemn it. For the Revolutionaries the classical past offered a body of meanings that they could draw upon to make meaningful their behavior and their goals. They didn't absorb it intact but drew upon it willy-nilly to fit their particular needs.

That's the way we still use ideas. Who reads a book and absorbs the whole thing? Rather, we select those parts that seem relevant or meaningful to us. We pick and choose the ideas from those available to us that seem most appropriate and that make our experience and circumstances most meaningful. But it is our experience that is determinative. Madison did not get his ideas for reforming the federal government in the 1780s from reading the trunks of books that Jefferson sent him from Paris. As I try to indicate in my "Interests and Disinterestedness" essay, his ideas were shaped by his experience in several sessions of the Virginia Assembly, and he used what ideas he could find, from David Hume as much as anyone, to justify and explain what he wanted to do in limiting the excesses of democracy in the state legislatures. His effort to use antiquity in order to justify the need for an upper house or senate, as described by historian Caroline Winterer at the conference, is another such example.

Moreover, as I suggest in the introduction to this volume, if we are using ideas to persuade someone of something, we have to select those ideas that will be most persuasive to whatever audience we are addressing. Of course, we can't just make up ideas out of whole cloth or concoct any old notion to make things meaningful. We have to draw upon those ideas, those sets of meanings, that are publicly available to us. For the Revolutionaries, the classical past offered a rich set of meanings to draw upon.

We borrow what we need from the ideas of the past, and in the process we inevitably distort those past ideas. Of course, the Founders' use of classicism was different from the classicism of antiquity, just as our use of the ideas of the Founding bears little resemblance to the thinking of the eighteenth century. But I would say that this sort of distortion went on with the ideas of the radical Whigs as well. In other words, ideas by themselves are never determinative of thought. Eighteenth-century Americans selected and used what they found relevant and appropriate in the ideas of Locke, Trenchard and Gordon, or James Burgh and in the process fit what they read into their circumstances. This is inevitably how ideas are used, and since our experience of reality is constantly changing, and we always have to make it meaningful, it is not surprising that our intellectual life is always dynamic and changing. Our intellectual quarrels are over what meanings we will give to our experience, to fulfill our present-day needs.

Yet by questioning whether the ideas of antiquity were determinative of the Founders' thinking, I do not mean to suggest that the classical past was unimportant to them. Even if ideas of an earlier era are not determinative of later thinking, it does not follow that these earlier ideas were simply ornamentation and had little influence. I believe that the classical past was much more than illustrative of the Founders' thoughts. Earlier ideas can, as I tried to indicate in the essay, influence and affect behavior.

CHAPTER THREE

CONSPIRACY *and the* PARANOID STYLE: CAUSALITY *and* DECEIT *in the* EIGHTEENTH CENTURY

*W*ERE THE AMERICAN REVOLUTIONARIES MENTALLY disturbed? Was the Revolution itself a consequence of anxieties buried deep in the psyches of its leaders? Bizarre and preposterous questions, it would seem, and scarcely the sorts of questions one expects to be asked about the Founding Fathers. Yet these are precisely the questions some historians are now suggesting we ought to be asking about the Revolution.

The Revolution seems to have become very much a psychological phenomenon. Recent writings on the subject are filled with psychological terms, and popular interpretations such as the "search for identity" on the part of insecure provincials are grounded in psychological conceptions.[1] With the growing interest in family history and child rearing, historians are making strenuous although contradictory efforts to explore the "interrelationship of private and public experience."[2] The upbringing of the colonists is being linked to their rejection of their "mother" country and "fatherly" king, and the familial relationship between Britain and the colonies is being wrung dry of every bit of psychological significance it may contain.[3] One by one the Founding Fathers are psychoanalyzed and their unconscious fears and drives brought to the surface.[4] The restraints of the British authorities, it now appears, threatened the colonists' "ego capacities" and aroused "large-scale personal anxiety, guilt, shame, and feelings of inadequacy that could only be overcome by a *manly* resistance to those restraints." Indeed, the colonists' widespread "fear of effeminacy," it has been suggested, may be "a source for some of the inner anxieties of many Americans" and "a useful clue to the psychological roots of the paranoid vision of the political world that dominated the politics of the period."[5] All of this psychologizing has been carried to the point where it is no longer strange or unreasonable to refer to the Revolution as "a cathartic event, . . . a psychological release" for a multitude of pent-up feelings and anxieties. It has even become possible to call the Revolution "a delusion explicable by the principles of psychology."[6]

No doubt much of this application of psychology to the Revolution can be explained by its influence on historical writing generally. Not only is psychohistory bidding to become a legitimate field, but psychological terms and theories have so insinuated themselves into our culture that we historians are often unaware that we are using them. Still, the recent impact of psychology on Revolutionary history writing is peculiarly intensive and cannot be accounted for simply by its effect on the discipline of history as a whole. What seems crucially important in explaining the extraordinary reliance on psychology in recent Revolutionary historiography is the coincidental publication in 1965 of two significant books— Bernard Bailyn's introduction to his *Pamphlets of the American Revolution* (subsequently enlarged and republished in 1967 as *The Ideological Origins of the American Revolution*) and Richard Hofstadter's *The Paranoid Style in American Politics*.[7] Neither of these works was influenced by the other, and each separately has strongly affected our understanding of American history. But when read together and interrelated in the thinking of historians, these books have taken on an unusual force in helping to shape our current interest in the Revolution as a psychological event.

Bailyn's interpretation of the origins of the Revolution is familiar enough. He argued that a pattern of ideas and attitudes bearing on the realities of colonial politics was "built into the very structure of political culture in eighteenth-century Britain and America" and provided "the sufficient background for understanding why there was a Revolution." A long-existing and integrated intellectual tradition drawn from various English sources, wrote Bailyn, prepared Americans for a particular interpretation of the welter of events that occurred in the 1760s and 1770s. "They saw about them, with increasing clarity, not merely mistaken, or even evil, policies violating the principles upon which freedom rested, but what appeared to be evidence of nothing less than a deliberate assault launched surreptitiously by plotters against liberty both in England and in America." It was the overwhelming evidence of a "design"—a conspiracy—"that was signaled to the colonists after 1763, and it was this above all else that in the end propelled them into Revolution."[8]

Bailyn's interpretation has had a powerful effect on our understanding of the Revolution, and every student of the Revolution has had to come to terms with it in one way or another. No one now can deny the prevalence of conspiratorial fears among the Revolutionaries. Indeed, historians largely take such fears for granted and have become preoccupied with explaining why the Revolutionaries should have had them. This need to make sense of these conspiratorial beliefs seems, more than anything else, to lie behind the extraordinary use of psychology in recent writing about the Revolution. While recognizing that there may be rational explanations for fears of conspiracy, most historians cannot help assuming that such fears are mainly rooted in nonrational sources. This assumption grew out of the experience of American politics, particularly McCarthyism, in the years following World War II—an assumption expressed in numerous sociological studies of those years and most strikingly in Hofstadter's conception of a "paranoid style."[9]

Hofstadter's book on the "paranoid style," which he found pervasive in American politics, demonstrated that the Revolutionary leaders were not unique in their fears of a conspiracy hatched by hidden diabolical forces. They were only one of many generations of Americans who have thought in terms of conspiracies throughout our history. Hofstadter became aware of Bailyn's interpretation when it was too late to integrate it into his argument, and thus he began his study of the "paranoid style" with the Bavarian Illuminati scare of the 1790s. He traced the style through the anti-Masonic, nativist, and Populist fears of the nineteenth century and concluded with an analysis of the beliefs in a communist conspiracy in the 1950s. By leaving the Revolution out of his story and by assuming that the "paranoid style" was "the preferred style only of *minority* movements" and marginal elements in American society, Hofstadter avoided the troubling implications of describing the Revolutionaries as paranoid personalities.[10]

Hofstadter said his use of "paranoid style" was not intended to suggest any medical or clinical significance; he meant only to use the term metaphorically to describe "a way of seeing the world and of expressing oneself." Medically, as he pointed out, paranoia is defined as a chronic mental disorder characterized by systematized delusions of persecution. However overly suspicious and apocalyptical in expression American paranoid spokesmen may have been, said Hofstadter, they could not be described as "certifiable lunatics." Yet—and it was a very big, drawn-out yet—this style was not quite normal; it was, Hofstadter wrote, "a distorted style" and thus "a possible signal that may alert us to a distorted judgment." It indicated that some kind of "political pathology" was at work; it was a recurrent mode of expression in American public life "which has frequently been linked with movements of suspicious discontent." Although believers in conspiracy may not have been crazy, they were persons, Hofstadter suggested, who had perverse and fanciful views of reality and were thus fit subjects for the application of some sort of "depth psychology."[11]

Other historians, sharing Hofstadter's assumption that politics was often "a projective arena for feelings and impulses that are only marginally related to the manifest issues," also sought to relate Americans' recurring fears of conspiracy to some underlying social or psychological process.[12] Some thought "that fear of conspiracy characterizes periods when traditional social and moral values are undergoing change" and therefore focused on the unusual fluidity of American society. People who were unsure of their identity and status, socially disrupted or alienated in some way, were, it seemed, especially susceptible to conspiratorial interpretations of events. Possibly, suggested David Brion Davis, who has most meticulously uncovered the conspiratorial fears of nineteenth-century Americans, various groups, from Anti-Masons to opponents of the Slave Power, found in the paranoid style a common means of expressing their different torments and troubles. Obviously, historians were careful to note, the great numbers of people who relied on such imagery of subversion—from Abraham Lincoln to Justice Robert H. Jackson—could not be dismissed as "charlatans, crackpots, and the disaffected." Davis in particular warned against any facile assumption "that the fear of subversion is always generated by internal, psychological needs." Despite such qualifications and cautions, however, the implications of these historical accounts of the paranoid style were clear: Americans seemed prone to fears of subversion, and these fears were symptomatic of severe social and psychological strains.[13]

Once America's paranoid style was revealed to be so prevalent, its connection with the ideology of the Revolution became inevitable. Not only was Bailyn's account of the colonists' fears of conspiracy widely reprinted, but historians now suggested that the Revolution had set "the basic pattern" of the paranoid style. "Is it possible," asked Davis, "that the circumstances of the Revolution conditioned Americans to think of resistance to a dark subversive force as the essential ingredient of their national identity?"[14] With the paranoid style associated with the ideology of the Revolution in this way, historians were quick to find traces of it everywhere in their sources. Although Bailyn had stressed in his *Ideological Origins* the rational basis of the colonists' fears, the term "paranoia" soon proliferated in historical writings on the Revolution. "The insurgent whig ideology," it now seemed clear, "had a frenzied, even paranoid cast to it," and leaders like John Adams and Thomas Jefferson were even accused of suffering from some form of paranoia.[15] The mounting evidence could lead to only one conclusion: "The era of the American Revolution was a period of political paranoia" in which "visions of conspiracy were endemic."[16]

In many cases these references to paranoia were clearly metaphorical. But given the current interest in psychohistory, it is not surprising that other references to paranoia have taken on an authentically psychological character, presuming a close connection between paranoid thinking and particular psychic sensibilities. Some historians, while acknowledging that the American Whigs' belief in a ministerial design against their liberties may have had some rational and conscious sources, have emphasized that "the fear of conspiracy also had roots buried deeply in the innermost recesses of the psyches of numerous Americans." Certain types of colonists unconsciously experienced tensions and anxieties over their personal autonomy and sexual identities "that may very well have shaped their public fears and fostered their sense of conspiracies endangering them."[17]

Other writers, taking Bailyn's argument as a "point of departure," have attempted a stark and quite literal "psychological interpretation of the coming of the Revolution," even going so far as to suggest that the Revolutionary leaders were clinically paranoiac—that is, that they were suffering from actual delusions of persecution and were unable to assess reality in a rational fashion. Far from being profoundly reasonable men, they were "prone to emotional instability, predisposed to psychological problems, vulnerable to them under the goad of an appropriate precipitant," like the Stamp Act, which left "in its wake the paranoid delusions that Britain was conspiring to enslave Americans."[18]

HOW MUCH FURTHER can we go? It is difficult to imagine that more psychological significance can be extracted from the conspiratorial beliefs of the Revolutionaries. Maybe it is time to pause in our psychological explorations, step back, and get a quite different, wider perspective on this mode of thinking—not to explain the Revolution but to explain why eighteenth-century Americans should have thought as they did. In other words, we need to reach through and beyond the Revolution to the larger culture of the English-speaking or, indeed, the entire Atlantic world of the eighteenth century. We may find that it was quite possible for all manner of people—not just British country-opposition groups and suspicious colonists, but "reasonable people," indeed the most enlightened minds of the day—to believe in malevolent conspiracies.[19]

There are explanations for the eighteenth century's conspiratorial beliefs that are rooted not in any modern notions of psychic strain or even in the peculiar suspicions of the radical Whigs and country-opposition tradition, but rather in the general presuppositions and conventions—in the underlying metaphysics—of eighteenth-century culture. Indeed, such conspiratorial beliefs grew so much out of the common ways in which enlightened thinkers conceived of events that they can scarcely be used to explain any particular happening of the period, including the Revolution. Such beliefs may accurately describe the American Revolutionaries' mode of thinking in the 1760s and 1770s, but they cannot account for the Revolution, and they cannot be used as evidence that the Revolutionaries were suffering from some emotional instability peculiar to themselves. For the one thing about conspiratorial interpretations of events that must impress all students of early modern Western history is their ubiquitousness: they can be found everywhere in the thought of people on both sides of the Atlantic.

More than any other period of English history, the century or so following the Restoration was the great era of conspiratorial fears and imagined intrigues. The Augustan Age, said Daniel Defoe, was "an Age of Plot and Deceit, of Contradiction and Paradox." Pretense and hypocrisy were everywhere, and nothing seemed as it really was. Politics, especially in the decades from the Restoration to the Hanoverian accession, appeared to be little more than one intrigue and deception after another. It had to be a "horrid plot," said Scrub in George Farquhar's *The Beaux' Stratagem* of 1707. "First, it must be a plot because there's a woman in't. Secondly, it must be a plot because there's a priest in't. Thirdly, it must be a plot because there's French gold in't. And fourthly, it must be a plot because I don't know what to make on't." With so many like Scrub wanting to know but with so little revealed, inferences of hidden designs and conspiracies flourished. So prevalent seemed the plotting that Jonathan

Swift in his inimitable fashion suggested that only the most ingenious scatological devices could uncover the many conspirators. Everywhere people sensed designs within designs, cabals within cabals; there were court conspiracies, backstairs conspiracies, ministerial conspiracies, factional conspiracies, aristocratic conspiracies, and by the last half of the eighteenth century even conspiracies of gigantic secret societies that cut across national boundaries and spanned the Atlantic. Revolutionary Americans may have been an especially jealous and suspicious people, but they were not unique in their fears of dark, malevolent plots and plotters.[20]

In the Anglo-American world at the time of the Revolutionary crisis there was scarcely a major figure who did not tend to explain political events in these terms. The American Whigs were not unique; opponents of the Revolution—American Tories and members of the British administration alike—were convinced that they themselves were victims of subversives who cloaked what George III called their "desperate conspiracy" in "vague expressions of attachment to the parent state and the strongest protestations of loyalty . . . whilst they were preparing for a general revolt." Others besides the deeply involved participants in the Revolutionary crisis saw the world in these same terms. John Wesley did. So, too, did sophisticated thinkers like Horace Walpole and Edmund Burke rely on hidden schemes to account for otherwise inexplicable events. Such conspiratorial thinking, moreover, was not confined to the English-speaking world. Some of the most grandiose and elaborate plots of the century were imagined by the French of various social ranks. Like the American Revolution, the French Revolution was born in an atmosphere of conspiratorial fears. There were plots by the ministers, by the queen, by the aristocracy, by the clergy; everywhere there were secret managers behind the scenes pulling the strings of the great events of the Revolution. The entire Revolution was even seen by some as the planned consequence of a huge Masonic conspiracy. The paranoid style, it seems, was a mode of expression common to the age.[21]

If all manner of people in the eighteenth century resorted readily to conspiratorial modes of explanation and habitually saw plots by dissembling men behind patterns of events, can the paranoid style carry the peculiarly American significance attributed to it? Can it have been, as we are told, the particular means by which certain kinds of disturbed people, especially unsettled Americans, released their hidden fears into the public arena? Yet if the prevalent eighteenth-century disposition to think in conspiratorial terms was not simply a symptom of American emotional instability, what then was it?

To understand how "reasonable people" could believe in the prevalence of plots, we should begin by taking their view of events at face value and examine what it rationally implied. It was obviously a form of causal explanation, a "tendency of many causes to one event," said Samuel Johnson. To us this is a crude and peculiar sort of causal explanation because it rests entirely on individual intentions or motives. It is, as Hofstadter pointed out, a "rationalistic" and "personal" explanation: "decisive events are not taken as part of the stream of history, but as the consequences of someone's will." To those who think in conspiratorial terms, things do not "just happen"; they are "brought about, step by step, by will and intention."[22] Concatenations of events are the products not, as we sophisticated historians might say, of "social forces" or "the stream of history" but of the concerted designs of individuals.

The paranoid style, in other words, is a mode of causal attribution based on particular assumptions about the nature of social reality and the necessity of moral responsibility in human affairs. It presumes a world of autonomous, freely acting individuals who are capable of directly and deliberately bringing about events through their decisions and actions, and who thereby can be held morally responsible for what happens. We are the heirs of this conception of cause, and its assumptions still permeate our culture, although, as our system of criminal punishment shows, in increasingly archaic and contradictory ways. Most of the eighteenth-century world of thought remains our world, so much so, indeed, that we have trouble perceiving how different we really are. We may still talk about causes and effects, but, as Hofstadter's invocation of "the stream of history" suggests, we often do so in ways the eighteenth century would not have understood. If we are to make sense of that period's predilection for conspiratorial thinking, we must suspend our modern understanding about how events ought to be explained and open ourselves to that different world.

There had, of course, been many conspiratorial interpretations of political affairs before the eighteenth century. Such interpretations rested on modes of apprehending reality that went back to classical antiquity. For centuries men had relied on "the spirit of classic ethical psychology, upon an *analyse du coeur humain*, not upon discovery or premonitions of historical forces," in explaining public events.[23] There was nothing new in seeing intrigue, deceit, and cabals in politics. From Sallust's description of Cataline through Machiavelli's lengthy discussion in his *Discourses*, conspiracy was a common feature of political theory. But classical and Renaissance accounts of plots differed from most of the conspiratorial interpretations of the eighteenth century. They usually described actions by which ambitious politicans gained control of governments: conspiracy was taken for granted as a normal means by which rulers were deposed. Machiavelli detailed dozens of such plots. Indeed, he wrote, "many more princes have lost their lives and their positions through them than through open war."[24] Such conspiracies occurred within the small ruling circles of a few great men—in limited political worlds where everyone knew everyone else. The classical and Renaissance discussions of conspiracies have a matter-of-fact quality. They were not imagined or guessed at; they happened. Cataline actually plotted to take over Rome; Brutus and Cassius really did conspire against Caesar.

During the early modern era, conspiracy continued to be a common term of politics. Seventeenth-century England was filled with talk and fears of conspiracies of all kinds. There were French plots, Irish plots, Popish plots, Whig plots, Tory plots, Jacobite plots; there was even the "Meal Tub Plot." Yet by this period many of the conspiracies had become very different from those depicted in earlier centuries of Western history. To be sure, some of them, like the Gunpowder Plot of 1605 to blow up Parliament or the "Rye House Plot" of 1683 to seize the king, were of the traditional sort described by Machiavelli, designed to subvert the existing government. But other references to conspiracy took a new and different form. The term was still pejorative and charged with suspicion, but now it became used more vaguely and broadly to refer to any combination of persons, including even members of the government itself, united for a presumed common end. The word acquired a more general and indeterminate meaning in political discourse. Its usage suggested confusion rather than certainty. Conspiracies like those of Charles II's Cabal became less matters of fact and more matters of inference. Accounts of plots by court or government were no longer descriptions of actual events but interpretations of otherwise puzzling concatenations of events. By the eighteenth century conspiracy was not simply a means of explaining how rulers were deposed; it had become a common means of explaining how rulers and others directing political events really operated. It was a term used not so much by those intimate with the sources of political events as by those removed from the events and, like Farquhar's Scrub, bewildered by them.

Unlike the schemes of antiquity and the Renaissance, which flowed from the simplicity and limitedness of politics, the conspiratorial interpretations of the Augustan Age flowed from the expansion and increasing complexity of the political world. Unprecedented demographic and economic developments in early modern Europe were massively altering the nature of society and politics. There were more people more distanced from one another and from the apparent centers of political decision making. The conceptual worlds of many individuals were being broadened and transformed. The more people became strangers to one another and the less they knew of one another's hearts, the more suspicious and mistrustful they became, ready as never before in Western history to see deceit and deception at work. Relationships between superiors and subordinates, rulers and ruled, formerly taken for granted, now became disturbingly problematical, and people became uncertain of who was who and who was doing what. Growing proportions of the population were more politically conscious and more concerned with what seemed to be the abused power and privileges of ruling elites. Impassioned efforts were made everywhere to arouse "the vigilance of the public eye" against those few men "who cannot exist without a scheme in their heads," those "turbulent, scheming, maliciously cunning, plotters of mischief." The warnings against rulers grew more anxious and fearful, the expressions of suspicion more frenzied and strident, because assumptions about how public affairs operated became more and more separated from reality. It was easy for a fifteenth-century nobleman, describing political events, to say that "it will be sufficient to speak of the high-ranking people, for it is through them that God's power and justice are made known."[25] But by the eighteenth century this tracing of all events back to the ambitions and actions of only the high-ranking leaders was being stretched to the breaking point. Society was composed not simply of great men and their retainers but of numerous groups, interests, and "classes" whose actions could not be easily deciphered. Human affairs were more complicated, more interdependent, and more impersonal than they had ever been in Western history.

Yet at this very moment when the world was outrunning man's capacity to explain it in personal terms, in terms of the passions and schemes of individuals, the most enlightened of the age were priding themselves on their ability to do just that. The widespread resort to conspiratorial interpretations grew out of this contradiction.

CONSPIRATORIAL INTERPRETATIONS—attributing events to the concerted designs of willful individuals—became a major means by which educated men in the early modern period ordered and gave meaning to their political world. Far from being symptomatic of irrationality, this conspiratorial mode of explanation represented an enlightened stage in Western man's long struggle to comprehend his social reality. It flowed from the scientific promise of the Enlightenment and represented an effort, perhaps in retrospect a last desperate effort, to hold men personally and morally responsible for their actions.

Personalistic explanations had, of course, long been characteristic of premodern European society and are still characteristic of primitive peoples. Premodern men lacked our modern repertory of explanations and could not rely on those impersonal forces such as industrialization, modernization, or the "stream of history" that we so blithely invoke to account for complicated combinations of events. They were unable, as we say, to "rise to the conception of movements."[26] For that different, distant world the question asked of an event was not "How did it happen?" but "Who did it?"

Yet despite this stress on persons rather than processes, premodern men always realized that much of what happened was beyond human agency and understanding. Even those classical and Renaissance writers who stressed that events were due to "the wisdoms and follies, the virtues and vices of individuals who made decisions" built their histories and tragic dramas around the extent to which such heroic individuals could prevail against unknown fortune. Ultimately the world seemed uncontrollable and unpredictable, ruled by mysterious forces of fate or chance, shadowed in inscrutability.[27]

At the opening of the modern era, Protestant reformers invoked divine providence and the omnipotence of God in order to stamp out the traditional popular reliance on luck and magic and to renew a sense of design and moral purpose in the world. Life, they held, was not a lottery but the working out of God's purpose and judgments, or "special providences." Men were morally responsible for events; even natural catastrophes like earthquakes and floods were seen as divine punishments for human misbehavior.[28] Still, it remained evident that life was uncertain and precarious and that God moved in very mysterious ways. As the Puritan Increase Mather observed as late as 1684, "Things many times come to pass contrary to humane probabilities and the rational Conjectures and expectations of men." Nature itself was not always consistent, for things sometimes acted "otherwise than according to their natures and proper inclinations." Humans might glimpse those parts of God's design that he chose to reveal, but ultimately they could never "be able fully to understand by what Rules the Holy and Wise God ordereth all events Prosperous and adverse which come to pass in the world." If there was comfort in knowing that what seemed chaotic, fortuitous, or accidental was in reality directed by God, it nonetheless remained true that the "ways of Providence are unsearchable."[29]

At the very time that Mather was writing, however, God was preparing to "let Newton be": the treatise that was to be enlarged into the first book of the *Principia* was completed in 1684. Of course, the scientific revolution of the seventeenth century—or, more accurately, the new Western consciousness of which that revolution was the most important expression—did not make all immediately light. Yet many people now had less fear of chaos and contingency and greater confidence in their ability to understand events, so much so that sophisticates like George Savile, marquis of Halifax, could even warn against "that common error of applying God's judgments upon particular occasions." The world lost some of its mystery and became more manipulable. Although the new science tended to remove man from the center of the physical universe at the same time it brought him to the center of human affairs in ways that even classical and Renaissance thinkers had scarcely conceived of. It promised him the capacity to predict and control not only nature but his own society, and it proceeded to make him directly and consciously responsible for the course of human events. Ultimately the implications of this momentous shift created the cultural matrix out of which eighteenth-century conspiratorial interpretations developed.[30]

The new science assumed a world of mechanistic cause and effect in which what happens does so only because something else happened before. Philosophers since Aristotle had talked of causes but never before in terms of such machine-like regularity, of such chains of consequences. "When the world became a machine," writes Jacob Bronowski, "[cause] became the god within the machine." Mechanistic causality became the paradigm in which the enlightened analysis of all behavior and events now had to take place. Cause was something that produced an effect; every effect had a cause; the cause and its effect were integrally related. Such thinking created a new world of laws, measurements, predictions, and constancies or regularities of behavior—all dependent on the same causes producing the same effects. "The knowledge of particular phenomena may gratify a barren curiosity," Samuel Stanhope Smith told a generation of Princeton students, "but they are of little real use, except, as they tend to establish some general law, which will enable the accurate observer to predict similar effects in all time to come, in similar circumstances, and to depend upon the result. Such general laws alone deserve the name of science."[31]

The change in consciousness came slowly, confusedly, and reluctantly. Few were immediately willing to abandon belief in the directing providence of God. Newton himself endeavored to preserve God's autonomy. "A God without dominion, providence, and final causes," he said, "is nothing but Fate and Nature." In fact, the Christian belief that nature was ordered by God's will was an essential presupposition of early modern science. Yet despite the continued stress by Newton's followers on God's control over the workings of nature, many eighteenth-century philosophers gradually came to picture the deity as a clockmaker, and some even went so far as to deny that God had anything at all to do with the physical movement of the universe. The logic of the new science implied a world that ran itself.[32]

To posit the independence of the natural world was exciting enough; to conceive of a human world without God's judgments and providences was simply breathtaking: it was in fact what centrally defined the Enlightenment. The work of John Locke and other philosophers opened reflective minds to the startling supposition that society, though no doubt ordained in principle by God, was man's own creation—formed and sustained, and thus alterable, by human beings acting autonomously and purposefully. It came to seem that if men could understand the natural order that God had made, then perhaps they could eventually understand the social order that they themselves had made. From the successes of natural science, or what the eighteenth century termed natural philosophy, grew the conviction that moral laws—the chains of cause and effect in human behavior—could be discovered that would match those of the physical world. Thus was generated eighteenth-century moral philosophy—the search for the uniformities and regularities of man's behavior that has proliferated into the various social sciences of our own time.[33]

Finding the laws of behavior became the consuming passion of the Enlightenment. In such a liberal and learned world there could no longer be any place for miracles or the random happenings of chance. Chance, it was now said, was "only a name to cover our ignorance of the cause of any event." God may have remained the primary cause of things, but in the minds of the enlightened he had left men to work out the causes and effects of their lives free from his special interventions. All that happened in society was to be reduced to the strictly human level of men's motivations and goals. "Humanity," said William Warburton in 1727, "is the only cause of human vicissitudes." The source of man's calamities, wrote Constantin François de Chasseboeuf, comte de Volney, in 1791, lay not in "the distant heavens . . . it resides in man himself, he carries it with him in the inward recesses of his own heart."[34] Such beliefs worked their way through every variety of intellectual endeavor in the age. They produced not only a new genre of literature—the novel with its authorial control and design—but also a new kind of man-centered causal history, one based on the same assumptions as the age's conspiratorial interpretations.[35]

English history since the Revolution of 1688, as Henry St. John, Viscount Bolingbroke, saw it from the vantage point of the 1730s, was "not the effect of ignorance, mistakes, or what we call chance, but of design and scheme in those who had the sway at that time." This could be proved by seeing "events that stand recorded in history . . . as they followed one another, or as they produced one another, causes or effects, immediate or remote." "History supplies the defects of our own experience" and demonstrates that there are really no such things as accidents; "it shows us causes as in fact they were laid, with their immediate effects: and it enables us to guess at future events." "History," said Edward Gibbon simply, "is the science of causes and effects."[36]

Extending this concept from the realm of natural phenomena into the moral world of human affairs was not an easy matter. Natural philosophers like Newton had sought to stave off the numbing necessitarianism implied in a starkly mechanistic conception of cause and effect by positing various God-inspired "active principles" as the causal agents of motion, gravity, heat, and the like. Even those later eighteenth-century scientists who saw nature as self-contained and requiring no divine intervention whatsoever still presumed various energizing powers in matter itself.[37] The need for some sort of active principle in human affairs was felt even more acutely, for the new mechanistic philosophy posed a threat to what Arthur O. Lovejoy has called the "intense ethical inwardness" of Western Christendom. The belief "that whatever moves and acts does so mechanically and necessarily" was ultimately incompatible with personalistic thinking and cast doubt on man's moral responsibility for his actions.[38] If human affairs were really the consequence of one thing repeatedly and predictably following upon another, the social world would become as determined as the physical world seemed to be. Theologians like Jonathan Edwards welcomed this logic and subtly used the new cause-and-effect philosophy to justify God's sovereignty. But other moral philosophers had no desire to create a secular version of divine providence or to destroy the voluntarism of either God or man, and thus sought to find a place for free will in the operations of the machine. They did so not by repudiating the paradigm of cause and effect but by trying to identify causes in human affairs with the motives, mind, or will of individuals. Just as natural scientists like Cadwallader Colden, believing that in a mechanistic physical world "there must be some power or force, or principle of Action," groped toward a modern concept of energy, so too did moral philosophers seek to discover the powers or principles of action that lay behind the sequences of human affairs—in effect, looking within the minds and hearts of men for the moral counterpart of Colden's physical energy.[39]

Such efforts to reconcile the search for laws of human behavior with the commitment to moral capability lay behind the numerous controversies over free will that bedeviled the eighteenth century. To be enlightened, it seemed, was to try one's hand at writing an essay on what David Hume called "the most contentious question of metaphysics"—the question of liberty and necessity. Despite all the bitter polemics between the libertarians and the necessitarians, however, both sides were caught up in the new thinking about causality. Both assumed, as Hume pointed out, that "the conjunction between motives and voluntary actions is as regular and uniform, as that between the cause and effect in any part of nature." Men's motives or will thus became the starting point in the sequential chain of causes and effects in human affairs. All human actions and events could now be seen scientifically as the products of men's intentions. If they were not, if men "are not necessarily determined by motives," then, said the Scottish moralist Thomas Reid, "all their actions must be capricious."[40] Only by identifying causes with motives was any sort of human science and predictability possible, and only then could morality be preserved in the new, mechanistic causal world.

Since it was "granted on all hands, that moral good and evil lie in the state of mind, or prevailing internal disposition of the agent," searching out the causes of social events meant discovering in these agents the motives, the "voluntary choice and design," that led them to act—the energizing principle, the inner springs of their behavior. "Every moral event must have an answerable cause. . . . Every such event must then have a *moral* cause."[41] Moral deeds implied moral doers; when things happen in society, individuals with particular intentions, often called "designs," must be at the bottom of them. All social processes could be reduced to specific individual passions and interests. "Ambition and avarice," wrote the Revolutionary historian Mercy Otis Warren, "are *the leading springs which generally actuate the restless mind. From these primary sources of corruption* have arisen all the rapine and confusion, the depredation and ruin, that have spread distress over the face of the earth from the days of Nimrod to Cesar, and from Cesar to an arbitrary prince of the house of Brunswick." This widespread belief that explanations of social phenomena must be sought in the moral nature of man himself ultimately reduced all eighteenth-century moral philosophy—its history and its social analysis—to what would come to be called psychology.[42]

Once men's designs were identified as the causes of human events, the new paradigm of causality worked to intensify and give a scientific gloss to the classic concern with the human heart and the ethical inwardness of Christian culture. Indeed, never before or since in Western history has man been held so directly and morally responsible for the events of his world. Because the new idea of causality presumed a homogeneous identity, an "indissoluble connection," between causes and effects, it became difficult to think of social effects, however remote in time, that were not morally linked to particular causes—that is, to particular human designs. There could be no more in the effects than existed in the causes. "Outward actions being determined by the will," they partook "of the nature of moral good or evil only with reference to their cause, viz. internal volition."[43]

It could now be taken for granted that the cause and the effect were so intimately related that they necessarily shared the same moral qualities. Whatever the particular moral character of the cause—that is, the motive or inclination of the actor—"the effect appears to be of the same kind."[44] Good intentions and beliefs would therefore result in good actions; evil motives caused evil actions. Of course, mistakes might happen, and occasionally actions "proceeded not from design." But continued or regular moral actions could follow only from similar moral intentions. Only by assuming this close relationship between causes and effects—"this *inference* from motives to voluntary actions; from characters to conduct," said Hume—was the eighteenth-century science of human behavior made possible.[45]

This presumed moral identity between cause and effect, between motive and deed, accounts for the excited reaction of moralists to Bernard Mandeville's satiric paradox of "private vices, publick benefits." Mandeville was unusual for his time in grasping the complexity of public events and the ways in which political effects could outrun and differ from their causes. "We ought," he wrote, "to forebear judging rashly of ministers and their actions, especially when we are unacquainted with every circumstance of an affair. Measures may be rightly concerted, and such casualties intervene, as may make the best design miscarry. . . . Humane understanding is too shallow to foresee the result of what is subject to many variations."[46] Such skepticism could not be easily tolerated by that enlightened and moral age. Mandeville and all those who would ignore private intentions in favor of public results threatened to unhinge both man's moral responsibility for his actions and the homogeneous relation that presumably existed between cause and effect. To break the necessary moral connection between cause and effect, to make evil the author of good and vice versa, would be, it was said, "to confound all differences of character, to destroy all distinction between right and wrong, and to make the most malicious and the most benevolent being of precisely the same temper and disposition."[47]

Mandeville clearly perceived that much of human activity had become an "incomprehensible Chain of Causes." But he, like others of his time, had no better way of describing the multitude of complicated and criss-crossing causal chains he saw than to invoke the traditional Protestant concept of "providence."[48] For those who would be enlightened and scientific, this resort to the mysterious hand of God was no explanation of human affairs at all but rather a step backward into darkness. Things happened, as John Adams noted, by human volition, either "by Accident or Design."[49] Some confusing event or effect might be passed off as an accident—the result of somebody's mistaken intention—but a series of events that seemed to form a pattern could be no accident. Having only the alternative of "providence" as an impersonal abstraction to describe systematic linkages of human actions, the most enlightened of the age could only conclude that regular patterns of behavior were the conse-quences of concerted human intentions—that is, the result of a number of people coming together to promote a collective design or conspiracy. The human mind, it seemed to Jonathan Edwards, had a natural disposition, "when it sees a thing begin to be," not only "to conclude certainly, that there is a *Cause* of it," but also, "if it sees a thing to be in a very orderly, regular and exact manner to conclude that some Design regulated and disposed it." Although Edwards was arguing here for God's "exact reg-ulation of a very great multitude of particulars," a similar leap from a

particular cause to a general design was made by eighteenth-century theorists who sought to account for the regularity of human actions by the
coincident purposes not of God but of human beings.[50]

Many enlightened thinkers of the eighteenth century could therefore
no more accept the seeming chaos and contingency of events than could
the Puritans. Like the Puritans, they presumed the existence of an ordering power lying beneath the apparently confused surface of events—not
God's concealed will, of course, but natural causes embodied in the hidden intentions and wills of men. Those who saw only random chance
in events simply did not know enough about these hidden human wills.
Just as devout Puritans believed that nothing occurred without God's
providence, so the liberal-minded believed that nothing occurred without
some person willing it. Earlier, men had sought to decipher the concealed
or partially revealed will of God; now they sought to understand the concealed or partially exposed wills of human beings. That, in a nutshell,
was what being enlightened was all about.

IT WAS PRECISELY these assumptions that lay behind American Whig
conspiratorial thinking, indeed all conspiratorial thinking, in the eighteenth century. To be sure, there was a long-existing Christian tradition that stressed, in the words of Revelation 12:9, the wiles of "that old
serpent, called the Devil, and Satan, which deceiveth the whole world." This
creature, whether called the dragon, the beast, or Satan, was easily pictured by
devout Christians and readers of John Milton as "the chief directing agent
in all the dark plots of tyranny, persecution and oppression." There is no
denying the importance of this religious tradition in preparing American
Protestants to detect a British ministeral plot that was "as black and dark
as the powder-treason plot." People who read their Bibles and heeded the
fervid millennial sermons of their ministers were conditioned to believe
that the forces of evil were like the frogs that issued from the mouth of
the satanic dragon, "slyly creeping into all the holes and corners of the
land, and using their enchanting art and bewitching policy, to lead aside,

the simple and unwary, from the truth, to prepare them for the shackles of slavery and bondage." Sermons of the period were filled with references to the "hidden intent," the "pernicious scheme," and the "intrigues and dark plots"—references that owed more to the apocalyptic beliefs of the clergy than to the Whig tradition of political jealousy and suspicion.[51] Nor can it be denied that the heated ideological atmosphere in America in the early 1770s intensified the colonists' readiness to suspect British intentions and to see deep dark plots at work. Yet ultimately it was neither the atmosphere of Whiggish suspicion and mistrust nor the Christian tradition of a deceitful Satan that was fundamental to the age's susceptibility to conspiratorial interpretations; for people who were neither radical Whigs nor devout Protestants nonetheless believed naturally in conspiracies. What was fundamental is that American secular thought—in fact, all enlightened thought of the eighteenth century—was structured in such a way that conspiratorial explanations of complex events became normal, necessary, and rational.

The rush of momentous events in the years leading to the Revolution demanded explanation, for, as the colonists told themselves, "these unheard of intolerable calamities spring not of the dust, come not causeless." Some Americans, of course, still relied on traditional religious presuppositions and warned of the necessity to "remain ignorant of the intentions of Providence, until the series of events explain them," so "vastly large, complicate and intricate" was God's design. Others, mostly Tories, doubted whether there was a design at all, whether in fact the actions of the British government added up to anything systematic. Most of the British acts, wrote the New York loyalist Peter Van Schaack as late as 1776, "seem to have sprung out of particular occasions, and are unconnected with each other." But most American patriots in the 1760s and 1770s gradually convinced themselves that the British actions were indeed linked in what Jefferson called "a deliberate, systematical plan of reducing us to slavery" and that this plan could be explained in terms not of the intentions of providence but of the intentions of British officials.[52]

Thus the central question for Americans from 1765 on was always:

what were the members of the British government up to? John Dickinson rested the entire argument of his famous *Letters from a Farmer in Pennsylvania* on the colonists' ability "to discover the intentions of those who rule over us." The colonists in effect turned their decade-long debate with the mother country into an elaborate exercise in the deciphering of British motives. To know what response to make to British acts, wrote James Iredell in 1776, "it was necessary previously to consider what might be supposed the sentiments and views of the administration of Great Britain, the fatal original authors of all these dire extremities." Had George Grenville, in promoting the Stamp Act of 1765, for example, "acted from *principle* and not from any *bad motive*"?[53]

This was the crux of the matter, not only for the American Revolutionaries but for all eighteenth-century thinkers: how were the real intentions of individuals—what John Adams referred to time and again as "the Secret Springs, Motives and Principles of human Actions"—to be discovered? Certainly the motives of most humble men, the "people," the multitude, were easily known from their expressions. Such simple, ordinary folk were "men of feeling": they wore their hearts on their sleeves and in their ignorance openly revealed their passionate, often violent, natures from which sprang the motives for their actions.[54] But the motives of others—the learned few, the gentlemanly elite, those who directed political affairs—were not so easily discovered. Some of these extraordinary men were, of course, "men of principle," acting benevolently out of disinterested judgment and with rational self-control; they revealed "sincerity" and "manly candor" in their actions. But others were men not of principle but of "policy," or concealed intentions, who exploited their reason and learning shrewdly and artfully to bring about selfish and wicked ends. Samuel Richardson's character Lovelace was an outwardly charming and respected gentleman, but he had "the plottingest heart in the universe." Such cultivated but evil-minded men could pretend they were something they were not and disguise their inner motives. They could smile and smile and yet be villains. "It is very hard under all these masks," wrote Defoe, "to see the true countenance of any man."[55]

Masquerades and hidden designs formed the grammar and vocabulary for much of the thought of the age. From Molière to Lord Chesterfield, intellectuals debated the advantages and disadvantages of politeness, frankness, and hiding one's true feelings in order to get along in the world. "Nothing in Courts is exactly as it appears to be," wrote Chesterfield. "Courts are unquestionably the seats of politeness and good-breeding; were they not so, they would be the seats of slaughter and desolation. Those who now smile upon and embrace, would affront and stab each other if manners did not interpose: but ambition and avarice, the two prevailing passions at Courts, found dissimulation more effectual than violence; and dissimulation introduced that habit of politeness which distinguishes the courtier from the country gentleman." Yet what was prudence and sociability to some became deceit and flattery to others. Perhaps never in Western history have the issues of hypocrisy and sincerity been more centrally engaged.[56] John Adams filled his diary and other writings with lengthy analyses of "Dissimulation," which he called "the first Maxim of worldly Wisdom," and anxiously tried to work out the extent to which a public figure could legitimately conceal his motives. The patronage politics of the age put a premium on circumspection, discretion, and the suppressing of one's real feelings in the interest of cultivating the friendship of patrons. This in turn encouraged an opposition politics dedicated to the unmasking of hypocrisy.

By the middle of the eighteenth century, if not earlier, this concern with the deceit and dissembling of sophisticated elites had turned "courtier" into a generic term of abuse and was leading some to suggest that common people, "men of feeling," despite their ignorance, brutality, and simplicity, might be better trusted in political affairs than men of learning. Such simple folk at least could be counted on to express their inner passions and motives spontaneously and honestly. "Ninety-nine parts out of one hundred of mankind, are ever inclined to live at peace, and cultivate a good understanding with each other." Only members of "the remaining small part"—those whose "considerable abilities" were "joined to an intriguing disposition"—were "the real authors, advisers, and perpetrators of wars, treasons, and those other violences, which have, in all ages, more or less disgraced the annals of man." It was "necessary," wrote historian Mercy Otis Warren, "to guard at every point, against the intrigues of artful or ambitious men," since such men were involved in a "game of deception . . . played over and over." Everywhere there seemed to be a frightening gap between public appearances and the inner motives of rulers.[57]

Because no one could ever actually penetrate into the inner hearts of men, true motives had to be discovered indirectly, had to be deduced from actions. That is, the causes had to be inferred from the effects. Since the scientific paradigm of causality presumed a homogenous connection, a moral likeness, between causes and effects, such deductions and inferences, however elaborate, were not only plausible but necessary. "The actions of men," wrote the novelist Henry Fielding in a concise essay on this Augustan theme of the separation of appearance and reality, "are the surest evidence of their character." The intentions of sophisticated and cunning men, especially those in public life, could be known neither by their countenances nor by their statements, for these were but masks. Although an "honest man," wrote a South Carolina polemicist in 1769, was supposed "to let his language express the real sentiments of his soul," words could no longer be trusted. Only men's outward actions could reveal their inner dispositions and expose deceit and dissembling. The "dark counsels" of the "Cabal" of Charles II's reign, wrote Hume in his *History of England*, "were not thoroughly known but by the event." "By their fruits so shall ye know them" was the common refrain of religious and secular thinkers alike.[58]

Americans in the 1760s and 1770s were far removed from the sources of what was happening—John Adams, for example, knew something was afoot "by somebody or other in Great-Britain"—and thus they necessarily fell back on this common inferential method of determining designs. "As in nature we best judge of causes by their effects, so," declared the Massachusetts minister Samuel Cooke in his Election Sermon of 1770, "rulers hereby will receive the surest information of the fitness of their laws and the exactness of their execution." For Americans, the execution of those laws provided the only way to discover whether Grenville and other ministers acted from principle or from bad motives. The intentions of the British officials, wrote Dickinson, were not to be judged by their declarations of good will; only "conduct . . . would in time sufficiently explain itself."[59] The British government's claim to have the interests of the colonies at heart, while its actions seemed clearly harmful to those interests, only confirmed its duplicity in colonial eyes. Indeed, it was this sort of discrepancy between the professed motives of an actor and the contrary effects of his actions that lay behind the eighteenth century's preoccupation with deception.

THE IDEA OF DECEPTION BECAME the means by which the Augustan Age closed the gaps that often seemed to exist between causes and effects, between men's proclaimed intentions and their contrary actions. Since cause and effect were inherently, mechanistically related, both possessing the same moral nature, any persistent discrepancy between the two presented a serious problem of explanation. Whenever effects seemed different from their ostensible causes, philosophers were certain, as Hume repeatedly pointed out, that "the contrariety of events" did "not proceed from any contingency in the cause but from the secret operation of contrary causes."[60] If bad effects continually resulted from the professedly benevolent intentions of an actor, then something was wrong. Some sort of deceit or dissimulation was to be suspected; the actor had to be concealing his real motives. It was, as Samuel Stanhope Smith said, the "arts of disguise" that made human actions complicated.[61]

This problem of deception was a source of continuing fascination in eighteenth-century Anglo-American culture. The Augustans, of course, did not invent the notion of deception, but because of their identification of cause and effect with human intentions and actions, and because of their assumption of man-made designs lying beneath the surface of seemingly contingent events, they made much more of it than other ages have. Given the influence of Locke's sensationalist epistomology, people were always in danger of mistaking false appearances for reality, words for things. Radical Whigs constantly warned of the ease by which the human mind was misled. If people were dependent for their knowledge on the information provided by their senses, then they had to be especially careful of what they saw and heard. Like jugglers fooling people by "sleight of Hand," artful political leaders knew how "to dally and play" upon the people's "Foibles" by using "fine Figures and beautiful Sounds" to "disguise and vanish Sense." What men often saw and heard was not reality. Beneath the surface of experience there existed, they had been told, a wonderful but invisible world of forces—gravity, electricity, magnetism, and fluids and gases of various sorts—that produced, said Joseph Priestley, "an almost infinite variety of visible effects."[62]

No wonder then that men were tempted to think that they were "formed to deceive and be deceived," that "Mankind are in Masquerade, and Falsehood assumes the Air of Reality." In a rapidly changing world of sense impressions, nothing seemed as it really was, and hypocrisy was a charge on everyone's lips. Men presumed, as did Robert Munford's hero in *The Patriots*, that "secrecy is generally the veil of iniquity" from which followed the "confident" conclusion of "some evil design." Sincerity, which Archbishop John Tillotson defined as making "our outward actions exactly agreeable to our inward purposes and intentions," became an ever more important ideal.[63] There even developed a politics of sincerity, with which republicanism became associated. With all social relationships in a free state presumably dependent on mutual trust, it is not surprising that the courts of eighteenth-century Massachusetts treated instances of cheating and deception far more severely than overt acts of violence.[64] The differences between appearance and reality, disguise and sincerity, were the stock themes of eighteenth-century literature and drama. The artful manipulation of innocent virtue was the traditional device by which most comic situations in novels and plays were created.

Satire, the kind of literature celebrated by the age—indeed, the eighteenth century was the greatest era of satire in Western history—presumed the prevalence of deception. It posited a distinction between appearance and reality—that the world we see is not the world that really exists—and rested on the discrepancy between what people profess to be and what they really are.[65] Satire was made for an enlightened age; it took for granted that individuals are autonomous rational beings fully responsible for the good and evil they bring about. Its object was always to expose to shame and ridicule any behavior contrary to what men of reason had a right to expect, to strip away the virtuous appearances that vice used to clothe itself. Since everyone professed to be pursuing truth and virtue, how was it, asked John Adams in one of his many discourses on this problem, that human affairs so often resulted "in direct opposition to both"? Only deception, including self-deception, could explain the discrepancy. "From what other source can such fierce disputations arise concerning the two things [truth and virtue] which seem the most consonant to the entire frame of human nature?"[66]

The conspiratorial interpretations of the age were a generalized application to the world of politics of the pervasive duplicity assumed to exist in all human affairs.[67] Only by positing secret plots and hidden machinations by governments was it possible, it seemed, to close the bewildering gaps between what rulers professed and what they brought forth. It was true, wrote Hume in his history of Charles II's court, that at first beliefs in conspiracies and cabals seemed preposterous and that often no concrete evidence could be found for them. "But the utter impossibility of accounting, by any other hypothesis, for those strange measures embraced by the court, as well as for the numerous circumstances which accompanied them obliges us to acknowledge, though there remains no direct evidence of it, that a formal plan was laid for changing the religion and subverting the constitution of England, and that the king and the ministry were in reality conspirators against the people."[68]

The same notion of deception lay behind Edmund Burke's celebrated "Thoughts on the Cause of the Present Discontents" (1770), which more than any other single piece of writing in the pre-Revolutionary period pinpointed the nature of the deceit at work in the early years of George

III's reign. There were, said Burke, no discernible causes that would explain the present discontents of the British nation—no great party agitations, no famine, no war, no foreign threat, no oppression. The effects, the national discontents, were out of all proportion to the apparent causes. They could be accounted for only by hidden causes—the existence of a "double cabinet," thought Burke, operating behind the scenes of George III's government against the will of the people. If enlightened thinkers like Hume and Burke could use such logic, it is not surprising that others relied on it as well.[69] As political consequences in an increasingly complicated world appeared more and more contrary to the avowed aims of rulers, only deception on a large scale seemed capable of resolving the mysterious discrepancies.

No wonder, then, that mistrust and jealousy grew, for, as the South Carolina merchant Henry Laurens noted in 1765, a "malicious Villain acting behind the Curtain . . . could be reached only by suspicion." Such suspicion could ripen into certainty through events. Words lost all capacity to reveal motives; only actions could reveal the secret designs of those in power. "What was their view in the beginning or [how] far it was Intended to be carried Must be Collected from facts that Afterwards have happened."[70] The more glaring the disparity between these facts and the professed good intentions of their perpetrators, the more shrill became the accusations of hidden designs and dark plots. Some might continue to suggest that "the ways of Heaven are inscrutable; and frequently, the most unlooked-for events have arisen from seemingly the most inadequate causes," and of course others continued to believe that motives and actions did not always coincide, trusting with Dr. Johnson in the old English proverb that "Hell is paved with good intentions."[71] But for those who knew how cause and effect really worked, deception and conspiracy were more morally coherent and intellectually satisfying explanations of the apparent difference between professions and deeds. When effects "cannot be accounted for by any visible cause," it was rational to conclude that "there must be, therefore, some men behind the curtain" who were secretly bringing them about.[72] This commonplace image of figures operating "behind the curtain" was the consequence of a political world that was expanding and changing faster than its available rational modes of explanation could handle.

SUCH WERE THE PRESUPPOSITIONS and circumstances that explain the propensity of Anglo-Americans and others in the eighteenth century to resort to conspiratorial interpretations of events. The belief in plots was not a symptom of disturbed minds but a rational attempt to explain human phenomena in terms of human intentions and to maintain moral coherence in the affairs of men. This mode of thinking was neither pathological nor uniquely American. Certainly, the American Revolution cannot serve as an adequate context for comprehending the obsession with conspiratorial beliefs. Perhaps we can perceive better their larger place in Western history by examining, however briefly, the newer modes of causal explanation that gradually came to replace them.

Well before the close of the eighteenth century, even while conspiratorial interpretations were flourishing under the aegis of enlightened science, alternative ways of explaining events were taking form, prompted by dynamic social changes that were stretching and contorting any simple linkage between human intentions and actions, causes and effects. The expanding, interdependent economic order obviously relied on the activity of thousands upon thousands of insignificant producers and traders whose various and conflicting motives could hardly be deciphered, let alone judged. The growing number of persons and interests participating in politics made causal evaluations ever more difficult. Causes seemed farther and farther removed from their consequences, sometimes disappearing altogether into a distant murkiness. As a result, the inferences of plots and deceptions used to close the widening gap between events and the presumed designs of particular individuals became even more elaborate and contrived. Many were still sure that every social effect, every political event, had to have a purposive human agent as a cause. But men now distinguished more frequently between "remote" and "proximate" causes and between "immediate" and "permanent" effects. Although many continued to assume that the relationship between causes and their effects was intrinsic and morally homogeneous, some moralists noted bewilderingly and sometimes cynically how personal vices like self-love and self-interest could have contrary, indeed beneficial, consequences for society. Men everywhere wrestled with the demands the changing social reality was placing on their thought. Some suggested that self-love might even be a virtue; others complained of "a kind of *mandevillian* chymistry" that converted avarice into benevolence; still others questioned the presumed identity between private motives and public consequences.[73]

Little of this was followed out in any systematic way in the Anglo-American world until the appearance in the latter half of the eighteenth century of that remarkable group of Scottish intellectuals who worked out, in an extraordinary series of writings, a new understanding of the relationship between individuals and events. These Scottish "social scientists" did not and could not by themselves create a new way of conceiving of human affairs, but their writings were an especially clear crystallization of the changes gradually taking place in Western consciousness during the last third of the eighteenth century. Adam Ferguson, Adam Smith, and John Millar sought to undermine what Duncan Forbes has called "a dominant characteristic of the historical thought of the age"— the "tendency to explain events in terms of conscious action by individuals." These Scottish moral philosophers had come to realize more clearly than most eighteenth-century thinkers that men pursuing their own particular aims were led by an "invisible hand" into promoting an end that was no part of their intentions. Traditional historians, complained Ferguson in his *History of Civil Society*, had seen all events as the "effect of design. An author and a work, like cause and effect, are perpetually coupled together." But reality was not so simple. Men, "in striving to remove inconveniencies, or to gain apparent and contiguous advantages, arrive at ends which even their imagination could not anticipate, . . . and nations stumble upon establishments, which are indeed the result of human action, but not the execution of any human design."[74]

Such momentous insights would in time help to transform all social and historical thinking in the Western world. But it took more than the writings of philosophers—it took the experiencing of tumultuous events—to shake most European intellectuals out of their accustomed ways of thinking. The French Revolution, more than any other single event, changed the consciousness of Europe. The Revolution was simply too convulsive and too sprawling, involving the participation of too many masses of people, to be easily confined within conventional personalistic and rationalistic modes of explanation. For the most sensitive European intellectuals, the Revolution became the cataclysm that shattered once and for all the traditional moral affinity between cause and effect, motives and behavior. That the actions of liberal, enlightened, and well-intentioned men could produce such horror, terror, and chaos, that so much promise could result in so much tragedy, became, said Shelley, "the master theme of the epoch in which we live." What the French Revolution revealed, wrote Wordsworth, speaking for a generation of disillusioned intellectuals, was "this awful truth" that "sin and crime are apt to start from their very opposite qualities."[75] Many European thinkers continued, of course, to describe what happened as the deliberate consequence of the desires and ambitions of individuals. But the scale and complexity of the Revolution now required conspiratorial interpretations of an unprecedented sort. No small group of particular plotters could account for its tumult and mass movements; only elaborately organized secret societies, like the Illuminati or the Freemasons, involving thousands of individuals linked by sinister designs, could be behind the Europe-wide upheaval.[76]

Although such conspiratorial interpretations of the Revolution were everywhere, the best minds—Hegel's in particular—now knew that the jumble of events that made up the Revolution were so complex and overwhelming that they could no longer be explained simply as the products of personal intention. For these thinkers, history could no longer be a combination of individual events managed by particular persons, but had to become a complicated flow or process, a "stream," that swept men along.

．　．　．

THE STORY OF THIS VAST TRANSFORMATION in the way men explain events is central to the history of modern Western thought. Indeed, so huge and complicated is it that our easy generalizations are apt to miss its confused and agonized significance for individuals and to neglect the piecemeal ways in which it was worked out in the minds of people—not great philosophers like Hegel or Adam Smith, but more ordinary people, workaday clergymen, writers, and politicians caught up in the problems and polemics of the moment.

Certainly late eighteenth-century Americans did not experience this transformation in consciousness as rapidly and to the same extent as Europeans, but it is evident that some were coming to realize that the social and moral order was not as intelligible as it once had been. Few active minds were able to resist the pressures a new complicated commercial reality was placing on familiar assumptions about human nature and morality. Even the cynical and worldly New York merchant-politician, Gouverneur Morris, found himself ensnared in an apparent conflict between motives and consequences and, in an unfinished essay, groped to make sense of the problematical nature of late eighteenth-century experience.

Morris began his essay on "Political Enquiries," as nearly all eighteenth-century writers did, with happiness and declared his agreement with the conventional belief that virtue and the avoidance of evil were the keys to realizing it: "To inculcate Obedience to the moral Law is therefore the best Means of promoting human Happiness." But immediately problems arose. Which should government encourage more, public or private virtue? "Can there be any Difference between them? In other Words," asked Morris, in a question that directly confronted Mandeville's paradox, "can the same Thing be right and wrong?" Could selfishness, for example, result in public benefits? If so, how should self-interest be judged? "If an Action be in its own Nature wrong," said Morris in a summary of the traditional moral view, "we can never justify it from a Relation to the public Interest." It had to be judged "by the Motive of the Actor." But then, "who can know his Motive?" Was motive the criterion of judgment after all? "From what Principle of the human Heart," wondered Morris, "is public Virtue derived?"[77]

Despite such scattered musings and questionings, most Americans found it as difficult as Morris to escape from the presuppositions of a traditional moral order. Only by assuming that the beliefs or motives of individuals caused events could those individuals be held morally accountable for what happened. These assumptions had underlain the Revolutionaries' charge of a British conspiracy, and they underlay every succeeding American notion of conspiracy. By the last decade of the eighteenth century, however, the polemics surrounding these continuing charges of conspiracy were unsettling older views and forcing new explorations into the problems of causation in human affairs.

The climax in America of the late eighteenth century's frenzy of plots and counterplots came in 1798 with the most serious crisis the young nation had yet faced. This crisis brought the country close to civil war and led, in New England at least, to Federalist accusations that the Republican Party was in league with an international Jacobinical conspiracy dominated by the Order of the Bavarian Illuminati. This Illuminati conspiracy, the Federalists charged, had not only brought about the French Revolution but was now threatening to subvert America's new government. In elaborating for their fellow Americans the nature of this plot, impassioned Federalists, especially those in the standing order of New England clergy, were compelled to expose the premises of their ideas about causality in an unprecedented manner.[78]

Federalist spokesmen in 1798 argued that Americans ought to be suspicious of the Illuminati and other similar organizations that claimed to have benevolent purposes. Had not the perpetrators of the French Revolution likewise professed a "fraternal intention" and made "splendid and passionate harangues on universal freedom and equality"? But everyone knew what "evil effects" they had produced. Such men were designing hypocrites, "void of sincerity" and not to be trusted.[79] Yet such suspicion and mistrust, such fears of duplicity, could just as easily be turned against any leaders, as the Federalists knew only too well. Throughout the 1790s the Republicans had accused them of just this sort of deception, of fomenting beneath their high-sounding professions of devotion to the new republic secret designs for monarchizing American society and government. In self-defense, therefore, the Federalists were pressed in the debates of the late 1790s into exploring the ways in which people could distinguish between hypocrisy and sincerity in their leaders. The public needed to be convinced that Federalist leaders were men whose words and motives could be trusted. The Federalists thus set out to show why people should confide their government only into the hands of honest, respectable, and well-bred gentlemen like themselves, who in contrast to the upstart and irreligious Republicans had the worth, religiosity, and status deserving of political authority.

The Federalists were thoroughly eighteenth-century minded (which is why they resorted to satire much more readily than did their Republican opponents). They assumed the existence of a rational moral order and a society of deliberately acting individuals who controlled the course and shape of events. They were sure that men's beliefs or motives mattered in determining actions and that such causes and effects were intrinsically related. "As the volitions and consequent actions of men are mainly governed by their prevailing belief," David Tappan, Hollis Professor of Divinity at Harvard, declared in 1798, "so he who steadily believes and obeys truth is a virtuous man; while he who chooses and obeys falsehood is a vitious character." Clinging to this traditional assumption that events were the direct consequence of individuals' intentions and opinions, which they summed up as "character," the Federalists could only conclude that the character of individuals, particularly of leaders, shaped the general character of society. Society in fact was only the individual writ large. "If each man conducts himself aright, the community cannot be conducted wrong," said Timothy Dwight, president of Yale. "If private life be unblamable, the public state must be commendable and happy." This being so, it followed that the established Federalist gentry, who even the Republicans admitted were honest and respectable men of character, were the best leaders for the society and could do it no harm. Good private motives, in other words, could have only good public consequences.[80]

Confronted with these self-serving arguments, Jeffersonian Republicans and others who opposed the privileged position of the Federalist gentry were eventually led to question and defy the Federalists' basic assumption: that men's intentions and beliefs—their private "character"— were necessarily and directly translated into public consequences. No one struggled more persistently with this issue than the fiery Connecticut Jeffersonian Abraham Bishop. Although Bishop eventually accused the Federalists of fomenting their own Illuminati conspiracy, he also tried in a series of speeches to work out an explanation for the perplexing discrepancy between causes and effects in human affairs. His thought was remarkable for both its boldness and originality.

Bishop at times fell back on the conventional notion of deception. "The great, the wise, rich and mighty men of the world" were always trying to delude those beneath them "with charming outsides, engaging manners, powerful address and inexhaustible argument." But Bishop admitted that such an explanation was not fully satisfactory. He knew that many of the Federalist leaders possessed "integrity in *private* life." Yet at the same time this private integrity had "no manner of connection with *political* character." How then to account for the difference between this respectable private character and its obnoxious public effects? Perhaps, Bishop suggested, honest and reputable men behaved differently in groups and organizations. "Thus committees of societies, selectmen and legislators will do certain things, officially, which would ruin them as individuals." It was hard to know how things happened; all we can know, said Bishop, is that men who exhibited no wicked passions at home or among their neighbors did so as politicians, as "evinced by correspondent actions."[81]

Perhaps, suggested Bishop, with an audacity rare among eighteenth-century Americans, personal character and intentions do not really count at all in explaining events. Since men always profess decent motives for their actions, he argued, we can never judge them by their motives. People seem to be caught up in a "system," and it is the "system," and not particular individuals, that we must combat and condemn. To account for the country's revolt against Great Britain, said Bishop, Americans in the 1770s had blamed the greater part of the respectable men in the British nation. "Did we by this intend to charge each of these men with a personal disposition to oppress, plunder and destroy us? Surely not!—But we charged to the system, which they supported, all these dispositions, and dreadful facts proved our charges to be well-founded."[82]

These kinds of thoughts were too new and too frightening in their moral implications to be easily followed up.[83] But at least one American saw very clearly what belief in conspiracies, like that of the Bavarian Illuminati, meant for men's understanding of events. In 1799, in a brilliant review of one of the many Federalist Fourth of July orations that laid out the diabolical designs of the Illuminati, the novelist and editor Charles Brockden Brown went right to the heart of the misconception that was at work.

Those who believe in such conspiracies, Brown wrote, have no idea how things really happen. They have no sense that "men are liable to error, and though they may intend good, may commit enormous mistakes in the choice of means." While enlightened philosophes, for example,

> imagine themselves labouring for the happiness of mankind, loosening the bonds of superstition, breaking the fetters of commerce, out-rooting the prejudice of birth, by which father transmits to son absolute power over the property, liberty and lives of millions, they may, in reality, be merely pulling down the props which uphold human society, and annihilate not merely the chains of false religion, but the foundations of morality—not merely the fetters of commerce, and federal usurpations upon property, but commerce and property themselves. The apology which may be made for such is, that though their activity be pernicious, their purposes are pure.

But those who believe in the Illuminati conspiracy deny liberal reformers "the benefits of this construction." They assume that all the disastrous consequences were produced by certain individuals and were "*foreseen* and *intended*." To avoid such simple-minded conspiratorial beliefs, wrote Brown, we must be "conscious of the uncertainty of history" and recognize that "actions and motives cannot be truly described," for they are not always integrally related.[84]

Brown returned again and again to this theme of what has been called "the unanticipated consequences of purposive action."[85] Indeed, his significance as a writer comes not from his creation of the American romance or the American gothic tale, but from his relentless attempts to probe Wordsworth's "awful truth," to examine the moral implications of evil caused by well-intentioned and benevolent persons. Unlike the oppressive didactic fiction of his American contemporaries, Brown's novels are intellectual explorations into causality, deception, and the moral complexity of life. In his fiction, not only do moral obligations such as sincerity and benevolence often contradict one another, but virtuous motives time and again lead to contrary consequences. Despite all the tedious analyses of motives his characters go through, none of them is able to avoid unfortunate results.[86] Each, like Wieland, finds he has "rashly set in motion a machine over whose progress [he] had no control." "How little cognizance have men over the actions and motives of each other!" Brown's character Edgar Huntly exclaims. "How total is our blindness with regard to our own performances!" Motives and intentions, Brown suggested, could no longer be crucial in judging moral responsibility, since "the causes that fashion men into instruments of happiness or misery, are numerous, complex, and operate upon a wide surface. . . . Every man is encompassed by numerous claims, and is the subject of intricate relations. . . . Human affairs are infinitely complicated."[87]

These American explorations into the relationship between aims and consequences were only small and modest examples of what was taking place generally in Western thought during the late eighteenth century. Others elsewhere were also becoming more and more conscious of the

complicatedness of human affairs. The growing awareness of the difficulty of delving into the human heart and the increasing unwillingness to
esteem men simply for their aristocratic character were forcing moralists,
sometimes imperceptibly, to shift the basis of judgment of human action
from the motives and personal qualifications of the actors to the public
consequences of their acts. The common practice of deducing motives
from their effects in actions only furthered this transition and blurred
what was happening. What counted now was less the beliefs and intentions, or the "character," of the actor and more the consequences of his
actions, or his contributions to human happiness. And any man, however
much he lacked "character," however ordinary and insignificant he may
have been, could make such contributions.

In just such shifts from motives to consequences was a democratic
consciousness strengthened and what came to be called utilitarianism created. Naturally, for most people there remained no discrepancy between
benevolent aims and good effects, and the familiar belief that private virtue was the obvious source of human happiness continued strong. But for
Jeremy Bentham and other stark utilitarians, there could no longer be
any such thing as good or bad motives: "If they are good or bad, it is only
on account of their effects, good on account of their tendency to produce
pleasure, or avert pain: bad, on account of their tendency to produce pain,
or avert pleasure."[88]

Many Americans were reluctant to separate motives from consequences, causes from effects, in this unequivocal utilitarian manner. But
by the early nineteenth century there were some, usually those most eager
to disparage "aristocratic" heroic individuals and to magnify the popular
"masses," who increasingly emphasized what Bishop had clumsily called
the "system" of society. Now it was described as the "natural order" or
the "aggregate result" of events formed out of the diverse and clashing
motives of countless insignificant individuals. Men no doubt caused this
"aggregate result," but they did so in large numbers and unthinkingly
by following their particular natural inclinations. This concept of the

social process eventually became identified with what Jacksonian Democrats called the "voluntary" or "democratic" principle—the principle that was able by itself "to work out the best possible general result or order and happiness from the chaos of characters, ideas, motives and interests: human society." Despite this separation of individuals' intentions from the consequences of their actions, the consequences nonetheless seemed to form a process or pattern that could be trusted. Perhaps, it was suggested, there was some kind of moral force in each person—sympathy or a moral feeling of some sort—that held the innumerable discordant individuals in a society together and, like gravity in the physical world, created a natural harmony of interests.[89]

Although this concept of the social process transcending the desires of particular individuals presaged a new social order, it was in some respects merely a throwback to a premodern Protestant understanding of divine sovereignty. Many Americans, even nonevangelicals like George Washington, had always been able to "trace the finger of Providence through those dark and mysterious events."[90] Now this traditional notion of providence took on a new importance and even among secular-minded thinkers became identified with "progress" and with the natural principles of society created by multiplicities of people following their natural desires free from artificial restraints, particularly those imposed by laws and government. Providence no longer meant, as it often had in the past, the special interpositions of God in the events of the world but was now increasingly identified almost wholly with the natural pattern these events seemed to form.[91] With such a conception, the virtuous or vicious character of individual beliefs and intentions in the movement of events no longer seemed to matter. Even the "pursuit of gold" could have beneficial results, for "by some interesting filiation, 'there's a Divinity, that shapes our ends.' "[92]

Although these ideas of a collective social process were strongly voiced by some Jacksonian Democrats and permeated some of the history writing of the romantic era, they were never able to dominate nineteenth-century American popular thinking.[93] Many Americans were too sure of the integral and homogeneous relationship between cause and effect, and too preoccupied with the moral purposes of men, to embrace fully and unequivocally any notion that stressed the impersonal and collective nature of the workings of society. Despite all the talk of usefulness and happiness as the consequence of behavior, most Americans in the early nineteenth century could scarcely conceive of a moral order that was not based on intentions. America as a republic, Timothy Dwight said, was necessarily "a government by motives, addressed to the understanding and affections of rational subjects, and operating on their minds, as inducements to voluntary obedience."[94] Many agreed with John Taylor that "it is unnatural that evil moral qualities, should produce good moral effects"; it was "a violation of the relation between cause and effect" and a denial of "the certainty with which moral inferences flow from moral causes." Traditionalists and moralists of all sorts clung determinedly to what Alexis de Tocqueville called the "aristocratic" assumption that society was still composed of autonomous individuals capable of deliberately causing good or evil events and therefore of being held morally accountable for them.[95]

In an oration of 1825 commemorating the fiftieth anniversary of the battle of Concord, Edward Everett paused to ponder the dilemma faced by anyone seeking to explain how things happened. It was difficult, Everett noted, to separate out of the processes of history "what is to be ascribed to the cooperation of a train of incidents and characters, following in long succession upon each other; and what is to be referred to the vast influence of single important events." Thoroughly captivated by the paradigm of mechanistic causality, Everett could readily perceive in the history of the American Revolution "a series of causes and effects, running back into the history of the dark ages in Europe." Yet at the same time he knew that on that particular day, April 19, 1775, in Concord, "the agency of individual events and men" was crucial in bringing on the Revolution. There seemed to be two distinct viewpoints—one a long-term distant perspective that traced a "chain of events, which lengthens, onward by blind fatality," involving innumerable participants; the other, a close-up perspective that focused on the heroic individuals and actions of the day itself, against which "every thing else seems lost in the comparison." Like many other Americans, Everett was reluctant to envelop the glorious and willful exploits of America's individual patriots in the deterministic processes of history. Despite their underlying sense that history was an orderly chain of causes and effects, most of America's early national historians continued to stress the contingency and openness of events and the moral responsibility of individual actors.[96]

As nineteenth-century society became more interdependent and complicated, however, sensitive and reflective observers increasingly saw the efficient causes of events becoming detached from particular self-acting individuals and receding from view. "Small but growing numbers of people," writes historian Thomas L. Haskell in the most perceptive account we have of this development, "found it implausible or unproductive to attribute genuine causal power to those elements of society with which they were intimately and concretely familiar."[97] As these ideas evolved, laying the basis for the emergence of modern social science, attributing events to the conscious design of particular individuals became more and more simplistic. Conspiratorial interpretations of events still thrived, but now they seemed increasingly primitive and quaint.

By our own time, dominated as it is by professional social science, conspiratorial interpretations have become so out of place that, as we have seen, they can be accounted for only as mental aberrations, as a paranoid style symptomatic of psychological disturbance. In our postindustrial, scientifically saturated society, those who continue to attribute combinations of events to deliberate human design may well be peculiar sorts of persons—marginal people, perhaps, removed from the centers of power, unable to grasp the conceptions of complicated causal linkages offered by sophisticated social scientists, and unwilling to abandon the desire to make simple and clear moral judgments of events. But people with such conspiratorial beliefs have not always been either marginal or irrational. Living in this complicated modern world, where the very notion of causality is in doubt, should not prevent us from seeing that at another time and in another culture most enlightened people accounted for events in just this particular way.

AFTERWORD TO CHAPTER 3

This article was stimulated first by the simultaneous appearance in 1965 of Richard Hofstadter's *The Paranoid Style in American Politics and Other Essays*; the introduction to Bernard Bailyn's *Pamphlets of the American Revolution*, which became *The Ideological Origins of the American Revolution* two years later; and then by the publication in 1976 of James H. Hutson's article "The American Revolution: The Triumph of a Delusion."

These works forced me to puzzle over the significance of conspiratorial thinking. I knew that Hofstadter's notion that such thinking was a distorted style that suggested some sort of political pathology at work was simply not applicable to the Founding Fathers. Whatever they were, the Revolutionary leaders were not fanciful or pathological thinkers; nor were they delusional, as Hutson suggested. Moreover, as Bailyn demonstrated, conspiratorial thinking was very prevalent in the eighteenth century. The Founders were not the only figures in the eighteenth century who thought in conspiratorial terms. The British leaders, including someone as sophisticated as Edmund Burke, did as well. I consequently became preoccupied with working out the questions of why so many people in the eighteenth century explained events in conspiratorial terms and why most sophisticated thinkers by the beginning of the nineteenth century had stopped doing so. My answer to these questions became the article here republished.

PART II

THE *Making* OF
THE *Constitution* AND
American Democracy

CHAPTER FOUR

INTERESTS *and* DISINTERESTEDNESS
in the MAKING *of the* CONSTITUTION

URING OUR BICENTENNIAL CELEBRATIONS of the Constitution, we will gather many times to honor the makers of that Constitution, the Federalists of 1787–1788. We have certainly done so many times in the past. We have repeatedly pictured the Founders, as we call them, as men of vision—bold, original, open-minded, enlightened men who deliberately created what William Gladstone once called "the most wonderful work ever struck off at a given time by the hand and purpose of man."[1] We have described them as men who knew where the future lay and went for it. Even those like Charles Beard who have denigrated their motives have seen the Founders as masters of events, realistic pragmatists who knew human nature when they saw it, farsighted, economically advanced, modern men in step with the movement of history.

In contrast, we have usually viewed the opponents of the Constitution, the Anti-Federalists, as very tame and timid, narrow-minded and parochial men of no imagination and little faith, caught up in the ideological rigidities of the past—inflexible, suspicious men unable to look ahead and see where the United States was going. The Anti-Federalists seem forever doomed to be losers, bypassed by history and eternally disgraced by their opposition to the greatest constitutional achievement in our nation's history.

But maybe we have got it all wrong. Maybe the Federalists were not men of the future after all. Maybe it was the Anti-Federalists who really saw best and farthest. Is it possible that all those original, bold, and far-sighted Federalists had their eyes not on what was coming, but on what was passing? Perhaps the roles of the participants in the contest over the Constitution in 1787–1788 ought to be reversed. If either side in the conflict over the Constitution stood for modernity, perhaps it was the Anti-Federalists. They, and not the Federalists, may have been the real harbingers of the moral and political world we know—the liberal, democratic, commercially advanced world of individual pursuits of happiness.

If this is true—if indeed the Founders did not stand for modernity—then it should not be surprising that they are now so lost to us that they should have become, as we continually lament, "a galaxy of public leaders we have never been able remotely to duplicate since."[2] Instead of being the masters, were they really the victims of events? Is it possible that their Constitution failed, and failed miserably, in what they wanted it to do?

Naturally, we are reluctant to admit that the Constitution may have failed in what it set out to do, and consequently we have difficulty in fully understanding its origins. To be sure, we readily accept the necessity for a new central government in 1787. Unable to imagine the United States as ever existing without a strong national government, we regard the creation of the new structure in 1787 as inevitable. (For us it is the Articles of Confederation that cannot be taken seriously.) But the new central government seems inevitable to us only for reasons that fit our modern preconceptions. As long as people in the 1780s explain the movement for the Constitution in terms of the weaknesses of the Confederation, we can easily understand and accept their explanations. But when people in the 1780s explain the movement for the Constitution in terms other than the palpable weaknesses of the central government—in terms of a crisis in the society—we become puzzled and skeptical. A real crisis? It hardly seems believable. The 1780s were, after all, a time of great release and expansion:

the population grew as never before, or since, and more Americans than ever before were off in pursuit of prosperity and happiness. "There is not upon the face of the earth a body of people more happy or rising into consequence with more rapid stride, than the Inhabitants of the United Stares of America," Charles Thomson told Jefferson in 1786. "Population is encreasing, new houses building, new lands clearing, new settlements forming, and new manufactures establishing with a rapidity beyond conception."3 The general mood was high, expectant, and far from bleak. No wonder then that historians of very different persuasions have doubted that there was anything really critical happening in the society.4

Yet, of course, we have all those statements by people in the 1780s warning that "our situation is critical and dangerous" and that "our vices" were plunging us into "national ruin." Benjamin Rush even thought that the American people were on the verge of "degenerating into savages or devouring each other like beasts of prey." But if we think that Rush is someone with a hyperactive imagination, here is the 1786 voice of the much more sober and restrained George Washington: "What astonishing changes a few years arc capable of producing. . . . From the high ground we stood upon, from the plain path which invited our footsteps, to be so fallen! so lost! it is really mortifying."5

What are we to make of such despairing and excited statements—statements that can be multiplied over and over and that were often made not in the frenzy of public debate, but in the privacy of letters to friends? Many of those historians who, like Charles Beard, believe that such statements are a gross exaggeration can conclude only that the sense of crisis was "conjured up" by the Federalists, since "actually the country faced no such emergency." But such a conspiratorial interpretation of the Constitution is hardly satisfying and tells us nothing of what such statements of alarm and foreboding meant. Why did some men, members of the elite—those who saved their letters for us to read—think America was in a crisis?6

Certainly it was not the defects of the Articles of Confederation that were causing this sense of crisis. These defects of the Confederation were remediable and were scarcely capable of eliciting horror and despair. To be sure, these defects did make possible the calling of the Philadelphia Convention to amend the Articles. By 1787 almost every political leader in the country, including most of the later Anti-Federalists, wanted something done to strengthen the Articles of Confederation. The Confederation had no power to pay its debts, no power to tax, and no power to regulate commerce, and it was daily being humiliated in its international relationships. Reform of the Articles in some way or other—particularly by granting the Congress a limited authority to tax and the power to regulate commerce—was in the air. This desire to do something about the central government was the Federalists' opportunity: it explains the willingness of people to accede to the meeting at Annapolis and the subsequent convening of delegates at Philadelphia. In fact, so acceptable and necessary seemed some sort of change in the Confederation that later Anti-Federalists were remarkably casual about the meeting at Philadelphia. William Findley of western Pennsylvania, for example, later claimed he was selected to go to the Convention but declined when he learned that "the delegates would have no wages." Thus the seven delegates Pennsylvania sent to the Convention were all residents of the city of Philadelphia (including even one, Gouverneur Morris, who was really a New Yorker), and no one at the time complained.[7]

Thus the defects of the Confederation were widely acknowledged, and many looked to the Philadelphia Convention for a remedy. But these defects do not account for the elite's expression of crisis, nor do they explain the ambitious nature of the nationalists' Virginia Plan that formed the working model for the Convention's deliberations. The nationalists' aims and the Virginia Plan went way beyond what the weaknesses of the Articles demanded. Granting Congress the authority to raise revenue, to regulate trade, to pay off its debts, and to deal effectively in international affairs did not require the total scrapping of the Articles and the creation of an extraordinarily powerful and distant national government, the like of which was virtually inconceivable to Americans a decade earlier. The Virginia Plan was the remedy for more than the obvious impotence of the Confederation; it was a remedy—and an aristocratic remedy—for what were often referred to as the excesses of American democracy. It was these excesses of democracy that lay behind the elite's sense of crisis.

What excesses of democracy? What on earth could have been happening to provoke fear and horror? Not Shays's Rebellion that broke out in the winter of 1786–1787. That was an alarming clincher for many Federalists, especially in Massachusetts, but it was scarcely the cause of the Federalists' pervasive sense of crisis, which existed well before they learned of Shays's Rebellion.[8] No, it was not mobs and overt disorder that really frightened the Founders. They knew about popular rioting, and had taken such occurrences more or less in stride for years. What bothered them, what they meant by the excesses of democracy, was something more insidious than mobs. It was something that we today accept as familiar, ordinary, and innocuous, but the Founders did not—good old American popular politics. It was popular politics, especially as practiced in the state legislatures, that lay behind the Founders' sense of crisis. The legislatures were unwilling to do "justice," and this, said Washington, is "the origin of the evils we now feel." The abuses of the state legislatures, said Madison, were "so frequent and so flagrant as to alarm the most stedfast friends of Republicanism," and these abuses, he told Jefferson in the fall of 1787, "contributed more to that uneasiness which produced the Convention, and prepared the public mind for a general reform, than those which accrued to our national character and interest from the inadequacy of the Confederation to its immediate objects."[9] Hard as it may be for us today to accept, the weaknesses of the Articles of Confederation were not the most important reasons for the making of the Constitution.

Throughout the whole period of crisis, Madison, the father of the Constitution if there ever was one, never had any doubt where the main source of the troubles lay. In his working paper drafted in the late winter of 1787 entitled "Vices of the Political System of the United States," Madison spent very little time on the impotence of the Confederation. What was really on his mind was the deficiencies of the state governments: he devoted more than half his paper to the "multiplicity," "mutability," and "injustice" of the laws passed by the states.[10] Particularly alarming and unjust in his eyes were the paper money acts, stay laws, and other forms of debtor-relief legislation that hurt creditors and violated individual property rights. And he knew personally what he was talking about. Although we usually think of Madison as a bookish scholar who got all his thoughts from his wide reading, he did not develop his ideas about the democratic excesses of the state governments by poring through the bundles of books that Jefferson was sending him from Europe. He learned about popular politics and legislative abuses firsthand—by being a member of the Virginia Assembly.

During the years 1784 through 1787 Madison attended four sessions of the Virginia legislature. They were perhaps the most frustrating and disillusioning years of his life, but also the most important years of his life, for his experience as a Virginia legislator in the 1780s was fundamental in shaping his thinking as a constitutional reformer.

Although Madison in these years had some notable legislative achievements, particularly with his shepherding into enactment Jefferson's famous bill for religious freedom, he was continually exasperated by what Jefferson years later (no doubt following Madison's own account) referred to as "the endless quibbles, chicaneries, perversions, vexations, and delays of lawyers and demi-lawyers" in the assembly. Really for the first time, Madison found out what democracy in America might mean. Not all the legislators were going to be like him or Jefferson; many of them did not even appear to be gentlemen. The Virginia legislators seemed so parochial, so illiberal, so small-minded, and most of them seemed to have only "a particular interest to serve." They had no regard for public honor or honesty. They too often made a travesty of the legislative process and were reluctant to do anything that might appear unpopular. They postponed taxes, subverted debts owed to the subjects of Great Britain, and passed, defeated, and repassed bills in the most haphazard ways. Madison had enlightened expectations for Virginia's port bill in 1784, but the other legislators got their self-serving hands on it and perverted it. It was the same with nearly all the legislative proposals he sought to introduce, especially those involving reform of the legal code and court system. "Important bills prepared at leisure by skilful hands," he complained, were vitiated by "crudeness and tedious discussion." What could he do with such clods? "It will little elevate your idea of our Senate," he wrote in weary disgust to Washington in 1786, to learn that the senators actually defeated a bill defining the privileges of foreign ambassadors in Virginia "on the principle . . . that an Alien ought not to be put on better ground than a Citizen."[11] This was carrying localism to absurdity.

It was not what republican lawmaking was supposed to be. Madison continually had to make concessions to the "prevailing sentiments," whether or not such sentiments promoted the good of the state or nation. He had to agree to bad laws for fear of getting worse ones, or give up good bills "rather than pay such a price" as opponents wanted. Today legislators are used to this sort of political horse-trading. But Madison simply was not yet ready for the logrolling and the pork-barreling that would eventually become the staples of American legislative politics. By 1786 he had "strong apprehensions" that his and Jefferson's hope for reforming the legal code "may never be systematically perfected." The legislature was simply too popular, and appealing to the people had none of the beneficial effects good republicans had expected. A bill having to do with court reform was, for example, "to be printed for consideration of the public"; but "instead of calling forth the sanction of the wise and virtuous," this action, Madison feared, would only "be a signal to interested men to redouble their efforts to get into the Legislature." Democracy was no solution to the problem; democracy was the problem. Madison repeatedly found himself having to beat back the "itch for paper money" and other measures "of a popular cast." Too often Madison had to admit that the only hope he had was "of moderating the fury," not defeating it.[12]

Madison, like other enthusiastic Revolutionary idealists, emerged from his experience with democratic politics in the mid-1780s a very chastened republican. It was bad enough, he wrote in his "Vices of the Political System of the United States," that legislators were often interested men or dupes of the sophistry of "a favorite leader" (like Patrick Henry).

Even more alarming for the fate of republican government, however, was the fact that such legislators were only reflecting the partial interests and parochial outlooks of their constituents. Too many of the American people could not see beyond their own pocketbooks or their own neighborhoods. "Individuals of extended views, and of national pride," said Madison (and he knew whom he meant), might be able to bring public proceedings to an enlightened cosmopolitan standard, but their example could never be followed by "the multitude." "Is it to be imagined that an ordinary citizen or even an assembly man of R. Island in estimating the policy of paper money, ever considered or cared in what light the measure would be viewed in France or Holland; or even in Massts or Connect? It was a sufficient temptation to both that it was for their interest."[13]

Madison's experience with the populist politics of the state legislatures was especially important because of his extraordinary influence in the writing of the federal Constitution. But his experience was not unusual; indeed, the Federalists could never have done what they did if Madison's experience was not widely shared. By the mid-1780s gentlemen up and down the continent were shaking their heads in disbelief and anger at the "private views and selfish principles" of the men they saw in the state assemblies, "men of narrow souls and no natural interest in the society." Selfish, ignorant, illiberal state legislators—"Characters too full of Local attachments and Views to permit sufficient attention to the general interest"—were bringing discredit upon popular government. They were promoting their own or their locality's particular interest, pandering "to the vulgar and sordid notions of the populace," and acting as judges in their own causes. "Private convenience, paper money, and ex post facto laws" were the "main springs" of these state lawmakers. Many of the delegates to the Philadelphia Convention were so ready to accept Madison's radical Virginia Plan and its proposed national authority to veto all state laws precisely because they shared his deep disgust with the localist and interest-ridden politics of the state legislatures. "The vile State governments are sources of pollution which will contaminate the American name for ages. . . . Smite them," Henry Knox urged Rufus King sitting in the Philadelphia Convention, "smite them, in the name of God and the people."[14]

We today can easily appreciate the concerns of the Founders with the weaknesses of the Confederation government: these seem real and tangible to us, especially in light of what we know our national government has become. But we have more difficulty in appreciating the fears the Founders expressed over the democratic politics of the state legislatures—the scrambling of different interest groups, the narrow self-promoting nature of much of the lawmaking, the incessant catering to popular demands. Surely, this behavior cannot be accurately described as the "wilderness of anarchy and vice." This "excess of democracy" is, after all, what popular politics is about, and it is not different from what Americans in time came to be very used to.[15]

It may not have been different from what Americans came to be used to, and it may not even have been different from what some of the Revolutionary leaders had occasionally experienced in their colonial assemblies. But for most of the Founding Fathers, popular political behavior in the states during the 1780s was very different from what they expected from their republican Revolution, and for them that difference was what made the 1780s a genuine critical period.

REPUBLICANISM WAS NOT SUPPOSED TO stimulate selfishness and private interests, but was to divert and control them. But in states up and down the continent various narrow factional interests, especially economic, were flourishing as never before, and, more alarming still, were demanding and getting protection and satisfaction from the democratically elected state legislatures. Although interest groups and factionalism had been common in the colonial legislatures, the interests and factions of post-Revolutionary politics were different: more numerous, less personal and family-oriented, and more democratically expressive of new, widespread economic elements in the society. The Revolution, it appeared, had unleashed acquisitive and commercial forces that no one had quite realized existed.

We are only beginning to appreciate the immense consequences that the Revolution and, especially, wartime mobilization had on American society. When all the articles and monographs are in, however, I think that we will find that the Revolutionary War, like the Civil War and the two World Wars, radically transformed America's society and economy. The war effort was enormous. The war went on for eight years (the longest in American history until that of Vietnam); it eventually saw one hundred thousand or more men under arms, and it touched the whole of American society to a degree that no previous event ever had. The inexhaustible needs of the army—for everything from blankets and wagons to meat and rum—brought into being a host of new manufacturing and entrepreneurial interests and made market farmers out of husbandmen who before had scarcely ever traded out of their neighborhoods. To pay for all these new war goods, the Revolutionary governments issued huge sums—four hundred million to five hundred million dollars—of paper money that made its way into the hands of many people who had hitherto dealt only in a personal and bookkeeping barter economy.[16] Under the stimulus of this wartime purchasing, speculative farmers, inland traders, and profiteers of all sorts sprang up by the thousands to circulate these goods and paper money throughout the interior areas of America. By 1778, wrote Henry Laurens, "the demand for money" was no longer "confined to the capital towns and cities within a small circle of trading merchants, but spread over a surface of 1,600 miles in length, and 300 broad." The war and rapidly rising prices were creating a society in which, as one bitter commissary agent complained, "Every Man buys in order to sell again."[17] No event in the eighteenth century accelerated the capitalistic development of America more than did the Revolutionary War. It brought new producers and consumers into the market economy, it aroused latent acquisitive instincts everywhere, it stimulated inland trade as never before, and it prepared the way for the eventual momentous shift of the basis of American prosperity from external to internal commerce.

The paper money and the enormous amounts of debts that all these inland entrepreneurs, traders, shopkeepers, and market farmers thrived on were the consequences neither of poverty nor of anticommercial behavior. Debt, as we of all generations in American history ought to know, was already emerging as a symptom of expansion and enterprise. Farmers, traders, and others in these Revolutionary years borrowed money, just as they married earlier and had more children than ever before, because they thought the future was going to be even better than the present. Common people had been increasingly buying consumer goods since at least the middle of the eighteenth century, but the Revolutionary War now gave many more ordinary farmers, often for the first time in their lives, the financial ability to purchase luxury goods that previously had been the preserve of the gentry—everything from lace finery to china dishware. It was this prospect of raising their standard of living and increasing their "pleasures and diversions" that got farmers to work harder and produce "surpluses" during the war, and there is evidence that when the availability of these "luxury" goods diminished during the war the farmers' productivity and their "surpluses" diminished too.[18] For ages men had thought that industry and frugality among the common people went together. Now suddenly in America the industriousness of ordinary people seemed dependent not on the fear of poverty, but on the prospect of luxury.[19]

The economic troubles of the 1780s came from the ending of the war and government purchasing. Too many people had too many heightened expectations and were into the market and the consumption of luxuries too deeply to make any easy adjustments to peace. The collapse of internal markets and the drying up of paper money meant diminished incomes, overextended businesses, swollen inventories of imported manufactures, and debt-laden farmers and traders. The responses of people hurt by these developments were very comprehensible; they simply wanted to continue what they had done during the war. The stay laws and other debtor-relief legislation and the printing of paper money were not the demands of backward-looking and uncommercial people. They were the demands of people who had enjoyed buying, selling, and consuming and desired to do more of it. In order to have prosperity, argued one defender of paper money in 1786, it was not enough to have an industrious people and a fertile territory; money was essential too. And for many ordinary people in the 1780s money—in the absence of gold and silver coin—meant paper money issued by governments or government loan offices. "By anticipating the products of several years labor," farmers were able to borrow loan office certificates based on land in order "to accelerate improvements" and "so to augment industry and multiply the means of carrying it on" and thereby "enrich" both themselves and the state.[20]

These calls for paper money in the 1780s were the calls of American business. The future of America's entrepreneurial activity and prosperity lay not with the hundreds of well-to-do creditor-merchants who dominated the overseas trade of the several ports along the Atlantic seaboard. Rather, it lay with the thousands upon thousands of ordinary traders, petty businessmen, aspiring artisans, and market farmers who were deep in debt and were buying and selling with each other all over America. For these people, unlike the overseas merchants who had their private bills of exchange, publicly created paper money was the only means "capable of answering all the *domestic* and *internal* purposes of a *circulating medium in a nation*" that lacked specie. The prosperity of a country, it was now argued, involved more than external commerce, more than having a surplus of exports over imports. "The *internal* commerce of the country must be promoted, by increasing its *real riches*," which were now rightly equated with the acquisitions, improvements, and entrepreneurial activity of ordinary people.[21]

There is no exaggerating the radical significance of this heightened awareness among Americans of the importance of domestic trade. Hitherto most Americans had thought of internal trade, as William Smith of New York put it in the 1750s, as publicly worthless—a mere passing of wealth around the community from hand to hand. Such exchanging, said Smith, "tho' it may enrich an Individual," meant that "others must be poorer, in an exact proportion to his Gains; but the collective Body of the People not at all."[22] Such was the traditional zero-sum mercantilist mentality that was now being challenged by the increased entrepreneurial activity of thousands of ordinary people. Farmers "in a new and unimproved country," it was now said, "have continual uses for money, to stock and improve their farms" or, as Madison noted, to "extend their consumption as far as credit can be obtained." And they now wanted more money than could be gotten by the old-fashioned means of applying "to a monied man for a loan from his private fortune." Consequently these farmers and other small-time entrepreneurs in state after state up and down the continent were electing representatives to their legislatures who could supply them with paper money, paper money which, as the preamble to a 1785 Pennsylvania statute establishing a loan office stated, was designed "to promote and establish the interests of internal commerce, agriculture and mechanic arts."[23] Not the defects of the Articles of Confederation, but this promotion of entrepreneurial interests by ordinary people—their endless buying and selling, their bottomless passion for luxurious consumption—was what really frightened the Federalists.

The Federalists in the 1780s had a glimpse of what America was to become—a scrambling business society dominated by the pecuniary interests of ordinary people—and they did not like what they saw. This premonition of America's future lay behind their sense of crisis and their horrified hyperbolic rhetoric. The wholesale pursuits of private interest and private luxury were, they thought, undermining America's capacity for republican government. They designed the Constitution in order to save American republicanism from the deadly effects of these private pursuits of happiness.

THE FOUNDERS DID NOT INTEND the new Constitution to change the character of the American people. They were not naive utopians; they were, as we have often noted, realistic about human nature. They had little or no faith in the power of religion or of sumptuary or other such laws to get people to behave differently. To be sure, they believed in education, and some of them put great stock in what it might do in reforming and enlightening American people. But still they generally approached their task in the 1780s with a practical, unsentimental appreciation of the givenness of human beings. They knew they lived in an age of commerce and interests. Although some of the landed gentry like Jefferson might yearn wistfully at times for America to emulate China and "abandon the ocean altogether," most of the Founders welcomed America's involvement in commerce, by which, however, they commonly meant overseas trade.[24] They believed in the importance of such commerce, saw it as a major agent in the refining and civilizing of people, and were generally eager to use the power of government to promote its growth. They knew too all about "interest," which Madison defined "in the popular sense" as the "immediate augmentation of property and wealth." They accepted the inevitability and the prevalence of "interest" and respected its power. "Interest," many of them said, "is the greatest tie one man can have on another." It was, they said, "the only binding cement" for states and peoples. Hamilton put it more bluntly: "He who pays is the master."[25]

Since 1776 they had learned that it was foolish to expect most people to sacrifice their private interests for the sake of the public welfare. For the Federalists there was little left of the Revolutionary utopianism of Samuel Adams. Already by the 1780s, Adams's brand of republicanism seemed archaic and Adams himself a figure from another time and place. Soon people would be shaking their heads in wonderment that such a person as Adams should have ever existed in America. "Modern times," it was said, "have produced no character like his." He was "one of Plutarch's men," a character out of the classical past. He was a Harvard-educated gentleman who devoted himself to the public. He had neither personal ambition nor the desire for wealth. He refused to help his children and gloried in his poverty. He was without interests or even private passions. Among the Revolutionary leaders he was unique. No other leader took classical republican values quite as seriously as Adams did.[26]

In fact, the other Revolutionary leaders were very quick to expose the unreality and impracticality of Adams's kind of republican idealism. As early as 1778 Washington realized that the Revolution would never succeed if it depended on patriotism alone. "It must be aided by a prospect of interest or some reward."[27] All men could not be like Samuel Adams.

It was too bad, but that was the way it was. Human beings were like that, and by the 1780s many of the younger Revolutionary leaders like Madison were willing to look at the reality of interests with a very cold eye. Madison's *Federalist* No. 10 was only the most famous and frank acknowledgment of the degree to which interests of various sorts had come to dominate American politics.

The Founders thus were not dreamers who expected more from the people than they were capable of. We in fact honor the Founding Fathers for their realism, their down-to-earth acceptance of human nature. Perhaps this is part of our despairing effort to make them one with us, to close that terrifying gap that always seems to exist between them and us. Nevertheless, in our hearts we know that they are not one with us, that they are separated from us, as they were separated from every subsequent generation of Americans, by an immense cultural chasm. They stood for a classical world that was rapidly dying, a world so different from what followed—and from our own—that an act of imagination is required to recover it in all its fullness. They believed in democracy, to be sure, but not our modern democracy; rather, they believed in a patrician-led classical democracy in which "virtue exemplified in government will diffuse its salutary influence through the society." For them government was not an arena for furthering the interests of groups and individuals but a means of moral betterment. What modern American politician would say, as James Wilson said in the Philadelphia Convention, that "the cultivation and improvement of the human mind was the most noble object" of government? Even Jefferson, who of all the Founders most forcefully led the way, though inadvertently, to a popular liberal future, could in 1787 urge a Virginia colleague: "Cherish . . . the spirit of our people, and keep alive their attention. Do not be too severe upon their errors, but reclaim them by enlightening them." All the Founding Fathers saw themselves as moral teachers.[28] However latently utilitarian, however potentially liberal, and however enthusiastically democratic the Founders may have been, they were not modern men.

Despite their acceptance of the reality of interests and commerce, the

Federalists had not yet abandoned what has been called the tradition of civic humanism—that host of values transmitted from antiquity that dominated the thinking of nearly all members of the elite in the eighteenth-century Anglo-American world. By the late eighteenth century this classical tradition was much attenuated and domesticated, tamed and eaten away by modern financial and commercial developments. But something remained, and the Federalists clung to it. Despite their disillusionment with political leadership in the states, the Federalists in 1787 had not yet lost hope that at least some individuals in the society might be worthy and virtuous enough to transcend their immediate material interests and devote themselves to the public good. They remained committed to the classical idea that political leadership was essentially one of character: "The whole art of government," said Jefferson, "consists of being honest."[29] Central to this ideal of leadership was the quality of *disinterestedness*—the term the Federalists most used as a synonym for the classic conception of civic virtue: it better conveyed the increasing threats from interests that virtue now faced.

Dr. Johnson defined "disinterested" as being "superior to regard of private advantage; not influenced by private profit"; and that was what the Founding Fathers meant by the term.[30] We today have lost most of this older meaning. Even educated people now use "disinterested" as a synonym for "uninterested," meaning indifferent or unconcerned. It is almost as if we cannot quite conceive of the characteristic that disinterestedness describes: we cannot quite imagine someone who is capable of rising above a pecuniary interest and being unselfish and unbiased where an interest might be present. This is simply another measure of how far we have traveled from the eighteenth century.

This eighteenth-century concept of disinterestedness was not confined either to Commonwealthmen or to the country tradition (which makes our current preoccupation with these strains of thought misleading). Nor did one have to be an American or a republican to believe in disinterestedness and the other classical values that accompanied it. Virtue or disinterestedness, like the concept of honor, lay at the heart of all prescriptions for political leadership in the eighteenth-century Anglo-American world. Throughout the century Englishmen of all political persuasions—Whigs and Tories both—struggled to find the ideal disinterested political leader amid the rising and swirling currents of financial and commercial interests that threatened to engulf their societies. Nothing more enhanced William Pitt's reputation as the great patriot than his pointed refusal in 1746 to profit from the perquisites of the traditionally lucrative office of paymaster of the forces. Pitt was living proof for the English-speaking world of the possibility of disinterestedness—that a man could be a governmental leader and yet remain free of corruption.[31]

This classical ideal of disinterestedness was based on independence and liberty. Only autonomous individuals, free of interested ties and paid by no masters, were capable of such virtue. Jefferson and other republican idealists might continue to hope that ordinary yeoman farmers in America might be independent and free enough of pecuniary temptations and interests to be virtuous. But others knew better, and if they did not, then the experience of the Revolutionary War soon opened their eyes. Washington realized almost at the outset that no common soldier could be expected to be "influenced by any other principles than those of Interest." And even among the officer corps there were only a "few . . . who act upon Principles of disinterestedness," and they were "comparatively speaking, no more than a drop in the Ocean."[32]

Perhaps it was as Adam Smith warned: as society became more commercialized and civilized and labor more divided, ordinary people gradually lost their ability to make any just judgments about the varied interests and occupations of their country; and only "those few, who, being attached to no particular occupation themselves, have leisure and inclination to examine the occupations of other people." Perhaps then in America, as well as in Britain, only a few were free and independent enough to stand above the scramblings of the marketplace. As "Cato" had written, only "a very small Part of Mankind have Capacities large enough to judge of the Whole of Things." Only a few were liberally educated and cosmopolitan enough to have the breadth of perspective to comprehend all the different interests, and only a few were dispassionate and unbiased enough to adjudicate among these different interests and promote the public rather than a private good. Virtue, it was said as early as 1778, "can only dwell in superior minds, elevated above private interest and selfish views." Even Jefferson at one point admitted that only those few "whom nature has endowed with genius and virtue" could "be rendered by liberal education worthy to receive, and able to guard the sacred rights and liberties of their fellow citizens."[33] In other words, the Federalists were saying that perhaps only from among the tiny proportion of the society the eighteenth century designated as "gentlemen" could be found men capable of disinterested political leadership.

This age-old distinction between gentlemen and others in the society had a vital meaning for the Revolutionary generation that we have totally lost. It was a horizontal cleavage that divided the social hierarchy into two unequal parts almost as sharply as the distinction between officers and soldiers divided the army; indeed, the military division was related to the larger social one. Ideally the liberality for which gentlemen were known connoted freedom—freedom from material want, freedom from the caprice of others, freedom from ignorance, and freedom from manual labor. The gentleman's distinctiveness came from being independent in a world of dependencies, learned in a world only partially literate, and leisured in a world of workers.[34] Just as gentlemen were expected to staff the officer corps of the Continental army (and expected also to provide for their own rations, clothing, and equipment on salaries that were less than half those of their British counterparts), so were independent gentlemen of leisure and education expected to supply the necessary disinterested leadership for government.[35] Since such well-to-do gentry were "exempted from the lower and less honourable employments," wrote the philosopher Francis Hutcheson, they were "rather more than others obliged to an active life in some service to mankind. The publick has this claim upon them." Governmental service, in other words, was thought to be a personal sacrifice, required of certain gentlemen because of their talents, independence, and social preeminence.[36]

In eighteenth-century America it had never been easy for gentlemen to make this personal sacrifice for the public, and it became especially difficult during the Revolution. Which is why many of the Revolutionary leaders, especially those of "small fortunes" who served in the Congress, continually complained of the burdens of office and repeatedly begged to be relieved from these burdens in order to pursue their private interests. Periodic temporary retirement from the cares and commotions of office to one's country estate for refuge and rest was acceptable classical behavior. But too often America's political leaders, especially in the North, had to retire not to relaxation in the solitude and leisure of a rural retreat, but to the making of money in the busyness and bustle of a city law practice.[37]

In short, America's would-be gentlemen had a great deal of trouble in maintaining the desired classical independence and freedom from the marketplace. There were not many American gentry who were capable of living idly off the rents of tenants as the English landed aristocracy did. Of course, there were large numbers of the Southern planter gentry whose leisure was based on the labor of their slaves, and these planters obviously came closest in America to fitting the classical ideal of the free and independent gentleman. But some Southern planters kept taverns on the side, and many others were not as removed from the day-to-day management of their estates as their counterparts among the English landed gentry. Their overseers were not comparable to the stewards of the English gentry; thus the planters, despite their aristocratic poses, were often very busy, commercially involved men. Their livelihoods were tied directly to the vicissitudes of international trade, and they had always had an uneasy sense of being dependent on the market to an extent that the English landed aristocracy, despite its commitment to enterprising projects and improvements, never really felt. Still, the great Southern planters at least approached the classical image of disinterested gentlemanly leadership, and they knew it and made the most of it throughout their history.[38]

In northern American society such independent gentlemen standing above the interests of the marketplace were harder to find, but the ideal remained strong. In ancient Rome, wrote James Wilson, magistrates and army officers were always gentleman farmers, always willing to step down "from the elevation of office" and reassume "with contentment and with pleasure, the peaceful labours of a rural and independent life." John Dickinson's pose in 1767 as a "Pennsylvania Farmer" is incomprehensible except within this classical tradition. Dickinson, the wealthy Philadelphia lawyer, wanted to assure his readers of his gentlemanly disinterestedness by informing them at the outset that he was a farmer "contented" and "undisturbed by wordly hopes or fears."[39] Prominent merchants dealing in international trade brought wealth into the society and were thus valuable members of the community, but their status as independent gentlemen was always tainted by their concern for personal profit.[40] Perhaps only a classical education that made "ancient manners familiar," as Richard Jackson once told Benjamin Franklin, could "produce a reconciliation between disinterestedness and commerce; a thing we often see, but almost always in men of a liberal education." Yet no matter how educated merchants were or how much leisure they managed for themselves, while they remained merchants they could never quite acquire the character of genteel disinterestedness essential for full acceptance as political leaders, and that is why most colonial merchants were not active in public life.[41]

John Hancock and Henry Laurens knew this, and during the imperial crisis each shed his mercantile business and sought to ennoble himself. Hancock spent lavishly, bought every imaginable luxury, and patronized everyone. He went through a fortune, but he did become the single most popular and powerful figure in Massachusetts politics during the last quarter or so of the eighteenth century. Laurens especially was aware of the bad image buying and selling had among Southern planters. In 1764 he advised two impoverished but aspiring gentry immigrants heading for the backcountry to establish themselves as planters before attempting to open a store. For them to enter immediately into "any retail Trade in those parts," he said, "would be mean, would Lessen them in the esteem of people whose respect they must endeavour to attract." Only after they were "set down in a Creditable manner as Planters" might they "carry on the Sale of many specie of European and West Indian goods to some advantage and with a good grace." In this same year, 1764, Laurens himself began to curtail his merchant operations. By the time of the Revolution he had become enough of an aristocrat that he was able to sneer at all those merchants who were still busy making money. "How hard it is," he had the gall to say in 1779, "for a rich, or covetous man to enter heartily into the kingdom of patriotism."⁴²

For mechanics and others who worked with their hands, being a disinterested gentleman was impossible. Only when wealthy Benjamin Franklin retired from his printing business, at the age of forty-two, did "the Publick," as he wrote in his *Autobiography*, "now considering me as a Man of Leisure," lay hold of him and bring him into an increasing number of important public offices. Other artisans and petty traders who had wealth and political ambitions, such as Roger Sherman of Connecticut, also found that retirement from business was a prerequisite for high public office.⁴³

Members of the learned professions were usually considered gentlemen, particularly if they were liberally educated. But were they disinterested? Were they free of the marketplace? Were they capable of virtuous public service? Hamilton for one argued strongly that, unlike merchants, mechanics, or farmers, "the learned professions . . . truly form no distinct interest in society"; thus they "will feel a neutrality to the rivalships between the different branches of industry" and will be most likely to be "an impartial arbiter" between the diverse interests of the society. But others had doubts. William Barton thought "a few individuals in a nation may be actuated by such exalted sentiments of public virtue, . . . but these instances must be rare." Certainly many thought lawyers did not stand above the fray. In fact, said Barton, "professional men of every description arc necessarily, as such, obliged to pursue their immediate advantage."⁴⁴

Everywhere, men struggled to find a way of reconciling this classical tradition of disinterested public leadership with the private demands of making a living. "A Man expends his Fortune in political Pursuits," wrote Gouverneur Morris in an introspective unfinished essay. Did he do this out of "personal Consideration" or out of a desire to promote the public good? If he did it to promote the public good, "was he justifiable in sacrificing to it the Subsistence of his Family? These are important Questions; but," said Morris, "there remains one more," and that one question of Morris's threatened to undermine the whole classical tradition: "Would not as much Good have followed from an industrious Attention to his own Affairs?" Hamilton, for one, could not agree. Although he knew that most people were selfish scavengers, incapable of noble and disinterested acts, he did not want to be one of them. Thus he refused to make speculative killings in land or banking "because," as he put it in one of his sardonic moods, "there must be some *public fools* who sacrifice private to public interest at the certainty of ingratitude and obloquy—because my *vanity* whispers I ought to be one of those fools and ought to keep myself in a situation the best calculated to render service." Hamilton clung as long and as hard to this classical conception of leadership as anyone in post-Revolutionary America.[45]

Washington too felt the force of the classical ideal and throughout his life was compulsive about his disinterestedness. Because he had not gone to college and acquired a liberal education, he always felt he had to live literally by the book. He was continually anxious that he not be thought too ambitious or self-seeking; above all, he did not want to be thought greedy or "interested." He refused to accept a salary for any of his public services, and he was scrupulous in avoiding any private financial benefits from his governmental positions.

Perhaps nothing more clearly reveals Washington's obsession with these classical republican values than his agonized response in the winter of 1784–1785 to the Virginia Assembly's gift of 150 shares in the James River and Potomac canal companies. Acceptance of the shares seemed clearly impossible. The shares might be "considered in the same light as a pension," he said. He would be thought "a dependant," and his reputation for virtue would be compromised. At the same time, however, Washington believed passionately in what the canal companies were doing; indeed, he had long dreamed of making a fortune from such canals. He thought the shares might constitute "the foundation of the *greatest* and most *certain* income" that anyone could expect from a speculative venture. Besides, he did not want to show "disrespect" to his countrymen or to appear "ostentatiously disinterested" by refusing the gift of the shares.[46]

What should he do? Few decisions in Washington's career called for such handwringing as this one did. He sought the advice of nearly everyone he knew. Letters went out to Jefferson, to Governor Patrick Henry, to William Grayson, to Benjamin Harrison, to George William Fairfax, to Nathanael Greene, to Henry Knox, even to Lafayette—all seeking "the best information and advice" on the disposition of the shares. "How would this matter be viewed then by the eyes of the world[?]" he asked. Would not his reputation for virtue be tarnished? Would not accepting the shares "deprive me of the principal thing which is laudable in my conduct?"—that is, his disinterestedness.

The story would be comic if Washington had not been so deadly earnest. He understated the situation when he told his correspondents that his mind was "not a little agitated" by the problem. In letter after letter he expressed real anguish. This was no ordinary display of scruples such as government officials today show over a conflict of interest: in 1784–1785 Washington was not even holding public office.[47]

These values, this need for disinterestedness in public officials, were very much on the minds of the Founding Fathers at the Philadelphia Convention, especially James Madison's. Madison was a tough-minded thinker, not given to illusions. He knew that there were "clashing interests" everywhere and that they were doing great harm to state legislative politics. But he had not yet given up hope that it might be possible to put into government, at the national if not at the state level, some "proper guardians of the public weal," men of "the most attractive merit, and most diffusive and established characters." We have too often mistaken Madison for some sort of prophet of a modern interest-group theory of politics. But Madison was not a forerunner of twentieth-century political scientists such as Arthur Bentley, David Truman, or Robert Dahl. Despite his hardheaded appreciation of the multiplicity of interests in American society, he did not offer America a pluralist conception of politics.

He did not see public policy or the common good emerging naturally from the give-and-take of hosts of competing interests. Instead he hoped that these clashing interests and parties in an enlarged national republic would neutralize themselves and thereby allow liberally educated, rational men, "whose enlightened views and virtuous sentiments render them superior to local prejudices, and to schemes of injustice," to promote the public good in a disinterested manner. Madison, in other words, was not at all as modern as we make him out to be."[48] He did not expect the new national government to be an integrator and harmonizer of the different interests in the society; instead he expected it to be a "disinterested and dispassionate umpire in disputes between different passions and interests in the State." Madison even suggested that the national government might play the same superpolitical, neutral role that the British king had been supposed to play in the empire.[49]

The Federalists' plans for the Constitution, in other words, rested on their belief that there were some disinterested gentlemen left in America to act as neutral umpires. In this sense the Constitution became a grand—and perhaps in retrospect a final desperate—effort to realize the great hope of the Revolution: the possibility of virtuous politics. The Constitution thus looked backward as much as it looked forward. Despite the Federalists' youthful energy, originality, and vision, they still clung to the classical tradition of civic humanism and its patrician code of disinterested public leadership. They stood for a moral and social order that was radically different from the popular, individualistic, and acquisitive world they saw emerging in the 1780s.

THE ANTI-FEDERALISTS, OF COURSE, saw it all very differently. Instead of seeing enlightened patriots simply making a Constitution to promote the national good, they saw groups of interested men trying to foist an aristocracy onto republican America. And they said so, just as the Federalists had feared, in pamphlets, newspapers, and the debates in ratifying conventions. Fear of aristocracy did become the principal shibboleth and rallying cry of the opponents of the Constitution. Already during the 1780s the classical demand that government should be run by rich, leisured gentlemen who served "without fee or reward" was being met by increasing contempt: "Enormous wealth," it was said even in aristocratic South Carolina, "is seldom the associate of *pure* and *disinterested virtue.*"⁵⁰ The Anti-Federalists brought this popular contempt to a head and refused to accept the claim that the Federalists were truly disinterested patriots. In fact, many of them had trouble seeing anyone at all as free from interests. If either side in the debate therefore stood for the liberal, pluralistic, interest-ridden future of American politics, it was the Anti-Federalists. They, not the Federalists, were the real modern men. They emerged from the confusion of the polemics with an understanding of American society that was far more hardheaded, realistic, and prophetic than even James Madison.

There were, of course, many different Anti-Federalist spokesmen, a fact that complicates any analysis of the opposition to the Constitution. Yet some of the prominent Anti-Federalist leaders, such as Elbridge Gerry, George Mason, and Richard Henry Lee, scarcely represented, either socially or emotionally, the main thrust of Anti-Federalists. Such aristocratic leaders were socially indistinguishable from the Federalist spokesmen and often were as fearful of the excesses of democracy in the state legislatures as the Federalists. Far more representative of the paper money interests of the 1780s and the populist opposition to the "aristocracy" of the Federalists was someone like William Findley—that pugnacious Scotch-Irishman from western Pennsylvania. Gerry, Mason, and Lee did not really point the way to the liberal, interest-ridden democracy of nineteenth-century America, but Findley did. Until we understand the likes of William Findley, we won't understand either Anti-Federalism or the subsequent democratic history of America.

Findley came to the colonies from northern Ireland in 1763, at age twenty-two, in one of those great waves of eighteenth-century emigration from the northern parts of the British islands that so frightened Dr. Johnson. After trying his hand at weaving, the craft to which he had been apprenticed, Findley became a schoolmaster and then a farmer—until he was caught up in the Revolutionary movement, moved through the ranks to a militia captaincy, and became a political officeholder in Pennsylvania. Findley was the very prototype of a later professional politician and was as much a product of the Revolution as were the more illustrious patriots like John Adams or James Madison. He had no lineage to speak of, he went to no college, and he possessed no great wealth. He was completely self-taught and self-made, but not in the manner of a Benjamin Franklin who acquired the cosmopolitan attributes of a gentleman: Findley's origins showed, and conspicuously so. In his middling aspirations, middling achievements, and middling resentments, he represented far more accurately what America was becoming than did cosmopolitan gentlemen like Franklin and Adams.[51]

By the middle eighties this red-faced Irishman with his flamboyant white hat was becoming one of the most articulate spokesmen for those debtor–paper money interests that lay behind the political turbulence and democratic excesses of the period. As a representative from the West in the Pennsylvania state legislature, he embodied that rough, upstart, individualistic society that eastern squires like George Clymer hated and feared. In the western counties around Pittsburgh, gentry like Clymer could see only avarice, ignorance, and suspicion, and a thin, weak society where there were "no private or publick associations for common good, every Man standing single."[52] Findley never much liked Clymer, but he reserved his deepest antagonism for two others of the Pennsylvania gentry—Hugh Henry Brackenridge and Robert Morris.

Findley's political conflicts with these two men in the Pennsylvania legislature in the 1780s foreshadowed and, indeed, epitomized the Anti-Federalists' struggle with the Federalists. It is perhaps not too much to say that Findley came to see the Constitution as a device designed by gentry like Brackenridge and Morris to keep men like himself out of the important affairs of government. This was especially galling to Findley because he could see no justification for the arrogance and assumed superiority of such men. Brackenridge and Morris were in reality, he believed, no different from him, and during the 1780s he meant to prove it.

Hugh Henry Brackenridge, born in 1748, was seven years younger than Findley. He was a Princeton graduate who in 1781 moved to western Pennsylvania because he thought the wilds of Pittsburgh offered greater opportunities for advancement than crowded Philadelphia. As the only college-educated gentleman in the area, he saw himself as an oasis of cultivation in the midst of a desert. He wanted to be "among the first to bring the press to the west of the mountains," so he helped establish a newspaper in Pittsburgh for which he wrote poetry, bagatelles, and other things.[53] He was pretty full of himself, and he never missed an opportunity to sprinkle his prose with Latin quotations and to show off his learning. This young, ambitious Princeton graduate with aristocratic pretensions was, in fact, just the sort of person who would send someone like William Findley climbing the walls.

William Findley was already a member of the state legislature in 1786 when Brackenridge decided that he too would like to be a legislator. Brackenridge ran for election and won by promising his western constituents that he would look after their particular interests, especially in favoring the use of state certificates of paper money in buying land. But then his troubles began. In Philadelphia he inevitably fell in with the well-to-do crowd around Robert Morris and James Wilson, who had cosmopolitan tastes more to his liking. Under the influence of Morris, Brackenridge voted against the state certificates he had promised to support and identified himself with the eastern establishment. He actually had the nerve to write in the *Pittsburgh Gazette* that the "eastern members" of the assembly had singled him out among all the "Huns, Goths and Vandals" who usually came over the mountains to legislate in Philadelphia and had complimented him for his "liberality." But it was a dinner party at Chief Justice Thomas McKean's house in December 1786, at which both he and Findley were guests, that really did him in. One guest suggested that Robert Morris's support for the Bank of North America seemed mainly for his own personal benefit rather than for the people's. To this Brackenridge responded loudly, "The people are fools; if they would let Mr. Morris alone, he would make Pennsylvania a great people, but they will not suffer him to do it."[54]

Most American political leaders already knew better than to call the people fools, at least aloud, and Findley saw his chance to bring Brackenridge down a peg or two. He wrote a devastating account of Brackenridge's statement in the *Pittsburgh Gazette* and accused him of betraying the people's trust by his vote against the state certificates. It was all right, said Findley sarcastically, for a representative to change his mind if he had not solicited or expected the office, "which is the case generally with modest, disinterested men." But for someone like Brackenridge who had openly sought the office and had made campaign promises—for him to change his vote could only arouse the "indignation" and the "contempt" of the people. Brackenridge may have professed "the greatest acquired abilities, and most shining imagination," but he was in fact a self-seeking and self-interested person who did not have the public good at heart.

Brackenridge vainly tried to reply. At first he sought to justify his change of vote on the classical humanist grounds that the people could not know about the "complex, intricate and involved" problems and interests involved in legislation. "The people at home know each man his own wishes and wants." Only an educated elite in the assembly could see the problems of finance whole; it required "the height of ability to be able to distinguish clearly the interests of a state." But was Brackenridge himself a member of this disinterested elite? Did he really stand above the various interests of the state? He admitted under Findley's assault that he had a "strong *interest* to prompt me to *offer* myself" for election, but his private interest was the same interest with that of the western country where he lived. "My object was to advance the country, and thereby advance myself."[55]

It was a frank and honest but strained answer, a desperate effort by Brackenridge to reconcile the presumed traditional disinterestedness of a political leader with his obvious personal ambition. The more he protested, the worse his situation became, and he never recovered from Findley's attack. The two men crossed swords again in the election of delegates to the state ratifying convention in 1788, and Brackenridge as an avowed Federalist lost to the Anti-Federalist Findley. Brackenridge then abandoned politics for the time being and turned his disillusionment with the vagaries of American democracy into his comic masterpiece, *Modern Chivalry.*

Findley sent Brackenridge scurrying out of politics into literature by attacking his pretensions as a virtuous gentlemanly leader. He attacked Robert Morris in a similar way, with far more ruinous consequences for Morris. Findley and Morris first tangled while they were both members of the Pennsylvania legislature in the 1780s. During several days of intense debate in 1786 over the rechartering of the Bank of North America, Findley mercilessly stripped away the mask of superior classical disinterestedness that Morris had sought to wear. This fascinating wide-ranging debate— the only important one we have recorded of state legislative proceedings in the 1780s—centered on the role of interest in public affairs.

Findley was the leader of the legislative representatives who opposed the rechartering of the bank. He and others like John Smilie from western Pennsylvania were precisely the sorts of legislators whom gentry like Madison had accused throughout the 1780s of being illiberal, narrow-minded, and interested in their support of debtor farmers and paper money. Now they had an opportunity to get back at their accusers, and they made the most of it. Day after day they hammered home one basic point: the supporters of the bank were themselves interested men. They were directors or stockholders in the bank, and therefore they had no right in supporting the rechartering of the bank to pose as disinterested gentlemen promoting the public good. The advocates of the bank "feel interested in it personally." Their defense of the bank, said Findley, who quickly emerged as the principal and most vitriolic critic of the bank's supporters, revealed "the manner in which disappointed avarice chagrins an interested mind."

Morris and his fellow supporters of the bank were embarrassed by these charges that they had a selfish interest in the bank's charter. At first, in George Clymer's committee report on the advisability of rechartering the bank, they took the overbearing line that the proponents of the bank in the general community "included the most respectable characters amongst us," men who knew about the world and the nature of banks. But as the charges of their selfishness mounted, the supporters of the bank became more and more defensive. They insisted they were men of "independent fortune and situations" and were therefore "above influence or terror" by the bank. Under the relentless criticism by Findley and others, however, they one by one grew silent, until their defense was left almost entirely in the hands of Robert Morris, who had a personal, emotional involvement in this debate that went well beyond his concern for the bank.[56]

Morris, as the wealthiest merchant in Pennsylvania and perhaps in all of North America, had heard it all before. The charges of always being privately interested had been the plague of his public career. No matter that his "Exertions" in supplying and financing the Revolution were "as disinterested and pure as ever were made by Mortal Man," no matter how much he sacrificed for the sake of the public, the charges of using public office for personal gain kept arising to torment him. No prominent Revolutionary leader had ever been subjected to such "unmeritted abuse," such bitter and vituperative accusations of selfishness, as he had.[57]

Now in 1786 he had to hear it all over again: that his support of the bank came solely from his personal interest in it. What could he do? He acknowledged that he was a shareholder in the bank, but he tried to argue that the bank was in the interest of all citizens in the state. How could he prove that he was not self-interested? Perhaps if he sold his bank stock? If he did, he assured his fellow legislators that he would be just as concerned with the bank's charter. At one point he gave up and said he would leave the issue of his self-interestedness to the members of the house to determine. But he could not leave it alone, and was soon back on his feet. Members have said "my information is not to be trusted, because I am interested in the bank: but surely," he pleaded, "I am more deeply interested in the state." He hoped, "notwithstanding the insinuation made, that it will never be supposed I would sacrifice the interest and welfare of the state to any interest I can possibly hold in the bank." Why couldn't his arguments for the bank be taken on their merits, apart from their source? he asked. Let them "be considered, not as coming from parties interested, but abstractedly as to their force and solidity."

Such nervous arguments were symptoms of his mounting frustration, and he finally exploded in anger and defiance. Once more he stated categorically: "I am not stimulated by the consideration of private interest, to stand forth in defence of the bank." If people supposed that he needed this bank, they were "grossly mistaken." He was bigger than the bank. If the bank should be destroyed, he on his "own capital, credit, and resources" would create another one; and even his enemies ("and God knows I seem to have enough of them") would have to deal with him, if only "for the sake of their own interest and convenience."⁵⁸

It was an excruciating experience for Morris. At one point in the debate he expressed his desire to retire from office and become a private citizen, "which suits both my inclination and affairs much better than to be in public life, for which I do not find myself very well qualified." But the lure of the public arena and what it represented in the traditional aristocratic terms of civic honor were too great for him, and instead he retired once and for all from his merchant business and like Hancock and Laurens before him sought to ennoble himself. In the late eighties and early nineties, he shifted all his entrepreneurial activities into the acquisition of speculative land—something that seemed more respectable for an aristocrat than trade. He acquired a coat of arms, patronized artists, and hired L'Enfant to build him a huge marble palace in Philadelphia. He surrounded himself with the finest furniture, tapestry, silver, and wines and made his home the center of America's social life. Like a good aristocrat, he maintained, recalled Samuel Breck, "a profuse, incessant and elegant hospitality" and displayed "a luxury . . . that was to be found nowhere else in America." When he became a United States senator in 1789, he—to the astonishment of listeners—began paying himself "compliments on his manner and conduct in life," in particular "his disregard of money." How else would a real aristocrat behave?⁵⁹

For Morris to disregard money was not only astonishing, however; it was fatal. We know what happened, and it is a poignant, even tragic story. All his aristocratic dreams came to nothing; the marble palace on Chestnut Street went unfinished; his dinner parties ceased; his carriages were seized; and he ended in debtors' prison. That Morris should have behaved as he did says something about the continuing power of the classical aristocratic ideal of disinterestedness in post-Revolutionary America. It also says something about the popular power of William Findley, for it was Findley, more than anyone else in the debate over the bank, who had hounded Morris into renouncing his interests in commerce.

Findley in the debate knew he had Morris's number and bore in on it. "The human soul," Findley said, "is affected by wealth, in almost all its faculties. It is affected by its present interest, by its expectations, and by its fears." All this was too much for Morris, and he angrily turned on Findley. "If wealth be so obnoxious, I ask this gentleman why is he so eager in the pursuit of it?" If Morris expected a denial from Findley, he did not get it. For Findley's understanding of Morris's motives was really based on an understanding of his own. Did he love wealth and pursue it as Morris did? "Doubtless I do," said Findley. "I love and pursue it— not as an end, but as a means of enjoying happiness and independence," though he was quick to point out that he had wealth "not in any proportion to the degree" Morris had. Not that this made Morris in any way superior to Findley. Indeed, the central point stressed by Findley and the other western opponents of the bank was that Morris and his patrician Philadelphia crowd were no different from them, were no more respectable than they were. Such would-be aristocrats simply had "more money than their neighbours." In America, said Findley, "no man has a greater claim of special privilege for his £100,000 than I have for my £5." That was what American equality meant.

Morris, like all aspiring aristocrats in an egalitarian society, tried to stress that social distinctions were not based on wealth alone. "Surely," he said in desperate disbelief, "persons possessed of knowledge, judgment, information, integrity, and having extensive connections, are not to be classed with persons void of reputation or character." But Morris's claims of superiority were meaningless as long as he and his friends were seen to be interested men, and on that point Findley had him. Findley and his western legislative colleagues had no desire to establish any claims of their own to disinterestedness. In fact they wanted to hear no more spurious patrician talk of virtue and disinterestedness. They had no objection to Morris's and the other stockholders' being interested in the bank's rechartering: "Any others in their situation . . . would do as they did." Morris and other legislators, said Findley, "have a right to advocate their own cause, on the floor of this house." But then they could not protest when others realize "that it is their own cause they are advocating; and to give credit to their opinions, and to think of their votes accordingly." In fact, said Findley, such open promotion of interests meant an end to the archaic idea that representatives should simply stand and not run for election. When a candidate for the legislature "has a cause of his own to advocate, interest will dictate the propriety of canvassing for a seat." Who has ever put the case for special-interest elective politics any better?[60]

These were the arguments of democratic legislators in the 1780s who were sick and tired of being told by the aristocratic likes of James Madison that they were "Men of factious tempers" and "of local prejudices" and "advocates and parties to the causes which they determine." If they were interested men, so too were all legislators, including even those such as Morris and Brackenridge who were supposed to be liberal-thinking genteel men of "enlightened views and virtuous sentiments." "The citizens," Findley later wrote, by which he meant citizens like himself, "have learned to take a surer course of obtaining information respecting political characters," particularly those who pretended to disinterested civic service. They had especially learned how to inquire "into the local interests and circumstances" of such characters and to point out those with "pursuits or interests" that were "inconsistent with the equal administration of government." Findley had seen the gentry up close, so close in fact that all sense of the mystery that had hitherto surrounded aristocratic authority was lost.[61]

The prevalence of interest and the impossibility of disinterestedness inevitably became a central argument of the Anti-Federalists in the debate over the Constitution. Precisely because the Constitution was designed to perpetuate the classical tradition of disinterested leadership in government, the Anti-Federalists felt compelled to challenge that tradition. There was, they said repeatedly, no disinterested gentlemanly elite that could feel "sympathetically the wants of the people" and speak for their "feelings, circumstances, and interests." Would-be patricians like James Wilson, declared William Findley, thought they were "born of a different race from the rest of the sons of men" and "able to conceive and perform great things." But despite their "lofty carriage," such gentry could not in fact see beyond "the pale of power and worldly grandeur." No one, said the Anti-Federalists, however elevated or educated, was free of the lures and interests of the marketplace. As for the leisured gentry who were "not . . . under the necessity of getting their bread by industry," far from being specially qualified for public leadership, they were in fact specially disqualified. Such men contributed nothing to the public good; their "idleness" rested on "other men's toil."[62]

But it was not just the classical tradition of leisured gentry leadership the Anti-Federalists challenged. Without realizing the full implications of what they were doing, they challenged too the whole social order the Federalists stood for. Society to the Anti-Federalists could no longer be a hierarchy of ranks or even a division into two unequal parts between gentlemen and commoners. Civic society should not in fact be graded by any criteria whatsoever. Society was best thought of as a heterogeneous mixture of "many different classes or orders of people, Merchants, Farmers, Planter Mechanics and Gentry or wealthy Men," all equal to one another. In this diverse egalitarian society, men from one class or interest could never be acquainted with the "*Situation* and Wants" of those from another. Lawyers and planters could never be "adequate judges of trademens concerns." Legislative representatives could not be just *for* the people; they actually had to be *of* the people. It was foolish to tell people that they ought to overlook local interests. Local interests were all there really were. "No man when he enters into society, does it from a view to promote the good of others, but he does it for his own good." Since all individuals and groups in the society were equally self-interested, the only "fair representation" in government, wrote the "Federal Farmer," ought to be one where "every order of men in the community . . . can have a share in it." Consequently, any American government ought "to allow professional men, merchants, traders, farmers, mechanics, etc. to bring a just proportion of their best informed men respectively into the legislature." Only an explicit form of representation that allowed Germans, Baptists, artisans, farmers, and so on each to send delegates of its own kind into the political arena could embody the pluralistic particularism of the emerging society of the early Republic.[63]

Thus in 1787–1788 it was not the Federalists but the Anti-Federalists who were the real pluralists and the real prophets of the future of American politics. They not only foresaw but endorsed a government of jarring individuals and interests. Unlike the Federalists, however, they offered no disinterested umpires, no mechanisms at all for reconciling and harmonizing these clashing selfish interests. All they and their Republican successors had was the assumption, attributed in 1806 to Jefferson, "that the public good is best promoted by the exertion of each individual seeking his *own good* in his own way."[64]

As early as the first decade of the nineteenth century it seemed to many gentlemen, like Benjamin Latrobe, the noted architect and engineer, that William Findley and the Anti-Federalists had not really lost the struggle after all. "Our representatives to all our Legislative bodies, National, as well as of the states," Latrobe explained to Philip Mazzei in 1806, "are elected by the majority *sui similes*, that is, *unlearned.*"

> For instance from Philadelphia and its environs we send to congress not *one* man of letters. One of them indeed is a lawyer but of no eminence, another a good Mathematician, but when elected he was a Clerk in a bank. The others are plain farmers. From the next county is sent a Blacksmith and from just over the river a Butcher. Our state legislature does not contain one individual of superior talents. The fact is, that superior talents actually excite distrust, and the experience of the world perhaps does not encourage the people to trust men of genius.[65]

This was not the world those "men of genius," the Founding Fathers, had wanted. To the extent therefore that the Constitution was designed to control and transcend common ordinary men with their common, ordinary pecuniary interests, it was clearly something of a failure. In place of a classical republic led by a disinterested enlightened elite, Americans got a democratic marketplace of equally competing individuals with interests to promote. Tocqueville saw what happened clearly enough. "Americans are not a virtuous people," he wrote, "yet they are free." In America, unlike the classical republics, "it is not disinterestedness which is great, it is interest." Such a diverse, rootless, and restless people—what could possibly hold them together? "Interest. That is the secret. The private interest that breaks through at each moment, the interest that moreover, appears openly and even proclaims itself as a social theory." In America, said Tocqueville, "the period of disinterested patriotism is gone . . . forever."[66]

No wonder the Founding Fathers seem so remote, so far away from us. They really are.

POSTSCRIPT

Were the Anti-Federalists right? Was no one in government without interests? Perhaps Brackenridge and Morris had interests, but did other Federalists? Were the "men of intelligence and uprightness" and "enlightened views and virtuous sentiments" that Federalists like James Wilson and James Madison spoke of also interested? Were such liberally educated cosmopolitans really no different from the debtor farmers of western Pennsylvania? These were essentially Charles Beard's questions, and they are still good ones.[67]

Most Federalist leaders certainly saw themselves as different from the likes of William Findley, and to a large extent they were different. They certainly had wealth and property; otherwise they could not have been the leisured gentlemen they aspired to be. But what was the nature of that property? How did most of them make their incomes? The Founding Fathers' sources of income is not a subject we know much about. How, for example, did Franklin actually support his genteel living through all those years of retirement? Merchants lived off the profits of their overseas trade, and Southern planters earned money by selling in transatlantic markets. Some gentry were landlords living off the earnings of tenants, and many others were professionals who earned money from fees. A few relied on the emoluments of government offices, though in the Revolutionary years this was not easy.

But with the exception of rents from property, most such direct sources of income were defiled by interest. That is, the income of most American gentlemen did not come without work and participation in commerce, as Adam Smith suggested it ought to for leaders to be truly disinterested. The "revenue" of the English landed aristocrats was unique, said Smith; their income from rents "costs them neither labour nor care, but comes to them as it were, of its own accord, and independent of any plan or project of their own." Thus would-be disinterested American public leaders struggled to find an equivalent, a reliable source of income that was not stained by marketplace exertion and interest. Many gentlemen of leisure found such a source in the interest from money they had lent out. It is not surprising that so many of the gentry used their wealth in this way. After all, what were the alternatives for investment in an underdeveloped society that lacked banks, corporations, and stock markets? Land, of course, was a traditional object of investment, but in America, as John Witherspoon pointed out in an important speech in the Continental Congress, rent-producing land could never allow for as stable a source of income as it did in England. In the New World, said Witherspoon, where land was more plentiful and cheaper than it was in the Old World, gentlemen seeking a steady income "would prefer money at interest to purchasing and holding real estate."[68]

The little evidence we have suggests that Witherspoon was correct. The probate records of wealthy individuals show large proportions of their estates out on loan. In fact, it was often through such loans to friends and neighbors that great men were able to build networks of dependents and clients. In 1776 Cadwallader Colden was the creditor of seventy-three different people. All sorts of persons lent money, said John Adams: merchants, professionals, widows, but especially "Men of fortune, who live upon their income." Because earning interest from loans was considered more genteel than most other moneymaking activities, John Dickinson reinforced the disinterestedness of his persona, the "Pennsylvania Farmer," by having him living off "a little money at interest." When merchants and wealthy artisans wanted to establish their status unequivocally as leisured gentlemen, they withdrew from their businesses and, apart from investing in property, lent their wealth out at interest. Franklin did it. So did Roger Sherman, John Hancock, and Henry Laurens. By 1783 Hancock had more than twelve thousand pounds owed him in bonds and notes. As soon as the trader Joseph Dwight of Springfield, Massachusetts, had any profits, he began removing them from his business and lending them out at interest. By the time of his death in 1768 he had more than 60 percent of his assets out on loan.[69]

As Robert Morris pointed out, in the years before the Revolutionary War, "monied men were fond, of lending upon bond and mortgage: it was a favourite practice; was thought perfectly safe." Even many of the great planters of the South earned more from such ancillary activities as lending money at interest than they did from selling their staple crops. Charles Carroll of Maryland had twenty-four thousand pounds on loan to his neighbors. A large landowner in the Shenandoah Valley, James Patton, had 90 percent of his total estate in the form of bonds, bills, and promissory notes due him. In this context all the bonds and loan office certificates sold by the state and congressional governments during the Revolution became just one more object of investment for gentlemen looking for steady sources of income.[70]

For these sorts of creditors and investors, inflation caused by the excessive printing of paper money could have only devastating consequences. "A depreciating Currency," warned John Adams, "will ruin Us." Indeed, for all those local creditors who were at the same time urban merchants or

Southern planters dealing in overseas trade with transatlantic obligations, excessive paper currency was doubly harmful: they received cheapened money from their debtors but had to pay their overseas creditors in rising rates of exchange. Washington was both a planter and a banker. In the 1780s he was angry at what his debtors and the promoters of inflation through paper money emissions had done to him while he was away fighting the Revolution. Such scoundrels, he complained more than once, had "taken advantage of my absence and the tender laws, to discharge their debts with a shilling or six pence in the pound," while to those whom he owed money, he now had "to pay in specie at the real value." Rather than enter into litigation, "unless there is every reason to expect a decision in my favor," he reluctantly agreed to accept paper money in place of specie for his rents and debts, "however unjustly and rascally it has been imposed." No wonder then, said Robert Morris, that wealthy men, at least those who had survived the Revolution, had stopped taking up bonds and mortgages; they were "deterred from lending again by the dread of paper money and tender laws."[71]

We have always known that the skyrocketing inflation fueled by the excessive printing of paper money during these years was devastating to creditors, but we have not always appreciated precisely what this meant socially and morally. Credit was the principal sinew of the society and was absolutely essential for the carrying on of any form of commerce. Establishing one's creditworthiness in this personally organized society was nearly equivalent to establishing one's existence as a person, which is why letters of recommendation were so important. The relationships between creditors and debtors were not supposed to be merely impersonal legal contracts. Such engagements, even when they spanned continents and oceans, depended ultimately, it seemed, on personal faith and trust. Debts were thus thought by many to be more than legal obligations; they were moral bonds tying people together. That is why defaulting debtors were still thought to be more than unfortunate victims of bad times; they were moral failures, violators of a code of trust and friendship who deserved to be punished and imprisoned.[72]

It is not surprising therefore that many of those whom George Clymer called "honest gentry of intrinsic worth" tended to see all actions interfering with this relationship between creditor and debtor as morally abhorrent. Inflation artificially induced by Rhode Island's printing of paper money threatened, said a Boston gentleman, nothing less than "the first principles of society." Paper money, Madison told his fellow Virginia legislators, was unjust, pernicious, and unconstitutional. It was bad for commerce, it was bad for morality, and it was bad for society: it destroyed "confidence between man and man." Thus most Federalists who stood up for credit and the honest payment of debts did not see themselves as just another economic interest in a pluralistic society. They were defending righteousness itself. "On one side," said Theodore Sedgwick, "are men of talents, and of integrity, firmly determined to support public justice and private faith, and on the other there exists as firm a determination to institute tender laws, paper money, . . . land in short to establish iniquity by law."73

The federal Constitution's abolition of the states' power to emit paper money was therefore welcomed by most gentry as the righting of a moral and social wrong. The wickedness of such inflationary state policies was so much taken for granted by the members of the Convention that this prohibition of the states' authority in Article I, Section 10 of the Constitution was scarcely debated. Even a proposal to grant authority to the federal Congress to emit bills of credit was thrown out by the Convention, nine states to two. The truth is there were almost no real Anti-Federalists such as William Findley present in the Convention to defend the states' paper money emissions of the 1780s. Of the delegates present, only eccentric Luther Martin spoke out against the prohibition of the states' emitting bills of credit. The Federalists morally controlled the debate over paper money in 1787–1788 and browbeat most potential defenders of it into silence. As William R. Davie pointed out to the North Carolina ratifying convention, gentlemen in their speeches attached such dishonesty and shame to paper money that even "a member from Rhode Island" (which was defiantly excessive in emitting paper money) "could not have set his face against such language."74 So dominant were classical values and so disturbing seemed the moral and social consequences of paper money that even those who defended paper emissions in the 1780s often did so in terms that conceded the Federalists' traditional argument against ordinary people's earning and spending money beyond their station.[75] Only in time, with the spread of paper-issuing banks and a new understanding of the economy, would Americans find the arguments to legitimate the position of men like William Findley.

Whatever the confusion of the Anti-Federalists, most Federalists believed they understood what their opponents were like. "Examine well the characters and circumstances of men who are averse to the new constitution," warned David Ramsay of South Carolina. Many of them may be debtors "who wish to defraud their creditors," and therefore, for some of them at least, Article I, Section 10 of the Constitution may be "the real ground of the opposition. . . . though they may artfully cover it with a splendid profession of zeal for state privileges and general liberty."[76] But even if this were not true, the Federalists at least knew that the end of the states' printing of paper money would be of "real service to the honest part of the community." If the new Constitution, said Benjamin Rush in 1788, "held forth no other advantages [than] that [of] a future exemption from paper money and tender laws, it would be eno' to recommend it to honest men." This was because "the man of wealth realized once more the safety of his bonds and rents against the inroads of paper money and tender laws."[77] That was putting it about as selfishly as it could be put.

Yet in the end it should not be put that way. To rest something as monumental as the formation of the federal Constitution on such crude, narrow, and selfish motives was Beard's mistake, and it should not be repeated. The Federalists certainly had far more fundamental concerns at stake in 1787 than their personal credit and their social status. They were defending not their personal interests (for they were often debtors as well as creditors), but rather a moral and social order that had been prescribed by the Revolution and the most enlightened thinking of the eighteenth century. So committed were they to these classical humanist values that they were scarcely capable of understanding, let alone admitting the legitimacy of, the acquisitive and enterprising world that paper money represented. They saw themselves, as sincerely and thoroughly as any generation in American history, as virtuous leaders dedicated to promoting the good of the nation. However strong and self-serving their underlying interests may have been, the Federalists always described their ideals and goals in the language of classical republican disinterestedness; and this language, these ideals and goals, repeated endlessly in private correspondence and public forums up and down the continent, inevitably controlled and shaped their behavior. Washington's agony over the canal shares and Morris's abandonment of his mercantile career are object lessons in the power of this culture to affect behavior. Self-interest that could not be publicly justified and explained was self-interest that could not be easily acted upon.

The Founders thus gave future Americans more than a new Constitution. They passed on ideals and standards of political behavior that helped to contain and control the unruly materialistic passions unleashed by the democratic revolution of the early nineteenth century. Even today our aversion to corruption, our uneasiness over the too-blatant promotion of special interests, and our yearning for examples of unselfish public service suggest that such ideals still have great moral power. Yet in the end we know that it was not the Federalists of 1787 who came to dominate American culture. Our wistful celebration of their heroic greatness, our persistent feelings that they were leaders the likes of whom we shall never see again in America, our ready acceptance of parties and interest-group politics—all tell us that it was William Findley and the Anti-Federalists who really belonged to the future. They, and not the Federalists, spoke for the emerging world of egalitarian democracy and the private pursuit of happiness.

AFTERWORD TO CHAPTER 4

This piece began as a lecture at a conference held in Philadelphia in October 1984 in preparation for the bicentennial celebration of the formation of the Constitution three years later. It was extensively revised and enlarged for publication in the 1987 volume that came out of the conference.

I probably made a mistake with the too-cute suggestion that maybe the Anti-Federalists were the ones who stood for the future of American politics better than did the Federalists. Many readers have tended to be very literal-minded, and they have taken me to task for trying to reverse our understanding of who was more important in the future development of American politics, the Federalists or the Anti-Federalists. Trying to assess individuals' or groups' responsibility for the future in this manner is probably not a very good way to write history. The historical process is too complicated for that sort of assessment.

CHAPTER FIVE

The ORIGINS of AMERICAN CONSTITUTIONALISM

*T*HE CONSTITUTIONALISM OF THE UNITED STATES is rather old hat these days. Since the country has the oldest written national constitution in the world, there doesn't seem to be much that is new and peculiar about it. Certainly the fact that the American Constitution is written is not unusual. Most constitutions these days are written, many of them during the past three decades. When people talk about a country like Afghanistan or Iraq getting a new constitution, they assume it will be a written one; it now seems that writing one out on paper is the only way to create a constitution these days. (I should point out that most newly written constitutions are a good deal longer than the eight thousand words of the American Constitution. Actually, the U.S. Constitution today has become as "unwritten" as those of Israel or Great Britain.)

It used to be that America's separation of powers was unusual, if not unique, among governments. Not anymore. Lots of governments now have independent judiciaries and presidents who are not members of their legislatures. But the parliamentary system of cabinet responsibility to the legislature still dominates in the world, and thus the American system of separation of powers still seems unusual.

There was a time when judicial review was peculiarly American, but no longer. Many states in the world now have judiciaries that review legislation and have the authority to declare statutes null and void. (Parenthetically, however, it is important to point out that many of these courts, unlike the American courts, are specialized constitutional courts.) Even the English courts, which have always been respectful of parliamentary sovereignty, have recently begun trying to use the European Convention on Human Rights as a basis for interpreting or limiting parliamentary statutes.

Foreign courts now routinely deal with the same issues that American courts deal with—right-to-life, freedom of speech, and equality. In fact, foreign courts sometimes critically scrutinize and use American court decisions in reaching their own decisions. Some judiciaries in the European states now declare more statutes void than does the U.S. Supreme Court. Many of these foreign courts, such as the Israeli Supreme Court, even consider cases justiciable that the American courts have avoided, especially those dealing with military matters. It is very unlikely that the U.S. Supreme Court would have taken on a case similar to one concerning the amount of food being provided to those holed up in the Church of the Nativity in Bethlehem while surrounded by the Israeli army. But the Israeli Supreme Court did, even without a written constitution!

Americans used to be known for their obsession with rights, but that obsession now seems to be shared more and more by other countries in the developed world. Most of the new constitutions of the past three decades have a core of basic rights and liberties to which judges can refer in their court decisions. Even the idea of separation of church and state, which Americans pioneered, has spread to other nations struggling with religious diversity. Federalism may have been a modern American invention, but it has been much copied. Indeed, federalism is so common throughout the world today that America's example is scarcely illuminating anymore. America may, in fact, be the most centralized of the many federal states and thus the least interesting model.

Despite all these modern similarities between the U.S. Constitution and other national constitutions, however, there are important differences. To better understand those differences and perhaps to make some sense of Americans' habitual ignorance of other constitutions in the world, it may be helpful to look at the origins of America's constitutionalism.

The first thing to emphasize is the fact that the Founders who created America's constitutional structure at the end of the eighteenth century were Englishmen with a strong sense that they were heirs of the English tradition of freedom. Although England had become corrupted during the eighteenth century, Americans believed that at one time it had been the dominant source of liberty and popular government in the world, its constitution celebrated by liberal intellectuals everywhere. Thus it was fitting that Anglo-Americans (the title most Europeans gave to Americans in the early nineteenth century) should become the beneficiaries of this popular tradition of English rights and English liberty. Americans thought that the torch of English freedom had been passed to them and that they had a responsibility to make it shine brighter and more enduringly than the English had been able to do.

The Americans were intent on avoiding the corruption they believed plagued the English constitution, and that meant that they had to deviate from the English constitutional tradition in a number of ways. In fact, comparing the Americans' constitutional developments at the end of the eighteenth century with the English constitutional system that they broke away from can help to illuminate just what is distinctive about American constitutionalism.

The most obvious difference between eighteenth-century English and American constitutionalism was the American Revolutionaries' conception of a constitution as a written document, as a fundamental law circumscribing the government. Before the American Revolution, a constitution was rarely distinguished from the government and its operations. Traditionally in English culture, a constitution referred both to the way the government was put together, or constituted, and to the fundamental rights the government was supposed to protect. The eighteenth-century English constitution was an unwritten mixture of laws, customs, principles, and institutions.

By the end of the Revolutionary era, however, the Americans' idea of a constitution had become very different. A constitution was now seen to be no part of the government at all: it was a written document distinct from and superior to all the operations of government. A constitution was, as Thomas Paine said in 1791, "a thing *antecedent* to a government; and a government is only the creature of a constitution." And, said Paine, it was "not a thing in name only; but in fact."

For Americans, a constitution was something fundamental. It was a written document, possessed by every family, and carried about like the Bible to be quoted and cited article by article. Such a constitution could never be an act of the legislature; it had to be the act of the people themselves, declared James Wilson—one of the principal framers of the Constitution of 1787—and "in their hands it is clay in the hands of a potter; they have the right to mould, to preserve, to improve, to refine, and to furnish it as they please." If eighteenth-century Britons thought this American idea of a constitution was, as the British writer Arthur Young caustically suggested in 1792, "a pudding made from a recipe," the Americans had become convinced that the English had no constitution at all.

As much as we now take for granted this idea of a constitution as written fundamental law, the idea was not easily arrived at. The American colonists began the debate with Great Britain in the 1760s thinking about constitutional issues in much the same way as their fellow Britons. Like the English, they believed that the principal threat to the people's ancient rights and liberties had always been the prerogative powers of the king— those vague and discretionary but equally ancient rights of authority that the king possessed in order to carry out his responsibility for governing the realm. Indeed, the eighteenth-century English saw their history as essentially a struggle between these ancient conflicting rights—between power and liberty, between an encroaching monarchy on one hand and the freedom-loving people on the other. Time and again in the colonial period, Americans, like their fellow Englishmen at home, had been forced to defend themselves against the intrusions of royal prerogative power. They relied for their defense on their colonial assemblies, their rights as English subjects, and what they called their ancient charters.

In the seventeenth century, many of the colonies had been established by crown charters—corporate or proprietary grants made by the king to groups such as the Massachusetts Puritans or to individuals such as William Penn and Lord Baltimore to found colonies in the New World. In subsequent years these charters gradually lost their original meaning in the eyes of the colonists and took on a new importance, both as prescriptions for government and as devices guaranteeing the rights of the people against their royal governors. In fact, the whole of the colonial past was littered with such charters and other written documents of various sorts to which the colonial assemblies repeatedly appealed in their squabbles with royal power.

In turning to written documents as confirmation of their liberties, the colonists acted no differently from other Englishmen. From almost the beginning of their history, the English had continually invoked written documents and charters in defense of their rights against the crown's power. "Anxious to preserve and transmit" their rights "unimpaired to posterity," declared a Connecticut clergyman on the eve of the Revolution, the English people had repeatedly "caused them to be reduced to writing, and in the most solemn manner to be recognized, ratified and confirmed," first by King John, then Henry III and Edward I, and "afterwards by a multitude of corroborating acts, reckoned in all, by Lord Cook, to be thirty-two, from Edw. 1st. to Hen. 4th. and since, in a great variety of instances, by the bills of right and acts of settlement." All of these documents, from the Magna Carta to the Bill of Rights of the Glorious Revolution of 1688–1689, were merely written evidence of those fixed principles of reason from which the English believed their constitution was derived.

Although the eighteenth-century English talked about the fundamental law of the English constitution, few of them doubted that Parliament, as the representative of the nobles and people and as the sovereign lawmaking body of the nation, was the supreme guarantor and interpreter of these fixed principles and fundamental law. Parliament was in fact the bulwark of the people's liberties against the crown's encroachments; it alone defended and confirmed the people's rights. The Petition of Right, the act of Habeas Corpus, and the Bill of Rights were all acts of Parliament, statutes not different in form from other laws passed by Parliament.

For the English, therefore, as William Blackstone, the great eighteenth-century jurist, pointed out, there could be no distinction between the "constitution or frame of government" and "the system of laws." All were of a piece: every act of Parliament was part of the constitution and all law, both customary and statute, was thus constitutional. "Therefore," concluded the English theorist William Paley, "the terms *constitutional* and *unconstitutional*, mean *legal* and *illegal*."

Nothing could be more strikingly different from what Americans came to believe. Indeed, it was precisely on this distinction between "legal" and "constitutional" that the American and English constitutional traditions diverged at the time of the Revolution. During the 1760s and 1770s the colonists came to realize that although acts of Parliament, like the Stamp Act of 1765, might be legal—that is, in accord with the acceptable way of making law—such acts could not thereby be automatically considered constitutional, or in accord with the basic principles of rights and justice that made the English constitution what it was. It was true that the English Bill of Rights and the Act of Settlement of 1701 were only statutes of Parliament, but surely, the colonists insisted, they were of "a nature more sacred than those which established a turnpike road."

Under this kind of pressure, the Americans came to believe that the fundamental principles of the English constitution had to be lifted out of the lawmaking and other institutions of government and set above them. "In all free States," said Samuel Adams in 1768, "the Constitution is fixed; and as the supreme Legislature derives its Powers and Authority from the Constitution, it cannot overleap the Bounds of it without destroying its own foundation." Thus in 1776, when Americans came to make their own constitutions for their newly independent states, they inevitably sought to make them fundamental and write them out in documents. These state constitutions of 1776–1777, which were immediately translated into several European languages, captured the imagination of the enlightened everywhere.

It was one thing, however, to define the constitution as fundamental law, different from ordinary legislation and circumscribing the institutions of government; it was quite another to make such a distinction effective. Since the state constitutions were created by the legislatures, they presumably could also be changed or amended by the legislatures. Some of the constitution makers in 1776 realized the problem and tried to deal with it. Delaware provided for a supermajority, five-sevenths of the legislature, when changing its constitution. Maryland said that its constitution could be amended only by a two-thirds vote of two successive legislatures. Most states, however, simply enacted their constitutions as if they were regular statutes. Clearly, everyone believed that the constitutions were special kinds of law, but no one knew quite how to make them so.

In the years following the Declaration of Independence, Americans struggled with this problem of distinguishing fundamental from statutory law, none more persistently than Thomas Jefferson. In 1779 Jefferson knew from experience that no legislature "elected by the people for the ordinary purposes of legislation only" could restrain the acts of succeeding legislatures. Thus he realized that to declare his great Statute for Religious Freedom in Virginia to be "irrevocable would be of no effect in law; yet we are free," he wrote into his 1779 bill in frustration, "to declare, and do declare, that . . . if any act shall be hereafter passed to repeal the present [act] or to narrow its operation, such act will be an infringement of natural right." In effect, he was placing a curse on the future legislators of Virginia.

But Jefferson realized that such a paper declaration was not enough and that something more was needed. By the 1780s both he and his friend James Madison were eager "to form a real constitution" for Virginia; the existing one, they said, was merely an "ordinance" with "no higher authority than the other ordinances of the same session." They wanted a constitution that would be "perpetual" and "unalterable by other legislatures." The only way that could be done was to have the constitution created, as Jefferson put it, "by a power superior to that to the legislature." By the time Jefferson came to write his *Notes on the State of Virginia* in the early 1780s, the answer had become clear. "To render a form of government unalterable by ordinary acts of assembly," wrote Jefferson, "the people must delegate persons with special powers. They have accordingly chosen special conventions or congresses to form and fix their governments."

Massachusetts in 1780 had shown the way. It had elected a convention specially designated to form a constitution and had then placed that constitution before the people for ratification. When the Philadelphia Convention drew up a new constitution for the nation in 1787, it knew what to do. It declared that the new Constitution had to be ratified by the people meeting in state conventions called for that purpose only. Constitutional conventions and the process of ratification made the people themselves the actual constituent power. As enlightened Europeans realized, these devices were some of the most distinctive contributions the American Revolution made to world politics.

But these were not the only contributions. With the conception of a constitution as fundamental law immune from legislative encroachment more firmly in hand, some state judges during the 1780s began cautiously moving in isolated cases to impose restraints on what the assemblies were enacting as law. In effect, they said to the legislatures—as George Wythe, judge of the Virginia supreme court, did in 1782—"Here is the limit of your authority; and hither shall you go, but no further." These were the hesitant beginnings of what would come to be called judicial review—that remarkable practice by which judges in the ordinary courts of law have the authority to determine the constitutionality of acts of the state and federal legislatures.

The development of judicial review came slowly. It was not easy for people in the eighteenth century, even those who were convinced that many of the acts of the state legislatures in the 1780s were unjust and unconstitutional, to believe that unelected judges could set aside acts of the popularly elected legislatures; this seemed to be an undemocratic usurpation of power. But as early as 1787, James Iredell, soon to be appointed an associate justice of the newly created Supreme Court of the United States, saw that the new meaning Americans had given to a constitution had clarified the responsibility of judges to determine the law. A constitution in America, said Iredell, was not only "a fundamental law" but also a special, popularly created "law in writing . . . limiting the powers of the Legislature, and with which every exercise of those powers must necessarily be compared." Judges were not arbiters of the constitution or usurpers of legislative power. They were, said Iredell, merely judicial officials fulfilling their duty of applying the proper law. When faced with a decision between "the *fundamental unrepealable* law" made specially by the people, and an ordinary statute enacted by the legislature contrary to the constitution, they must simply determine which law was superior. Judges could not avoid exercising this authority, concluded Iredell, for in America a constitution was not "a mere imaginary thing, about which ten thousand different opinions may be formed, but a written document to which all may have recourse, and to which, therefore, the judges cannot witfully blind themselves."

Although Iredell may have been wrong about the number of different opinions that could arise over a constitution, he was certainly right about the direction judicial authority in America would take. The way was prepared for Supreme Court Justice John Marshall's decision in *Marbury v. Madison* in 1803 and the subsequent but bitterly contested development of the practice of judicial review—a practice that Europeans soon became aware of.

Unlike the European and Israeli constitutional courts, the American federal courts are not special courts with constitutional responsibilities separate from ordinary law adjudication. This is an important point of distinction whose implications are not easy to spell out. Because the European and Israeli constitutional courts are so special, they are usually protected from partisanship by elaborate mechanisms of appointment. The Israeli system of appointment is indirect and largely removed from the politics of the Knesset. As we know only too well from recent events,

Americans have no such indirect method of appointing judges. Thus the filibustering of appointments by the U.S. Senate becomes a crude requirement of a supermajority for federal court appointments. Of course, this is simply a measure of how significant judges have become in our constitutional system.

As important as the idea of a written constitution distinguishable from ordinary statute law was in the eighteenth century, however, it was not the most significant constitutional deviation the Americans made from their inherited English traditions. More important in distinguishing American constitutionalism from that of the English, and most other democratic nations in the world today, was the idea of separation of powers.

Montesquieu, in his *Spirit of the Laws*, had praised the English constitution for separating the executive, legislative, and judicial powers of government. But Montesquieu did not understand precisely what was happening to the English constitution in the eighteenth century. The legislature (that is, Parliament) and the executive (that is, the king's ministry) were in fact becoming blurred as England stumbled into what eventually became its modern parliamentary system of responsible cabinet government. The key to the British system is the fact that the ministers of the crown are simultaneously members of Parliament. It was this linkage, which the American colonists labeled "corruption" and David Hume called "influence," that the Americans in 1776 were determined to destroy.

Thus, in their state constitutions of 1776, they excluded from their assemblies all members of the executive branch, so that, as the New Jersey constitution declared, "the legislative department of this Government may, as much as possible, be preserved from all suspicion of corruption." This separation was repeated in the federal Constitution in Article I, Section 6—preventing the development of responsible cabinet government in America. In this respect, at least, American constitutionalism has not been influential at all, for most democratic governments in the world have tended to follow the British parliamentary model of government.

But beneath these obvious differences between the constitutionalism of Great Britain and of America are even more fundamental deviations that help to make America's conception of government and politics different from nearly every other nation in the world. These differences began with the concept of representation.

During the debates over the nature of the empire in the 1760s and 1770s, the British vainly tried to justify Parliament's taxation of the colonies. They argued that the American colonists, like Britons everywhere, were subject to acts of Parliament through a system of what they called "virtual" representation. Even though the colonists, like "nine-tenths of the people of Britain, did not in fact choose any representative to the House of Commons," they said, they were undoubtedly "a part, and an important part of the Commons of Great Britain: they are represented in Parliament in the same manner as those inhabitants of Britain are who have not voices in elections."

To most of the mainstream English at home, this argument made a great deal of sense. Centuries of history had left Britain with a confusing mixture of sizes and shapes of its electoral districts. Some of the constituencies were large, with thousands of voters, but others were small and more or less in the pocket of a single great landowner. Many of the electoral districts had few voters, and some so-called rotten boroughs had no inhabitants at all. One town, Dunwich, continued to send representatives to Parliament even though it had long since slipped into the North Sea. At the same time, some of England's largest cities, such as Manchester and Birmingham, which had grown suddenly in the mid-eighteenth century, sent no representatives to Parliament. The British justified this hodgepodge of representation by claiming that each member of Parliament represented the whole British nation and not just the particular locality he supposedly came from. Parliament, as Edmund Burke said, was not "a *congress* of ambassadors from different and hostile interests, which interests each must maintain, as an agent and advocate, against other agents and advocates; but Parliament is a deliberative assembly of *one* nation, with *one* interest, that of the whole." Requirements that the members of Parliament (MPs) reside in the constituencies they represented had long since been ignored and of course are still not necessary for MPs today. According to this idea of virtual representation, people were represented in England not by the process of election, which was considered incidental to representation, but rather by the mutual interests that members of Parliament were presumed to share with all Britons for whom they spoke—including those, like the colonists, who did not actually vote for them.

The Americans strongly rejected these British claims that they were "virtually" represented in the same way that the nonvoters of cities like Manchester and Birmingham were. They challenged the idea of virtual representation with what they called "actual" representation. If the people were to be properly represented in a legislature, the colonists declared, not only did the people have to vote directly for the members of the legislature, but they also had to be represented by members whose numbers were proportionate to the size of the population they spoke for. What purpose is served, asked James Otis of Massachusetts in 1765, by the continual attempts of the English to defend the lack of American representation in Parliament by citing the examples of Manchester and Birmingham, which returned no members to the House of Commons? "If those now so considerable places are not represented," said Otis, "they ought to be."

What was meaningful in England made no sense in America. Unlike in England, electoral districts in the New World were not the products of history that stretched back centuries, but rather were recent and regular creations that were related to changes in population. When new towns in Massachusetts and new counties in Virginia were formed, new representatives customarily were sent to the respective colonial legislatures. This system of actual representation stressed the closest possible connection between the local electors and their representatives. Unlike the English, Americans believed that representatives had to be residents of the localities they spoke for and that people of the locality had the right to instruct their representatives. The representatives were to be in effect what Burke had said they should never be, ambassadors from their localities. Since Americans thought it only fair that their localities be represented more or less in proportion to their population, they wrote that requirement into their Revolutionary constitutions. In short, the American belief in actual representation pointed toward the fullest and most equal participation of the people in the process of government that the modern world had ever seen.

Since this actual representation was based on the people's mistrust of those they elected, they pushed for the most explicit and broadest kind of consent, which generally meant voting. The mutuality of interests that made virtual representation meaningful in England was in America so weak and tenuous that the representatives could not be trusted to speak for the interests of their constituents unless those constituents actually voted for them. Actual representation thus made the process of election not incidental but central to representation.

Actual representation became the key to the peculiarities of American constitutionalism and government. People wanted elected officials that were like them in every way, not only in ideas but in religion, ethnicity, or social class. The people in Philadelphia in 1775 called for so many Presbyterians, so many artisans, and so many Germans on the Revolutionary committees. Already Americans were expressing the idea that the elected representatives not only had to be *for* the people, they also had to be *of* the people.

Mistrust became the source of American democracy. Indeed, the mistrust at times became so great that the representative process itself was brought into question, and mobs and extralegal associations emerged to claim to speak more authentically for the people than their elected representatives. The people, it seemed, could be represented in a variety of ways and in a variety of institutions. But no officials, however many votes they received, could ever fully represent the people.

Ultimately, these contrasting ideas of representation separated the English and American constitutional systems. In England Parliament came to possess sovereignty—the final, supreme, and indivisible lawmaking authority in the state—because it embodied the whole society, all the estates of the realm, within itself, and nothing existed outside of it.

In America, however, sovereignty remained with the people themselves, and not with any of their agents or even with all their agents put together. The American people, unlike the British, were never eclipsed by the process of representation.

When Americans referred to the sovereignty of the people, they did not just mean that all government was derived from the people. Instead, they meant that the final, supreme, and indivisible lawmaking authority of the society remained with the people themselves, not with their representatives or with any of their agents. In American thinking, all public officials became delegated and mistrusted agents of the people, temporarily holding bits and pieces of the people's power out, so to speak, on always recallable loan.

It may be important to point out why the Constitutional Convention failed to include a bill of rights with the Constitution it drafted in 1787. At the end of the Convention one delegate suggested that one was required. But the motion was defeated by every state delegation. The rationale for not having a bill of rights was that—unlike in England, where the crown's prerogative power preexisted and had to be limited by a bill of rights—all power in America existed in the people, who doled out only scraps of it to their various agents, so no such fence or bill of rights was necessary. This was a bit too precious an argument for many, however, and Madison and other supporters eventually had to concede the need for amendments, the first ten of which became the Bill of Rights.

By thinking of the people in this extraordinary way, Americans were able to conceive of federalism—that is, the remarkable division of power between central and provincial governments. By creating two legislatures with different powers operating over the same territory—the Congress and the separate state legislatures—the Americans offered the world a new way of organizing government. In subsequent decades, nineteenth-century libertarian reformers everywhere in Europe and Latin America, struggling to put together central governments in the face of strong local loyalties, appealed to the American example of federalism. German reformers in 1848 cited the American example in their efforts to build a confederation, and liberal reformers in Switzerland called the United States Constitution "a model and a pattern for the organization of the public life of republics in general, in which the whole and parts shall both be free and equal. . . . The problem," they said, with more enthusiasm than accuracy, given America's growing federal crisis that resulted in the Civil War, "has been solved by the new world for all peoples, states and countries."

Only by conceiving of sovereignty remaining with the people could Americans make sense of their new constitutional achievements, such as the idea of special constitution-making conventions and the process of popular ratification of constitutions. In America the notion that sovereignty rested in the people was not just a convenient political fiction; the American people, unlike the English, retained an actual lawmaking authority. The English did not need conventions and popular ratifications to change their constitution because Parliament was fully and completely the people and the people did not exist politically or constitutionally outside of it, except at the moment of election.

Once election became for Americans the sole criterion of representation, it was natural to think of all elected officials as somehow representative of the people. As early as the 1780s, many Americans were referring to their elected senates as double representations of the people; some began claiming that their governors, because they were elected by all the people, were the most representative officials in the state. Soon all elected officials were being designated representatives of the people, and the term originally applied to the various "houses of representatives" in the state constitutions and the federal Constitution became an awkward reminder that Americans had once thought of representation as the English had: as confined to the lower houses of their legislatures.

The people inevitably included even judges as their various agents. When, in order to justify judicial review, Alexander Hamilton in *The Federalist* No. 78 referred to judges as agents of the people and not really inferior to the people's other agents in the legislature, he opened up a radically new way of thinking of the judiciary. If judges were indeed the people's agents, as many soon concluded, then rightfully they ought to be elected, especially since election had become the sole measure of representation. Consequently, it was only a matter of time before the states began electing their judges. Conceiving of judges as just another one of their agents perhaps helps explain why Americans eventually became so accepting of judicial review, including even having the Supreme Court decide who will be president.

Since in the American system the people were never fully embodied in government, all sorts of strange political institutions and practices could and did emerge. The primaries, referendums, processes of recall, and ballot initiatives introduced by Progressive reformers at the beginning of the twentieth century were only extensions of the ideas of popular sovereignty and acute actual representation created at the Founding of the United States. These efforts to reach beyond actual representation to some kind of pure democracy were based on popular mistrust of elected officials, as were the original ideas of actual representation. As one account of 1896 put it, California had "only one kind of politics and that was corrupt politics. It didn't matter whether a man was a Republican or Democrat. The Southern Pacific Railroad controlled both parties."

In the past several decades the number of ballot initiatives in some of the western states has soared, to the point where they seem to rival the number of statutes passed by the legislatures. Ironically, the Southern Pacific Railroad, now just another special-interest group, in 1990 promoted a ballot initiative to issues billions in bonds in support of rail transportation. Although Oregon has had more ballot initiatives than California, California's have become the most notorious. The recall of Governor Gray Davis and the election of Arnold Schwarzenegger as governor of California in 2003 are the kinds of popular actions not likely to be duplicated in any other developed democracy in the world today (with the possible exception of Switzerland). But once we grasp the peculiar American idea of the sovereignty of the people, based on a deeply rooted mistrust of all elected officials, these extraordinary political events begin to make some sense. Whether these efforts at direct democracy are sensible ways of running a modern democratic state, however, remains to be seen.

AFTERWORD TO CHAPTER 5

Like many of these collected essays, this one began as a lecture presented at a conference on constitutionalism at the University of Chicago Law School in January 2004. Although it has never previously been published, it highlights themes that have been part of my thinking and writing over the past half century.

The history of American constitutionalism in the eighteenth century is very important, if only because of recent events. Over the past two decades or so, sixty-nine countries—from the nations of post-communist Central and Eastern Europe, to South Africa, to Afghanistan and Iraq—have drafted constitutions. At the same time many other states have revised their constitutions on paper, and even the European Union has tried to get a written constitution ratified. Consequently, only a few states in the world are without written constitutions. Indeed, it is almost impossible for many people today to conceive of a constitution as anything but a written document. And it all essentially began with America a little over two centuries ago.

For more on the influence of American constitutionalism over the past two centuries, see the monumental study by George Athan Billias, *American Constitutionalism Heard Round the World, 1776–1789: A Global Perspective* (New York: New York University Press, 2009).

A German scholar, Horst Dippel, is in the midst of a huge project of editing and publishing all constitutions written between the period 1776 and 1860. Entitled *Modern Constitutionalism and Its Sources*, it will be an enormously helpful resource when completed.

CHAPTER SIX

The MAKING *of*
AMERICAN DEMOCRACY

O NE OF THE MOST PROFOUND REVOLUTIONS of the past two centuries or so has been the introduction of ordinary people into the political process. For America and the rest of Western Europe this revolution was most dramatically expressed at the end of the eighteenth century—"the age of the democratic revolution," as historian R. R. Palmer once called it.[1] This bringing of the people into politics took place in the several decades following the American Revolution, while in Europe it took much longer, requiring for many nations the greater part of the nineteenth century. And for the rest of the world the process is still going on. Indeed, since the end of World War II we have witnessed what has been called a "participation explosion"—the rapid incorporation into the political process of peoples who hitherto had been outside of politics— in hurried, sometimes even desperate, efforts by underdeveloped nations to catch up with the modern developed states.[2] During the first decade of the twenty-first century various organizations have estimated that the great majority of all the states in the world have become electoral democracies, with the number of presumed democracies hovering around 120 or so. Of course, these democracies differ greatly from one another. Indeed, *The Economist* puts the number of full-fledged democracies at only twenty-eight, with eighty-four considered to be either flawed democracies or hybrid regimes. *The Economist* labels the governments of fifty-five countries as authoritarian.

Still, the growth of democracies throughout the world over the past six or seven decades is impressive. In fact, this incorporation of common people into politics is what sets the modern world apart from what went on before. Eighteenth-century Revolutionary Americans were in the vanguard of this modern development. Within decades following the Declaration of Independence, Americans were calling their government a democracy; they legitimated the term and set the rest of the world on the path of democratization.

To be sure, it was the ancient Greeks who had actually invented democracy—that is, rule directly by the people themselves—and who had passed the word on to the eighteenth-century Western world. But the Greek idea of democracy inherited by the West was regarded with suspicion and hostility. The great Greek writers whose works the Western Europeans most read—Thucydides, Plato, and Aristotle—had found democracy wanting to one degree or another. They believed that the people trying to rule by themselves would inevitably lead to anarchy and violence, ending in dictatorship and tyranny. At best, Aristotle had contended, democracy might be part of a mixed government, acceptable if it were balanced by monarchy and aristocracy.

And that is how the eighteenth-century English on both sides of the Atlantic tended to employ the word "democracy": as a term almost always used in conjunction with "monarchy" and "aristocracy"—as an essential part of a mixed or balanced constitution. Indeed, the eighteenth-century English constitution was so famous precisely because it mixed or balanced the three pure types of government—monarchy, aristocracy, and democracy—in its crown, House of Lords, and House of Commons.

By itself a pure democracy—"a government of all over all," as James Otis called it—was not much valued.[3] It meant not a government electorally derived from the people, but one actually administered by the people themselves. Enlightened Britons might agree that ideally the people ought to govern themselves directly, but they realized that democracy in this literal sense had been approximated only in the Greek city-states and in the New England towns; actual self-government or simple democracy was not feasible for any large community. As one American polemicist stated in 1776, even the great radical Whig Algernon Sidney had written that he had known of "no such thing" as "in the strict sense, . . . a pure democracy, where the people in themselves and by themselves, perform all that belongs to government," and if any had ever existed in the world, he had "nothing to say for it."4 Neither Alexander Hamilton nor James Madison in *The Federalist* had any good words for the kind of pure democracy that existed in antiquity. "Such Democracies," wrote Madison in *The Federalist* No. 10, "have ever been spectacles of turbulence and contention; have ever been found incompatible with personal security, or the rights of property; and have in general been as short in their lives, as they have been violent in their deaths." Consequently, most eighteenth-century Britons in both the mother country and the colonies were so uneasy over the impracticality and instability of pure democracy that the term "democracy" was commonly used vituperatively to discredit any untoward tendency toward popular government.

The English had invented the idea of representation, imagining their elected House of Commons to be the democratic part of the mixed constitution. But, as we have seen in the previous essay, it was the Americans who expanded the idea of representation to all parts of their federal and state governments. This expansion did not happen immediately. The original Revolutionary state constitutions of 1776 were intended to be republican versions of the mixed or balanced constitution of the former mother country. This is why we call the lower houses of our federal and state legislatures "houses of representatives" and set them against our senates, executives, and judiciaries, as if they were the only representative bodies in our governments. But eventually, in the several years following the Declaration of Independence, Americans came to think of all their elected governmental institutions as representative of the people, and the term "republic," which meant government derived from the people, became identified with the term "democracy." By the first decade or so of the nineteenth century the two terms became interchangeable.

Because representation of the people was based so exclusively on popular election, voting in America, as we have noted, became the sole criterion of representation. Americans believed that unless they actually voted for their agents, they could not be adequately represented by them. This peculiar notion of actual representation in turn made the suffrage seem to be the necessary and sufficient measure of democratic politics—which accounts for our often naive notion that simply giving people the vote in a developing country is tantamount to creating a democracy. Although the right to vote is clearly a prerequisite for democratic politics, it is hardly all there is to it. In fact, voting is only the exposed tip of an incredibly complicated political and social process. How this process came about and how the people became involved in politics are questions that lie at the heart of the American Revolution.

The American Revolution was both a consequence and a cause of democracy. It marked a decisive change in the way political activity was carried on in America and gave new legitimacy to the involvement of common people in politics. It was not, however, simply a matter of enfranchising new voters. The franchise in most colonies prior to the Revolution was already extensive. Although the right to vote in colonial America was restricted by property qualifications (usually a personal estate worth forty pounds or a freehold worth forty shillings a year) as it was in eighteenth-century England, property owning was so widespread in America that the colonists enjoyed the broadest suffrage of any people in the world: perhaps as many as 60 to 80 percent of adult white males in the colonies could legally vote. The legal exclusion of the propertyless from the franchise was based not on the fear that these people without property might confiscate the wealth of the aristocratic few, but on the opposite fear: that the aristocratic few might manipulate and corrupt the poor for their own ends. Only men who were independent, owned stable amounts of property, and were free from influence should have the vote. The same reasoning lay behind the exclusion from the franchise of women, minors, and others who were considered to be dependent and to have no will of their own.

Despite the breadth of suffrage in colonial America, however, the fact remains that most of those legally enfranchised did not exercise their right to vote. And when they did vote, they usually voted for the same prominent families. It turns out that the property holders in colonial America were not as independent and as free from influence as the law presumed. The social structure and social values were such that colonial politics, at least when compared to politics in post-Revolutionary America, was remarkably stable; the percentage of people actually voting and participating in politics remained small, and the political leadership remained in a remarkably limited number of hands.

Established social leaders expected deference from those below them and generally got it, and were habitually reelected to political office. Yet this acquiescence that people gave to those who by their wealth, influence, and independence were considered best qualified to rule was based not simply on traditional habits of deference but, more important, on the substantial dependency that patronage and economic and social power created. In 1773 in the Mohawk district of Tryon County, New York, at least four hundred men had the franchise. Yet in an election for five constables, only fourteen electors turned out to vote; all fourteen were closely tied by interest or patronage to Sir William Johnson, the local grandee of the area, and all fourteen naturally voted for the same five candidates.[5]

Translating the personal, social, and economic authority of the leading gentry into political patronage and power was essentially what eighteenth-century politics was about. The process was self-intensifying: social authority created political power, which in turn created more social influence. Some members of the gentry, such as the Tidewater planters of Virginia or the wealthy landholders of the Connecticut River valley, had enough patronage and influence to overawe entire communities. Connecticut River valley gentry like Israel Williams and John Worthington, so imposing as to be called "river gods," used their power to become at one time or another selectmen of their towns, representatives to the

Massachusetts General Court, members of the Massachusetts Council, provincial court judges, justices of the peace, and colonels of their county regiments. It became impossible to tell where the circle of their authority began: the political authority to grant licenses for taverns or mills, to determine the location of roads and bridges, or to enlist men for military service was of a piece with their wealth and social influence.

It was likewise substantial paternalistic and patronage power, and not merely the treating of the freeholders with toddy at election time, that enabled the great Virginia planters to mobilize their "interest" and to maintain law and order over their local communities without the aid of police forces. The leading Virginia gentry were the vestrymen of their parishes and the lay leaders of the Anglican Church, so that the sacredness of religion and the patronage of poor relief further enhanced the hierarchy of authority. All this was the stuff of which aristocracies were made.

Colonial society had no organized political parties and no professional politicians in today's sense of these terms. Large planters, established merchants, and wealthy lawyers held the major offices and ran political affairs as part of the responsibility of their elevated social position. It was rare for a tavern keeper or a small farmer to gain a political office of any consequence. Men were granted political authority in accord not with their seniority or experience in politics but with their established economic and social superiority. Thus Thomas Hutchinson, scion of a distinguished Boston mercantile family, was elected to the Massachusetts House of Representatives at the age of twenty-six and almost immediately became its speaker. So too could Jonathan Trumbull, an obscure country merchant, be catapulted in 1739 into the speakership of the Connecticut assembly at age twenty-eight and into the prestigious Council of Assistants the following year simply by the fact that his marriage into the ancient and esteemed Robinson family had given him, as eighteenth-century historian Samuel Peters put it, "the prospect of preferment in civil life."[6] Social and political authority was indivisible, and men moved horizontally into politics from society rather than (as is common today) moving up vertically through an exclusively political hierarchy.

Yet politics in eighteenth-century colonial America was unstable enough in many areas that members of the elite struggled for political power and precedent among themselves. The social hierarchy was often sufficiently confused at the top that it was never entirely clear who was destined to hold political office and govern. It was obvious that well-to-do lawyers or planters from distinguished families were superior to, say, blacksmiths, but within the group of well-to-do lawyers or wealthy planters, superiority was not so visible and incontestable. Indeed, in some colonies social superiority was so recent and so seemingly arbitrary that contesting it was inevitable. These contests for office and power created the grinding factionalism—the shifting competing congeries of the leading gentry's personal and family "interests"—that characterized much of eighteenth-century colonial politics.[7]

Before the 1730s and 1740s, many of these contests were transatlantic in character and focused on the metropolitan center of the empire (London). In the early decades of the eighteenth century, elite factions opposed to the royal governors often sought political leverage from the imperial arena; in other words, they resorted to the use of imperial interests and transatlantic connections in order to win local political battles in their colonies. They used extralegal channels in the home country, such as merchant groups in London, in order to undermine the royal governors' political positions from the rear. Or they formed alliances with other imperial agents, such as those representing the Church of England, in order to bypass the governors. Colonial opposition leaders even made personal journeys to London to lobby for the reversal of gubernatorial decisions or even the removal of a governor. This kind of Anglo-American politics was open-ended. Since there were many transatlantic avenues of influence and connection and many appeals over the heads of local officials to Whitehall, few decisions made in the colonies themselves could be final.[8]

But after 1740 or so this open-ended character of American politics began to close up, and the colonists' ability to influence English politics sharply declined. Communications to the mother country became more formal, and personal appeals declined. The colonial lobbying agents who earlier had been initiators of colonial policy were now hard put to head off colonial measures begun by others in Britain. As the earlier transatlantic channels and avenues of influence clogged up or closed off, the royal governors were left as the only major link between the colonies and Great Britain. If opposition groups in the colonies were going to contest their governors, they would have to find leverage within their own colonies.[9]

Under these changed circumstances dissident factions in the colonies were forced to turn inward, toward the only source of authority other than the king recognized by eighteenth-century Anglo-American political theory: the people. Opposition groups now began to mobilize the electorate in their colonies as never before, using the popular elective assemblies as their main instrument of opposition against the royal governors. Consequently, the number of contested elections for the colonial assemblies rapidly multiplied. In Boston, for example, in the decade of the 1720s, only 30 percent of elections were contested; by the 1750s, 60 percent were. With the growth of contested elections came greater voter participation and more vitriolic political rhetoric and propaganda. Groups began forming tickets, caucuses, and political clubs, and hiring professional pamphleteers to attack their opponents for being overstuffed men of wealth and learning. In these mid-eighteenth-century developments we can see the beginnings of what would eventually become typically American egalitarian electoral propaganda and modern political campaigning.[10]

But of course nobody had the future in mind. By appealing to the people, these elite families and factions were not trying to create the democratic world of the nineteenth century; they were simply using whatever weapons they had at their disposal—together with inflammatory popular Whig rhetoric—to get at their opponents. All of their appeals to the people were merely tactical devices for gaining office. The colonial assemblies that earlier had been virtual closed clubs now became more sensitive to the public out-of-doors. In the 1750s they began publishing compilations of their laws and revealing how their members voted on particular issues. In the 1760s they began building galleries in the legislative halls to allow the people to witness debates. Some even began calling for a widening of the franchise. Those who opposed these measures were labeled "enemies of the people."[11]

Democracy in America thus began not as the result of the people arousing themselves spontaneously and clamoring from below for a share in political authority. Instead, democracy was initially created from above. The people were cajoled, persuaded, even sometimes frightened into getting involved. Although normally many of the towns of Massachusetts—sometimes as many as one-third—did not even bother to send their representatives to the General Court, they "have it in their power upon an extraordinary Emergency," warned Governor William Shirley in 1742, "to double and almost treble their numbers [of representatives], which they would not fail to do if they should be desirous of disputing any point with His Majesty's governor which they might suspect their ordinary members would carry against his influence in the House."[12] Each competing faction tried to outdo its opponents in posing as a friend of the people, defending popular rights and advancing popular interests against those of the crown. Yet over time what began as a pose eventually assumed a reality that had not been anticipated. The people once mobilized could not easily be put down.

Thus by the 1760s American politics were already primed for the Revolutionary transformation from monarchy to republicanism. As patriot leaders began contesting the authority of the English government, the earlier practices of mobilizing the people into politics increased dramatically. As we have seen, the imperial debate not only challenged traditional British authority but compelled Americans to articulate an idea of actual representation that they have never lost. This idea of actual representation led to heightened demands to expand the franchise and to the unprecedented conviction that representation in government ought to be equal and more or less in proportion to population. Initially provided for in the Revolutionary state constitutions of 1776, this conviction resulted in the federal Constitution's mandate that a census be taken every ten years. Eventually, as we have noted in the previous essay on "The Origins of American Constitutionalism," the belief inherent in the concept of actual representation that voting itself was the sole criterion of representation tended to transform all elected officials, including governors and members of upper houses, into other kinds of representatives of the people, placing them, at least in name, in an awkward relationship to the original houses of representatives.

Actual representation had more than constitutional importance for American politics. It had social significance as well. Even before the Revolutionary turmoil had settled, some Americans, as we have seen, began arguing that mere voting by ordinary men was not a sufficient protection of ordinary men's interests if only members of the elite continued to be the ones elected. It was coming to be thought that in a society of diverse and particular interests, men from one class or group, however educated and respectable, could not be acquainted with the needs and interests of other classes and groups. Wealthy college-educated lawyers or merchants could not know the concerns of poor farmers or small tradesmen. As we have seen, the logic of actual representation required that ordinary men be represented by ordinary men, indeed, by men of the same religion, ethnic group, or occupation.

Such an idea—lying at the heart of the radicalism of the American Revolution—constituted an extraordinary transformation in the relationship between society and government. It expressed egalitarian forces released by the Revolution that could not be easily contained.

At the outset of the Revolution, equality to most Americans had meant an equality of legal rights and the opportunity to rise by merit through clearly discernible ranks. But in the hands of competing politicians seeking to diminish the credentials of their opponents and win votes, the idea of equality was soon expanded in ways that few of its supporters had originally anticipated—to mean that one man was as good as another. This meaning of equality soon dissolved the identity between social and political leadership and helped to give political power to the kinds of men who hitherto had never held it. Politics was transformed, and political upstarts—obscure men with obscure backgrounds who had never been to college—launched vigorous attacks on the former attributes of social

superiority (names, titles, social origins, family connections, even education) and bragged that their own positions were based not on relatives
or friends but only on what their hard work and money had made for
them.

The confrontation in the 1780s between John Rutledge, a distinguished social and political leader in South Carolina, and William
Thompson, an unknown Charleston tavern keeper, graphically illus-
trates the new emerging post-Revolutionary culture. Rutledge had sent
a female servant to Thompson's tavern to watch a fireworks display from
the roof. Thompson denied the servant admittance and sent her back to
Rutledge. Rutledge was infuriated and demanded that Thompson come
to his house and apologize. Thompson refused and, believing that his
honor had been affronted by Rutledge's arrogant request, challenged
Rutledge to a duel. Since the social likes of Rutledge did not accept chal-
lenges from tavern keepers, Rutledge went to the South Carolina House
of Representatives, of which he was a member, and insisted that it pass a
bill banishing Thompson from the state for insulting an officer of its government. Thompson took to the press for his defense and in 1784 made
what can only be described as a classic expression of American resentment against social superiority—a resentment voiced, said Thompson,
not on behalf of himself but on behalf of the people generally, or "those
more especially, who go at this day under the opprobrious appellation of
the Lower Orders of Men."

In his newspaper essays Thompson did not merely attack the few aristocratic "nabobs" who had humiliated him; he actually assaulted the very
idea of a social hierarchy ruled by a gentlemanly elite. In fact, he turned
traditional eighteenth-century opinion upside down and argued that the
social aristocracy was peculiarly unqualified to rule politically. In other
words, social authority should have no relation to political authority; it
was in fact harmful to political authority. Rather than preparing men for
political leadership in a free government, said Thompson, "signal opu-
lence and influence," especially when united "by intermarriage or otherwise," were really "calculated to subvert Republicanism." The "persons

and conduct" of the South Carolina nabobs like Rutledge "in private life may be unexceptionable, and even amiable, but their pride, influence, ambition, connections, wealth, and political principles ought in public life," Thompson contended, "ever to exclude them from public confidence." Since in a republican government "consequence is from the public opinion, and not from private fancy," all that was needed in republican leadership, said Thompson, was "being good, able, useful, and friends to social equality."

Thompson sarcastically went on to recount how he, a mere tavern keeper, "a wretch of no higher rank in the Commonwealth than that of Common-Citizen," had been debased by what he called "those self-exalted characters, who affect to compose the grand hierarchy of the State, . . . for having dared to dispute with a John Rutledge, or any of the NABOB tribe." The experience had been degrading enough to Thompson as a man, but as a former militia officer it had been, he said, "insupportable"—indicating how Revolutionary military service had affected social mobility and social expectations. Undoubtedly, wrote Thompson, Rutledge had "conceived me his inferior." But like many others in these years—tavern keepers, farmers, petty merchants, small-time lawyers, former militia officers—Thompson could no longer "comprehend the inferiority."[13]

Many new politicians in the following years, likewise not being able to comprehend their inferiority, began using the popular and egalitarian ideals of the Revolution to upset the older hierarchy and bring ordinary people like themselves into politics. This was not always easy, for as some politicians complained, "the poorer commonality," even when they possessed the legal right to vote, seemed apathetic to appeals and too accepting of traditional authority. Their ideas of government had too long been "rather aristocratical than popular." "The rich," said one polemicist, "having been used to govern, seem to think it is their right," while the common people, "having hitherto had little or no hand in government, seemed to think it does not belong to them to have any."[14] To convince the people that they rightfully had a share in government became the task of hustling egalitarian politicians in the decades following the Revolution.

Everywhere, but especially in the North, these middling politicians urged the people to shed their political apathy and "keep up the cry against Judges, Lawyers, Generals, Colonels, and all other designing men, and the day will be our own." They demanded that they do their "utmost at election to prevent all men of talents, lawyers, rich men from being elected."[15]

The increased competition between candidates and parties in the early nineteenth century meant more and more contested elections for both federal and state officials, which sent the turnout of voters skyrocketing. In many places, especially in the North, the participation of eligible voters went from 20 percent or so in the 1790s to 80 percent or more in the first decade of the nineteenth century.[16]

As voting took on a heightened significance, the states that had not already done so began to expand the franchise by eliminating property qualifications or transforming the requirement into the mere paying of taxes. In the eighteenth century, landed property had been a justifiable qualification for voting because it had been seen as a source of independence and authority. But as property in the fast-moving economy of the early Republic became more and more a commodity to be exchanged in the marketplace, property as a requirement for officeholding and suffrage steadily lost its meaning. Who could believe that "property is . . . any proof of superior virtue, discernment or patriotism"? asked the New York Democratic-Republicans in 1812.[17] By 1825, under this kind of popular pressure, every state but Rhode Island, Virginia, and Louisiana had more or less achieved universal white male suffrage; by 1830 only Rhode Island, which had once been the most democratic place in North America, retained the old forty pounds–forty shillings freehold qualification for voting. With the exception of a brief period in New Jersey (1790–1807) no state granted women suffrage. By modern standards the system was far from democratic, but by the standards of the early nineteenth century, America possessed the most popular electoral politics in the world.[18]

Many of the spokesmen for popular interests who emerged in these years made no pretense to having any special personal or social qualifications to rule. They were not wealthy men, they had not gone to Harvard or Princeton, and they were often proud of their parochial and localist outlook. When Simon Snyder, the ill-educated son of a poor mechanic, ran successfully for governor of Pennsylvania in 1808, opponents mocked his obscure origins and called him and his followers "clodhoppers." Snyder and his supporters quite shrewdly picked up the epithet and began proudly wearing it. Being a clodhopper in a society of clodhoppers became the source of much of Snyder's political success. Like other such popular political figures, his claim to office was based solely on his ability to garner votes and satisfy the interests of his constituents. No longer could political office be the consequence of a gentleman's previously established wealth and social authority. If anything, holding office in America was becoming the source of that wealth and social authority.

In the 1780s James Madison had hoped that government might become a "disinterested & dispassionate umpire in disputes between different passions & interests in the State."[19] But this hope seemed increasingly visionary. Few elected officials sought to stand above the competing interests of the marketplace and, like an umpire, make impartial judgments about what was good for the whole society. In fact, elected officials were bringing the partial, local interests of their constituents, and sometimes even their own interests, right into the workings of government. State legislators often became what Madison in the 1780s had most feared: judges in their own causes. In Connecticut the subscription list of the Hartford Bank, suggested one shrewd subscriber in 1791, had to be left open, or seem to be open—that is, if the bank hoped to be incorporated by the Connecticut legislature. There were "a number in the Legislature who would wish to become subscribers, and would, of course, advocate the bill while they supposed they could subscribe, and, on the contrary, if it was known the subscription was full, they would oppose it violently."[20]

Everywhere legislators responded to the interests of those who elected them. Since every town in the country seemed to want a bank, banks proliferated. In 1813 the Pennsylvania legislature in a single bill authorized the incorporation of twenty-five new banks. After the governor vetoed this bill, the legislature in 1814 passed over the governor's veto another bill incorporating forty-one banks. By 1818 Kentucky had forty-three new banks, two of them in towns that had fewer than one hundred inhabitants.

Early nineteenth-century politics increasingly assumed modern characteristics, and partisanship and parties—using government to promote partial interests—acquired a legitimacy that they had not had before. Congressmen began referring to those who sought to influence them as "a commanding lobby," and the term "lobbyist" took on its modern meaning. The word "logrolling" in the making of laws (that is, the trading of votes by legislators for each other's bills) likewise began to be used for the first time, to the bewilderment of conservative Federalists. "I do not well understand the Term," said an Ohio Federalist, "but I believe it means bargaining with each other for the little loaves and fishes of the State." The modern problem of taxation in a democracy had already emerged. As one Virginia congressman complained in 1814, "Everyone is for taxing every body, except himself and his Constituents."[21]

If representatives were elected to promote the particular interests and private causes of their constituents, then the idea that such representatives were simply disinterested gentlemen, squire worthies called by duty to shoulder the burdens of public service, became archaic. Many now began running for office, not, as earlier, simply standing for election. The weakening of the older social hierarchy and the erosion of the traditional belief in elite rule made the rise of political parties both necessary and possible. Indeed, the United States was the first nation to develop modern political parties dealing with mass electorates. Individuals cut loose from traditional ties to the social hierarchy were now forced to combine in new groups for political ends. Political office was no longer set by social ascription, but rather was won by political achievement within the organization of the party and through the winning of votes.

In time new arts of persuasion, using cheap newspapers and mass meetings, were developed, and politics assumed carnival-like characteristics that led during the nineteenth century to participation by higher percentages of the legal electorate than ever again was achieved in American politics. In such an atmosphere of stump-speaking and running for office, the members of the older gentry were frequently at a considerable disadvantage. In fact, by the early nineteenth century, being a gentleman or professing the characteristics of a gentleman, even having gone to college, became a liability in elections in some parts of the country.

In his Jeffersonian Republican campaign for governor of New York in 1807, Daniel Tomkins, prosperous lawyer and graduate of Columbia College, knew that portraying himself as a simple "farmer's boy" would contrast successfully with the character of his opponent, Morgan Lewis, who was an in-law of the aristocratic Livingston family. In 1810 the New York Federalists tried to retaliate and combat Tomkins and the Jeffersonian Republicans with their own plebeian candidate, Jonas Platt, "whose habits and manners," said the Federalists, "are as plain and republican as those of his country neighbors." Unlike Tompkins, Platt was not "a city lawyer who rolls in splendor and wallows in luxury."[22]

By the middle decades of the nineteenth century, this kind of popular antielitism coming out of the Revolution was as strong as ever, as the 1868 election campaign for the fifth congressional district of Massachusetts vividly demonstrates. The fifth congressional district—Essex County—was the former center of Massachusetts Brahmin Federalism, but by the mid-nineteenth century it was increasingly filled with Irish immigrants. The campaign was essentially between Richard Henry Dana Jr., a well-to-do and Harvard-educated descendent of a distinguished Massachusetts family and author of *Two Years Before the Mast*, and Benjamin Butler, son of boardinghouse keeper who had never been to college and was one of the most flamboyant demagogues American politics has ever produced. (One gets some idea of Butler's standing with the Massachusetts elite by realizing that he was the first governor of Massachusetts in over two centuries not invited to a Harvard College commencement.) In the congressional campaign, Butler showed Dana what nineteenth-century electoral politics was all about. While Dana was talking to tea groups about bond payments, Butler was haranguing the Irish shoe workers of

Lynn, organizing parades, turning out the fire and police departments, hiring brass bands, distributing hundreds of pamphlets, and charging his opponent with being a Beau Brummel in white gloves. Dana was simply no match for him.

When Dana was finally forced to confront audiences of workingmen, he gave up talking about bonds and tried desperately to assure his audiences that he too worked hard. All the while, Butler mocked his wearing of white gloves and his efforts to make common cause with the people. During one speech Dana told the Irish shoe workers that when he spent two years before the mast as a young sailor he too was a worker who didn't wear white gloves. "I was as dirty as any of you," he exclaimed. With such statements it is not surprising that Dana ended up with less than 10 percent of the vote in a humiliating loss to Butler.[23]

By vying for political leadership and competing for votes, new men— not necessarily as colorful as Butler but having the same social obscurity and doomed in any other society to remain in obscurity—became part of the political process. The most important criterion of their leadership was their ability to appeal to voters.

It was the American Revolution that had helped to make possible and to accelerate these changes in our politics. As a result of the republican revolution, Americans essentially denied any other status than citizen. The people were all in politics and all of the people were equal. Any sort of unequal restrictions on the rights of citizenship—on the right to run for office or to vote, for example, theoretically were anomalies, relics of an older society that now had to be eliminated. In the early decades of the nineteenth century, competing political parties searched out groups of people hitherto uninvolved in politics and brought them in: renters initially denied the franchise because they were not freeholders, poor men who lacked the necessary property qualifications, and newly arrived immigrants—anyone who might become a voter and supporter of the party, or even one of its leaders. If they could not yet legally vote, the vote could be given them. If they could legally vote but did not bother, then they could be persuaded that they ought to. In these ways American politicians in the decades following the Revolution worked to establish universal male suffrage and democratic politics.

We take these developments for granted and easily forget how far ahead of the rest of the world the United States was in the early nineteenth century. Tavern keepers and weavers were sitting in our legislatures while most European states were still trying to disentangle voting and representation from an incredible variety of estate and corporate statuses. In 1792 Kentucky entered the Union with a constitution allowing universal suffrage for all free adult males. A generation later the English were still debating whether voting was a privilege confined to a few; in fact, England had to wait until 1867 before workingmen got the vote and became, in William Gladstone's words, "our fellow subjects." In many parts of the world today people are still waiting to become citizens and full participants in the political process.

Yet, as we know all too well, America's record in integrating the people into politics has not been an untainted success story. The great aberration amidst all the Revolutionary talk of equality, voting, and representation was slavery. Indeed, it was the Revolution itself, not only with its appeal to liberty but with its idea of citizenship of equal individuals, that made slavery in 1776 suddenly seem anomalous to large numbers of Americans. What had been taken for granted earlier in the eighteenth century as part of the brutality and inequality of life—regarded as merely the most base and degraded status in a society of numerous degrees and multiple ranks of freedom and unfreedom—now seemed conspicuous and peculiar. In a republic, as was not the case in a monarchy, there could be no place for subjection and degrees of freedom or dependency. In the North, where slavery was considerable but not deeply rooted, the exposure of the anomaly worked to abolish it. By 1804 all the Northern states had legally ended slavery, and by 1830 there were fewer than 3,000 black slaves remaining out of a Northern black population of over 125,000.[24] In the South the suddenly exposed peculiarity of slavery threw Southern whites, who had been in the vanguard of the Revolutionary movement and among the most fervent spokesmen for its libertarianism, onto the defensive. Although the South was able to maintain dominance over much of the federal government in the antebellum period by manipulating the Constitution, its leadership was hollow, increasingly desperate, and without firm foundation in the country as a whole; in time, the peculiarity of slavery gradually separated the section from the mainstream of America's egalitarian developments.

Yet the very egalitarianism of America's republican ideology—the egalitarianism that undercut the rationale of slavery—worked at the same time to inhibit integrating the free black man into the political process. Since republican citizenship implied equality for all citizens, a person once admitted as a citizen into the political process was put on a level with all other citizens and regarded as being as good as the next man—uneducated tavern keepers were as good as wealthy college-educated planters. With the spread of these republican assumptions, Northern whites began to view black voters with increasing apprehension, unwilling to accept the equality that suffrage and citizenship dictated. In the 1790s in several states of the North, free blacks possessed the right to vote (often as a result of the general extension of the franchise that took place during the Revolution), and they exercised it in some areas with particular effectiveness. But in subsequent years, as the white electorate continued to expand through changes in the laws and the mobilization of new voters, blacks found themselves being squeezed out.

There is perhaps no greater irony in the democratization of American politics in the early nineteenth century than the fact that as the poor white man gained the right to vote, the free black man lost it. By the heyday of Jacksonian democracy, white popular majorities in state after state in the North had moved to eliminate the remaining property restrictions on white voters while at the same time concocting new restrictions taking away the franchise from black voters who in some cases had exercised it for decades. No state admitted to the Union after 1819 allowed blacks to vote. By 1840, 93 percent of Northern free blacks lived in states that completely or practically excluded them from suffrage and hence from the participation in politics.[25]

This exclusion of blacks from politics was largely a consequence of white fears of the equality that republican citizenship demanded. But it was also a product of competitive democratic politics. In some states, like Pennsylvania, black exclusion was the price paid for lower-class whites gaining the right to vote, universal male suffrage having been opposed on the grounds that it would add too many blacks to the electorate. In other states, like New York, exclusion of blacks from the franchise was an effective way for Democratic Party majorities to eliminate once and for all blocs of black voters who too often had voted first for Federalist and then for Whig candidates. Since the Democratic Party—as the spokesman for the popular cause against elitism and aristocracy—was in the forefront of the effort to expand suffrage, it seemed to be good politics for the party not only to attract new voters to its ranks but to take away voters who supported its opponents. It was this kind of political pressure that led to the peculiar situation in some states in which immigrant aliens were granted the right the vote before they had become citizens while blacks who had been born and bred in the United States had their right to vote abolished—a development often based on a shrewd assessment by politicians of what particular party new immigrants and blacks would support. Such were the strange and perverse consequences of democracy.

For a republican society it was an impossible situation, and Americans wrestled with it for decades. Federal officials in the first half of the nineteenth century could never decide the precise status of free blacks, sometimes arguing that blacks were not citizens in possessing the right to vote but were citizens in having the right to secure passports. Others tried to discover some sort of intermediate legal position for free blacks as denizens standing between aliens and citizens. But the logic of republican equality would not allow these distinctions, and sooner or later many sought to escape from the dilemma posed by black disfranchisement by denying citizenship to all blacks, whether slave or free, a position Chief Justice Roger Taney and the Supreme Court tried to establish in the *Dred Scott* decision of 1857. Suffrage had become sufficiently equated with representation in America that if a person was not granted the right to vote then he was not represented in the community; and not being represented in a republican community was equivalent to not being a citizen. In the end, enslaved blacks without liberty and free blacks without citizenship were such contradictions of the Revolutionary ideals that sooner or later they had to tear the country apart.

When Northerners came to debate methods of Southern reconstruction at the end of the Civil War, they moved often reluctantly but nonetheless steadily toward black enfranchisement, impelled both by the logic of the persisting ideals of the Revolution and by the circumstances of politics. Although some historians have believed that the Republican Party's espousal of black suffrage in the aftermath of the war was based on a cynical desire to recruit new voters to the party, it was obviously based on much more than that. In terms of political expediency alone, the Republicans' sponsorship of black suffrage ran the risk even in the North of what we later came to call "white backlash." Many advocates of black suffrage sincerely believed, as Wendell Phillips put it, that America could never be truly a united nation "until every class God has made, from the lakes to the Gulf, has its ballot to protect itself."[26]

Nevertheless, there can be little doubt that black enfranchisement after the Civil War was bolstered, like all reforms, by political exigencies, and that many Northerners and Republicans favored it grudgingly and only as a means of preventing the resurgence of an unreconstructed South controlled by a Democratic Party that would threaten the dominance of the Republican Party. Hence there resulted an awkward gap between the Fourteenth Amendment, which defined citizenship for the first time and gave it a national emphasis that it had hitherto lacked, and the Fifteenth Amendment, which enfranchised blacks but unfortunately linked their enfranchisement not to their citizenship but to their race. This linkage allowed a state to impose any voting qualifications it chose as long as they were not based on race. This created a tangled situation that Americans only began to unravel a century later.

Although Americans have hesitated to make the connection between citizenship and the right to vote explicit and unequivocal, everything in American history has pointed to that connection. During the 1960s, largely under the impetus of the civil rights movement but going beyond that, Americans became more and more interested in political and voting rights, and the logic of principles concerning suffrage and the representation first articulated in the Revolution were finally drawn out. The voting rights acts and the anti–poll tax amendment were based on a deeply rooted belief that no nation like ours could in conscience exclude any of its citizens from the political process. That same legacy from the Revolution led the Supreme Court in a series of reapportionment decisions to apply the idea of "one person, one vote" to congressional and state legislative districting. As a result, senates in many states finally became the fully representative bodies they had not been intended to be in 1776. Of course, as one wag has observed, our periodic redistricting can sometimes turn democracy on its head. Instead of the voters choosing their political leaders, the leaders get to choose their voters.[27]

Many Americans became concerned with large and unequal campaign contributions precisely because they seemed to negate the effects of equal suffrage and violate the equality of participation in the political process. Despite an electorate that at times seems apathetic, interest in suffrage and in the equality of consent has never been greater than it has over the past generation. Such a concern naturally puts a terrific burden on our political system, but it is a burden we should gladly bear (and many other nations would love to have it), for it bespeaks an underlying popular confidence in the processes of politics that surface events and news headlines tend to obscure.

In fact, our concern with suffrage and with the formal rights of consent has assumed such a transcendent significance that it has sometimes concealed the substance of democratic politics and has tended to exaggerate the real power of the legal right to vote. Suffrage has become such a symbol of citizenship that its possession seems necessarily to involve all kinds of rights. Thus acquiring the vote has often seemed to be an instrument of reform or a means of solving complicated social problems. The women's rights movement of the nineteenth century—premised on the belief, as one woman put it in 1848, that "there is no reality in any power that cannot be coined into votes"—came to focus almost exclusively on the gaining of suffrage.[28] And when the Nineteenth Amendment granting women the franchise was finally ratified in 1920 and did not lead to the promised revolution, the sense of failure set the feminist movement back at least half a century. As late as the 1960s, this formal integration into the political process through suffrage continued to be regarded as a panacea for social ills. Certainly this assumption lay behind the response to the youth rebellions of the late 1960s and the eventual adoption of the Twenty-sixth Amendment giving eighteen-year-olds the vote.

This special fascination with politics and this reliance on political integration through voting as a means of solving social problems are legacies of our Revolution, and they are as alive now as they were then. The Revolution not only brought ordinary people into politics; it also created such confidence in suffrage as the sole criterion of representation that we have too often forgotten just what makes the right to vote workable in America. In our dealings with newly developing nations, we are too apt to believe that the mere institution of the ballot in a new country will automatically create a viable democracy, and we are often confused and disillusioned when this rarely happens.

The point is that we have the relationship backward. It is not suffrage that gives life to our democracy; it is our democratic society that gives life to suffrage. American society is permeated by the belief in (and, despite extraordinary differences of income, in the reality of) equality that makes our reliance on the ballot operable. It was not the breadth of the franchise in the nineteenth century that created democratic politics. The franchise was broad even in colonial times. Rather, it was the egalitarian process of politics that led to the mobilization of voters and the political integration of the nation. It was the work of countless politicians recruited from all levels of society and representing many diverse interests, attempting to win elections by exhorting and pleading with their electors, that in the final analysis shaped our democratic system. Any state can grant suffrage to its people overnight, but it cannot thereby guarantee to itself a democratic

polity. As American history shows, such a democracy requires generations of experience with electoral politics. More important, it requires the
emergence of political parties and egalitarian politicians none of whom
have too much power and most of whom ought to run scared—politicians
whose maneuvering for electoral advantage, whose courting of the electorate, and whose passion for victory result, in the end, in grander and more
significant developments than they themselves can foresee or even imagine. Politicians are at the heart of our political system, and insofar as it is
democratic, they have made it so.

AFTERWORD TO CHAPTER 6

This essay is a much-revised and updated version of a lecture originally
given before the Kentucky legislature in Frankfort, Kentucky, on January
9, 1974, which perhaps accounts for the rather exuberant paean to politicians at the end. The event was arranged by the American Enterprise
Institute, which sponsored a series of lectures by scholars and other intellectual figures at different venues as part of the bicentennial celebration of
the American Revolution.

These lectures were collected and published as *America's Continuing
Revolution: An Act of Conservation* (Washington, D.C.: American Enterprise Institute, 1975).

CHAPTER SEVEN

The RADICALISM *of* THOMAS JEFFERSON *and* THOMAS PAINE CONSIDERED

*B*Y 1792 THOMAS PAINE already sensed that the world might not give him as much credit for his endeavors on behalf of the American Revolution as he thought he deserved, and thus he thought he ought to set the world straight. "With all the inconveniences of early life against me," he wrote in *The Rights of Man: Part the Second*, "I am proud to say that with a perseverance undismayed by difficulties, a disinterestedness that compelled respect, I have not only contributed to raise a new empire in the world, founded on a new system of government, but I have arrived at an eminence in political literature, the most difficult of all lines to succeed and excel in, which aristocracy with all its aids, has not been able to reach or to rival." Paine sensed the future correctly. By 1800 there were few Americans left who were willing to recognize Paine's contribution to their Revolution. Thomas Jefferson was the great exception. Paine, he said in 1801, had "steadily labored" on behalf of liberty and the American Revolution "with as much effect as any man living."[1]

Naturally, it was Jefferson who celebrated Paine when everyone else was scorning him, for he and Paine thought alike. Indeed, no two prominent American Revolutionaries shared so many ideas as did Jefferson and Paine. Yet no two Revolutionaries were more different in background and temperament.

Jefferson was a wealthy slaveholding aristocrat from Virginia who was as well connected socially as anyone in America. His mother was a Randolph, perhaps the most prestigious family in all of Virginia, and positions in his society came easy to him. Personally, he was cool, reserved, and self-possessed. He disliked personal controversy and was always charming in face-to-face relations with both friends and enemies. Although he played at being casual, he was utterly civilized and genteel. He mastered several languages, including those of antiquity, and he spent his life trying to discover (and acquire) what was the best and most enlightened in the world of the eighteenth century. He prided himself on his manners and taste; indeed, he became an impresario for his countrymen, advising them on what was proper in everything from the arts to wine. There was almost nothing he did not know about. "Without having quitted his own country," this earnest autodidact with a voracious appetite for learning had become, as the French visitor Chevalier de Chastellux noted in the early 1780s, "an American who . . . is at once a Musician, a Draftsman, Surveyor, Astronomer, Natural Philosopher, Jurist, and Statesman."[2]

By contrast, Paine was a free-floating individual who, as critics said, lacked social connections of any kind. He came from the ranks of the middling sorts, and unlike, say, Benjamin Franklin, he never really shed his obscure and lowly origins. He had some education but did not attend college, and he knew no languages except English. He spent the first half of his life jumping from one job to another, first a stay maker like his father, then a teacher, next a failed businessman, then back to stay making, followed by two failed attempts as an excise collector; he also tried running a tobacco shop. He was slovenly and lazy and was described as "coarse and uncouth in his manners."[3] His temperament was fiery and passionate, and he loved his liquor and confrontations of all sorts. He came to America at age thirty-seven full of anger at a world that had not recognized his talents.

Yet as dissimilar as Jefferson and Paine were from one another, they shared a common outlook on the world. As a British dinner partner observed in 1792, Jefferson in conversation was "a vigorous stickler for revolutions and for the downfall of an aristocracy. . . . In fact, like his friend T. Payne, he cannot live but in a revolution, and all events in Europe are only considered by him in the relation they bear to the probability of a revolution to be produced by them."[4]

Jefferson and Paine were good republicans who believed in the rights of man. They thought that all government should be derived from the people and that no one should hold office by hereditary right. No American trusted the people at large or outside of government more than did these two radicals, Jefferson and Paine.

This confidence flowed from their magnanimous view of human nature. Both men had an extraordinary faith in the moral capacity of ordinary people. Being one of the ordinary people, Paine had a natural tendency to trust them. But even Jefferson, the natural aristocrat, on most things trusted ordinary people far more than he trusted his aristocratic colleagues, who, he believed, were very apt to become wolves if they could. Unlike the elite, common people were not deceptive or deceitful; they wore their hearts on their sleeves and were sincere. An American republican world dominated by common folk would end the deceit and dissembling so characteristic of courtiers and monarchies. "Let those flatter who fear: it is not an American art," said Jefferson.[5]

Paine agreed that everyone shared a similar social or moral sense. Appeals to common sense, he said, were "appeals to those feelings without which we should be incapable of discharging the duties of life or enjoying the felicities of it."[6] Reason might be unevenly distributed throughout society, but everyone, even the most lowly of persons, had senses and could feel. In all of his writings, Paine said, his "principal design is to form the disposition of the people to the measures which I am fully persuaded it is their interest and duty to adopt, and which need no other force to accomplish them than the force of being felt."[7]

But Paine and Jefferson went further in their trust in common people. By assuming that ordinary people had personal realities equal to their own, Paine and Jefferson helped to give birth to what perhaps is best described as the modern humanitarian sensibility—a powerful force that we of the twenty-first century have inherited and further expanded. They, like most other Revolutionary leaders, shared the liberal premises of Lockean sensationalism: that all men were born equal and that only the environment working on their senses made them different. These premises were essential to the growing sense of sympathy for other human creatures felt by enlightened people in the eighteenth century. Once the liberally educated came to believe that they could control their environment and educate the vulgar and lowly to become something other than what the traditional society had presumed they were destined to be, then the enlightened few began to expand their sense of moral responsibility for the vice and ignorance they saw in others and to experience feelings of common humanity with them.

Thus, despite their acceptance of differences among people, both Jefferson and Paine concluded that all men were basically alike, that they all partook of the same common nature. It was this commonality that linked people together in natural affection and made it possible for them to share each other's feelings. There was something in each human being—some sort of moral sense or sympathetic instinct—that made possible natural compassion and affection. Indeed, wrote Paine, "[i]nstinct in animals does not act with stronger impulse, than the principles of society and civilization operate in man." Even the lowliest of persons, even black slaves, Jefferson believed, had this sense of sympathy or moral feeling for others. All human beings, said Jefferson, rich and poor, white and black, had "implanted in their breasts" this "moral instinct," this "love of others." Everyone, whatever their differences of education, instinctively knew right from wrong. "State a moral case to a ploughman and a professor," said Jefferson; the ploughman will decide it as well, and often better, than the professor, "because he has not been led astray by artificial rules."[8]

This belief in the equal moral worth and equal moral authority of every individual was the real source of both Jefferson's and Paine's democratic equality, an equality that was far more potent than merely the Lockean idea that everyone started at birth with the same blank sheet.

Jefferson's and Paine's assumption that people possessed an innate moral or social sense had important implications. It lay behind their belief in the natural harmony of society and their advocacy of minimal government. People, they claimed, had an inherent need to socialize with one another and were naturally benevolent and affable. This benevolence and sociability became a modern substitute for the ascetic and Spartan virtue of the ancient republics. This new modern virtue, as David Hume pointed out, was much more in accord with the growing commercialization and refinement of the enlightened and civilized eighteenth century than the austere and severe virtue of the ancients.

The classical virtue of antiquity had flowed from the citizen's participation in politics; government had been the source of the citizen's civic consciousness and public-spiritedness. But the modern virtue of Jefferson, Paine, and other eighteenth-century liberals flowed from the citizen's participation in society, not in government. Society to eighteenth-century liberals was harmonious and compassionate. We today may believe that society—with its class antagonisms, business and capitalist exploitation, and racial prejudices—by itself breeds the ills and cruelties that plague us. But for eighteenth-century radicals, society was benign; it created sympathy, affability, and the new domesticated virtue. By mingling in drawing rooms, clubs, and coffeehouses, by partaking in the innumerable interchanges of the daily comings and goings of modern life, people developed affection and fellow feeling, which were all the adhesives really necessary to hold an enlightened people together. Some even argued that commerce, that traditional enemy of classical virtue, was in fact a source of modern virtue. Because it encouraged intercourse and confidence among people and nations, commerce actually contributed to benevolence and fellow feeling.

The opening paragraph of Thomas Paine's *Common Sense* articulated brilliantly this distinction between society and government. Society and government were different things, said Paine, and they have different origins. "Society is produced by our wants and government by our wickedness." Society "promotes our happiness *positively* by uniting our affections"; government affects us *"negatively* by restraining our vices. The one encourages intercourse, the other creates distinctions. . . . Society in every state was a blessing; but government even in its best state was but a necessary evil; in its worst state an intolerable one."⁹ The most devout republicans like Paine and Jefferson believed that if only the natural tendencies of people to love and care for one another were allowed to flow freely, unclogged by the artificial interference of government, particularly monarchical government, society would prosper and hold itself together.

These liberal ideas that society was naturally autonomous and self-regulating and that everyone possessed a common moral and social sense were no utopian fantasies but the conclusions of what many enlightened thinkers took to be the modern science of society. While most clergymen continued to urge Christian love and charity upon their ordinary parishioners, many other educated and enlightened people sought to secularize Christian love and find in human nature itself a scientific imperative for loving one's neighbor as oneself. There seemed to be a natural principle of attraction that pulled people together, a moral principle that was no different from the principles that operated in the physical world. "Just as the regular motions and harmony of the heavenly bodies depend upon their mutual gravitation towards each other," said the liberal Massachusetts preacher Jonathan Mayhew, so too did love and benevolence among people preserve "order and harmony" in the society.¹⁰ Love between humans was the gravity of the moral world, and it could be studied and perhaps even manipulated more easily than the gravity of the physical world. Enlightened thinkers like Lord Shaftesbury, Francis Hutcheson, and Adam Smith thus sought to discover these hidden forces that moved and held people together in the moral world—forces, they believed, that could match the great eighteenth-century scientific discoveries of the hidden physical forces (gravity, magnetism, electricity, and energy) that operated in the physical world. Out of such dreams was born modern social science.

Their complete reliance on "a system of social affections" is what made Paine and Jefferson such natural republicans.[11] Republics demanded far more morally from their citizens than monarchies did of their subjects. In monarchies each man's desire to do what was right in his own eyes could be restrained by fear or force, by patronage or honor, by the distribution of offices and distinctions, and by professional standing armies. By contrast, republics could not use the traditional instruments of government to hold the society together; instead, they had to hold themselves together from the bottom up, ultimately, from their citizens' willingness to sacrifice their private desires for the sake of the public good—their virtue. This reliance on the moral virtue of their citizens, on their capacity for self-sacrifice and their innate sociability, was what made republican governments historically so fragile.

Jefferson and Paine had so much confidence in the natural harmony of society that they sometimes came close to denying any role for government at all in holding the society together. To believe that government contributed to social cohesion was a great mistake, said Paine. "Society performs for itself almost every thing which is ascribed to government." Government had little or nothing to do with civilized life. Instead of ordering society, government "divided it; it deprived it of its natural cohesion, and engendered discontents and disorder, which otherwise would not have existed."[12] Both Paine and Jefferson believed that all social abuses and deprivations—social distinctions, business contracts, monopolies and privileges of all sorts, even excessive property and wealth, anything and everything that interfered with people's natural social dispositions—seemed to flow from connections to government, in the end from connections to monarchical government. Everywhere in the Old World, said Paine, we "find the greedy hand of government thrusting itself into every corner and crevice of industry, and grasping the spoil of the multitude."[13]

Both Jefferson and Paine believed deeply in minimal government—not as nineteenth-century laissez-faire liberals trying to promote capitalism, but as eighteenth-century radicals who hated monarchy, which was the only kind of government they had known. Calling them believers in minimal government is perhaps too tame a way of describing their deep disdain for hereditary monarchical government. Monarchy for Paine was "a silly contemptible thing" whose fuss and formality, when once exposed, became laughable. Jefferson felt the same; when he was president he went out of his way to mock the formalities and ceremonies of the court life of the European kings. His scorn of the European monarchs knew no bounds. They were, he said, all fools or idiots. "They passed their lives in hunting, and dispatched two couriers a week, one thousand miles, to let each other know what game they had killed the preceding days."[14]

But what really made Jefferson and Paine hate monarchy was its habitual promotion of war. As far as they were concerned, as Paine put it, "all the monarchical governments are military. War is their trade, plunder and revenue their objects."[15] Angry liberals everywhere in the Western world thought that monarchy and war were intimately related. Indeed, as the son of the Revolutionary War general Benjamin Lincoln declared, "Kings owe their origin to war."[16] This recent Harvard graduate, like Jefferson and Paine, spoke out of a widespread eighteenth-century liberal protest against developments that had been taking place in Europe over the previous three centuries.

From the sixteenth century through the eighteenth century, the European monarchies had been busy consolidating their power and marking out their authority within clearly designated boundaries while at the same time protecting themselves from rival claimants to their power and territories. They erected ever-larger bureaucracies and military forces in order to wage war, which is what they did through most decades of these three centuries. This meant the building of more centralized governments and the creation of more elaborate means for extracting money and men from their subjects. These efforts in turn led to the growth of armies, the increase in public debts, the raising of taxes, and the strengthening of executive power.

Such monarchical state building was bound to provoke opposition, especially among the English who had a long tradition of valuing their liberties and resisting crown power. The country-Whig-opposition ideology that arose in England in the late seventeenth and early eighteenth centuries was directed against these kinds of monarchical state-building efforts taking place rather belatedly in England. When later eighteenth-century British radicals, including Thomas Paine, warned that the lamps of liberty were going out all over Europe and were being dimmed in Britain itself, it was these efforts at modern state formation that they were talking about.

Liberals and republicans like Jefferson and Paine assumed that kings brought their countries into war so frequently because wars sustained monarchical power. The internal needs of monarchies—the requirements of their bloated bureaucracies, their standing armies, their marriage alliances, their restless dynastic ambitions—lay behind the prevalence of war. Eliminate monarchy and all its accoutrements, many Americans believed, and war itself would be eliminated. A world of republican states would encourage a different kind of diplomacy, a peace-loving diplomacy—one based not on the brutal struggle for power of conventional diplomacy but on the natural concert of the commercial interests of the people of the various nations. "If commerce were permitted to act to the universal extent it is capable," said Paine, "it would extirpate the system of war, and produce a revolution in the uncivilized state of governments."[17] In other words, if the people of the various nations were left alone to exchange goods freely among themselves—without the corrupting interference of selfish monarchical courts, irrational dynastic rivalries, and the secret double-dealing diplomacy of the past—then, as Jefferson, Paine, and other radical liberals hoped, international politics would become republicanized, pacified, and ruled by commerce alone, and a universal peace might emerge. Old-fashioned political diplomats might not even be necessary in this new commercially linked world.

Both men naturally and enthusiastically supported the French Revolution; indeed, both of them were close to Lafayette and his liberal circle and participated in the early stages of that Revolution. They had no doubt that the republican ideals of the American Revolution were simply spreading eastward and would eventually republicanize all of Europe. Although Paine became a member of the French National Convention and participated in its affairs, he turned out to be somewhat less fanatical than Jefferson. Paine never said anything comparable to Jefferson's comment of January 1793, in which the American secretary of state declared that he "would have seen half the earth desolated" rather than have the Revolution in France fail. "Were there but an Adam and an Eve left in every country, and left free, it would be better than as it is now." Indeed, while Paine bravely argued in the National Convention that the life of King Louis XVI ought to be spared, Jefferson viewed the king's execution as "punishment like other criminals." He hoped that France's eventual triumph would "bring at length kings, nobles and priests to the scaffolds which they have been so long deluging with human blood."[18]

For hardheaded realists like Alexander Hamilton, these radical ideas of Jefferson and Paine were nothing but "pernicious dreams." By abandoning the main instruments by which eighteenth-century monarchical governments held their turbulent societies together and ruled— patronage, ceremonies and rituals, aristocratic titles, and force—dreamers like Jefferson and Paine, said a disgruntled Hamilton, were offering "the bewitching tenets of the illuminated doctrine, which promises men, ere long, an emancipation from the burdens and restraints of government." By the early 1790s Hamilton was alarmed by the extraordinarily utopian idea coming out of the French Revolution "that but a small portion of power is requisite to Government." And some radicals like William Godwin believed that "even this is only temporarily necessary" and could be done away with once "the bad habits" of the ancien régime were eliminated. Unfortunately, said Hamilton, there were wishful thinkers in both France and America who assumed that, "as human nature shall refine and ameliorate by the operation of a more enlightened plan" based on a common moral sense and the spread of affection and benevolence, "government itself will become useless, and Society will subsist and flourish free from its shackles."[19]

With all the "mischiefs . . . inherent in so wild and fatal a scheme," Hamilton had hoped that "votaries of this new philosophy" would not push it to its fullest. But the new Jefferson administration that took over the federal government in 1801 was trying to do just that. "No army, no navy, no *active* commerce—national defence, not by arms but by embargoes, prohibition of trade &c.—as little government as possible." These all added up, said Hamilton in 1802, to "a most visionary theory."[20] Consequently, Hamilton and the other opponents of the Jefferson administration never tired of ridiculing the president and his supporters as utopians who walked with their heads in the clouds trying to extract sunbeams from cucumbers. Jefferson, the quixotic president, may have been ideally suited to be a college professor, they declared, but he was not suited to be the leader of a great nation.

But like many college professors, both Jefferson and Paine were optimists, believing in the promise of the future rather than in the dead hand of the past. Both loved inventions, like Paine's iron bridge, that made life and commerce easier. Both detested primogeniture and other aristocratic inheritance laws that treated new generations of children unequally. They hated charters and corporations that gave the few monopoly privileges that were not shared by the many. They were, said Paine, "charters, not of rights, but of exclusion."[21] The idea that corporate charters were vested rights that were unalterable by subsequent popular legislatures was, said Jefferson, a doctrine inculcated by "our lawyers and priests" that supposed "that preceding generations held the earth more freely than we do; had a right to impose laws on us, unalterable by ourselves, and that we, in like manner, can make laws and impose burdens on future generations, which they will have no right to alter; in fine, that the earth belongs to the dead and not the living."[22] Neither Jefferson nor Paine, in other words, had any patience with the sophisticated defense of prescription set forth by Edmund Burke.

Even the two men's religious views were similar—as radical as the enlightened eighteenth century allowed. Although Jefferson never publicly attacked orthodox religion in the extreme way Paine did in his *Age of Reason* (1794)—"Of all the systems of religion that ever were invented," Paine declared, "there is none more derogatory to the Almighty, more unedifying to man, more repugnant to reason, and more contradictory in itself than this thing called Christianity"—Jefferson privately shared Paine's scorn for traditional Christianity. Members of the "priestcraft," he wrote to friends he could trust, had turned Christianity "into mystery and jargon unintelligible to all mankind and therefore the safer engine for their purposes." The Trinity was nothing but "Abracadabra" and "hocus-pocus . . . so incomprehensible to the human mind that no candid man can say he has any idea of it." Ridicule, he said, was the only weapon to be used against it. But because he had been badly burned by some indiscreet remarks about religion in his *Notes on the State of Virginia*, he had learned to share his religious thoughts with only those he could rely on. "I not only write nothing on religion," he told a friend in 1815, "but rarely permit myself to speak on it, and never but in a reasonable society."[23]

Paine's outrageous statements about Christianity in his *Age of Reason* helped to destroy his reputation in America. These views, coupled with his vicious attack on George Washington, meant that when he returned from Europe to America in 1802, he had few friends left in the country, but Thomas Jefferson was one of them.

Jefferson was the president and a political figure and that made all the difference between the two men. On nearly every point of political and religious beliefs the two enlightened radicals were in agreement. Where they differed was in Paine's need to voice his ideas publicly and in Jefferson's need to confine them to private drawing rooms composed of reasonable people. Paine was America's first modern public intellectual, an unconnected social critic, who knew, he said, "but one kind of life I am fit for, and that is a thinking one, and of course, a writing one."[24] By aggressively publishing his ideas, Paine aimed to turn the contemplative life into an active one. Jefferson could not do this. Since he had a political career that depended on popular elections, he could not afford to spell out his radical ideas in pamphlets and books in the forceful way Paine could. Yet if he had written out in any systematic manner what he believed about politics, it would have resembled Paine's *The Rights of Man: Part the Second*. As a politician, Jefferson continually had to compromise his beliefs—on minimal government, on banks, on the debt, on patronage, and perhaps on slavery. When he was speaking with his liberal friends abroad, he certainly took the correct line in opposition to slavery, but he was unable to become the kind of outspoken opponent of slavery that Paine became. Yet the intensity with which Jefferson enforced his embargo—his grand experiment in "peaceful coercion" as an alternative to war—reveals just how dedicated a radical he could be on some issues.

Although Jefferson was certainly cosmopolitan in an enlightened eighteenth-century manner, he was at heart a Virginian and an American deeply attached to his country. Paine was different. By the time he left America to return to the Old World in 1787, he had emotionally cut loose from his adopted home and had turned into an intellectual progenitor of revolutions. "It was neither the place nor the people [of America], but the Cause itself that irresistibly engages me in its support," he told the president of the Continental Congress as early as 1779, "for I should have acted the same part in any other country could the same circumstance have arisen there which have happened here." He had come to see himself as little better than "a refugee, and that of the most extraordinary kind, a refugee from the Country I have befriended." In the end he became a man without a home, without a country, and literally, as he said, "a citizen of the world."[25]

Because Paine after 1787 became as eager to reform the Old World as he had the New, his writings eventually took on issues that he had not dealt with earlier. Thinking of England and its huge numbers of landless people and its extremes of wealth and poverty, he proposed systems of public welfare and social insurance financed by progressive taxation in his *Rights of Man: Part the Second* and in his *Agrarian Justice*. Jefferson, as the patriot who believed that agrarian America was already an egalitarian paradise, felt no need to express such radical views publicly. Yet as early as 1785 he privately suggested various measures to ensure that property in a state not become too unequally divided. Indeed, he declared, so harmful was gross inequality of wealth that "legislators cannot invent too many devices for subdividing property." In addition to proposing that all children inherit property equally, he, like Paine, advocated the progressive taxation of the rich and the exemption of the poor from taxes. Even in America, he said, "it is not too soon to provide by every possible means that as few as possible shall be without a little portion of land. The small landholders are the most precious part of a state."[26]

In the end, Americans treated the two men who shared so many ideas very differently. Although Americans have erected a huge memorial to Jefferson in Washington, D.C., and celebrated him as the premier spokesman for democracy, they have scarcely noticed Thomas Paine. He died in obscurity in the United States in 1809 and ten years later William Cobbett took his bones away to England. Although Jefferson declared in 1801 that Paine had labored on behalf of liberty and the American Revolution "with as much effort as any man living," Paine still remains a much-neglected Founder.[27] Perhaps it is time for that to change.

AFTERWORD TO CHAPTER 7

This was a paper presented at a conference in London in 2009 celebrating the bicentennial of Thomas Paine's death. Although not written with that intent, the paper may help refurbish the reputation of Jefferson in some small way. It is not easy, since Jefferson has come in for some very brutal and often deserved bashing by historians over the past half century. Although he has traditionally been seen as America's premier spokesman for democracy, he was an aristocratic slaveholder, and the irony of that conjunction has been too much for many historians to bear, especially as historians have made slavery the central fact in the founding of the nation. Jefferson seems to be the ultimate hypocrite, and because he has been such a symbol of America, his hypocrisy has tainted the nation's reputation as well.

Although it took courage for young Jefferson, raised in a slave society, to speak out against the institution, there is ultimately no defending Jefferson on slavery or race. He did indeed oppose slavery as a young man, and he even tried to do something about limiting it, but his suspicions of black inferiority and racial distinctiveness expressed in his *Notes on the State of Virginia* are so abhorrent that his moral credentials appear to be fatally compromised. Yet despite his repugnant views on race, Jefferson still has something to say to us Americans today. Indeed, I think that he deserves his traditional reputation as America's supreme apostle of democracy.

Paine may be able to help redeem Jefferson. Since it is clear that Jefferson and Paine thought alike on virtually every issue, Paine's radical and democratic credentials may allow historians, especially those of the left, to see Jefferson in a somewhat more favorable light, or at least see him in light of the eighteenth century, and not in today's light.

So taken with Jefferson's hypocrisy are recent historians that some of them have even suggested that Jefferson's advocacy of minimal government was merely a device for defending slavery. Since a small government presumably would have less opportunity to interfere with the institution of slavery, some Southern Jeffersonian Republicans certainly found minimal government appealing. But that was not Jefferson's motive or the motive of his many Northern followers. Jefferson's ideas of minimal government were widely shared by eighteenth-century radicals such as Paine, William Godwin, and others who certainly had no brief for slavery. The fact of the matter is that late eighteenth-century Anglo-American radicalism demanded a belief in minimal government, and historians who do not appreciate that fact reveal their ignorance of the period.

Jefferson's standing as the spokesman for democracy rests on his belief in equality. It is why Lincoln paid "all honor to Jefferson." He and others subsequently have drawn inspiration from the Declaration of Independence and its claim that all men are created equal. But Jefferson went much further than simply claiming that all men were created equal—that was a cliché among the enlightened in the late eighteenth century. As I try to point out in this article, both he and Paine believed that people were not just created equal but were actually equal to everyone else throughout their lives. Not that Jefferson and Paine denied the obvious differences among individuals that exist—how some individuals are taller, smarter, more handsome than others—but rather both radicals posited that at bottom, every single individual, men and women, black and white, had a common moral or social sense that tied him or her to other individuals. None of the other leading Founders believed that—not Washington, not Hamilton, not Adams. And since no democracy can intelligibly exist without some such magnanimous belief that at heart everyone is the same, Jefferson's position as the apostle of American democracy seems not only legitimate but necessary to the well-being of the nation.

PART III

THE *Early Republic*

CHAPTER EIGHT

MONARCHISM *and* REPUBLICANISM *in* EARLY AMERICA

*D*URING THE DEBATE over the new proposed Constitution in 1787–1788, many Americans were fearful that the entire Revolutionary project of 1776 was being threatened. Opponents thought that the Constitution threatened to undermine the republican experiment and create a monarchical tyranny that would eventually take away America's liberty. They especially objected to "the mighty and splendid President," who possessed power "in the most unlimited manner" that could be easily abused.[1]

It was true that the Convention had decided on an extraordinarily strong and single executive. The president was to stand alone, unencumbered by an executive council except one of his own choosing. With command over the armed forces, with the authority to direct diplomatic relations, with power over appointments to the executive and judicial branches that few state governors possessed, and with a four-year term of office (longer than that of any state governor) and perpetually reeligible for reelection, the president was a magistrate who, as Patrick Henry charged, could "easily become king."[2] Many of the opponents of the Constitution believed that the country was being led down the garden path to monarchy.

These opponents of the new Constitution were not entirely wrong. By 1787–1788 many of those who supported the new Constitution—the Federalists, as they called themselves—did have aspects of monarchy on their minds. By the time the Constitutional Convention met in Philadelphia in 1787, many members of the elite had lost faith in the Revolutionary dream of 1776—that America could exist as a confederation of thirteen states with a minimum of government. Some New England Federalists, "seeing and dreading the evils of democracy," according to one English traveler at the time, were even willing to "admit monarchy, or something like it." The wealthy New England merchant Benjamin Tappan, father of the future abolitionists, was not alone in thinking that a good dose of monarchism was needed in 1787 to offset the popular excesses of the American people. Even though Henry Knox, Washington's close friend, had given Tappan "a gentle check" for openly voicing such an opinion, Tappan told Knox that he "cannot give up the Idea that monarchy in our present situation is become absolutely necessary to save the states from sinking into the lowest abyss of misery." Since he had "delivered my sentiment in all companies" and found it well received, he believed that "if matters were properly arranged it would be easily and soon effected," perhaps with the aid of the Society of the Cincinnati, the fraternal organization of former Revolutionary War officers. Even if nothing were done, Tappan intended to continue to be "a strong advocate for what I have suggested."³

There were many more Americans in 1787 thinking like Tappan than we have been prepared to admit. This new federal government marked as great a change as the Revolution itself. Such a strong national government as the Constitution prescribed had certainly not been anticipated by anyone in 1776. No one in his wildest dreams had even imagined such a powerful government.

In 1776 the Revolutionaries had established not a single republic but thirteen of them. The Declaration of Independence was in fact a declaration of thirteen separate states. All of these states in 1776 had immediately set about constructing their own constitutions. These Revolutionary constitutions were modeled on what Americans thought the mixed or balanced constitution of the so-called English commonwealth ideally ought to have been. Thus most of the state constitution makers created mixtures of governors, senates, and houses of representatives, which they identified with the monarchy, aristocracy, and democracy of the English constitution. The new republican governors may have been elected, but they were still thought to embody the monarchical element in society. In the same way, the senates or upper houses of the legislatures were thought to embody the aristocratic element.

Of course, the American constitution makers wanted to avoid the corruption of the English constitution, which they believed flowed from the misuse of patronage by the crown. Hence they forbade members of the legislatures from simultaneously holding office in the government or executive branch. This prohibition, repeated in Article I, Section 6 of the federal Constitution, prevented the development of ministerial responsibility to the legislatures and, as we saw in a previous essay, sent Americans off on a very different constitutional path from the English.

Although Americans in 1776 attempted to model their republican state constitutions on the balanced English monarchical constitution, they knew only too well that republican and monarchical governments were designed for very different societies. Republicanism put a premium on the homogeneity and cohesiveness of its society. By contrast, monarchies could comprehend large territories and composite kingdoms and peoples with diverse interests and ethnicities. Monarchies had their unitary authority, kingly honors and patronage, hereditary aristocracies, established national churches, and standing armies to hold their diverse societies together. Republics had none of these adhesive elements. Instead, republics were supposed to rely for cohesion on the moral qualities of their people—their virtue and their natural sociability. Monarchy imagined its society in traditional and prenational terms, as a mosaic of quasicorporate communities, and thus had little trouble in embracing African slaves and Indians as subjects. But republicanism created citizens, and since citizens were all equal to one another, it was difficult for the Revolutionaries to include blacks and Indians as citizens in the new republican states they were trying to create. This emphasis on republican homogeneity and equal citizenship meant that republics, as Montesquieu had indicated, should be small in size.

For this reason, none of the Revolutionaries in 1776 had had any idea of making the thirteen United States anything other than a confederation. Hence they created in 1777 and ratified in 1781 the Articles of Confederation. It was a league of friendship among thirteen independent states, in character not all that different from the present European Union. In this Confederation each of the states had equal representation and a single vote. The individual states may have been republics, but the Confederation government was something else—a union of republics. Although the Confederation Congress was not a king, it was designed to play the same role the former king had been supposed to play in the empire. It inherited most of the prerogative powers that the British king had exercised over the colonies—namely, the powers to conduct foreign policy, to declare and wage war and to make peace, to handle Indian affairs, and to settle disputes between the states. The Congress, composed of equal representation from each state, was not intended to be a legislature but rather a superintending executive of the Confederation. It became in effect a stand-in for the former monarchy, which is why it was not given the powers to tax or regulate trade: these powers were not prerogative powers and had not been exercised unilaterally by the king.

By the early 1780s the vicissitudes of the war forced the Congress to create separate departments of war, finance, and foreign affairs, with single individuals appointed to head them; in other words, the Congress created something akin to modern executive departments. This development turned the Congress, which was supposed to play the central magisterial role the crown had played in the empire, into something resembling a legislature. And when this happened, many began complaining that now this congressional legislature did not proportionally represent the people in the various states. All of this prepared the way for the disposing of the Articles and the creation of an entirely new government with the Constitution of 1787—the present existing government of the United States.

In the decade following the Declaration of Independence, many of the Revolutionary leaders had become increasingly disillusioned with the consequences of their republican revolution. The Confederation lacked the powers to tax and to regulate trade and was unable to stand up for the United States in international affairs. But, more important, the states themselves were not behaving as the leaders had expected. By the mid-1780s, as we have seen, many of them had become convinced that not only was the Confederation too weak to accomplish its tasks, but, more alarming, the states themselves were unable to function as stable and just republics.

James Madison and other leaders had concluded that legislative majorities in the states were acting irresponsibly, flooding the states with poorly drafted and mutable laws that victimized minorities and violated individual rights. Most alarming, these state legislators were simply acting in accord with the sentiments of the voters who elected them. Such abuses of popular power, these excesses of democracy, were not easily remedied, for they struck at the heart of what the Revolution was about. These legislative evils, said Madison, "brought into question the fundamental principle of republican Government, that the majority who rule in such governments are the safest Guardians both of public Good and private rights."[4] To Madison and to other leaders it thus seemed as if the entire American experiment in republicanism was at stake.

Thus the crisis of the 1780s was a real one for many of the country's leaders. There was too much democracy in the states, and this excessive democracy had to be curbed—without doing violence to republican principles. At first many reformers had concentrated on changing the Revolutionary state constitutions. They urged taking power back from the houses of representatives and giving it to the senates and the governors—the aristocratic and monarchical elements of their constitutions. Although Americans in 1776 had created their mixed or balanced state governments in emulation of the famed English constitution, the reformers soon discovered that they could no longer justify strengthening their governors and senates by talking in traditional terms of infusing more monarchy and aristocracy into their state constitutions. Since any public reference to monarchy and aristocracy was vehemently denounced as unrepublican and un-American, reformers had to find new justifications for the senates and the governors. Within a few years they began describing all parts of the original mixed state governments—governors and senators, and not just the houses of representatives—as representative agents of the people. As we have seen, this forced Americans into an entirely new understanding of the sovereign people and the people's relationship to government.

Many reformers, however, soon realized that even changing the state constitutions would not solve the problems of majoritarian factionalism and minority rights in the state legislatures. They soon began to look beyond the state level for what Madison called "a republican remedy for those diseases most incident to republican government." Those who wanted to reform the states were able to come together with the growing numbers of those who were urging reform of the Confederation. Indeed, by the mid-1780s nearly the entire political nation agreed that some specific powers needed to be added to the Confederation Congress—namely, the powers to levy customs duties and to regulate trade.

Thus almost everybody welcomed the calling of the Convention in Philadelphia in May 1787 in order to amend the Articles of Confederation. But the Convention offered an opportunity as well to those who were most concerned with the problems of democracy in the states. Although it was the widespread desire to reform the Confederation that made the calling of the Convention possible, it was the problems of democracy in the states that actually drove the plans of the Convention's leaders, including Madison, who more than anyone was responsible for the new Constitution. It was, Madison told his friend Jefferson, the abuses of the state legislatures, "so frequent and so flagrant as to alarm the most stedfast friends of Republicanism," that "contributed more to that uneasiness which produced the Convention, and prepared the public mind for a general reform, than those which accrued to our national character and interest from the inadequacy of the Confederation to its immediate objects."[5] Instead of merely adding some powers to the Articles of

Confederation, the Convention, under Madison's leadership, scrapped the Articles and drew up an entirely new Constitution. Which, of course, it had no authority to do.

The new Constitution created not a confederation of separate states but a new powerful national republic operating directly on the people; in other words, it created a nation instead of a union, although the supporters scrupulously avoided using the terms "nation" and "national" in the Constitution. Given the prevailing assumption that republics were supposed to be small in size and homogeneous in character, justifying this huge extended republic posed some problems. All experience and all theory were against the kind of extended national republic that Americans in 1787 were attempting to erect. Not only did Americans know from their experience under the British Empire what far-removed central power could mean, but they also knew that conventional wisdom required that republics be small and homogeneous.

The new nation was hardly that. By 1787 Americans were already a very large and diverse people with a dazzling variety of ethnicities and religions. Not only were over 20 percent of the population of African descent, but the white population was composed of virtually every European nationality. Only about half the population was English in origin. Yet, unlike today, the defenders of the Constitution could scarcely stress America's multicultural diversity—not in the face of the conventional wisdom that republics were supposed to have a homogeneous society. So in order to justify their new extended republic, they had to stretch the truth in emphasizing that Americans were actually one people with one destiny.

Although most supporters of the new Constitution stressed the homogeneity of the American people, some of them sought to turn conventional wisdom on its head. Some, including Madison, argued (following David Hume) that perhaps a large republic with many varying interests was better able to sustain itself than a small republic—largely because the varying interests would neutralize one another and allow for a common good to emerge.

Whatever the nature of the arguments, however, all the Federalists knew that if democracy were to be curbed, then what was needed in the new government was more power. And power in eighteenth-century Anglo-American political theory essentially meant monarchy. In the conventional thinking of an eighteenth-century balanced or mixed constitution, too much democracy required the counterbalancing of some more monarchy.

Just as the state reformers had been inhibited from speaking frankly about the need for more monarchical and aristocratic principles in the state constitutions, so too were the Federalists unwilling to say openly that the new national government required more aristocratic and monarchical elements. Nevertheless, there is little doubt that many of them had come to believe that some aristocracy and especially some monarchism were needed to offset the democratic excesses of the American people. In 1790 Benjamin Rush described the new government as one "which unites with the vigor of monarchy and the stability of aristocracy all the freedom of a simple republic."[6] Even Madison, who was as devoted to republicanism as any of the Founders, was in 1787 sufficiently disillusioned with the democratic consequences of the Revolution to see some advantages in monarchy. With his dream of "the purest and noblest characters" of the society in power in his new extended republic, he expected that the new federal government would play the same superpolitical neutral role that the British king had been supposed to play in the empire. Like a good constitutional monarch, he wrote, the new national government would be "sufficiently neutral between the different interests and factions, to control one part of the society from invading the rights of another, and at the same time sufficiently controlled itself, from setting up an interest adverse to that of the whole society."[7]

That a moderate like Madison should see some benefits to monarchy was a measure of the crisis of the 1780s. Other Federalists like Alexander Hamilton were even more disillusioned with the democratic consequences of the Revolution and wanted even stronger doses of monarchy injected into the body politic. In fact, Hamilton and other high-toned

Federalists, who in the 1790s clung to the name of the supporters of the Constitution, wanted to create a centralized fiscal-military state that would eventually rival the great monarchical powers of Europe on their own terms. Yet they knew that whatever aspects of monarchy they hoped to bring back into America would have to be placed within a republican framework. Perhaps, as some historians have suggested, the Federalists really intended to create another Augustan Age. Augustus had, after all, sought to incorporate elements of monarchy into the Roman Empire while all the time talking about republicanism.

If some monarchical power were to be instilled in the new system, the energetic center of that power would be the presidency. For that reason it was the office of the president that made many Americans most suspicious of the new government. The executive or chief magistracy was, after all, the traditional source of tyranny and, as Benjamin Franklin pointed out, the source in America from which monarchy would naturally emerge.

Although Americans were used to congresses, the presidency was a new office for them. A single, strong national executive was bound to remind them of the king they had just cast off. When James Wilson at the Philadelphia Convention had moved that the executive "consist of a single person," a long, uneasy silence had followed. The delegates knew only too well what such an office implied. John Rutledge complained that "the people will think we are leaning too much towards Monarchy." The creation of the presidency, warned Edmund Randolph, "made a bold stroke for monarchy."[8] But the Convention resisted these warnings and went on to make the new chief executive so strong, so kinglike, precisely because the delegates expected George Washington to be the first president.

Many people, including Jefferson, expected that Washington might be president for life, that he would be a kind of elective monarch— something not out of the question in the eighteenth century.[9] Indeed, we will never understand events of the 1790s until we take seriously, as contemporaries did, the possibility of some sort of monarchy developing in America. From our vantage point, the idea of America becoming a monarchy may seem absurd, but in 1789 it did not seem so at all. After all, Americans had been raised as subjects of monarchy and, in the opinion of some, still seemed emotionally to need to look up to a single patriarchal figure. Republicanism was new and untried. Monarchy still prevailed almost everywhere; it was what much of the world was used to, and history showed that sooner or later most republics tended to develop into kingly governments. As ancient Rome had shown, the natural evolution of societies and states seemed to be from simple republican youth to complex monarchical maturity.

William Short, viewing the new Constitution from France, was not immediately frightened by the power of the executive. But he thought that "the President of the eighteenth century" would "form a stock on which will be grafted a King in the nineteenth." Others, like George Mason of Virginia, believed that the new government was destined to become "an elective monarchy," and still others, like Rawlins Lowndes of South Carolina, assumed that the government so closely resembled the British form that everyone naturally expected "our changing from a republic to monarchy."[10] To add to the confusion, the line between monarchical and republican governments in the eighteenth century was often hazy at best, and some were already talking about monarchical republics and republican monarchies.

From the outset, Washington's behavior often savored of monarchy. His journey from Mount Vernon to the capital in New York in the spring of 1789, for example, took on the air of a royal procession. He was saluted by cannons and celebrated in elaborate ceremonies along the way. Everywhere he was greeted by triumphal rejoicing and acclamations of "Long live George Washington!" With Yale students debating the advantages of an elective over a hereditary king, suggestions of monarchy were very much in the air. "You are now a King, under a different name," James McHenry told Washington in March 1789, and wished that he "may reign long and happy over us."[11] It was not surprising therefore that some people referred to his inauguration as a "coronation."[12]

So prevalent was the thinking that Washington resembled an elected monarch that some people even expressed relief that he had no heirs.[13] Washington was sensitive to these popular anxieties about monarchy, and for a while he had thought of holding the presidency for only a year or so and then resigning and turning the office over to Vice President John Adams. In the initial draft of his inaugural address he pointed out that "the Divine Providence hath not seen fit, that my blood should be transmitted or name perpetuated by the endearing though sometimes seducing channel of immediate offspring." He had, he wrote, "no child for whom I could wish to make a provision—no family to build in greatness upon my country's ruins." Madison talked him out of this draft, but Washington's desire to show the public that he harbored no monarchical ambitions remained strong.[14] His protests testified to the widespread sense that monarchy was a distinct possibility for America.

Sensitive to charges that he had royal ambitions, Washington was often uncertain about the role he ought to play as president. He realized that the new government was fragile and needed dignity, but how far in a monarchical European direction ought he to go to achieve it? Aware that whatever he did would become a precedent for the future, Washington sought the advice of those close to him, including the vice president and the man he would soon make his secretary of the treasury, Alexander Hamilton.

How often should he meet with the public? How accessible should he be? Should he dine with members of Congress? Should he host state dinners? Could he ever have private dinners with friends? Should he make a tour of the United States? The only state ceremonies that late eighteenth-century Americans were familiar with were those of the European monarchies. Were they applicable to the young republic?

Hamilton thought that most people were "prepared for a pretty high tone in the demeanour of the Executive," but probably not as high a tone as Hamilton thought desirable. "Notions of equality," he said, were as "yet . . . too general and too strong" for the president to be properly distanced from the other branches of the government. (Note the "yet"; Federalists thought time was on their side.) In the meantime, suggested

Hamilton, the president ought to follow the practice of "European Courts" as closely as he could. Only department heads, high-ranking diplomats, and senators should have access to the president. "Your Excellency," as Hamilton referred to Washington, might hold a half-hour levee no more than once a week, and then only for invited guests. He could give up to four formal entertainments a year, but must never accept any invitations or call on anyone.[15] Vice President John Adams for his part urged Washington to make a show of "splendor and majesty" for his office. The president needed an entourage of chamberlains, aides-de-camp, and masters of ceremonies to conduct the formalities of his office.[16]

Washington realized that he had to maintain more distance from the public than the presidents of the Confederation Congress had. They had reduced their office to "perfect contempt," having been "considered in no better light than as a maitre d'hotel . . . for their table was considered as a public one and every person who could get introduced conceived that he had a right to be invited to it." He knew that too much familiarity was no way "to preserve the dignity and respect that was due to the first magistrate."[17]

As uncomfortable as he often was with ceremony, Washington knew that he had to make the presidency "respectable," and when he became president he spared few expenses in doing so. Although he was compelled to accept his $25,000 presidential salary—an enormous sum for the age—he spent nearly $2,000 of it on liquor and wine for entertaining. In his public appearances he rode in an elaborately ornamented coach drawn by four and sometimes six horses, attended with four servants in livery, followed by his official family in other coaches.[18] In his public pronouncements he referred to himself in the third person, and he sat for dozens of state portraits, all modeled on those of European monarchs; these were hung in prominent public places throughout the nation with the hope of thereby encouraging respect for the new regime. Indeed, much of the iconography of the new nation, including its civic processions, was copied from monarchical symbolism.[19] Washington may have been a simple republican—at heart just a country gentleman who was in bed every night by 9:30—but there is no doubt that he was concerned with "the style proper for the Chief Magistrate." He conceded that a certain monarchical tone had to be made part of the government, and he was willing up to a point to play the part of a republican king. He was, as John Adams later caustically remarked, "the best actor of presidency we have ever had."[20]

Obsessed with the new government's weakness, other Federalists were even more eager than Washington to bolster its dignity and respectability. Most believed that this could be best done by adopting some of the ceremony and majesty of monarchy—by making, for example, Washington's birthday celebrations rival those of the Fourth of July. Like the king of England speaking to Parliament from the throne, the president delivered his inaugural address personally to the Congress, and like the two houses of Parliament, both houses of Congress formally responded and then waited upon the president at his residence.

The English monarchy was the model for the new republican government in other respects as well. The Senate, the body in the American government that most closely resembled the House of Lords, voted that writs of the federal government ought to run in the name of the president—just as writs in England ran in the name of the king. Although the House refused to go along, the Supreme Court used the Senate's form for its writs. The Senate also tried to have all American coins bear the head of the president, as was the case with the European monarchs.

Although the high-toned Federalists eventually lost this proposal to put the president's impression on the coins, they made many such attempts to surround the new government with some of the trappings of monarchy. They drew up elaborate monarchlike rules of etiquette at what soon came to be denounced as the "American Court."[21] They established formal levees for the president where, as critics said, Washington was "seen in public on Stated times like an Eastern Lama."[22] Led by Vice President Adams, the Senate debated for a month in 1789 the proper title for the president. He could not be called simply "His Excellency," for governors of the states were called that. "A royal or at least a princely title," said

Adams, "will be found indispensably necessary to maintain the reputation, authority, and dignity of the President." Only something like "His Highness, or, if you will, His Most Benign Highness" would do.[23] Eventually, under Adams's prodding, a Senate committee reported the title "His Highness the President of the United States of America, and Protector of their Liberties." When Jefferson learned of Adams's obsession with titles and the Senate's action, he could only shake his head and recall Benjamin Franklin's now-famous characterization of Adams as someone who was always an honest man, often a wise one, but sometimes on some things absolutely out of his mind.[24]

But apparently not the only one out of his mind, for Washington himself had supposedly initially favored for a title "His High Mightiness, the President of the United States and Protector of Their Liberties."[25] But when the president heard the criticism that such titles smacked of monarchy, he changed his mind and was relieved when the House of Representatives under Madison's leadership succeeded in fixing the simple title of "Mr. President." Still, the talk of royalizing the new republic continued and heightened the fears of many Americans. The financial program of Secretary of the Treasury Hamilton, with its funded debt and Bank of the United States, was modeled on that of the British monarchy. Indeed, like the British ministers of His Majesty George III's government, Hamilton sought to use patronage and every other source of influence to win support for his and Washington's programs. To many other Americans, however, it looked as if British monarchical corruption had spread to America.

Because of these very real apprehensions of monarchy and monarchical corruption, the first decade or so under the new American Constitution could never be a time of ordinary politics. In fact, the entire period was wracked by a series of crises that threatened to destroy the national government that had been so recently and painstakingly created. The new expanded republic of the United States was an unprecedented political experiment, and everyone knew that. No similar national republic in modern times had ever extended over such a large extent of territory. Since all theory and all history were against the success of this republican experiment, the political leaders worried about every unanticipated development. With even President Washington's having suggested at the conclusion of the Constitutional Convention that the new federal government might not last twenty years, most political leaders in the 1790s had no great faith that the Union would survive. In such uneasy and fearful circumstances, politics could never be what we today regard as normal.

The political parties that emerged in the 1790s—the Federalists and the Republicans—were not modern parties, and competition between them was anything but what some scholars used to call "the first party system." No one thought that the emergence of parties was a good thing; indeed, far from building a party system in the 1790s, the nation's leaders struggled to prevent one from developing. The Federalists under the leadership of Washington, Adams, and Hamilton never saw themselves as a party but as the beleaguered legitimate government beset by people allied with Revolutionary France out to destroy the Union. Although the Republicans, under the leadership of Jefferson and Madison, did reluctantly describe themselves as a party, they believed they were only a temporary one, designed to prevent the United States from becoming a Federalist-led British-backed monarchy. Since neither the Federalists nor the Republicans accepted the legitimacy of the other, partisan feelings ran very high, making the bitter clash between Hamilton and Jefferson, for example, more than just personal. Indeed, the 1790s became one of the most passionate and divisive decades in American history.

This is the best context for understanding the 1790s and Jefferson's election as president in 1800. Otherwise we can never make full sense of the extraordinary events and behavior of people in the period: the many riots and the burning of officials in effigy; the viciousness of the press; the many duels; the fighting and wrestling in the halls of Congress; the Alien and Sedition Acts that gave the government extraordinary powers to deal with aliens and to prosecute libel against federal officials; the astonishingly improper and indiscreet actions of officials in dealing with foreign powers, actions that in our own time might be labeled treasonous. Only by taking seriously the feeling of many Americans that the

Federalists in the 1790s were well on their way to reintroducing monarchy in America can we understand the significance of the election of Thomas Jefferson as president in 1800. Jefferson sincerely believed that his "revolution of 1800" was, as he later said, "as real a revolution in the principles of our government as that of 1776 was in its form."[26] He thought, with some justification, that he had saved the republic from monarchy.

From our present perspective, it is hard to take seriously Jefferson's belief in the revolutionary significance of his election (especially since the kind of fiscal-military quasimonarchical state the Federalists wanted for the United States has actually come into being; Hamilton surely would have loved the Pentagon and the CIA, and America's huge standing army). From our viewpoint, then, Jefferson's election does not seem all that bold and radical. At the outset he struck a note of conciliation: We are all republicans—we are all federalists, he said; and some Federalists were soon absorbed into the Republican Party. Jefferson's administration, as historian Henry Adams delighted in pointing out, did deviate from strict Republican principles. Thus the continuities are impressive, and the Jefferson "revolution of 1800" has blended nearly imperceptibly into the main democratic currents of American history.

However, compared to the consolidated and centralized state that the Federalists wanted to build in the 1790s, the Republicans after 1800 proved that something akin to a real revolution did take place. Jefferson radically reduced the power of the federal government. He turned it into something resembling the Articles of Confederation more than the European-type state the Federalists desired. In fact, the Jeffersonian Republicans sought to create a general government that would rule without the traditional attributes of power.

From the outset Jefferson was determined that the new government would lack even the usual rituals of power. He purposefully set a new tone of republican simplicity in contrast to the stiff formality and regal ceremony with which the Federalists, in imitation of European court life, had surrounded the presidency. Since the Federalist presidents (Washington and Adams), like the English monarch, had personally delivered their addresses to the legislature "from the throne," Jefferson chose to submit his in writing (a practice that was continued until the presidency of Woodrow Wilson). Unlike Washington and Adams, he made himself easily accessible to visitors. In order to contrast his administration with those of his predecessors, he sought greater casualness in the White House, even to the point of greeting the British minister in carpet slippers. He replaced the protocol and distinctions of European court life with egalitarian rules of pell-mell, or "first into their seats."

Jefferson left unbuilt Washington's plans for a magnificent capital befitting the new American empire. Jefferson wanted the national government to be insignificant. The federal government, he declared in his first message to Congress in 1801, was "charged with the external affairs and mutual relations only of these states." All the rest—the "principal care of persons, our property, and our reputation, constituting the great field of human concerns"—was to be left to the states. He and his Republicans set about reversing a decade of Federalist policy. Although the Federalist establishment was minuscule by even eighteenth-century standards (the War Department, for example, consisted of only the secretary, an accountant, fourteen clerks, and two messengers), Jefferson thought the bureaucracy had become "too complicated, too expensive," and offices under the Federalists had "unnecessarily multiplied."[27] Thus the roll of federal officials was severely cut back. All tax inspectors and collectors were eliminated. The diplomatic establishment was reduced to three missions—to Britain, France, and Spain. The Federalist dream of creating a European-type army and navy disappeared; the military budget was cut in half. The army, stationed only in the West, was reduced to 3,000 men and 172 officers. The navy was cut back to several hundred gunboats for defensive purposes only. Hamilton's financial program was dismantled or allowed to lapse and all federal taxes were eliminated. For most people, the national government's presence was reduced to the delivery of the mail.

When the Republicans under President James Madison came to fight the War of 1812 with Great Britain, they refused to strengthen the government's capacity to wage it. Better that the enemy burn the nation's capital than surrender to a Hamiltonian enhancement of federal power. Thus the Republicans sought to fight the war without having to raise taxes, increase the debt, enlarge the military forces, or expand the executive. They wanted to prove that even war could be waged without the usual instruments of power.

When Andrew Jackson became president in 1828, the republican principles of the United States seemed so secure that the Jacksonian Democrats felt they could reassert some the older aspects of monarchism inherent in the presidency without fear of political retribution. Perhaps the Jacksonian era is less the era of the common man and more the era of consolidation and reintegration than we have usually allowed. The Jacksonians developed the use of patronage—the "spoils system"—to a fine art; they built up the federal bureaucracy, and under Jackson's leadership they turned the presidency into the most popular and powerful office in the nation. Jackson's opponents, in retaliation, called him "King Andrew" and called themselves Whigs, invoking the old English name for the opponents of bloated crown power. But the earlier fear of monarchy was now gone, and the Whigs could never really capitalize on their antimonarchical ideology.

Yet monarchism was latent in the powerful office of the presidency and it has been revived by various presidents over the subsequent decades of American history. Article II of the Constitution is so vague that many presidents under wartime conditions have expanded executive authority to unanticipated lengths. Much of the so-called unitary executive was there at the outset. It may even be possible to argue that the presidency created in 1787 inherited all the prerogative powers of the English king save those that were explicitly assigned to the Congress, such as the powers to declare war, erect courts, and coin money. As we know from the history of the past half century, even the power to declare war has slipped back into the president's hands.

Thus the imperial presidency of the twentieth century and early twenty-first century was built into the office from the beginning. One could argue that republicanism has survived in the United States not by repudiating but by absorbing some of the essential elements of monarchy. Vice President John Adams may have had little sense of political correctness, but he was honest to the core and maybe very accurate indeed when he called the United States a republican monarchy.

AFTERWORD TO CHAPTER 8

This paper began as the Bernard Bailyn Lecture given at La Trobe University in Australia in 2000 and was published separately by La Trobe University. It has been much revised since then. In addition to the expansion of the president's powers during wartime mentioned in the essay, the president's role in domestic affairs from the New Deal on has grown as well. Sometimes the Congress has fought back against this executive aggrandizement, creating its own budget office, for example, to counter the executive's dominance over finance. But the crisis-ridden nature of modern life makes resisting the expansion of executive energy difficult. Over the past seven decades the president, like a royal monarch, has taken the country into war six times without the formal congressional declaration of war that is mandated by the Constitution. More recently the president has moved aggressively into the economy, asserting, for example, unprecedented control over the automobile and banking industries. The monarch-like character of the United States government seems more evident today than ever before.

CHAPTER NINE

ILLUSIONS *of* POWER *in* *the* AWKWARD ERA *of* FEDERALISM

T HE NATIONAL GOVERNMENT created by the Constitution was inaugurated in 1789 with more optimism and more consensus among the American people than at any time since the Declaration of Independence. A common enthusiasm for the new Constitution momentarily obscured the deep differences that existed among the national leaders and the states and sections they represented. The unanimous election of Washington as the first president gave the new government an immediate respectability it otherwise would not have had. A sense of beginning anew, of putting the republican experiment on a new and stronger foundation, ran through communities up and down the continent. By 1789 even the leading opponents of the Constitution, the Anti-Federalists, had come to accept it, though of course with an expectation of its soon being amended. In fact, none of the Anti-Federalists in 1787 had been opposed to some sort of strengthening of the national government; they simply had not anticipated as strong a central government as the Constitution had created. Consequently, the former opponents of the Constitution were really in no position to oppose the new national government without giving it a chance.

It was a liberal, humanitarian, and cosmopolitan age. The country's leaders saw America's "rising empire" fulfilling at long last the promises of the Enlightenment. Freemasonry flourished, and orators everywhere promised an end to ignorance and superstition and the beginnings of a new era of reason, benevolence, and fraternity. It was a heroic age in which men talked of the aristocratic passions—of greatness, honor, and the desire for fame. It was a neoclassical age, an Augustan Age, as historian Linda K. Kerber has called it, an age of stability following a revolutionary upheaval in which art and literature would thrive.[1] Never in American history have the country's leaders voiced such high expectations for the cultural achievements of the nation as did Americans in the 1790s. The arts and sciences were inevitably moving across the Atlantic to the New World and bringing America into a golden age.

By whatever term the Federalist age might be called, it was in fact a very brief one. It disappeared so fast that we have a hard time recovering or understanding it. The consensus and optimism of 1789 quickly evaporated, and the decade that had begun so hopefully turned into one of the most passionate and divisive periods of American history. By the end of the 1790s the United States was on the verge of civil war, and the "whole system of American Government," in the opinion of the British foreign secretary, was "tottering to its foundations."[2]

The decade of the 1790s is the most awkward in American history. It seems unrelated to what preceded or followed it, a fleeting moment of heroic neoclassical dreams that were unsupported by American reality. The self-conscious, self-molded, self-controlled character of George Washington was the perfect symbol for the age, for, like Washington himself, the entire Federalist project was a monumental act of will in the face of contrary circumstances. The Federalists stood in the way of popular democracy as it was emerging in the United States, and thus they became heretics opposed to the developing democratic faith. Everything seemed to turn against them. They thought they were creating a classically heroic state, and they attempted everywhere to symbolize these classical aims. Instead they left only a legacy of indecipherable icons, unread poetry, antique place names, and a proliferation of Greek and Roman temples. They despised political parties, but parties nonetheless emerged to shatter the remarkable harmony of 1789. They sought desperately in the 1790s to avoid conflict with the former mother country to the point that they appeared to be compromising the independence of the new nation, only to discover in the end that the war with Great Britain they had avoided was to be fought anyway in 1812 by the subsequent administration of their opponents. By the early nineteenth century, Alexander Hamilton, the brilliant leader of the Federalists, who more than anyone pursued the heroic dreams of the age, was not alone in his despairing conclusion "that this American world was not meant for me."[3]

The Federalist age was awkward because so many of America's leaders were heroically confident they were in control of events. No generation in American history was so acutely conscious that what it did would affect future generations, or, in the common phrase of the day, "millions yet unborn." The leaders felt an awesome responsibility not only for America's governments and political institutions but for its art, literature, and manners—indeed, for the entire culture.

But of course they were never in charge of events or circumstances. Everything was moving and changing much too fast. Indeed, it is the gap between the leaders' pretensions of control and the dynamic reality of the forces they were attempting to deal with that accounts for the strangeness and awkwardness of the decade. Subsequent generations of American leaders usually have had a much less heroic attitude about themselves. Mid-nineteenth-century leaders always had a sense of being caught up by forces larger than themselves, of being carried along by inevitable elements—whether called providence, progress, public opinion, or simply the popular masses. But most American leaders of the 1790s still clung to an older hierarchical-gentry world that assumed that a few men at the top could control and manipulate events and shape circumstances. The decade of the 1790s was the last gasp of an American eighteenth-century patrician world quickly lost and largely forgotten—a world of aristocratic assumptions, heroic leadership, and powdered wigs and knee breeches. It was a world soon to be overwhelmed by the most popular, most licentious, and most commercially ridden society history had ever known.

Most of what happened in the period was unanticipated and unwanted by the Founding Fathers. The sudden transformation of the electoral college in the election of the president, which had been the consequence of complicated and painstaking compromises by the Philadelphia Convention, was only the most graphic example of the best-laid plans gone amiss.

It may be hard for us today to see how much in the decade turned out differently from what the leaders at the time expected, for many of their hopes and dreams did eventually get realized, even if decades or centuries after being formulated. Consequently, we tend to give the Federalists and other leaders of the decade credit for foresight and for laying the proper foundations for the future even if they were unable to bring about much in their own lifetimes. The city of Washington, D.C., is a good example. The plans for it were truly monumental, but the implementation of those plans was a long time coming. For a good part of the nineteenth century the national capital remained the butt of jokes, a city of open spaces and long distances, "bearing," as one observer said, "the marks of partial labour and general desertion."[4] Only after mid-century, or perhaps only at the beginning of the twentieth century—some might say only in the past fifty years—did the Federal City begin to resemble what L'Enfant and others originally had hoped for it. Other dreams of the 1790s have likewise been gradually realized in time. But the fact that many of the hopes and aspirations of the Federalist era have eventually come to pass should not obscure the extent of disillusionment and unfulfilled expectation that dominated that bizarre and stormy decade.

Many of the issues of the decades reveal to one degree or another the gap that existed between the leaders' plans and purposes on one hand and the reality of dynamic social circumstances on the other. Few of the public decision makers, whether Hamilton or Jefferson, whether Federalist or Republican, clearly understood the complicated historical forces they were dealing with, or if they did, were able to control or manipulate those forces.

The problem can be most fully seen in the ways in which the national government was created in the 1790s. Certainly the political leaders had high hopes for the launching of the ship of state. But though they commonly resorted to a nautical image of launching a new ship, they also realized that in 1789 much of their ship existed only on the drawing boards. Not only was the ship of state largely unbuilt, but the plans and blueprints for it were general and vague enough that the size and shape of the ship still remained uncertain; it was not even clear what the ship would be designed to do. Everyone realized that the nature, purposes, and strength of the new national government all had to be worked out, and beneath the outward consensus of 1789 nearly everyone had his own ideas about what these ought to be.

Because the government was so unformed and the future so problematical, the stakes were high, and men knew that precedents were being set. Consequently, every issue, no matter how trivial, seemed loaded with significance. Many members of the Senate did not think they were wasting their time in spending a month debating the proper title for addressing the president. From that title, whether "His Highness" or simply "Mr. President," might flow the very character of the future government and state.

In such uncertain circumstances the advantage lay with those whose vision was clearest, whose purposes were most certain, and this meant the Federalist leaders, and in particular Alexander Hamilton, the secretary of the treasury. From 1787 the most nationally minded of the Federalists had wanted the United States to be no mere confederation of disparate states but a republican government in its own right with the power to act energetically in the public sphere—to be a mercantilist state. In building such an integrated national state, the Federalist leaders saw their principal political problem as one of adhesion: how to keep people in such a large sprawling republic from flying apart in pursuit of their partial local interests. This, of course, as Montesquieu had said, was the central problem for any republic, but it was especially a problem for a huge extended republic like the United States. Republics were supposed to rely for cohesion on the moral qualities of their people—their virtue and their natural sociability; unlike monarchies they had to be held together from below, by their natural affection and benevolence and by their willingness to sacrifice their partial and private interests for the sake of the public good.

In today's language, what was essential for republics was the existence of a civil society—all those voluntary associations and institutions that stand between the state and the individual. In our own time it has been the new states of Eastern Europe and the Middle East that have revived this Scottish Enlightenment emphasis on the importance of a civil society. In light of efforts of the ex-communist states of Eastern Europe and the states of the Middle East to erect viable democratic societies, we today can perhaps more fully understand the significance of a civil society to the workings of a popular government. Certainly we are in a better position than previous generations of Americans to appreciate the weaknesses of republics and the advantages of monarchies and authoritarian governments in holding peoples of diverse backgrounds, interests, and ethnicities together.

By 1789 many of the Federalists, particularly Hamilton, had no confidence whatsoever left in the virtue or the natural sociability of the American people as adhesive forces: to rely on such wild schemes and visionary principles, as radicals like Jefferson and Paine did, to tie the United States together, the Federalists said, was to rely on nothing. Hence Hamilton and the other Federalist leaders had to find things other than republican virtue and natural sociability to make the American people a single nation.

Tying people together, creating social cohesiveness, making a single nation out of disparate sections and communities without relying on idealistic republican adhesives—this was the preoccupation of the Federalists, and it explains much of what they did—from Washington's proposals for building canals to Hamilton's financial program. As we saw in the previous essay, many of the Federalists actually thought in terms of turning the government of the United States into a surrogate monarchy, of devising substitutes for traditional monarchical ligaments and placing them within a republican framework.[5]

In place of the impotent confederation of separate states that had existed in the 1780s, the Federalists envisioned a strong, consolidated, and prosperous national state, united, as Hamilton said, "for the accomplishment of great purposes" and led by an energetic government composed of the best and most distinguished men in the society.[6] As we have seen, they aimed to bolster the dignity of this government by adopting some of the ceremony and majesty of monarchy. Many of the Federalists, in short, aimed to make the United States in time a grand, illustrious nation and a rival of the great monarchies of Europe. Hamilton especially envisioned the new national government in traditional European fashion as a great military power. The federal government for him was not to be, as it was for James Madison, simply a disinterested umpire making judicial-like decisions among a number of competing interests. Hamilton wanted to use central state power positively in order to turn the United States into "something noble and magnificent." He and some other Federalists dreamed of making the United States the equal of the European monarchies on their own terms—terms that, as Washington said, were "characteristic of wise and powerful Nations."[7] This meant a strong central government that reached to all parts of an integrated nation with a powerful army and navy that commanded the respect of all the world.

Hamilton's model was England, and he consciously set out to duplicate the great English achievement of the eighteenth century. England had emerged from the chaos and civil wars of the seventeenth century that had killed one king and deposed another to become the most dominant power in the world. That this small island on the northern edge of Europe with a third of the population of France was able to build the biggest empire since the fall of Rome was the miracle of the century, even surpassing the astonishing achievement of the Netherlands in the previous century. The English "fiscal-military state," in John Brewer's apt term, could mobilize wealth and wage war as no state in history ever had. Its centralized administration had developed an extraordinary capacity to tax and borrow from its subjects without impoverishing them.[8] Hamilton saw that the secret of England's success was its system of funded debt together with its banking structure and its market in public securities. He aimed to do for the United States what English ministers had done for the former mother country. His financial program followed directly from this aim.

Hamilton was undoubtedly concerned with the commercial prosperity of the United States—with furthering "the interests of a great people"—but he was scarcely the capitalist promoter of America's emerging business culture that he is often described as being. He was a traditional eighteenth-century statesman, willing to allow ordinary people their profits and property, their interests and their petty pursuits of happiness, but wanting honor and glory for himself and his country. He was very much the mercantilist who believed deeply in the "need" in government for "a common directing power." He had only contempt for those who believed in laissez-faire and thought that trade and interests could regulate themselves. "This," he said, "is one of those wild speculative paradoxes which have grown into credit among us, contrary to the uniform practice and sense of the most enlightened nations. . . . It must be rejected by every man acquainted with commercial history."[9]

Of course, he accepted the prevalence of interests—indeed, he thought there could be no other tie but interest between most people in the society. He himself, however, was extraordinarily scrupulous as secretary of the treasury in maintaining his personal disinterestedness and freedom from corruption. Let others, including congressmen, become "speculators" and "peculators," but not he. He was determined to stand above all the interested men and try to harness and use them. He agreed with the eighteenth-century British economic philosopher Sir James Steuart that "self-interest . . . is the main spring and only motive which a statesman should make use of, to engage a free people to concur in the plans which he lays down for their government." Although he later and rather defensively denied that he had ever made self-interest "the weightiest motive" behind his financial program, there is no doubt that he thought the debt and other financial measures would strengthen the national government "by increasing the number of ligaments between the Government and the interests of Individuals."[10]

In effect, in the opposition language of the eighteenth-century Anglo-American world, Hamilton set out to "corrupt" American society, to use monarchical-like governmental influence to tie existing commercial interests to the government and to create new hierarchies of interest and dependency that would substitute for the absence of virtue and the apparently weak republican adhesives existing in America. In local areas, Hamilton and the Federalist leaders built up followings among Revolutionary War veterans and members of the Society of the Cincinnati. They appointed important and respectable local figures to the federal judiciary and other federal offices. They exploited the patronage of the treasury department and its seven hundred or more customs officials, revenue agents, and postmasters with particular effectiveness. By 1793 or so the Federalists had formed groups of "friends of government" in most of the states. Their hierarchies of patronage and dependency ran from the federal executive through Congress down to the various localities. It was as close to monarchy and a British system of corruption and influence made famous by Prime Minister Robert Walpole as America was ever to have.

At the same time the Federalists sought to wean the people's affections away from their state governments and to get them to feel the power of what they hoped would become a consolidated national government. The Constitution had attempted to reduce drastically the power of the states. Article I, Section 10, among other things, had forbidden the states from levying tariffs or duties on imports or exports and had barred them from issuing paper money or bills of credit. As these were the principal means by which premodern governments raised money, their prohibition cut deeply into the fiscal competency of the state governments. Some Federalists hoped to go further and eventually reduce the states to mere administrative units of the national government. Hamilton, at the time the Constitution was drafted, had hoped that the new federal government would "triumph altogether over the state governments and reduce them to an intire subordination, dividing the larger states into smaller districts."[11] Washington thought that the states might in time have no occasion for taxes and "consequently may abandon all the subjects of taxation to the Union." The federal excise taxes, especially the tax on whiskey, were designed to make people feel the authority of the national government. In a like way, the raising of nearly 15,000 militiamen by the national government to put down the Whiskey Rebellion flowed from Hamilton's assumption, voiced in 1794, that "government can never [be] said to be established until some signal display, has manifested its power of military coercion."[12]

But the national government could not rely on military force to keep people in line. Other more subtle and more ostensibly republican means were needed to control the surging democratic passions of the people. The Federalists found one answer in the judiciary. They were eager to make judges a bulwark against the unruly democratic consequences of the Revolution. Since the 1780s, those concerned about rampaging state legislatures and their abuses of private property and minority rights, particularly those of creditors, had conducted a propaganda campaign to strengthen the judiciary.

Judges in colonial America had been relatively insignificant members of government; they had been viewed largely as appendages or extensions of the royal governors or chief magistrates, who usually appointed them at the pleasure of the crown. At the time of the Revolution, Americans had done little to enhance the judiciary's negligible status. In their Revolutionary state constitutions of 1776 they had taken away the appointment of judges from the governors and had given it to the state legislatures, and through codification schemes they had tried further to reduce the importance of judges by turning them into what Jefferson called "a mere machine."[13]

In the following decades all this was reversed. Suddenly in the 1780s and 1790s, the judiciary in America emerged out of its earlier insignificance to become a full-fledged partner in what was now defined as the tripartite system of American government—sharing power equally with legislatures and executives. Many, in fact, thought that the judiciary had become the principal means for controlling popular legislatures and protecting private rights. The most dramatic institutional transformation in the early Republic was this rise of what was commonly referred to as an "independent judiciary." It is a fascinating story still not fully told.

It is not surprising, therefore, that the Federalists should have been concerned with creating strong judiciaries, not only in the states but especially in the new federal government. No institution of the new national government would be less susceptible to popular democratic pressure and yet touch the lives of ordinary people in their localities more than a federal court system. Thus the Federalists fought hard to create a separate national court structure in which, they hoped, the common law of crimes would run. The Judiciary Act of 1789, which gave concurrent original jurisdiction to the state courts, was scarcely satisfactory to the more nationally minded Federalists, and throughout the 1790s they struggled to expand the power and jurisdiction of the federal courts. The Judiciary Act of 1801 and the broadened and constructive interpretations of national law by federal judges in the 1790s, including that of treason, were manifestations of these efforts. The actions of the Marshall Court in subsequent years—as its repudiation of the idea that the common law of crimes ran in the federal courts and its limited definition of treason in the Burr trial show—were far from being extensions of national power and were in fact retreats from the advanced and exposed positions that the Federalists of the 1790s attempted to stake out for the national judiciary.[14]

All these grand and grandiose aims of the Federalist leaders, particularly of the high-toned Federalists, are a measure of their disillusionment with what the Revolution had done to American society and their confidence that they now had the national solution to the problems of the country. Their disillusionment had in fact been widely shared among America's gentry leadership in 1787 and had helped create the Constitution. But the degrees of disillusionment were vastly different among even fervent supporters of the Constitution. James Madison, for example, certainly shared Hamilton's misgivings about democracy and his desire to reduce popular state power; and he surely wanted a commercially strong mercantilist national government that would be able both to pass navigation acts and protect minority creditor rights in the several states. But he and others who had created and supported the Constitution, particularly in the Southern and mid-Atlantic states, did not share Hamilton's vision of the United States becoming a consolidated European-like "fiscal-military" power. Nor did they ever really doubt the popular basis of America's governments.[15] Indeed, Madison, Jefferson, and the Republicans never accepted the newly emerging European idea of the modern state, with its elaborate administrative structures, large armies and navies, high taxes, and huge debts. The Republicans' rejection of this modern state had immense implications for America's future.

The high-toned High-Federalists' attempts to impose such a state on America eventually divided the gentry-leaders of the nation and led to passionate factional splits throughout the country. Jefferson and the Republicans came to believe quite sincerely that Hamilton and the Federalists were out to create a monarchy in America. Although Hamilton with equal sincerity denied that that was ever his aim, popular Republican resistance to his projects only made him and the High-Federalists more desperate. By the end of the decade the Federalists had become truly frightened by the popular direction of events and felt compelled to pass alien and sedition acts and to make plans for war involving the creation of armies in the tens of thousands and the calling of Washington back into uniform as commander of these troops. Hamilton even toyed with the idea of dismantling the states.

We know how it all turned out—with Jefferson's election in 1800 and peaceful accession to power in 1801—and consequently we find it hard to take the fears of either the Federalists or the Republicans very seriously. But both had good reason to be frightened, for there were forces at work in the 1790s that neither the Federalists nor the Republicans fully understood or could control. The consequence was that many of their best intentions went awry.

The men who wrote the Constitution had expected to attract to the national government the best people, "men who possess the most attractive merit and the most diffusive and established characters," in Madison's words, or "men of discernment and liberality," as Washington described them.[16] They knew whom they meant even if we have a hard time defining such people. They meant men pretty much like themselves, gentlemen of talent and distinction, with all that the term "gentlemen" implied in the eighteenth century. Such gentlemen should ideally be educated in the liberal arts at a good college like Harvard or Princeton, or if not, at least self-cultivated and with sufficient wealth and independence that they did not have to earn a living in too blatant or mercenary a fashion. Madison was apprehensive that the First Congress was going to be composed of the same sorts of illiberal and narrow-minded men who had sat in the state legislatures, and he was relieved at the character of most of the congressmen he met. But it soon became evident that his elevated republic was not going to be high enough to keep out permanently the middling and other ordinary and interested people who had caused so much difficulty in the state legislatures in the 1780s. In the northern parts of America, at least, all levels of government were steadily being democratized and occupied by people with interests to promote. By the Second Congress, even William Findley, an ex-weaver from Pennsylvania and a prototype of the plebeian Anti-Federalists, made it into the elevated national government that was designed to keep his type out.

The problem was that Washington's "men of discernment and liberality" were hard to find and even when found lacked sufficient income to behave as disinterested gentlemen in government were supposed to behave. By 1795 President Washington was having trouble recruiting proper men for the highest federal offices, including the cabinet. Federalists in the House of Representatives charged that Jefferson, Hamilton, and Henry Knox had all resigned from the cabinet "chiefly for one reason, the smallness of the salary."[17] Although this was not at the case with Jefferson, both Knox and Hamilton did have trouble maintaining a genteel standard of living on their government salaries. There were of course plenty of claimants for the middle and lower offices of the government, but these were lesser sorts of men who were quite openly seeking the offices in order to make a living from them.

The truth was that the entire Federalist scheme rested on a false understanding of America's gentry. Washington, like other Federalists, conceived of his "men of discernment and liberality" in classically republican terms, as gentlemen of leisure and independence who were generally free of direct market interests and who therefore could take up the burden of public office as a disinterested obligation of their social rank. By proposing in the Philadelphia Convention that all members of the executive be barred from receiving any salaries or fees, Benjamin Franklin was simply expressing an extreme version of this classical republican view of officeholding. But the fact of the matter was that members of the American aristocracy, with the exception of a few wealthy individuals like Franklin and many Southern gentry like Washington and Jefferson, were incapable of living up to the classical image of a leisured patriciate serving in public office without compensation.

Heaven knows many of them tried to live up to the classical image, often with disastrous consequences for themselves and their families. Merchants who wanted to hold high public office usually had to ennoble themselves and put their mercantile property into a rentier form—John Hancock and Robert Morris being notable examples. As we have seen, the goal was to get enough wealth, preferably in the form of land, so that one did not have to work at accumulating money on a regular basis and in an acquisitive manner. All the desperate efforts of men like Morris, James Wilson, and Henry Knox to find genteel independence for themselves through land speculation—efforts that ended in ruin and sometimes debtors' prison—are measures of the power of that classical image of a leisured patriciate. For it was evident to the eighteenth-century gentry, even if not to us, that one could not acquire real independence of the marketplace without having that independence based on what historian George V. Taylor, in reference to eighteenth-century France, calls "proprietary wealth."[18]

Such proprietary wealth was composed of static forms of property— "unearned income," as we might call it: rents from tenants, bonds, interest from money out on loan—that allowed its holders sufficient leisure to assume the burdens of public office without expecting high salaries. These kinds of proprietary property holders were those Washington had in mind when he used the term "the monied gentry."[19] These monied gentry, with their static proprietary wealth, were of course very vulnerable to inflation, which is why the printing of paper money was so frightening to them. Although these proprietary gentry, like their counterparts in England, were often involved in various commercial ventures, they were not risk-taking entrepreneurs or businessmen in any modern sense. Instead, they were social leaders whose property was the source of their personal authority and independence; inflation therefore threatened not simply their livelihood but their very identity and social position. Until we grasp this point, we will never appreciate the depth of moral indignation behind the gentry's outcry against paper money and other debtor-relief legislation in the 1780s.

Of course, not only was this kind of proprietary wealth very hard to come by in America—where, compared to England, land was so plentiful and tenantry so rare—but commerce and trade were creating new forms of property that gave wealth and power to new sorts of people. This new property was anything but static: it was risk-taking, entrepreneurial capital—not money out on loan, but money borrowed. It was in fact all the paper money that enterprising people clamored for in these years. It was not "unearned income" that came to a person, as Adam Smith defined the rents of the English landed gentry, without exertion, but "earned income" that came *with* exertion—indeed, came with labor, production, and exchange. This was the property of businessmen and protobusinessmen—of commercial farmers, artisan-manufacturers, traders, shopkeepers, and all who labored for a living and produced and exchanged things, no matter how poor or wealthy they might be.

The increasing distinctions drawn in these years between, in the words of the uneducated New England farmer William Manning, "those that labour for a Living and those that git a Living without Bodily Labour," which included all gentry-professionals, expressed the rise of this new kind of property.[20] Unlike proprietary wealth, this new kind of dynamic, fluid, and evanescent property could not create personal authority or identity; it was, said Joseph Story, "continually changing like the waves of the sea."[21] Hence it was meaningless to rely on it as a source of independence. Once this was understood, then property qualifications for participation in public life either as voters or officeholders lost their relevance and rapidly fell away. The William Mannings and the William Findleys who spoke for these new kinds of entrepreneurial and labor-produced property—for "earned income"—were precisely the sorts of illiberal and parochial men that liberal gentry like Madison in the 1780s had condemned.[22]

But Madison, Jefferson, and other Southern gentry leaders of the Republicans no more understood what was happening to American society and to property than did Hamilton and the Federalists. Nor did Hamilton and Jefferson understand very clearly the direction the American economy was taking. Both assumed that the future prosperity of the United States lay essentially with foreign trade, and they were both wrong: it lay mainly with domestic or internal trade, with the United States becoming "a world within themselves."[23] Eighteenth-century leaders had difficulty putting great value on internal trade because of their lingering zero-sum mercantilist assumption that a nation's wealth as a whole could grow only at the expense of another nation; that is, the country as a whole could prosper only by selling more abroad than it bought.[24]

Domestic trade was thought to benefit only individuals or regions but not the country as a whole; it simply moved wealth about without increasing its total. Those involved in domestic commerce, however, had a different sense of where the future prosperity of the country lay, but they needed paper money to carry on their internal trading—lots of it. Article I, Section 10 of the Constitution had prohibited the states from printing bills of credit, but the needs and desires of all the protobusinessmen and domestic traders were too great to be stymied by a paper restriction. So the states, under popular pressure, got around the constitutional prohibition by chartering banks, hundreds upon hundreds of them, which in turn issued the paper money people wanted. Hamilton no more predicted or wanted this proliferation of banks and paper money than did Jefferson;

he and other Federalists had in fact thought the Bank of the United States would absorb the state banks and have a monopoly on banking and the issuing of currency.[25]

Both Hamilton and Jefferson equally underestimated the importance of artisan-manufacturing. As historian Joyce Appleby has told us, Jefferson and the Republican Party benefited from artisan and business support in the mid-Atlantic states, but Jefferson never fully grasped this point; he never appreciated the nature of the popular commercial forces he was presumably leading.[26] Hamilton's biggest political mistake was to ignore the interests of the artisan-manufacturers. Despite his 1791 "Report on Manufactures," which presumably recognized the importance of domestic commerce, Hamilton, as John R. Nelson has told us, never had his heart in manufacturing and never pushed to implement his report; instead, his program actually favored moneyed men and import merchants at the expense of domestic producers and traders.[27] Consequently, artisans in the mid-Atlantic states who had been fervent Federalists in 1787–1788 were eventually driven into the ranks of the Republican Party—except in New England. The exception is illuminating. Too many of the New England artisans were too closely tied to patron-client relationships with wealthy overseas merchants in New England's port cities to develop as sharp a sense of their separate interests as that possessed by the mid-Atlantic artisans. From 1793 to 1807 New England's interests and prosperity were almost entirely absorbed in overseas trade. As a result, the emphasis Hamilton's program placed on overseas trade skewed Federalist support toward New England and helped to mask the fact that the future prosperity of the United States lay largely in the development of domestic commerce and not in international shipping.

In other areas as well, gentry leaders of all sections and both parties lived with illusions and misunderstood the realities of American society. Many leaders in the 1790s, for example, thought that slavery was on its way to ultimate extinction. The American Revolution had unleashed enlightened principles of liberty that seemed to make the disappearance of slavery just a matter of time: David Ramsay of South Carolina thought there would "not be a slave in these states fifty years hence."[28] Liberal opinion everywhere in the world condemned the institution. When even Southerners like Jefferson, Patrick Henry, and Henry Laurens deplored the injustice of slavery, from "that moment," many believed, "the slow, but certain, death-wound was inflicted upon it."[29]

Of course, as we know, such predictions could not have been more wrong: far from being doomed, slavery in the United States in the 1790s was on the verge of its greatest expansion. But such self-deception, such mistaken optimism, among the Revolutionary leaders was understandable, for they wanted to believe the best, and there was some evidence that slavery was dying away. The Northern states, where slavery was not inconsequential, were busy trying to eliminate the institution, and by 1804 all had done so. There were indications that the same thing was happening in the Southern states, especially in the Upper South. More antislave societies existed in the South than in the North, and manumissions in the South were becoming more frequent.

Virginia, being the richest and most populous state in the nation, not only dominated the presidency but seemed to be setting the tone for the country. In Virginia alone the number of free blacks increased from 3,000 in 1780 to 13,000 by 1790. Between 1790 and 1810 the free black population in the United States grew faster than the slave population. By the 1790s all the states, including South Carolina, had ended the international slave trade. Many hoped that abolishing the importation of slaves from abroad would eventually kill off the institution of slavery. But faith in the future was not enough: the Founding Fathers had simply not counted on the remarkable demographic capacity of the old slave states themselves, especially Virginia, to produce slaves for the expanding areas of the Deep South and Southwest. Believing that slavery was dying a natural death was the most fatal of the Founders' many illusions.

Perhaps we can muster some sympathy for the Founding Fathers' difficulty in predicting the future when we take into account the breathtaking speed of events and complexity of circumstances in the 1790s. Nowhere was this speed and complexity more obvious than in the settlement of the

West, and nowhere was the gap between the leaders' illusions and reality more conspicuous than in the way they dealt with the West.

The Federalists at least were not mistaken in their sense of the fragility of the United States. It was the largest republic since ancient Rome, and as such it was continually in danger of falling apart. Indeed, fear for the integrity of the United States lay behind the Continental Congress's passage of the Northwest Ordinance of 1787. Despite its progressive promises, this plan for the colonization of American territories was actually quite reactionary. Its proposals for garrison governments with authoritarian leadership for the new western colonies resembled nothing so much as those failed seventeenth-century English efforts at establishing military governments over the obstreperous colonists.[30] The ordinance was an indication of how fearful eastern leaders were of the unruly westerners leaving the union, lured away perhaps by one European power or another.

These fears that westerners could be separated from the United States by European powers were not entirely illusory—not when popular societies were toasting the right of everyone to "remove out of the limits of these United States" at will.[31] There were indeed conspiracies involving Britain and Spain on the western borders. In fact, some British officials in Canada were convinced that they could reverse the Revolution and put the North American British Empire back together again. American fears of foreign influence help account both for the hasty admission into the Union in the 1790s of Vermont, Kentucky, and Tennessee, and for the later violations of the Northwest Ordinance's procedures for orderly territorial advancement to statehood. Since Britain in Canada was regarded as by far the more dangerous power, Americans felt they had to organize the Northwest Territory as soon as possible. Spain, on the other hand, was thought to be so decrepit, its hold on its empire so weak, that its Southern and Southwestern territories could be left to fall into American hands like so many ripe fruit. Natural demographic pressures would see to that, it being a common assumption in the 1790s that most western migrants would come from the burgeoning Southern states. This was one of several mistaken ideas that American leaders had about the future of the West.

The Federalists' western policy, including the working of the Northwest Ordinance and treatment of the Indians, rested on the assumption that settlement of the western territories would be neat and orderly. Many of the Federalist leaders were scrupulously concerned for the fate of the Indians; indeed, the statements of Secretary of War Henry Knox about the need for just treatment of the native Americans might even be deemed politically correct by a modern anthropologist. But purchasing the Indians' rights to the land and assimilating or protecting them in a civilized manner depended on an orderly and steady pace of white settlement.

So too did both the hopes for governmental revenue from the land and the plans of land speculators depend on gradual, piecemeal, and wellregulated settlement of the West. The federal government hoped to gain steady revenues by selling its western land to land companies and speculators. The speculators in turn counted on the settlers slowly filling in the territory surrounding the land they held, which would raise its value and bring them the promised returns on their investments.

Everything was built on illusions.[32] The people moving west ignored the federal government's Indian policies and refused to buy land at the expensive prices at which it was being offered. They shunned the speculators' land, violated Indian treaty rights, and moved irregularly, chaotically, unevenly, jumping from place to place and leaving huge chunks of unsettled land and pockets of hemmed-in Indians behind them. The government responded, and continued to respond until the Homestead Act of 1863, in a series of desperate efforts to keep up with popular pressures. It continually lowered the price of land, increased the credit it offered, and reduced the size of the parcels of land people had to buy; and still people complained and ignored the laws. Eventually the federal government recognized the rights of squatters to preempt the land, and finally it just gave the land away. It took more than a half century for governmental leaders to come to terms fully with the reality of popular settlement of the West.

For the Federalists of the 1790s it took less than that for most of their heroic plans and dreams to be exploded. Even if Jefferson had been somehow technically denied the presidency in 1800, most of the Federalists' blueprints for America were already doomed. They were too out of touch with the surging popular and commercial realities of American life. The demographic and economic forces at work were too powerful for any gentry leadership to overcome or any election to reverse. The secret of Jefferson's success, insofar as he had any, was his unwitting surrender to these popular commercial forces. He abandoned the Federalist goals of creating a strong, mercantilist, European-like state, reduced the power of the national government in a variety of ways, and in effect left everyone free to pursue his happiness as he saw fit. It remained for later generations of Americans—in some cases even the generation following World War II—to fulfill many of the dreams and schemes of the Federalists of the 1790s.

Perhaps our history since 1800 has been one long effort to do in two centuries what the Federalists unsuccessfully tried to do in a decade: bring under control the powerful and unruly popular and commercial forces unleashed by the Revolution and create a strong integrated nation. When we look at the huge, prosperous, and unitary fiscal-military state that we have built—the most powerful state the world has ever known— we might conclude that Hamilton and the Federalists of the 1790s have had the last laugh after all.

AFTERWORD TO CHAPTER 9

This began as a lecture opening the symposium on "Launching the 'Extended Republic'" held in the early 1990s under the auspices of the United States Capitol Historical Society. It was later published in Ronald Hoffman and Peter J. Albert, eds., *Launching the "Extended Republic": The Federalist Era* (Charlottesville: University Press of Virginia, 1996). By creating and organizing their extraordinarily successful project, *Perspectives on the American Revolution* (supported by the United States Capitol Historical Society), Hoffman and Albert have made an enormous contribution to our understanding of the Revolution and the early Republic.

For nearly twenty years, from the early 1980s to the end of the twentieth century, Hoffman and Albert, supplemented by occasional guest editors, brought out almost a dozen and a half volumes on various important issues connected with the American Revolution and its aftermath—everything from women, slavery, and Indians to religion, social developments, and patterns of consumption. It is a stunning achievement.

CHAPTER TEN

The AMERICAN ENLIGHTENMENT

T HE RATIFICATION OF the United States Constitution in 1788 was greeted with more excitement and more unanimity among the American people than at any time since the Declaration of Independence a decade earlier. "'Tis done!" declared Benjamin Rush in July 1788. "We have become a nation." This was an extravagant claim, to say the least. Yet Rush thought the new United States had become a nation virtually overnight. Everywhere in America, he said, there was "such a tide of joy as has seldom been felt in any age or country. . . . Justice has descended from heaven to dwell in our land, and ample restitution has at last been made to human nature by our new Constitution of all the injuries she has sustained in the old world from arbitrary government, false religions, and unlawful commerce." The new nation represented the "triumph of knowledge over ignorance, of virtue over vice, and of liberty over slavery."[1]

What gave Revolutionaries like Rush confidence in America's instant nationhood was their belief in America's enlightenment. As early as 1765 John Adams had declared that all of previous American history had pointed toward the eighteenth-century Enlightenment. The seventeenth-century settlement of America, he said, had opened up "a grand scene and design in Providence for the illumination of the ignorant, and the emancipation of the slavish part of mankind all over the earth."[2] The Revolution had become the climax of this great historic drama. Enlightenment was spreading everywhere in the Western world, but nowhere more so than in America. With the break from Great Britain complete and the Constitution ratified, many Americans in the 1790s thought that the United States had become the "most enlightened" nation in the world.[3]

For the people of these obscure provinces—"so recently," as Samuel Bryan of Pennsylvania declared, "a rugged wilderness and the abode of savages and wild beasts"—for these provincial people to claim to be the most enlightened nation on earth and to have "attained to a degree of improvement and greatness . . . of which history furnishes no parallel" seemed scarcely credible.[4] The United States in 1789, in comparison with the former mother country, was still an underdeveloped country. Americans had no sophisticated court life, no magnificent cities, no great concert halls, no lavish drawing rooms, and not much to speak of in the way of the fine arts. Its economy was primitive. There was as yet nothing comparable to the Bank of England; there were no stock exchanges, no large trading companies, no great centers of capital, and no readily available circulating medium of exchange. Nineteen out of twenty Americans were still employed in agriculture, and most of them lived in tiny rural communities. In 1790 there were only twenty-four towns in the entire United States with a population of 2,500 or more, and only five of these urban areas were cities with populations over 10,000. It took over two months for news of a foreign event in London to reach Philadelphia.[5] No wonder many Europeans thought of the United States as a remote wilderness at the very edges of Christendom, three thousand miles from the centers of Western civilization.

Nevertheless, as far removed from the centers of civilization as they were, many Americans persisted in believing not only that they were the most enlightened people on earth but also that because they were enlightened they were by that fact alone a nation. Indeed, America became the first nation in the world to base its nationhood solely on Enlightenment values. Gertrude Stein may have been right when she said that America was the oldest country in the world.

It was a strange kind of nationalism Revolutionary Americans asserted. For Americans to identify their nation with the Enlightenment was to identify it with transnational—indeed, universal and ecumenical—standards. They had little sense that their devotion to the universal principles of the Enlightenment was incompatible with loyalty to their state or to the country as a whole. Historian David Ramsay claimed he was "a citizen of the world and therefore despise[d] national reflections." Nevertheless, he did not believe he was being "inconsistent" in hoping that the professions would be "administered to my country by its own sons." Joel Barlow did not think he was any less American just because he was elected to the French National Convention in 1792–1793. The many state histories written in the aftermath of the Revolution were anything but celebrations of localism and the diversity of the nation. Indeed, declared Ramsay, these histories were testimonies to the American commitment to enlightened nationhood; they were designed to "wear away prejudices—rub off asperities and mould us into an homogeneous people."[6]

Homogeneous people! This is a phrase that seems to separate us most decisively from that different, distant eighteenth-century world. Because we today can take our nationhood for granted, we can indulge ourselves in the luxury of celebrating our multicultural diversity. But two hundred years ago Americans were trying to create a nation from scratch and had no such luxury. They were desperately trying to make themselves one people, and the best way they could do that was to stress their remarkable degree of enlightenment. Since the Enlightenment emphasized the value of homogeneity and of being a single people, by describing themselves as the most enlightened people in the world Americans assumed that they would thereby be a nation. More than anything else, their deep desire to be a nation is what accounts for their impassioned insistence that they were especially enlightened.

But why would they assume that they were especially enlightened? Of course, they had many European radicals like Richard Price filling their heads with the idea that they had actually created the Enlightenment. "A Spirit" that had originated in America, Price told Benjamin Franklin in 1787, was now spreading throughout the Atlantic world. This spirit, said Price, promised "a State of Society more favourable to peace, virtue, Science, and liberty (and consequently to human happiness and dignity) than has yet been known. . . . The minds of men are becoming more enlighten'd, and the silly despots of the world are likely to be forced to respect human rights and to take care not to govern too much lest they should not govern at all."[7]

But it was not simply compliments like Price's that made Americans believe that they were the most enlightened people on earth. They thought they had ample reason for their confidence. They may not have been correct in their reasoning, but it is important for us to know why they thought as they did. By doing so we can understand not only something about the origins of the United States but also something of what the Enlightenment meant to many people in the eighteenth-century Atlantic world.

Americans had no doubt that they were living in an age of Enlightenment. Everywhere the boundaries of darkness and ignorance were being pushed back and light and reason were being extended outward. More than most people in the Atlantic world, Americans were keenly aware that savagery and barbarism were giving way to refinement and civilization. Precisely because they were provincials living on the periphery of civilization, living, as historian Franco Venturi once pointed out, in a place "where the contact between a backward world and modern world was chronologically more abrupt and geographically closer," they knew what the process of becoming enlightened really meant.[8] The experience of becoming refined and civilized was more palpable and immediate for them than it was for those living in the metropolitan centers of the Old World.

Americans told themselves over and over that they were a young and forming people. And because they inhabited a New World and were in a plastic state, they were more capable of refinement and education than people stuck in the habits and prejudices of the Old World. In writings, orations, poetry—in every conceivable manner and in the most extravagant and rapturous rhetoric—Revolutionary Americans told themselves that they were more capable than any people in the world of making themselves over.

As republicans attempting to build a state from the bottom up, they were necessarily committed to Lockean sensationalism—that knowledge came less from reason and more from sense experience. Not only did such Lockean sensationalism give a new significance to the capacities of ordinary people, since all people had senses, but it also opened up the possibility of people being educated and improved by changing the environments that operated on their senses.

These views lay behind the enlightened assumption that all men were created equal. Even those as aristocratic as William Byrd and Governor Francis Fauquier of Virginia now conceded that all men, even men of different nations and races, were born equal and that, as Byrd wrote, "the principal difference between one people and another proceeds only from the differing opportunities of improvement." "White, Red, or Black; polished or unpolished," declared Governor Fauquier in 1760, "Men are Men."[9] The American Revolutionary leaders were primed to receive these ideas that culture was socially constructed and that only education and cultivation separated one man from another. In fact, their receptivity to these explosive ideas, which became the basis of all modern thinking, helps explain why they should have become the most remarkable generation of leaders in American history. Because they were men of high ambition and yet of relatively modest origins, they naturally were eager to promote the new enlightened standards of gentility and learning in opposition to the traditional importance of family and blood. They saw themselves sharply set apart from the older world of their fathers and grandfathers. They sought, often unsuccessfully but always sincerely, to be what Jefferson called "natural aristocrats"—aristocrats who measured their status not by birth or family but by enlightened values and benevolent behavior. To be a natural aristocrat meant being reasonable, tolerant, honest, virtuous, and candid. It implied as well being cosmopolitan, standing on elevated ground in order to have a large view of human affairs, and being free of the prejudices, parochialism, and religious enthusiasm of the vulgar and barbaric. It meant, in short, having all those characteristics that we today sum up in the idea of a liberal arts education.

Almost all the Revolutionary leaders—including the second and third tiers of leadership—were first-generation gentlemen. That is to say, almost all were the first in their families to attend college and to acquire a liberal arts education that was now the new mark of an enlightened eighteenth-century gentleman. Jefferson's father, Peter Jefferson, was a wealthy Virginia planter and surveyor who married successfully into the prestigious Randolph family. But he was not a refined and liberally educated gentleman: he did not read Latin, he did not know French, he did not play the violin, and, as far as we know, he never once questioned the idea of a religious establishment or the owning of slaves.

His son Thomas was very different. Indeed, all the Revolutionaries knew things that their fathers had not known, and they were eager to prove themselves by what they believed and valued and by their virtue and disinterestedness.

Most important, these Revolutionary leaders felt a greater affinity with the people they spoke for than did elites in Europe. Not for them "the withdrawal of the upper classes" from the uncultivated bulk of the population that historian Peter Burke speaks about. Because the American gentry were establishing republics, they necessarily had to have a more magnanimous view of human nature than their European counterparts. As we have seen, monarchies could comprehend large territories and composite kingdoms and rule over people who were selfish, corrupt, and diverse in interests and ethnicities. But republics required societies that were not only enlightened but were cohesive, virtuous, and egalitarian. It seemed as if the American people were ideally suited for republicanism; they necessarily possessed a unanimity and a oneness that other peoples did not have. As Joel Barlow noted in 1792, the "people" had come to mean something very different in America from what it did in Europe.

In Europe the people remained only a portion of the society; they were the poor, the rabble, the *misérables*, the *menu peuple*, the *Pöbel*.[10] But in America the people were the whole society. In republican America there could be no subjects, no orders, no aristocracy, no estates separate from the people. The people had become everything.

Perhaps some American gentry in the privacy of their dining rooms continued to express the traditional elitist contempt for ordinary folk. But it was no longer possible in public for an American leader to refer to the people as the common "herd." During the Virginia ratifying convention in June 1788, Edmund Randolph had used just this term in reference to the people, and Patrick Henry immediately jumped on him. By likening the people to a "herd," said Henry, Randolph had "levelled and degraded [them] to the lowest degree," reducing them "from respectable independent citizens, to abject, dependent subjects or slaves." Randolph was forced to rise at once and defensively declare "that he did not use that word to excite any odium, but merely to convey an idea of a multitude."[11]

From this moment no American political leader ever again dared in public to refer to the people in such disparaging terms. Instead, in their orations and writings they exulted in the various ways the American people as a whole were more enlightened than the rest of mankind.

In these attempts to justify their enlightenment, Americans created the sources of their belief in their exceptionalism, in their difference from the peoples of the Old World. Americans, they told themselves, were without both the corrupting luxury of Europe and its great distinctions of wealth and poverty. "Here," said the French immigrant and author Hector St. John de Crèvecoeur in one of his typical ecstatic celebrations of the distinctiveness of the New World, "are no aristocratical families, no courts, no kings, no bishops, no ecclesiastical dominion, no invisible power giving to a few a very visible one, no great manufactures employing thousands, no great refinements of luxury. The rich and the poor are not so far removed from each other as they are in Europe." There was nothing in America remotely resembling the wretched poverty and the gin-soaked slums of London. America, continued Crèvecoeur, was largely made up of "cultivators scattered over an immense territory," each of them working for himself. Nowhere in America, he said, ignoring for the moment the big houses of the Southern planters and the slave quarters of hundreds of thousands of black Africans, could one find "the hostile castle and the haughty mansion, contrasted with the clay-built hut and miserable cabin, where cattle and men help to keep each other warm and dwell in meanness, smoke and indigence."[12]

Precisely because Americans were separated from Europe and, as Jefferson said in 1787, "remote from all other aid, we are obliged to invent and execute; to find means within ourselves, and not to lean on others." The result of this American pragmatism, this ability, said Jefferson, "to surmount every difficulty by resolution and contrivance," was a general prosperity.[13] White Americans enjoyed the highest standard of living in the world, and goods of all sorts were widely diffused throughout the society. Indeed, the enlightenment of a society could be measured by the spread of material possessions, by seeing whether most people possessed what Jefferson called those things "applicable to our daily concerns." Did people eat with knives and forks instead of with their hands? Did they sleep on feather mattresses instead of straw? Did they drink out of china cups instead of wooden vessels? These were signs of prosperity, of happiness, of civilization. Jefferson believed that to know the real state of a society's enlightenment one "must ferret the people out of their hovels, . . . look into their kettle, eat their bread, loll on their beds under pretence of resting yourself, but in fact to find out if they are soft."[14]

The Revolution had made Americans a more intelligent people. It had given "a spring to the active powers of the inhabitants," said David Ramsay in 1789, "and set them on thinking, speaking, and acting far beyond that to which they had been accustomed."[15] Three-quarters of all the books and pamphlets published in America between 1640 and 1800 appeared in the last thirty-five years of the eighteenth century. By eighteenth-century standards, levels of literacy, at least for white Americans in the North, were higher than almost any other place on earth and were rapidly climbing, especially for white women. All their reading made them enlightened. Jefferson was convinced that an American farmer rather than an English farmer had conceived of making the rim of a wheel from a single piece of wood. He knew it had to be an American because the idea had been suggested by Homer, and "ours are the only farmers who can read Homer."[16]

Unlike in England where conservative aristocrats opposed educating the masses for fear of breeding dissatisfied employees and social instability, American elites wholeheartedly endorsed education for ordinary people. American leaders issued a torrent of speeches and writings on the importance of popular education that has rarely been matched in American history or in the history of any other country. Their goal, as Benjamin Rush put it, was not to release the talents of individuals as much as it was to produce "one general and uniform system of education" in order to "render the mass of the people more homogeneous, and thereby fit them more easily for uniform and peaceable government."[17]

Formal schooling was only part of the educational process of rendering the people more homogeneous and enlightened. Because information of all sorts had to be spread throughout the sprawling nation, Americans began creating post offices faster than any other people in the world. One of the consequences of this expanding postal system was an astonishing increase in the circulation of newspapers. "In no other country on earth, not even in Great Britain," said Noah Webster, "are Newspapers so generally circulated among the body of the people, as in America." By 1810 Americans were buying over twenty-two million copies of 376 newspapers annually—even though half the population was under the age of sixteen and one-fifth was enslaved and prevented from reading. This was the largest aggregate circulation of newspapers of any country in the world.[18]

Because republics, as Benjamin Rush said, were naturally "peaceful and benevolent forms of government," Americans inevitably took the lead in promoting humane reforms. Jefferson in fact thought that America was the most compassionate nation in the world. "There is not a country on earth," he said, "where there is greater tranquillity, where the laws are milder, or better obeyed . . . , where strangers are better received, more hospitably treated, & with a more sacred respect."[19] In the several decades following the Revolution, Americans took very seriously the idea that they were peculiarly a people of sentiment and sensibility, more honest, more generous, more caring than other peoples.

They eagerly began creating charitable and humanitarian societies by the hundreds and thousands. Indeed, there were more such societies formed in the decade following the Revolution than were created in the entire colonial period. These multiplying societies treated the sick, aided the industrious poor, housed orphans, fed imprisoned debtors, built huts for shipwrecked sailors, and, in the case of the Massachusetts Humane Society, even attempted to resuscitate those suffering from "suspended animation"—that is, those such as drowning victims who appeared to be dead but actually were not. The fear of being buried alive was a serious concern at this time. Many, like Washington on his death bed, asked that their bodies not be immediately interred in case they might be suffering from suspended animation.

The most notable of the humanitarian reforms coming out of the Revolution involved new systems of criminal punishment. Jefferson and other leaders drew up plans for liberalizing the harsh and bloody penal codes of the colonial period. Since people learned from what they saw, the cruel and barbaric punishments of monarchies carried out in public, said Thomas Paine, hardened the hearts of their subjects and made them bloodthirsty. "It is [monarchy's] sanguinary punishments which corrupt mankind."[20] Maybe it was sensible for Britain to have over two hundred crimes punishable by death, for monarchies were based on fear and had to rely on harsh punishments. But, said Paine, republics were different. They were capable of producing a kinder and gentler people.

People were not born to be criminals, it was now said; they were taught to be criminals by sensuously experiencing the world around them. If the characters of people were produced by their environments, as Lockean liberal thinking suggested, perhaps criminals were not entirely respon- sible for their actions. Maybe impious and cruel parents of the criminal were at fault, or maybe even the whole society was to blame. "We all must plead guilty before the bar of conscience as having had some share in corrupting the morals of the community, and levelling the highway to the gallows," declared a New Hampshire minister in 1796.[21] If criminal behavior was learned, then perhaps it could be unlearned. "Let every criminal, then, be considered as a person laboring under an infectious disorder," said one writer in 1790. "Mental disease is the cause of all crimes."[22] If so, then it seemed that criminals could be salvaged, and not simply mutilated or executed.

These enlightened sentiments spread everywhere and eroded support for capital punishment in the new republican states. Not that the reformers had become soft on crime. Although Jefferson's code called for the death penalty only for treason and murder, he did propose the lex talionis, the law of retaliation, for the punishment of other crimes. So the state would poison the criminal who poisoned his victim, and would castrate men guilty of rape or sodomy; guilty women would have a half-inch hole bored through their noses. In Massachusetts in 1785 a counterfeiter was no longer executed. Instead, he was set in the pillory, taken to the gallows where he stood with a rope around his neck for a time, whipped twenty stripes, had his left arm cut off, and finally was sentenced to three years' hard labor.

Although most states did something to change their codes of punishment, Pennsylvania led the way in the 1780s and 1790s in the enlightened effort, as its legislation put it, "to reclaim rather than destroy," "to correct and reform the offenders" rather than simply to mark or eliminate them. Pennsylvania abolished all bodily punishments such as "burning in the hand" and "cutting off the ears" and ended the death penalty for all crimes except murder. In their place the state proposed a scale of punishments based on fines and years of imprisonment. Criminals were now to feel their personal guilt by being confined in prisons apart from the excited environment of the outside world, in solitude where, declared a fascinated French observer, the "calm contemplation of mind which brings on penitence" could take place.[23]

Out of these efforts was created the penitentiary, which turned the prison into what Philadelphia officials called "a school of reformation." By 1805 New York, New Jersey, Connecticut, Virginia, and Massachusetts had followed Pennsylvania in constructing penitentiaries based on the principle of solitary confinement. Nowhere else in the Western world, enlightened philosophers recognized, were such penal reforms carried as far as they were in America.[24]

Not only did the Americans believe that they possessed a more intelligent, more equal, more prosperous, and more compassionate society than those of other countries, they also thought that they were less superstitious and more rational than the peoples of the Old World. They had actually destroyed religious establishments and created a degree of religious liberty that European liberals could only dream about. Many Americans thought that their Revolution, in the words of the New York constitution of 1777, had been designed to end the "spiritual oppression and intolerance wherewith the bigotry and ambition of weak and wicked priests" had "scourged mankind."[25]

Although it was the proliferation of different religious groups that made possible this religious freedom, Americans generally did not celebrate their religious diversity; indeed, the fragmentation of religion in America appalled most people. Most Americans accepted differences of religion only insofar as these differences made toleration and freedom of conscience possible. Even an enlightened reformer like Jefferson hoped that eventually everyone would become a Unitarian.

Since refugees from the tyrannies of Britain and Europe were entering the United States in increasing numbers in the 1790s, Americans had every reason to believe that their country had become the special asylum of liberty. In the spring of 1794 the United Irishmen of Dublin sent the renowned scientist Joseph Priestley their best wishes as he fled from persecution in England to the New World. "You are going to a happier world—the world of Washington and Franklin. . . . You are going to a country where science is turned to better uses."

All of this immigration meant that representatives of all the peoples of Europe were present in America, which in turn helped to fulfill the fraternal dream of the Enlightenment, as Benjamin Rush described it, of "men of various countries and languages . . . conversing with each other like children of one father."[26] Not that American leaders celebrated the ethnic diversity of America in any modern sense. Far from it. What impressed the Revolutionary leaders was not the multicultural diversity of these immigrants but rather their remarkable acculturation and assimilation into one people. John Jay lived in New York City, the most ethnically and religiously diverse place in all America, and was himself three-eighths French and five-eighths Dutch, without any English ancestry. Nevertheless, Jay could declare with a straight face in *The Federalist* No. 2 that "Providence has been pleased to give this one connected country to one united people—a people descended from the same ancestors, speaking the same language, professing the same religion, attached to the same principles of government, very similar in their manners and customs and who, by their joint counsels, arms, and efforts . . . have nobly established general liberty and independence."[27]

The Revolutionary leaders' idea of a modern state, shared by enlightened British, French, and German eighteenth-century reformers as well, was one that was homogeneous, not one that was fractured by differences of language, ethnicity, and religion. Much of Europe in the eighteenth century was still a patchwork of small duchies, principalities, and city-states—nearly 350 of them. Even those nation-states that had begun consolidating were not yet very secure or homogeneous. England had struggled for centuries to bring Wales, Scotland, and Ireland under its control. Only in the Act of Union in 1707 had it created the entity known as Great Britain, and as events showed, its struggle to create a single nation was far from over. France was even worse off. Its eighteenth-century ancien régime was a still a hodgepodge of provinces and diverse peoples and by modern standards scarcely a single nation at all. Spain had just recently begun assimilating the kingdoms of Castile and Aragon into a single state, but the Basque provinces and Navarre still maintained an extraordinary degree of independence from the central monarchy.

European reformers everywhere wanted to eliminate these differences within their national boundaries and bind the people of their state together in a common culture. The American Revolutionary leaders were no different. They thought that Americans had become the most enlightened nation in the world precisely because they were a more rational and homogeneous society. They had done away with the various peasant customs, craft holidays, and primitive peculiarities—the morris dances, the charavaries, the bear-baiting, and other folk practices—that characterized the societies of the Old World. The New England Puritans had banned many of these popular festivals and customs, and elsewhere the mixing and settling of different peoples had worn most of them away. In New England, all that remained of Old World holidays was Pope's Day, November 5—the colonists' version of Guy Fawkes Day. Since enlightened elites everywhere regarded most of these different plebeian customs and holidays as remnants of superstition and barbarism, their relative absence in America seemed to be another sign of the new nation's enlightenment and oneness.[28]

In various ways, Americans appeared to be more of a single people than the nations of Europe. Nothing made enlightened eighteenth-century Americans prouder than the fact that most people in America spoke the same language and could understand one another everywhere. That this was not true in the European nations was one of the great laments of enlightened reformers in the Old World. Europeans, even those within the same country, were cut off from one another by their regional and local dialects. A Yorkshireman could not be understood in Somerset and vice versa. On the eve of the French Revolution, the majority of people in France did not speak French.

Americans by contrast could understand each other from Maine to Georgia. It was very obvious why this should be so, said John Witherspoon, president of the College of New Jersey (later Princeton). Since Americans were "much more unsettled, and mov[ed] frequently from place to place, they are not as liable to local peculiarities, either in accent or phraseology."[29]

In England, said Noah Webster, language was what divided the English people from one another. The court and the upper ranks of the aristocracy set the standards of usage and thus put themselves at odds with the language spoken by the rest of the country. America was different, said Webster. Its standard was fixed by the general practice of the nation, and therefore Americans had "the fairest opportunity of establishing a national language, and of giving it [more] uniformity and perspicuity . . . [than] ever [before] presented itself to mankind." Indeed, Webster was convinced that Americans already "speak the most pure English now known in the world." Within a century and a half, he predicted, North America would be peopled with a hundred million citizens, "all speaking the same language." Nowhere else in the world would such large numbers of people "be able to associate and converse together like children of the same family."[30]

Others had even more grandiose visions for the spread of America's language. John Adams was among those who suggested that American English would eventually become "the next universal language." In 1789 even a French official agreed; in a moment of giddiness he actually predicted that American English was destined to replace diplomatic French as the language of the world. Americans, he said, "tempered by misfortune," were "more human, more generous, more tolerant, all qualities that make one want to share the opinions, adopt the customs, and speak the language of such a people."[31] We can only assume that this Frenchman's official career was short-lived.

It was understandable that American English might conquer the world, because Americans were the only true citizens of the world. To be enlightened was to be, as Washington said, "a citizen of the great republic of humanity at large." The Revolutionary generation was more eager to demonstrate its cosmopolitanism than any subsequent generation in American history. Intense local attachments were common to peasants and backward peoples, but educated and enlightened persons were supposed to be at home anywhere in the world. Indeed, to be free of local prejudices and parochial ties was what defined an enlightened gentleman.

One's humanity was measured by one's ability to relate to strangers, to enter into the hearts of even those who were different. Americans prided themselves on their hospitality and their treatment of strangers. In America, as Crèvecoeur pointed out, the concept of "stranger" scarcely seemed to exist. "A traveller in Europe becomes a stranger as soon as he quits his own kingdom; but it is otherwise here. We know, properly speaking, no strangers; this is every person's country; the variety of our soils, situations, climates, governments, and produce hath something which must please everyone."[32]

The truth, declared Thomas Paine in *Common Sense*, was that Americans were the most cosmopolitan people in the world. They surmounted all local prejudices. They regarded everyone from different nations as their countrymen and ignored neighborhoods, towns, and counties as "distinctions too limited for continental minds."[33] Because they were free men, they were brothers to all the world.

These were the enlightened dreams of Americans two hundred years ago. Looking back from our all-knowing postmodern perspective, we can only marvel at the hubris and hypocrisy involved in the building of their enlightened empire of liberty. Precisely because the United States today has become the greatest and richest empire the world has ever known, we can see only the limits of their achievement and the failures of their imaginations. All their talk of enlightenment and the promise of America seems hypocritical in light of their unwillingness to abolish slavery, promote racial equality, and treat the native peoples fairly. But in fact it was the Americans' commitment to being enlightened that for the first time on a large scale gave them both the incentive and the moral capacity to condemn their own treatment of the Indians and Africans in their midst. However brutally white Americans treated Indians and Africans in the decades following the Revolution—and no one can deny the brutality—that treatment was denounced as a moral evil by more and more enlightened Americans in ways that had not been done in premodern pre-Enlightenment times.

Since these Enlightenment ideals still constitute the source of American nationhood, we need to understand them and their origins. Despite all our present talk of diversity and multiculturalism, we are, because of these Enlightenment ideals, still in the best position among the advanced democracies to deal with the massive demographic changes and movements taking place throughout the world. All the advanced democracies of Europe are finding it very difficult to assimilate immigrants and are experiencing serious crises of national identity. Whatever problems we have in this respect pale in comparison with those of the European nations.

We, of course, are not the only country to base its nationhood on Enlightenment values. France also claims to be grounded in universal Enlightenment principles. But, ironically, the French have taken the Enlightenment desire for a single homogeneous nation so seriously that their collective sense of national oneness leaves little room for the existence of Arab and other ethnic minorities. Precisely because America ultimately came to conceive of itself not as a single entity but as a nation of individuals—in our better moments, open to anyone in the world—it is better able to handle this explosive demographic future. The coming decades will test just how much of an enlightened nation of immigrants we Americans are willing to be.

AFTERWORD TO CHAPTER 10

In recent years historians have been approaching the Anglo-American Enlightenment in new ways. They have tended to conceive of it as much more than a movement involving reason and deism and the works of high-level philosophers like David Hume and Adam Smith. Instead, they have taken seriously what contemporaries thought being enlightened meant. It turns out contemporaries talked a great deal about the growth of what they called politeness and civility. Thus historians of eighteenth-century Anglo-American life have given a new significance to such mundane subjects as tea parties and letter writing. On this expanded conception of the Enlightenment, see Richard L. Bushman, *The Refinement of America: Persons, Houses, Cities* (1992); David S. Shields, *Civil Tongues and Polite Letters in British America* (1997); and Lawrence E. Klein, *Shaftesbury and the Culture of Politeness: Moral Discourse and Cultural Politics in Early Eighteenth-Century England* (1994).

This paper began as a lecture at the Institute of United States Studies at the University of London in 2002. It was revised and later published in *America and Enlightenment Constitutionalism*, edited by Gary L. McDowell and Johnathan O'Neill (New York: Palgrave Macmillan, 2006).

$\mathscr{A}$ HISTORY *of* RIGHTS
in EARLY AMERICA

E AMERICANS TODAY talk all the time about rights—everyone has rights—and we believe that they trump all other claims and values. Much of the time we seem to regard our preoccupation with rights as something new, something recent, something that began with, say, the Warren Court and the civil rights movement. But our obsession with rights is not new at all. From the very beginning of our history we have been very rights conscious.

The history of rights in America began, as much of our history did, in England. It is not very fashionable these days to talk about the contributions of Western Europeans to American culture, but in the case of our preoccupation with rights, we owe most of our consciousness to our English heritage. The English had a concern for rights and a Bill of Rights long before our Bill of Rights of 1791. As Chief Justice Thomas Hutchinson told a Massachusetts grand jury in 1769, "The bare Mention of the Word *Rights* always strikes an Englishman in a peculiar manner."[1] Medieval and early modern Englishmen valued their rights to their personal liberty and property—rights that were embedded in their common law. The common law had deeply held principles, including, for example, the notions that no one could be a judge in his own cause and that no one, even the king, could legally take another's property without that person's consent. These rights and liberties belonged to all the people of England, and they adhered in each person as a person. Their force did not depend on their written delineation; they existed in the customary or unwritten law of England that went back to time immemorial.

It was not just the people who had rights; the king did too, usually referred to as the king's prerogatives. These prerogatives, or royal rights, to govern the realm were as old and sacred as the privileges and liberties of the people. In that distant medieval world, the king had sole responsibility to govern, to provide for the safety of his people, and to see that justice was done—that is, that the people's rights were protected. The king's courts were expected to adjudicate the law common to those courts and to the realm, hence the development of the term "common law."

The king's highest court of all—Parliament—arose sometime in the thirteenth century and was composed both of the feudal nobles that eventually became the House of Lords and of agents from the boroughs and counties of the realm that eventually became the House of Commons. Unlike the modern English Parliament, its medieval predecessor was convened by the king only sporadically and did not have as yet any direct responsibility for governing the country. Instead, its responsibility was mainly limited to voting supplies to the king to enable him to govern, presenting petitions to the king for the redress of popular grievances, and, as the highest court in the land, correcting and emending the common law so as to ensure that justice was done. This correcting and emending of the law was not regarded as legislation in any modern sense, for medieval men thought of law not as something invented but as something discovered in the customs and precedents of the past. The modern idea of law as the command of a legislative body was as yet inconceivable; indeed, law was equated with justice, and its purpose was to protect the rights of people from each other and from the king.

Thus the king had his rights to govern, and the people had their equally ancient and equally legitimate rights to their liberties and their property. Indeed, it is perhaps not too much to say that the whole of

English constitutional history can be seen as a struggle between these two competing sets of rights. The courts, including the high court of Parliament, were supposed to adjudicate between these conflicting sets of rights. Because the king, in trying to fulfill his responsibility of governing the realm, often infringed upon the customary rights of the people, the English periodically felt the need to have the king recognize their rights and liberties in writing. These recognitions in the early Middle Ages took the form of coronation oaths and assizes and charters issued by the crown. In 1215 the barons compelled King John to sign what became the most famous written document in English history—the great charter, or Magna Carta. In it the king explicitly acknowledged many of the customary rights of the English people, including the right of a freeman not to be imprisoned, exiled, or executed "unless by the lawful judgment of his peers, or by the law of the land." This meant a judgment by the common-law courts or by Parliament, the highest court in the land.

The succeeding centuries of English history saw more struggles over rights and more attempts by the English people to place limits on their kings. These struggles came to a climax in the seventeenth century. When, in 1627, King Charles I attempted to raise money by forced loans, five English knights resisted, and Charles had the resisters arbitrarily imprisoned. This in turn led to the popular reinvocation of the Magna Carta and the reiteration of the rights of a subject to his property and to no imprisonment without the legal judgment of his peers. In 1628 the House of Commons presented these grievances in a Petition of Right, which the king was compelled to accept.

Yet this hardly resolved the conflict between the rights of the king and the liberties of the people. Only after a bloody civil war and one king had been beheaded and another driven from his throne was the struggle between king and people finally settled, in the Glorious Revolution of 1688–1689. In 1688–1689 the Convention-Parliament set forth a Declaration of Rights that quickly became enshrined in English constitutionalism. In this listing of rights, which became a statute or a Bill of Rights when the new king, William III, approved them, Parliament declared illegal certain actions of the crown, including its dispensing with laws, using prerogative power to raise money, and maintaining a standing army without the consent of Parliament. At the same time, Parliament asserted certain rights and freedoms possessed by the English, including the right to bear arms, to petition the king, to have free elections and frequent Parliaments in which speech would be free, and to have no excessive bail or fines.[2]

It is important to understand that this delineation of rights in 1689 was an act of Parliament consented to by the king. The English Bill of Rights was designed to protect the subjects not from the power of Parliament but from the power of the king. Indeed, it was inconceivable that Parliament could endanger the subjects' rights. Only the crown could do that. As the highest court in the land, Parliament was therefore the bulwark and guardian of the people's rights and liberties; there was no point in limiting it. Consequently, there were no legal or constitutional restrictions placed on the actions of the English Parliament, and, despite the efforts of some British judges to invoke the declarations of the European Union, there are still none today, which makes the English Parliament one of the most powerful governmental institutions in the world.

So convinced were the English, in the decades following 1689, that tyranny could come only from a single ruler that they could hardly conceive of the people tyrannizing themselves. Once Parliament became sovereign, once the body that represented and spoke for them—the House of Commons—had gained control of the crown authority that had traditionally threatened their liberties, the English people lost much of their former interest in codifying and listing their personal rights. Since the people themselves now controlled the government, charters defining the people's rights, and contracts between the people and government, no longer made sense. If the high court of Parliament represented or embodied the whole nation, then its judgments became in effect the sovereign commands of the whole nation, and what formerly had been adjudication now became legislation binding everyone and encompassing everyone's rights. Since Parliament was the protector of the people's rights, it could be no threat to them.

· · ·

BY THE TIME OF the American Revolution, most educated Britons had become convinced that their rights existed only against the crown. Against their representative and sovereign Parliament, which was the guardian of these rights, they existed not at all. Although the American colonists did not have quite the same confidence in Parliament that the English at home did, they did equally fear the powers of the crown and saw their own local representative assemblies as the bulwarks of their rights. Like the English in relation to Parliament, very few colonists saw any need to protect their rights from their colonial assemblies. Following the Zenger trial in 1735, for example, no royal governor dared bring a case of seditious libel against anyone. But the colonial assemblies, which presumably spoke for the people, continued to punish individuals for seditiously libeling the legislatures under the common law. In other words, liberty of the press existed against the crown but not against the representatives of the people; any libel against them was ipso facto seditious.[3]

In the 1760s and 1770s, during the crisis that eventually tore apart the British Empire, the American colonists had the long English heritage of popular rights to draw upon. Like all Britons, they were familiar with the persistent struggle of the English people to erect written barriers against encroaching crown power. Their own colonial past was littered with written documents delineating their rights. From the "Laws and Liberties" of Massachusetts Bay in 1648 to New York's "Charter of Liberties and Privileges" in 1683, the early colonial assemblies had felt the need to acknowledge in writing what William Penn called "those rights and privileges . . . which are the proper birth-right of Englishmen."[4]

As government and law stabilized in the eighteenth century, however, the need in the colonies for these sorts of explicit codifications of rights declined just as they had in the mother country. But the Englishman's instinct to defend his rights against encroachments of the governmental power of the crown was always latently present and was easily aroused. And getting the ruler to recognize these rights on paper was part of that instinct. By the time of the imperial crisis, it was natural for colonists like Arthur Lee of Virginia to call in 1768 for "a bill of rights" that would "merit the title of the Magna Carta Americana."[5]

Indeed, as historian John Reid has reminded us, the colonial resistance movement of the 1760s and 1770s was all about the colonists' defense of their rights as Englishmen.[6] By the eve of the Revolution, the charters that the crown had granted to many of the colonies in the previous century had come to be seen as just so many miniature Magna Cartas, designed, as one New Englander declared, "to reduce to a certainty the rights and privileges we were entitled to" and "to point out and circumscribe the prerogatives of the crown." Their several charters (or, where these were lacking, "their commissions to their governors have ever been considered as equivalent securities") had become transformed into what, "from their subject matter and the reality of things, can only operate as the evidence of a compact between an English King and the American subjects." These charters, continued Joseph Hawley of Massachusetts, were no longer franchises or grants from the crown that could be unilaterally recalled or forfeited: "Their running in the stile of a grant is mere matter of form and not of substance." They were reciprocal agreements "made and executed between the King of England, and our predecessors," contracts between ruler and people, outlining the rights of each but particularly the rights of the people.[7]

This imagined contract between the rights of the king and the people was not John Locke's contract, which was a contract among the people to form a society; instead, it was the Whig contract that ran through much of eighteenth-century English thinking and justified the people's obeying the prerogative decrees and edicts of the king. This contract was an agreement, legal or mercantile in character, between rulers and people—equal parties with equal sets of rights—in which protection and allegiance were the considerations. "Allegiance," wrote James Wilson in 1774, "is the faith and obedience, which every subject owes to his prince. This obedience is founded on the protection derived from government: for protection and allegiance are the reciprocal bonds, which connect the prince and his subjects." This allegiance was not the same as consent. "Allegiance to the king and obedience to the parliament," said Wilson, "are founded on very different principles. The former is founded on protection, the latter on representation. An inattention to this difference," said Wilson, "has produced . . . much uncertainty and confusion in our ideas concerning the connexion, which ought to subsist between Great Britain and the American colonies."[8]

ALL OF THIS CONTRACTUAL IMAGERY between two equal parties, not to mention the familial imagery of a patriarchal king and the mother country, suggested that for many eighteenth-century Anglo-Americans the public and private realms were still largely indistinguishable. Indeed, the colonists never regarded the struggle between the rights of the crown and the rights of the people as one between public and private rights. For even as late as the eve of the Revolution, the modern distinction between public and private was still not clear. The people's ancient rights and liberties were as much public as private, just as the king's rights—his prerogatives—were as much private as they were public. So-called public institutions had private rights and private persons had public obligations. The king's prerogatives, or his premier rights to govern the realm, grew out of his private position as the wealthiest of the wealthy and the largest landowner in the society; his government had really begun as an extension of his royal household. But in a like manner all private households or families—"those small subdivisions of Government," one colonist called them—had public responsibilities to help the king govern.[9]

All of this meant that the colonists were used to a great deal of communal or "public" control and management of what we today would call "private" rights. Governments in this premodern colonial society regulated all sorts of personal behavior, especially the moral and religious behavior of people, without any consciousness that they were depriving people of their private liberty or rights. Of the nearly 2,800 prosecutions in the superior and general sessions courts of Massachusetts between

1760 and 1774, over half involved sexual and religious offenses, such as fornication and using profanity. Many of the other prosecutions involved drunkenness, slander, and various violations of decency and good manners. At the same time, the colonial governments spent very little time on what we today would call public matters. Royal governors did not have legislative policies, and assemblies did not enact legislative programs. Many of the governments' activities were private, local, and adjudicative. The colonial assemblies still saw themselves more as courts making judgments rather than as legislatures making law. They spent a good deal of their time hearing private petitions, which often were the complaints of one individual or group against another. In historian William Nelson's survey of the Massachusetts General Court in 1761 ("as typical a year as any," he says), he could find "only three acts that were arguably legislative in the sense that they changed law or made new law."[10]

Indeed, to the colonists the separation of legislative, executive, and judicial powers that we value so greatly was far from clear. Since there was no modern bureaucracy and few modern mechanisms of coercion—a few constables and sheriffs scarcely constituted a police force—it was often left to the courts to exercise what governmental coercion there was and to engage in an extraordinary number of administrative and even legislative tasks, usually drawing on the communities for help.

Much of this judicial or magisterial activity—in fact, much of the government—was carried on without direct compensation. No one as yet conceived of politics as a paid profession or a permanent civil service. Most officeholding was still regarded, with varying degrees of plausibility, as a public obligation that private persons *serving gratis or generously* owed the community.[11] Every private person in the society had an obligation to help govern the realm commensurate with his social rank—the king's being the greatest because he stood at the top of the social hierarchy.

As legal historian Hendrik Hartog has written, all government in the colonial period was regarded essentially as the enlisting and mobilizing of the power of private persons to carry out public ends. "Governments," writes Hartog, "did not so much act as they ensured and sanctioned the actions of others."[12] If the eighteenth-century city of New York wanted its streets cleaned or paved, for example, it did not hire contractors or create a "public works" department; instead, it issued ordinances obliging each person in the city to clean or repair the street abutting his house or shop. In the same way, if the colony of Connecticut wanted a college, it did not build and run the college itself, but instead gave legal rights to private persons to build and run it—in short, creating what were called corporations.

Most public action—from the building of wharves and ferries to the maintaining of roads and inns—depended upon private energy and private funds. Governments were always short of revenue and instead tended to rely mostly on their legal authority to mobilize the community and compel private persons to fulfill public obligations. They issued sanctions against private persons for failure to perform their public duties, and they enticed private persons into fulfilling public goals by offering corporate charters, licenses, and various other legal immunities together with fee-collecting offices.[13] Since the government, including the king, was only one property holder in a world of property holders, it could not take "private" property for "public" purposes without the consent of the owner of that property; in other words, it had no modern power of eminent domain.

The Revolution was designed to dramatically change all this. By creating republics, Americans brought into play the tradition of neo-Roman Whig thinking that emphasized the collective public liberty of the people.[14] In stressing the power of the republican commonwealth in this way, Americans suddenly became much more conscious of private individual rights and interests that stood in opposition to the public good. Since the earlier mobilizing of "private" power for "public" ends was now viewed as "corruption"—that is, the exploitation of the "public" for "private" gain—it had to cease. It was now hoped that governments would no longer grant monopoly charters, licenses, and fee-collecting offices to private individuals in order to induce them to carry out public goals. Instead, the new republican leaders expected select individuals to become public servants working for the state and generally for a salary. State power in America began assuming some of its modern character as an autonomous entity capable of hiring agents to carry out public tasks. The Revolutionaries now claimed the primacy of the public good over all private individual rights and interests; indeed, it sought to separate the public from the private in a new manner and to prevent the former intrusion of private rights and interests into what was now seen as a distinct public realm. With such goals, Revolutionary Americans had to conceive of state power and individual liberty in radically new ways.

It would be difficult to exaggerate what this new idea of republican state power meant. No longer could government be seen as the exercise of someone's personal authority, as the assertion of prerogative rights or of the rights of those with economic and social superiority. Rulers suddenly lost their traditional personal rights to rule, and personal allegiance as a civic bond became meaningless. The long-existing Whig image of government as a contract between rulers and ruled disappeared virtually overnight. The Revolutionary state constitutions eliminated the crown's prerogatives outright or re-granted them to the state legislatures. These constitutional grants of authority, together with the expanded notion of consent underlying all government, gave the new state legislatures a degree of public power that the colonial assemblies had never claimed or even imagined. Although the new state assemblies, to the chagrin of many leaders, continued to act in a traditional courtlike manner—interfering with and reversing judicial decisions and passing private acts affecting individuals—they now became as well sovereign embodiments of the people with legislative responsibility for exercising an autonomous public authority.

In republican America, government would no longer be merely private property and private interests writ large as it had been in the colonial period. Public and private spheres that earlier had been mingled were now presumably to be starkly separated. *Res publica* became everything.

The new republican states saw themselves promoting a unitary public interest that was to be clearly superior to the many private interests and rights of the people.

At the beginning of the Revolution, few Americans imagined that there could be any real conflict between this unitary public good expressed by the representative state legislatures and the rights of individuals. When in 1775 a frightened Tory warned the people of Massachusetts that a popular revolutionary legislature could become as tyrannical as the crown and deprive the people of their individual liberties, John Adams dismissed the idea out of hand. That the people might tyrannize themselves and harm their own rights and liberties was illogical, declared Adams. "A democratic despotism is a contradiction in terms."[15]

With their new heightened sense of the public good, the Revolutionary republican legislatures were determined to bring what were seen as the private rights of selfish individuals under communal control. Many Americans now viewed with suspicion the traditional monarchical practice of enlisting private wealth and energy for public purposes. Especially objectionable was the issuing of corporate privileges and licenses to private persons. In a republic, it was said, no person should be allowed to exploit the public's authority for private gain. Indeed, several of the states wrote into their Revolutionary constitutions declarations, like that of New Hampshire, that "government is instituted for the common benefit, protection, and security of the whole community, and not for the private interest or emolument of any one man, family, or class of men." And some of the states, like North Carolina, declared that "perpetuities and monopolies are contrary to the genius of a State, and ought not to be allowed."[16]

Because they wanted to avoid any taint of corruption by allowing private individuals to undertake public tasks, the new republican state governments sought to assert their newly enhanced public power in direct and unprecedented ways—doing for themselves what they had earlier commissioned private persons to do. The state assemblies began legislating—making and changing law—as never before. Indeed, as Madison complained in

1787, the states passed more laws in the single decade following independence than they had in the entire colonial period. And these laws had less
and less to do with private matters (moral and religious issues) and more
and more with public matters (economic development and commercial
convenience).

"Improvement" was on every Revolutionary's mind, and most leaders
naturally assumed that the new state governments would take the lead
in promoting it. The states now carved out exclusively public spheres
of action and responsibility where none had existed before. They drew
up plans for improving everything from trade and commerce to roads
and waterworks and helped to create a science of political economy for
Americans. And they formed their own public organizations with paid
professional staffs supported by tax money, not private labor. The city of
New York, for example, working under the authority of the state legislature, now set up its own public workforce to clean its streets and wharves
instead of relying, as in the past, on the private residents to do these tasks.
By the early nineteenth century, as Hartog has told us in a brilliant work
of legal history, the city of New York had become a public institution
financed primarily by public taxation and concerned with particularly
public concerns. Like other post-Revolutionary governments, New York
City acquired what it had not had before: the modern power of eminent
domain—the authority to take private property for the sake of the public
good without the consent of the particular property owner.[17]

Many thought that the new state legislatures, as the representatives of
the people, could do for the public whatever the people entrusted them
to do. Some argued that the needs of the public could even override the
rights of individuals. Did not the collective power of the people expressed
in their representative legislatures supersede the rights of the few? Of
course, under monarchy the people could legitimately defend their rights
against encroachments from the prerogative rights and privileges of the
king. But in the new republics, where there were no more prerogative
rights, could the people's personal rights meaningfully exist apart from
the people's sovereign power expressed in their assemblies? In other

words, did it any longer make sense to speak of negative liberty where the people's positive liberty was complete and supreme? To be sure, as the Pennsylvania constitution and other Revolutionary constitutions declared, "no part of a man's property can be justly taken from him, or applied to public uses, without his consent," but this consent, in 1776 at least, meant "that of his legal representatives."[18]

IN 1776 IT WAS NOT at all clear that people had rights against their own representatives. Five states drew up bills of rights in 1776, and several other states listed the people's rights in the bodies of their constitutions. But because the Revolutionary constitutions so circumscribed the governors or rulers, many of the states felt no need any longer to protect the people's rights by separately listing them; their popular legislatures were surely no danger to individual liberties. This accounts for the confusion Americans in 1776 had in not being entirely sure against whom their state bills of rights were directed. In English history, declarations of rights had been directed against the crown and its prerogatives. But in republican America, where there was no longer any crown or any prerogatives, did bills of rights make sense? What was the need of protecting the people's rights from themselves? Monarchies might become despotic, but democracies, when they ran to excess, could only become anarchical and licentious. Or so everyone since the ancient Greeks had assumed.

We know what happened. Within a decade, the democratic despotism and the threat to individual rights from popular legislatures that had seemed so illogical and contradictory to John Adams and other American Whigs in 1775–1776 had become only too real—at least for many gentry leaders. Consequently, many of these leaders were faced with the great constitutional dilemma of limiting popular government and protecting private property and individual rights without, at the same time, denying the sovereign public power of the majority of the people.

This dilemma led some Americans to think freshly about a number of constitutional issues, including those that justified the creation of a new federal Constitution in 1787. Most difficult of all was the formulating of a defense of individual rights and liberties against the people themselves— against Parliament, so to speak. There were no precedents for this in English history or in their own colonial histories. And they had to do all this in the face of their own republican revolutionary ideology—their belief in the autonomous power of the republican community to determine the public good.

It was not easy limiting the popular legislatures without denigrating the people and everything the American Revolution had been about. If the people weren't capable of protecting their own rights and liberties, then what was the value of republican government? Many realized only too keenly that the violations of individual rights in the 1780s did not arise because the people had been forsaken by their legislative representatives, but, as a Boston newspaper declared, those violations occurred because the people's "transient and indigested sentiments have been too implicitly adopted."[19]

James Madison certainly agreed. The rampaging legislatures of the 1780s, he said in 1787, were not acting against the will of the people; they were acting on behalf of that will. Unfortunately, the legislators were only too representative, only too democratic, reflecting only too accurately the narrow views and parochial outlooks of their constituents. Good republicans had not expected this at the outset of the Revolution. "According to Republican Theory," said Madison, "Right and power being both vested in the majority, are held to be synonimous." But experience since 1776 had shown the contrary. "Wherever the real power in a Government lies," he told his friend Thomas Jefferson, residing in Paris, "there is the danger of oppression. In our Governments the real power lies in the majority of the Community, and the invasion of private rights is chiefly to be apprehended, not from any acts of Government contrary to the sense of its constituents, but from acts in which the Government is the mere instrument of the major number of the constituents." As we have seen, that was why for Madison the crisis of the 1780s was truly frightening. The legislative abuses and the many violations of individual rights, he said, "brought into question the fundamental principle of republican Government, that the majority who rule in such governments are the safest Guardians both of public Good and private rights."[20]

From his post in France, Jefferson scarcely grasped what Madison was saying. His confidence in the people was too great for him ever to question their judgment. Instead, in his mind he drew a distinction between the representative legislatures and the people themselves. Jefferson had no doubt that all officials in government, even the popularly elected representatives in the lower houses of the legislatures, could act tyrannically; "173 despots would surely be as oppressive as one," he said of the Virginia House of Delegates in 1785. "An *elective despotism* was not the government we fought for."[21] But this kind of tyranny was not really the people's fault. Jefferson always thought that the people themselves, if undisturbed by demagogues like Patrick Henry, would eventually set matters right. He saw little potential conflict between positive and negative liberty, between the people at large and individual rights. He was one of those who paid no attention to what Madison called that "essential distinction, too little heeded, between assumptions of power by the General Government, in opposition to the will of the constituent body, and assumptions by the constituent body through the Government as the organ of its will."[22] For Jefferson, it could never be the people themselves but only their elected agents that were in error.

Whatever doubts American leaders had privately about the virtue or good sense of the people, few of them by 1787 were willing to express such doubts publicly. Questioning the judgment of the people themselves had become too politically risky for most. Hence publicly, at least, they began drawing the same distinction between the people and their elected delegates as Jefferson had, and sought to exploit that distinction in their efforts to curb the state legislatures. Indeed, that distinction became the basis of all the major arguments mounted by the defenders of the new Constitution in 1787–1788, or the Federalists, as they called themselves. Confronted with arguments from the opponents of the Constitution, or the Anti-Federalists, that raised the question of where sovereignty—the final supreme indivisible lawmaking authority—would lie under the new

Constitution, the Federalists, as we have seen, denied that sovereignty would be taken away from the state legislatures and given to the Congress. Unlike Britain, where sovereignty rested with the king-in-Parliament, sovereignty in America, they said, belonged to no institution of government, including the so-called houses of representatives, or even to all of the institutions together; it remained with the people themselves. In America, representative government could never fully embody the people.

By opening up and exaggerating the distinction between the sovereign people and their elected governments, the Federalists tended to homogenize political power and turn all government officials, in both the state and federal governments, into equally mistrusted agents of the people. Once people came to regard all political power as essentially similar, once they came to view all governmental officials, whether executive, judicial, or even legislative, as, in Jefferson's words, "three branches of magistracy," equally mistrusted, then it became possible to protect individual rights from the popularly elected legislatures without doing violence either to the Americans' republican theory or even to their English heritage. For hadn't the English always sought to protect their rights from the magistracy of the crown?[23]

Leaders anxious about individual liberties and the rights of property could now identify the popular legislatures with the former monarchical or magisterial power (which is what they meant by the term "democratic despotism"), and they could invoke the traditional language of the rights of the English in these new republican circumstances.

Not every American, of course, was willing to follow this line of thinking, and many opponents of the Constitution rose in defense of the peculiar popular character of the state legislatures and denied that their will could be limited in any way. After all, they represented the people. But now the Federalists had a ready answer to this traditional argument. In *The Federalist*, Alexander Hamilton rebuked these defenders of the state legislatures by caustically observing that "the representatives of the people, in a popular assembly, seem sometimes to fancy that they are the people themselves." And he went on to suggest ways the people's rights

embodied in the constitutions could be protected from the legislatures—
by relying on other agents of the people, the courts. Since the people
created constitutions, not the legislatures, it could never "be supposed,"
he said, "that the constitution could intend to enable the representatives
of the people to substitute their *will* to that of their constituents. It is far
more rational to suppose that the courts were designed to be an intermediate body between the people and the legislature, in order, among other
things, to keep the latter within the limits assigned to their authority."[24]

Already many others besides Hamilton had begun looking to the
once-feared judiciary as a principal means of restraining the rampaging
and unstable popular legislatures. Why not? It was just another kind of
agent of the people, after all, ideally situated to protect the people's rights
against the oppressive actions of some of their other agents in the legislatures. As early as 1786, William Plummer, a future U.S. senator and
a governor of New Hampshire, concluded that the very "existence" of
America's elective governments had come to depend upon the judiciary:
"That is the only body of men who will have an effective check upon a
numerous Assembly."[25]

Thus was launched the massive rethinking out of which in a matter
of decades emerged America's strong independent judiciary, a judiciary
that became primarily concerned with protecting individual rights. In
the years following the Revolution, judges shed their earlier broad and ill-
defined political and magisterial roles and adopted ones that were much
more exclusively legal. They withdrew from politics, promoted the development of law as a mysterious science known best by trained experts, and
restricted their activities to the regular courts, which became increasingly
professional and less burdened by popular juries. Many of those who were
suspicious of democracy thought that this withdrawal from politics made
the judiciary a far better protector of the rights of individuals than the
popular legislatures could ever hope to be. As early as 1787, Alexander
Hamilton argued in the New York assembly that the state constitution
prevented anyone from being deprived of his rights except "by the law of
the land" or, as a recent act of the assembly had put it, "by due process of

law," which, said Hamilton, in an astonishing and novel twist, had "a precise technical import": these words were now "only applicable to the process and proceedings of the courts of justice; they can never be referred to an act of legislature," even though the legislature had written them.[26]

The view expressed by Hamilton did not, of course, immediately take hold. The attorney general of North Carolina, for example, argued in 1794 that the clauses of the state constitution referring to due process and the law of the land were not limitations on the legislature; they were "declarations the people thought proper to make of their rights, not against a power they supposed their own representatives might usurp, but against oppression and usurpation in general . . . by a pretended prerogative against or without the authority of law." Thus the phrase that no one could be deprived of his property except by the law of the land meant simply "a law for the people of North Carolina, made or adopted by themselves by the intervention of their own legislature." This view was accepted by the North Carolina superior court.[27]

It is not surprising that the argument Hamilton put forth in 1787 was opposed by others, for his argument was truly extraordinary, to say the least—one of the first of many imaginative readings in our history to be given to that important phrase "due process of law." Parliament, which included the House of Commons, had always protected the rights of the English, including their property rights, from the crown's encroachments. That was what the Bill of Rights of 1689 had been all about. But the English had never thought it necessary to protect these rights from the power of the people themselves—that is, from the legislative power of Parliament. Blackstone had agreed that one of the absolute rights of an individual was "the right of property: which consists in the free use, enjoyment and disposal of all his acquisitions, without any control or diminution, *save only by the laws of the land.*"[28]

Of course, for Blackstone the laws of the land included those laws enacted by the legislature (Parliament). Not so any longer for Hamilton and many other Americans. As far as many Americans were concerned, the legislatures had become legally or constitutionally no different from the former crown. But, as brilliant as some of the Federalists' arguments were, it was never easy to see popularly elected legislatures as threats to individual rights. And since the Federalists tended to be conventional supporters of strong government, they themselves were confused. Because their opponents, the Jeffersonian Republicans, had so often invoked the "rights of man" against the oppressions of government, some Federalists could only conceive of retaliating in traditional terms—by seeking a strengthening of government against the licentiousness of the people whose rights had run amok. But other shrewder Federalists saw that they might be better off appropriating the rights talk of their Jeffersonian opponents and using it in their own behalf against the popular power of the state legislatures. Indeed, they perceived that the liberties of individuals— that is, negative liberty—could actually be turned against positive liberty or self-government. In the United States, the laws of the land were not just what the popular legislatures commanded; indeed, some laws, it seemed, were not under the purview of the legislatures at all.

Many Federalists now argued that the laws of the land concerning individual rights belonged exclusively to the courts. And the reason they belonged exclusively to the courts was that they involved private matters, not public, and private matters concerning individual rights required adjudication, not legislation. As legal historian William Nelson has pointed out, the courts in the early Republic became eager to leave "to legislatures the resolution of conflicts between organized social groups"—that is, conflicts of politics—and instead to concentrate on protecting the rights of individuals.[29]

Those Federalists and even those Republicans who were worried about democratic despotism and the legislative abuses of private rights argued that the popular state legislatures should stick to the great public responsibilities of being a republic and not "take up private business, or interfere in disputes between contending parties," as the colonial assemblies had habitually done. The evils of such legislative meddling were "heightened when the society is divided among themselves;—one party praying the assembly for one thing, and opposite party for another thing. . . . In such circumstances, the assembly ought not to interfere by any exertion of leg-islative power, but leave the contending parties to apply to the proper tribunals [that is, to the judiciary] for a decision of their differences."[30]

These efforts to separate private issues from public ones, to remove some questions from legislative politics and transform them into contests of individual rights, contributed to the emergence of a powerful indepen-dent judiciary in the early Republic. Almost overnight the judiciary in America became not only the principal means by which popular legisla-tures were controlled and limited but also the most effective instrument for sorting out individual disputes within a private sphere that the other institutions of government were forbidden to enter.

BY CARVING OUT an exclusively public sphere for the promotion of repub-lican state power, the Revolutionaries had necessarily created a private sphere as well—a private sphere of individual rights that was to be the domain solely of judges. The idea that there was a sphere of private rights that lay absolutely beyond the authority of the people themselves, espe-cially in a republican government, was a remarkable innovation. Few colo-nists had ever believed that there were individual rights that could stand against the united will of the community expressed in its representative assemblies. But the Revolution had prepared Americans to accept this innovation in their conception of rights. And it had done so with its radi-cal commitment to the right of religious freedom. Once Americans were able to limit state authority in religious matters—an area of such impor-tance that no state had hitherto ever denied itself the power to regulate—they set in motion the principle that there were some realms of private rights and individual liberties into which executives and legislatures had no business intruding. If formerly public religious corporations created by the state became private entities immune from further state tampering, then why couldn't other formerly public corporations be treated in a like manner?[31]

Indeed, that's what happened, as the economy of the early Republic became privatized, which meant turning public responsibilities into private rights. As Oscar and Mary Handlin, Louis Hartz, and others pointed out six or seven decades ago, the new Revolutionary states had expected to involve themselves directly in the economy. But the states attempted to do more than they could handle. As Hartz wrote in reference to Pennsylvania, "[T]he objectives of the state in the economic field were usually so broad that they were beyond its administrative powers to achieve."[32] And not just beyond its administrative powers, but its fiscal powers as well. Because the new democratically elected legislatures were often unwilling to raise taxes to pay for all that the governmental leaders desired to do, the states were forced to fall back on the traditional premodern monarchical practice of enlisting private wealth to carry out public ends. Instead of doing the tasks themselves, as many devout republicans had expected, the states ended up doing what the crown and all premodern governments had done, granting charters of incorporation to private associations and groups to carry out a wide variety of endeavors presumably beneficial to the public: in banking, transportation, insurance, and other enterprises. The states did not intend to abandon their republican responsibility to promote the public good; they simply lacked the money to do it directly. And, of course, there were many private interests that were only too eager to acquire these corporate privileges.

Yet because of the republican aversion to chartered monopolies, the creation of these corporations did not take place without strenuous opposition and heated debate. As a consequence, these corporations were radically transformed. The popular state legislatures began giving out these charter rights freely to a variety of clamoring interests, religious groups as well as business groups. If a group in Boston received a bank charter, then a group in Newburyport wanted one too; and then other groups in both cities requested and received bank charters as well. Before long there were chartered banks all over the state of Massachusetts. Not only did the number of corporations rapidly multiply, but their earlier monopolistic privileged character changed as well. Whereas all the colonies together had chartered only about a half dozen business corporations, the new states began creating them in astonishing numbers, numbers that were unmatched anywhere else in the world. From an exclusive privilege granted at the behest of the state to a few highly visible, socially distinguished recipients to carry out a public purpose, corporate charters eventually became an equal right available to virtually everyone. The states issued 11 charters of incorporation between 1781 and 1785, 22 more between 1786 and 1790, and 114 between 1791 and 1795. Between 1800 and 1817 they created nearly 1,800 corporate charters. With this multiplication not only was the traditional exclusivity of the corporate charters destroyed, but the public power of the state governments was also dispersed. If "government, unsparingly and with an unguarded hand, shall multiply corporations, and grant privileges without limitation," then, declared a concerned Governor Levi Lincoln of Massachusetts, sooner or later "only the very shadow of sovereignty" would remain.[33]

At the same time as these corporations increased in number and shed their exclusivity, they lost much of their earlier public character as well and were more and more regarded as private property. As private property—as rights vested by the legislatures in private individuals— these corporations now became exempt from further legislative interference. This idea that the corporate charter was a species of private property was expressed early. "In granting charters," declared William Robinson in the Pennsylvania assembly in 1786 in defense of the charter of the Bank of North America, "the legislature acts in a ministerial capacity"; that is, it acted as the crown had acted in mobilizing private resources for public purposes. This bestowing of charters, said Robinson, "is totally distinct from the power of making laws, and it is a novel doctrine in Pennsylvania that they can abrogate those charters so solemnly granted." There was a difference between laws and charters. Laws were general rules for the whole community; charters "bestow particular privileges upon a certain number of people. . . . Charters are a species of property. When they are obtained, they are of value. Their forfeiture belongs solely to the courts of justice."[34] This argument did not convince the Pennsylvania assembly in 1786, but it was a brilliant anticipation of what was to come.

The more the state legislatures could be demonized as monarch-like tyrants, the more their grants could be regarded as rights vested in individuals that could not be taken back by the legislatures. "The proposition that a power to do, includes virtually, a power to undo, as applied to a legislative body," wrote Hamilton in 1802, "is generally but not universally true. All *vested* rights form an exception to the rule."[35] This protection of vested rights, as Edward S. Corwin once pointed out, became "the basic doctrine of American constitutional law."[36] So much had legislative grants seem to have become contracts that Senator Gouverneur Morris used the analogy to oppose the Jeffersonian Republicans' elimination of the circuit court positions created by the Federalists' Judiciary Act of 1801. When you give an individual the right to make a toll road or bridge, said Morris, "can you, by a subsequent law, take it away? No; when you make a compact, you are bound by it."[37] This thinking prepared the way for the argument that corporations were actually contracts immune from state tampering by the contract clause in Article I, Section 10 of the Constitution, a position eventually endorsed by the Supreme Court in the *Dartmouth College* case in 1819.

Of course, many resisted these efforts to turn chartered corporations into species of private property. Jefferson may have been especially dedicated to equal rights, but he did not believe that a corporate charter was one of those rights. To his dying day he never accepted the idea that corporations were private property that could not be touched or modified by the legislative body that chartered them. That idea, he said, "may perhaps be a salutary provision against the abuses of a monarch, but is most absurd against the nation itself." Others agreed. "It seems difficult to conceive of a corporation established for merely private purposes," declared a North Carolina judge in 1805. "In every institution of that kind the ground of the establishment is some public good or purpose to be promoted."[38] This increasing stress on the need for a "public purpose" behind the state's activity, however, only worked to further privatize the business corporations. Eventually people felt compelled to distinguish between corporations such as banks, bridges, and insurance companies that were now considered private because they were privately endowed, and those such as towns or counties that remained public because they were tax-based. Even in Massachusetts, which retained its established church until 1833, religious dissenters transformed religious corporations into private voluntary associations that acted beyond the state but were entitled to legal recognition and protection by the state.[39]

There was a curious paradox in these developments. Just as the public power grew in these years of the early Republic, so too did the private rights of individuals. Those who sought to protect the rights of individuals did not deny the public prerogatives of the states. Instead, they drew boundaries around the rights of private individuals, including business corporations, which judges eventually transformed into private, rights-bearing "persons." In fact, the heightened concern for the private vested rights of persons was a direct consequence of the enhanced public power the republican Revolution had given to the states and municipalities. The bigger the public domain, the bigger the private domain of private rights had to be to protect itself. Although the power of the federal government certainly declined in the decades following Jefferson's election as president, the public authority and the police powers and regulatory rights of the states and their municipalities grew stronger.

Separating the political from the legal, the public from the individual, actually allowed for more vigorous state action as long as that action served what was called a "public purpose." Individuals may have had rights, but the public had rights as well—rights that grew out of the sovereignty of the state and its legitimate power to police the society. The state of New York, for example, remained deeply involved in the society and economy. Not only did the state government of New York distribute its largess to individual businessmen and groups in the form of bounties, subsidies, stock ownership, loans, corporate grants, and franchises, but it also assumed direct responsibility for some economic activities, including building the Erie Canal.[40] Even when the states, lacking sufficient tax funds, began dissipating their modern public power by reverting to the premodern practice of enlisting private wealth to carry out public ends by issuing increasing numbers of corporate charters, they continued to use their ancient police power to regulate their economies. Between 1780 and 1814, the Massachusetts legislature, for example, enacted a multitude of laws regulating the marketing of a variety of products—everything from lumber, fish, tobacco, and shoes, to butter, bread, nails, and firearms. The states never lost their inherited responsibility for the safety, economy, morality, and health of their societies.[41] The idea that there was a public good that could interfere with some private rights remained very much alive.

Despite all this state police power legislation and municipal regulation, however, it was usually left to the courts to sort out and mediate the conflicting claims of public authority and the private rights of individuals. The more the state legislatures enacted statutes to manage and regulate the economy, the more judges found it necessary to exert their authority in order to do justice between individuals and to make sense of what was happening. Following the lead of William Blackstone and Lord Mansfield in eighteenth-century England, American judges in the early Republic interpreted the common law flexibly in order to mitigate and correct the harm done by the profusion of conflicting statutes passed by unstable democratic legislatures.[42] Judges were often able to play down the importance of precedents and to emphasize instead reason, equity, and convenience in order to bring the law into accord with changing commercial circumstances.[43]

They were able to do this and to expand their authority by transforming many public issues of the economy into private ones, turning political questions into questions of individual rights that could only be judicially determined. If an enterprising and improving society needed certainty in the law, then the courts seemed more capable than popular legislatures in assuring it. The success of the courts in promoting commercial and economic development in the early Republic was due in large part to their ability to separate the legal issues of individual rights from the tumultuous and chaotic world of democratic politics. As Chief Justice John Marshall said in his *Marbury* decision of 1803, some questions were political; "they respect the nation, not individual rights," and thus were "only politically examinable" by elected legislatures. But questions involving the vested rights of individuals were different; they were in their "nature, judicial, and must be tried by the judicial authority."[44] But these efforts to protect the rights of individuals from political abuse were not just Federalist-inspired. Even the strongly Jeffersonian Virginia court of appeals in 1804 took the position that the state legislature could do many things, but it could not violate private and vested rights of property.[45]

In the late 1780s, Madison had yearned for some enlightened and impartial men who would somehow transcend the interest-group politics that plagued the state legislatures. In *The Federalist* No. 10 he had used judicial imagery in describing the problems of America's legislative politics. Madison accepted the fact that the regulation of different commercial interests had become the principal task of modern legislation. This meant, he wrote, that in the future the spirit of party and faction was likely to be involved in the ordinary operations of government. Since in traditional fashion he continued to think of all legislative acts as "so many judicial determinations, not indeed concerning the rights of single persons, but concerning the rights of large bodies of citizens," he could only conclude pessimistically that legislators would become "both judges and parties at the same time." The best solution he could offer to prevent these parties from becoming judges in their own causes and violating the rights of individuals and minorities was to enlarge the arena of politics so that no party could dominate, thus allowing only disinterested and impartial men to exercise power and make decisions. He hoped against hope that the new elevated federal government might assume a judicial-like character and become a "disinterested and dispassionate umpire in disputes between different passions and interests" within the individual states.[46] By the early decades of the nineteenth century, he, along with many other Americans, came to the conclusion that perhaps the judiciary was the only governmental institution that even came close to playing this role. It is a conclusion that in our history we have reached time and time again.

AFTERWORD TO CHAPTER 11

This paper is actually a revised composite of several different lectures and articles. It began as a lecture at the American Antiquarian Society in October 1991 celebrating the bicentennial of the Bill of Rights. This lecture was later published in the *Proceedings of the American Antiquarian Society*, 101, Part 2 (1992), 255–274. Some of the material in that paper found its way into the McCorkle Lecture given at the University of Virginia School of Law in March 1999, and was later published as "The Origins of Vested Rights in the Early Republic" in the *Virginia Law Review*, 85 (1999), 1421–1445. This article was in turn heavily revised and presented as a lecture at Colgate University in 2001 and published as "The History of Rights in Early America" in *The Nature of Rights at the American Founding and Beyond*, edited by Barry Alan Shain (Charlottesville: University of Virginia Press, 2007), 233–257. Anyone interested in the development of rights in early America can do no better than to consult the other papers in this volume, all written by distinguished political scientists and historians.

The AMERICAN REVOLUTIONARY TRADITION, *or* WHY AMERICA WANTS *to* SPREAD DEMOCRACY AROUND *the* WORLD

HE REVOLUTION BEGAN on April 19, 1775, with, as Emerson put it in the mid-nineteenth century, a "shot heard round the world." That, in fact, was how the nineteenth century saw the Revolution—as an event of worldwide significance. It was an event that opened up a new era in politics and society, not just for Americans but eventually for everyone in the world. It is a perspective on the American Revolution not always grasped, even by Americans, and it is the perspective of this essay.

It was "America's destiny," said the Hungarian patriot Louis Kossuth in 1852, "to become the cornerstone of Liberty on earth." "Should the Republic of America ever lose this consciousness of this destiny," Kossuth went on in a speech given while he was in the United States trying to raise money for the 1848 Hungarian revolution, "that moment would be just as surely the beginning of America's decline as the 19th of April 1775 was the beginning of the Republic of America."

I don't know if that moment of decline is at hand or not, but in the aftermath of September 11 and our involvement in Iraq and Afghanistan, we are certainly at a significant moment in our history. We now dominate the world as no nation in history ever has. Our military expenditures are nearly equal to those of all the other nations in the world put together. We have over a million men and women under arms and we have troops in at least forty countries. This may not be an empire in the traditional meaning of that term, but it is an extraordinary degree of dominance over the world that we are exercising. Is this the fulfillment of our destiny, as Kossuth saw it, to build liberty everywhere? Or is it a repudiation of our destiny? Have we lost our consciousness of being the bearers of liberty? Have we become just another great imperial power? Did our invasion of Iraq in order to bring democracy to the Middle East mark the end of our Revolutionary tradition, or, instead, was it the fulfillment of it?

It is hard for many people to think of the United States as a revolutionary nation operating out of a revolutionary tradition. For the past six or seven decades or more the United States has so often stood on the side of established governments and opposed to revolutionary movements that to describe America as a revolutionary state seems to be an oxymoron. So reactionary did many intellectuals think American policy was during the Cold War that they could only conclude that our involvement in the world was due solely to American capitalism and its needs. Many people continue to believe that our involvement in the Middle East can be explained simply in terms of oil. No doubt such economic explanations can make sense of particular events at particular times, but they cannot do justice to the incredibly complicated and ideological relationship we have had with the rest of the world throughout our history. Economic considerations, for example, can never adequately explain America's tragic involvement in Vietnam. But America's revolutionary tradition can.

The Revolution is important to us Americans for many reasons, not least because it gave us our obsessive concern with our own morality and our messianic sense of purpose in the world. In short, the Revolution made us an ideological people.

We do not like to think of ourselves as an ideologically minded people. Ideology seems to have no place in American thinking. The word even sounds European. It conjures up systems of doctrinaire ideas and dogmatic, abstract theories. It could hardly have much to do with the practical, pragmatic people we Americans have generally thought ourselves to be. And certainly ideology, it used to be thought, could not have been involved in that most practical of revolutions—the American Revolution.

Few historians of the Revolution believe that anymore. It now seems clear that the Revolution was very much an ideological movement, involving a fundamental shift in ideas and values. In fact, I would go so far as to say that the American Revolution was as ideological as any revolution in modern Western history, and as a consequence, we Americans have been as ideological-minded as any people in Western culture.

Of course, we Americans have vaguely known all along that we are peculiarly dedicated to intellectual principles, and that adherence to these intellectual principles has been the major adhesive holding us together. We Americans do not have a nationality the way other peoples do. Our sense of being a distinct ethnicity was not something we could take for granted, the way most Europeans could—which of course is why we can absorb immigrants more easily than they can. A nation like ours, made up of so many races and ethnicities, could not assume its identity as a matter of course. The American nation had to be invented or contrived.

At the end of the Declaration of Independence, the members of the Continental Congress mutually pledged to each other their lives, their fortunes, and their sacred honor. There was nothing else but themselves they could dedicate themselves to—no patria, no fatherland, no nation as yet.

In comparison with the 235-year-old United States, many European states are new, some created in the twentieth century. Yet these European states, new as they may be, are undergirded by peoples who had a preexisting sense of their own distinctiveness, their own nationhood. In the United States, the process was reversed. We Americans created a state before we were a nation, and much of our history has been an effort to define the nature of that nationality. In an important sense, we have never been a nation in any traditional meaning of the term. It is the state, the Constitution, the principles of liberty, equality, and free government that make us think of ourselves as a single people. To be an American is not to be someone, but to believe in something.

What is the nature of this ideology created by the American Revolution? Looking back from our vantage point at the beginning of the twenty-first century, what strikes me as most extraordinary about the Revolution is the world-shattering significance the Revolutionaries gave to it. In light of the fact that we did eventually become the greatest power the world has ever seen, it requires an act of imagination to recover the audacity and presumptuousness of Americans in 1776 in claiming that their little colonial rebellion possessed universal importance. After all, those thirteen colonies made up an insignificant proportion of the Western world, numbering perhaps two million people, huddled along a narrow strip of the Atlantic coast, three thousand miles from the centers of civilization. To believe that anything they did would matter to the rest of the world was the height of arrogance. Yet the Revolutionaries and their heirs in the nineteenth century sincerely believed that they were leading the world toward a new libertarian future. Our conception of ourselves as the leader of the free world began in 1776.

What made this presumptuous attitude possible, what made Americans in 1776 think they were on the edge of a new era in history, pointing the way toward a new kind of politics and society and a new sort of world, what, in short, transformed their Revolution into something more than a colonial rebellion was the revolutionary ideology of republicanism.

It has been only in the past generation or so that we have come to understand just how ideologically charged with republicanism the eighteenth century was. (For the term "republicanism" we today have to substitute the word "democracy," or we won't understand what was meant in the eighteenth century. After all, the Chinese today live in a republic, as do the Syrians and the Cubans. And for monarchy we have to think of authoritarian governments, since a good proportion of the states of Western Europe are monarchies.) Where republicanism today is taken so much for granted and where much of the monarchy that remains seems so benign, it is difficult to appreciate the power republicanism had for eighteenth-century intellectuals. Indeed, republicanism was as radical for the eighteenth century as Marxism was for the nineteenth. Republicanism and the republican tradition framed for all sorts of political and social critics of eighteenth-century Europe the moral perspective with which they confronted the dominant monarchism and materialism of the age.

This republicanism was not an indigenous ideology peculiar only to Americans, but was in fact a product of a long-existing heritage of civic humanism, originating in the classical Latin literature of antiquity—with Livy, Cicero, Tacitus, Sallust, and others—revived by Machiavelli and others in the Renaissance and carried into the eighteenth century by nearly everyone who claimed to be enlightened. These republican values articulated most vociferously but not exclusively by the popularizers and heirs of the seventeenth-century republicans—Harrington, Milton, and Sidney—promised far more than the elimination of kings and new elective governments. Republicanism, in fact, promised an entirely new morality. It necessarily involved the character and culture of the society and thus possessed immense significance for any people who should decide to become republican.

Everyone in the eighteenth century knew that republicanism required a special kind of people, a people who possessed virtue, who were willing to surrender their private interests for the sake of the whole. As we have seen in the earlier essays in this collection, monarchy or authoritarian governments were so prevalent because they were based on the assumption that people were incapable of this kind of virtue. Monarchy presumed that people were selfish and corrupt and that without the existence of the strong, unitary authority of monarchy, the society would fall apart. Theorists of the eighteenth century like Montesquieu would have understood perfectly what happened in the Soviet Union and in Yugoslavia in the 1990s when a strong unitary authority was removed. They would have understood too why the states of Iraq and Afghanistan and elsewhere are having such trouble sustaining themselves. People assert their various selfish ethnicities, religions, and interests, and the society cannot hold together and falls apart. Montesquieu would have said that the people of these states lacked sufficient virtue to hold their societies together.

Monarchies thus had advantages that republics lacked, which is why they have existed everywhere since the beginning of history and why authoritarian governments still flourish around the world. Monarchies were utterly realistic or cynical about human nature. Supporters of monarchy did not expect humans to be anything but corrupt and selfish. Authoritarian kings possessed a number of means for holding their diverse and corrupt societies together. Monarchies had powerful single executives, a multitude of offices, complicated social hierarchies, titles of honor, standing armies, and established churches to maintain cohesion.

But republics possessed few of the adhesive attributes of monarchies. Therefore, order, if there were to be any in republics, would have to come from below, from the virtue or selflessness of the people themselves. Yet precisely because republics were so utterly dependent on the people, they were also the states most sensitive to changes in the moral character of their societies. In short, republics were the most delicate and fragile kinds of states. There was nothing but the moral quality of the people themselves to keep republics from being torn apart by factionalism and division. Republics were thus the states most likely to experience political death.

To the eighteenth century the decay and death of states seemed as scientifically grounded as the decay and death of human beings. "It is with states as it is with men" was a commonplace of the day. "They have their infancy, their manhood, and their decline." The study of the life cycle of states, focusing on political disease, was of central concern to the Enlightenment, for through such political pathology, people could further their knowledge of political health and prevent the process of decay. With these kinds of concerns, the whole world, including the past, became a kind of laboratory in which the sifting and evaluating of empirical evidence would lead to an understanding of social sickness and health. Political science became a kind of diagnostics, and history became an autopsy of the past. Those states that had died would be cut open, so to speak, and examined in order to discover why they had died.

Of course, the most important states that had died were the republics of antiquity, especially the ancient republic of Rome. The death of Rome fascinated eighteenth-century thinkers. Almost every intellectual, including Montesquieu, tried his hand at writing about the decline and fall of Rome. Reading the great Latin writers of antiquity, the eighteenth century came to realize that the Roman republic became great not simply by the force of its arms; nor was it destroyed by military might. Both Rome's greatness and its eventual fall were caused by the character of its people. As long as the Roman people maintained their love of virtue, their simplicity and equality, their scorn of great distinctions, and their willingness to fight for the state, they attained great heights of glory. But when they became too luxury-loving, too obsessed with refinements and social distinctions, too preoccupied with money, and too effeminate to take up arms on behalf of the state, their politics became corrupted, selfishness predominated, and the dissolution of the state had to follow. Rome fell not because of the invasions of the barbarians from without, but because of decay from within.

The lesson for the Revolutionaries in 1776 was obvious. If their experiment in republicanism were to succeed, the American people had to avoid the luxury and corruption that had destroyed ancient Rome. They had to be a morally virtuous people.

Americans had good reason to believe that they were ideally adapted for republican government. Most of them, at least the white portion, were independent yeoman farmers, Jefferson's "chosen people of God," who were widely regarded as the most incorruptible sorts of citizens and the best foundation for a republic. There were no titled aristocrats in America and none of the legal distinctions and privileges that encumbered the European states. All in all, Americans in 1776 thought they were the special kind of simple, austere, egalitarian, and virtuous people that enlightened social science said was essential for the sustenance of a republic. Their moral quality thus became a measure of their success as a society, and this inevitably gave their new Republic an experimental and problematical character.

The Americans thus began their Revolution in a spirit of high adventure. They knew they were embarking on a grand experiment in self-government. That experiment remained very much in doubt during the first half of the nineteenth century, especially during the Civil War, when monarchy still dominated all of Europe. Hence we can understand the importance of Lincoln's Gettysburg Address, in which he described the Civil War as a test of whether a nation conceived in liberty could long endure. This idea that republican government was a perilous experiment was part of America's consciousness from the beginning.

All of this republican ideology assumed tremendous moral force. When fused with Protestant millennialism, it gave Americans the sense that they were chosen people of God, possessing peculiar qualities of virtue, with a special responsibility to lead the world toward liberty and republican government.

Americans began their experiment in republicanism with very high hopes that other peoples would follow their lead in throwing off monarchy. But they also knew that it wouldn't be easy, since republicanism required a particular moral quality in its people. Naturally, at first they saw the French Revolution as a copy of their own Revolution, and they welcomed the effort. Lafayette sent the key to the Bastille to Washington in gratitude for America's having inspired the French Revolution. But its rapid perversion and excesses, ending in Napoleonic despotism, disillusioned many Americans about the ability of Europeans to emulate them in becoming republican. They came to see the French Revolution as simply an abortive attempt to imitate the successful American effort at establishing republicanism. Far from changing things for the better in Europe, the French Revolution had failed. And thus the Americans' optimism about the future was tempered by doubts.

These doubts soon played into American attitudes toward the Latin

American colonial rebellions that broke out in the early decades of the nineteenth century. If any revolutions were emulations of the American Revolution, these certainly seemed to be. And, of course, Americans like John Adams and Thomas Jefferson welcomed them. But at the same time they were skeptical of the South Americans' ability to create free republican governments. Did they have the stuff, the virtue, that republicans were made of? "I feared from the beginning," wrote Jefferson in 1821, "that these people were not as yet sufficiently enlightened for self-government; and that after wading through blood and slaughter, they would end in military tyrannies, more or less numerous. Yet as they wished to try the experiment [in republicanism], I wish them success in it."

Thus Americans from the outset had an ambiguous attitude toward republican revolutions in other parts of the world. Naturally there was no hostility, only sympathy and enthusiasm mixed with some skepticism, a well-wishing mingled with a kind of patronizing pessimism bred of an anxiety that other peoples would not have the sort of social and moral qualities necessary to carry through a successful republican revolution. Nevertheless, Americans continued to believe that they, and not the French, were the revolutionary nation par excellence.

And some Europeans agreed with them. Count Metternich, the chief minister of the Austrian-Hungarian Empire, excoriated the United States for proclaiming in 1823 the Monroe Doctrine, which told the Europeans that they no longer had any role to play in the New World:

> In their indecent declarations [these United States] have cast blame and scorn on the institutions of Europe most worthy of respect. . . . In permitting themselves these unprovoked attacks, in fostering revolutions wherever they show themselves, in regretting those which have failed, in extending a helping hand to those which seem to prosper, they lend new strength to the apostles of sedition and re-animate the courage of every conspirator. If this flood of evil doctrines and pernicious examples should extend over the whole of America, what would become of

our religious and political institutions, of the moral forces of our governments, and of the conservative system which has saved Europe from complete dissolution?

Despite promising not to intervene in Europe's internal affairs and expressing a desire to have no entangling alliances with Europe, most Americans remained very concerned with what went on there. Yet they were reluctant to get directly involved in any revolutionary ventures that might endanger their own republican experiment. Believing that people who were ready for republicanism would sooner or later become republicans as they had, Americans in the nineteenth century concluded that they could best accomplish their mission of bringing free governments to the rest of the world simply by existing as a free government, by being an exemplar to the world.

William Wirt of Virginia put this very nicely in a speech in Baltimore in 1830. "We stand under a fearful responsibility to our Creator and our fellow citizens," Wirt told his audience. "It has been his divine pleasure that we should be sent forth as the harbinger of free government on the earth, and in this attitude we are now before the world. The eyes of the world are upon us; and our example will probably be decisive of the cause of human liberty."

So Americans watched and encouraged all the nineteenth-century revolutions. They did not intervene in deed, but they did in every other way. Individuals raised money for the rebels and some went off to fight on behalf of revolutionary movements. In all the European revolutions of the century—the Greek revolt of 1821, the French constitutional transformation of 1830, the general European insurrections of 1848, and the overthrow of the Second French Empire and the establishment of the Third French Republic in 1870—the United States was usually the first state in the world to extend diplomatic recognition to the new revolutionary regimes.

After all, in the Americans' eyes these European revolutions were simply efforts by oppressed peoples to become like them, all species of the same revolutionary *genus Americanus*. Americans never felt threatened by these revolutions and had no fear whatsoever of the spread of revolutionary ideas. There was, of course, one exception to this enthusiasm for revolution: the Haitian revolution that created in 1804 the second republic in the New World. We did not recognize the Haitian republic until Lincoln's administration. But we welcomed all the others and toasted those revolutionary patriots like Kossuth when they came to America in search of money and support.

Naturally, this encouragement of revolution did not endear us to the European monarchies. But nineteenth-century Americans in their geographical separation simply did not care. We were proud of our revolutionary example and simply assumed that we were the cause of all the revolutionary upheavals in nineteenth-century Europe. When the Hapsburg monarchy protested American sympathy with the Hungarian revolution of 1848, Secretary of State Daniel Webster did not resort to any traditional polite diplomatic evasion. Quite the contrary—he claimed nothing less than full American responsibility for the upheavals. He told the Austrian Hungarian minister in Washington "that the prevalence on the other continent of sentiments favorable to republican liberty is the result of the reaction of America upon Europe; and the source and center of that reaction has doubtless been, and now is, in these United States." Webster then went on to add, in one of those gratuitous insults for which American diplomatic messages in the nineteenth century were famous, that in comparison with the great extent of the United States, the Hapsburg monarchy was "but a patch on the earth's surface."

Because nineteenth-century Americans frequently resorted to such spread-eagled bombast but actually did very little to aid the revolutions, many historians have concluded that America's revolutionary sympathy was something of a fraud. But I think such a conclusion misunderstands the peculiar character of America's nineteenth-century revolutionary tradition. Because of their republican assumptions, Americans believed that any revolution in Europe would have to come from the oppressed peoples themselves and from the moral force of America's example as a republic. But they never had any doubt that America was the center of the international revolution. This American ethnocentricity is mind-boggling. The best example I know of is a message from President Grant to the French government sent in response to the French overthrow of the Second Empire and the establishment of the Third Republic in 1870. Despite America's determination not to intervene in Europe's affairs, President Grant told the French, "We cannot be indifferent to the spread of American political ideas in a great and civilized country like France." It was as if France had no revolutionary tradition of its own to call on. One wonders what the officials at the French foreign office thought of this extraordinary message.

Because of the slowness with which republicanism spread, however, nineteenth-century Americans increasingly concluded that they were destined to be the only successful republican state in a corrupt world. Millions of people in the world seemed to think so too. The migration to the United States between 1820 and 1920 of over thirty-five million refugees from monarchism gave the Americans' conception of themselves as a chosen people a less divine and more literal meaning and confirmed for them their preeminence as a revolutionary people.

It is within this nineteenth-century context, this revolutionary tradition of republicanism, and this belief of Americans that they were in the vanguard of history leading the world toward liberty that we can begin to comprehend the extraordinary American reaction to the Russian Revolution of 1917. In the full sweep of American history up to that time, no foreign event had such a dramatic and searing effect on Americans as did the Bolshevik revolution of November 1917. After that momentous event, our understanding of ourselves and the world became very confused.

At first, with the March 1917 overthrow of the tsar and the formation of the provisional government, Americans welcomed the Russian Revolution as they had welcomed earlier antimonarchical European revolutions. Seven days after the tsar abdicated, the United States extended diplomatic recognition to the new Russian government, the first power in the world to do so. President Wilson now thought he had "a fit partner for a league of honor," a league which Wilson hoped would be a means for the worldwide extension of republicanism. In May 1917 the American ambassador in Moscow wrote back to the United States that he expected Russia to come out of its ordeal "as a republic, and with a government . . . founded on correct principles"—that is to say, principles similar to those of the American Republic.

Yet with the Bolshevik takeover of the revolution in the fall of 1917, all this initial American enthusiasm quickly disappeared. Instead of the Russian Revolution's firmest friend, the United States suddenly became its most bitter enemy. Instead of quickly extending diplomatic recognition to the new republican regime, as American governments had traditionally done throughout the nineteenth century, the United States withheld diplomatic recognition from the Soviet Union for sixteen years and four American presidencies, making the United States not the first but the last major Western power to recognize the revolutionary regime.

In light of America's earlier revolutionary tradition, this was a remarkable turnabout—a turnabout, however, that is explicable only in terms of that earlier revolutionary tradition. What was now different, what caused this abrupt change of attitude, was the nature of the Bolshevik appeal, the new character of the communist ideology. The Russian Revolution was not another species of the revolutionary *genus Americanus*; it was a new revolutionary genus altogether. The Bolsheviks claimed not simply to be leading another antimonarchical republican revolution in emulation of the American or French models of the late eighteenth century. The Bolsheviks said that their communist revolution represented a totally new departure in world history. Others saw what this meant. The Swiss playwright and essayist Herman Kesser said in 1918 that "it is [now] certain that mankind must make up its mind either for Wilson or for Lenin."

The great antagonism that immediately sprang up between the United States and the Soviet Union rested not simply on the exigencies of power politics, or the circumstances of contrasting marketing systems, but, more important, on the competitiveness of two very different revolutionary traditions. The Cold War really began in 1917. The Soviet Union threatened nothing less than the displacement of the United States from the vanguard of history. The Russians, not the Americans, now claimed to be pointing the way toward the future (and, more alarming still, there were some American intellectuals in the 1920s and 1930s who agreed with that claim).

For the first time since 1776, Americans were faced with an alternative revolutionary ideology with universalist aspirations equal to their own. This ideological threat was far more serious to us than anything the Russians did technologically, either in developing the H-bomb or in launching Sputnik. For it seemed to make America's heritage irrelevant. If we Americans were not leading the world toward liberty and free government, what then was our history all about?

With this dramatic emergence of an opposing revolutionary ideology, Americans in the twentieth century grew more and more confused about themselves and their place in history. They could not very well stand against the idea of revolution, but at the same time they could no longer be very enthusiastic about revolutions that they assumed would be communist. With the enunciation of the Truman Doctrine in 1947, the United States for the first time in its history committed itself to supporting established governments of "free peoples" against the threat from subversion from "armed minorities"—presumably communist—within the state. Our Cold War struggle with the Soviet Union eventually culminated in our disastrous intervention in Vietnam in the 1960s. Most Americans thought they were simply following President Kennedy's call in 1961 to "pay any price, bear any burden, meet any hardship, support any friend or oppose any foe to assure the survival and the success of liberty." Only this time, support for liberty meant supporting an existing government against revolution.

The fundamental threat to the meaning of our history posed by a rival revolutionary ideology blinded us to the nationalistic and other ethnocultural forces at work in the world. In such an atmosphere it became difficult for us not to believe that every revolution was in some way communist, and consequently our definition of "free" governments was stretched to extraordinary lengths to cover eventually any government that was noncommunist. The ironies, of course, are abundant: we Americans spent ten years between 1979 and 1989 helping the Taliban in Afghanistan withstand a Soviet takeover.

It would be a mistake, however, to see our support of corrupt or reactionary regimes as the direct response of American capitalism or as the result of some deep-rooted abhorrence of revolution. Many of our Cold War actions, clumsy and misguided as they often may have been, represented our confused and sometimes desperate efforts to maintain our universalist revolutionary aspirations in the world.

Our Point Four Program accompanied the Truman Doctrine; the Peace Corps coincided with our involvement in Vietnam. All were linked; all were cut from the same ideological cloth; all were expressions of what was becoming an increasingly dimly perceived sense of America's revolutionary mission in the world.

Suddenly, in 1989, this all changed. The Soviet Union collapsed; with it, its revolutionary aspirations to make the world over as communist collapsed as well. Joel Barr, an American engineer who had defected to the Soviet Union in 1950, told a *Los Angeles Times* reporter in 1992 that he had been wrong about communism. "I believe that now history will show that the Russian Revolution was a tremendous mistake. It was a step backward," he said. "The real revolution for mankind that will go down for many, many years was the American Revolution."

We're living at an extraordinary moment in our history. It is not at all clear what the consequences of the momentous events we're living through will be. At first September 11 seemed to have increased, not weakened, our desire to dominate the world. President George W. Bush came into office opposed to nation building. Then he became determined to do just that in Iraq. Lots of intelligent Americans, like Tom Friedman of the *New York Times* and the editors of the *New Republic*, initially welcomed the idea of bringing democracy to the Middle East. But after a long, frustrating struggle, we are now merely hoping against hope that as we get out of Iraq, it will become perhaps not a democracy but at least a functioning state. In Afghanistan we don't even talk about democracy. All we can hope for there is the establishment of a reasonably stable state capable of resisting the Taliban, or perhaps not even that— just a state capable of resisting Al Qaida. These Middle East wars seem to have drained away most of our idealism about changing the world. Yet what is happening in Egypt and elsewhere in the Middle East is reviving the hope of democracy re-emerging in the region, however tenuously.

We seem to be very much an all-or-nothing people. It is very difficult for us to maintain a *realpolitik* attitude toward the world. We have to be either saving the world or shunning it. In the 1990s some intellectuals were bitterly opposed to any of the messianic impulses coming out of our revolutionary tradition. Some, including Irving Kristol, thought that we had become a middle-aged nation not all that different from the nations of Europe. But still others, such as Secretary of State Madeleine Albright, contended that we were still the indispensable nation. Now, at the beginning of the second decade of the twenty-first century, we seem to be in a quandary about what to do, about what our role in the world ought to be. We remain the sole superpower but still unsure of quite how to use that power.

What the future will be is impossible to tell. All we can do with our history is to remember that the United States has always been to ourselves and to the world primarily an idea. However many troops we can muster around the world will mean little if, in using them, we erode that idea, that moral authority which is the real source of our strength and our ability to gain the admiration and support of other peoples.

Our revolutionary heritage still commands the attention of many people in the world—our devotion to liberty and equality, our abhorrence of privilege, our fear of abused political power, our faith in constitutionalism and individual liberties. This was brought home to me over three decades ago at a talk I gave in Warsaw in 1976—during the bicentennial of the American Revolution. It was an incident that I will never forget. It was well before the end of the Cold War, even several years before the emergence of Solidarity, the movement in 1980 that was the beginning of the end of communism in Poland.

At the end of my very ordinary lecture on the American Revolution, a young Polish intellectual rose to tell me that I had left out the most important part. Naturally, I was stunned. She said I had not mentioned the Bill of Rights—the constitutional protection of individual liberties against the government. It was true. I had taken the Bill of Rights for granted. But this young Polish woman living under a communist regime could not take individual rights for granted.

We forget—we take for granted—the important things. This example of the Polish intellectual showed me that our republic was still a potent experiment in liberty worth demonstrating to the rest of the world. We can only hope that that idea of America will never die.

ACKNOWLEDGMENTS

Since these essays were written at various times over the past half century, I have incurred a host of debts that I can never adequately repay. The individuals who have helped over the decades are too many to name, but they certainly include the administrative staff of the History Department at Brown University; I am grateful to all of the staff through the years, and most recently Karen Mota, Cherrie Guerzon, Mary Beth Bryson, and Julissa Bautista. My former editor at Penguin and now agent, Scott Moyers, has been especially helpful. He is a brilliant editor, and he is responsible for the titles of several of my books, including this one. I can't thank him enough. Laura Stickney, my new editor at Penguin, has been encouraging and patient, with a keen eye for what's appropriate and what's not, and I am grateful for her able assistance in bringing out this book. I am grateful too for Cathy Dexter's excellent copyediting. I am also very grateful to Barbara Campo at Penguin for all of her help in seeing the book into production. Of course, I owe the most to my editor in chief, my wife, Louise, who has borne with me all these years.

NOTES

INTRODUCTION

1. Isaiah Berlin, *The Hedge and the Fox: An Essay on Tolstoy's View of History* (New York: Simon and Schuster, 1953), 1–2.
2. James H. Broussard, "Historians and the Early Republic: SHEAR's Origins and Prospects," *Journal of the Early Republic*, II (1982), 66.
3. Winthrop D. Jordan, *White Over Black: American Attitudes Toward the Negro, 1550–1812* (Chapel Hill: University of North Carolina Press, 1968); James M. Banner Jr., *To the Hartford Convention: The Federalists and the Origins of Party Politics in Massachusetts, 1789–1815* (New York: Knopf, 1970).
4. Broussard, "Historians and the Early Republic," 66.
5. William Nesbit Chambers, *Political Parties in a New Nation: The American Experience, 1776–1809* (New York: Oxford University Press, 1963); Seymour Martin Lipset, *The First New Nation: The United States in Historical and Comparative Perspective* (New York: Basic Books, 1963).
6. On the differing historical views of the early Republic, see Gordon S. Wood, "The Significance of the Early Republic," *Journal of the Early Republic*, VIII (1988), 1–20, from which some of this introduction is derived.
7. Jim Cullen, review of Gordon Wood's *Empire of Liberty: A History of the Early Republic, 1789–1815* (New York: Oxford University Press, 2009), on *History News Network*, December 1, 2009.
8. See in particular Richard Hofstadter, *The Progressive Historians: Turner, Beard, Parrington* (New York: Knopf, 1968). Before his untimely death in 1970, Hofstadter planned a multivolume history of the late eighteenth through early nineteenth centuries—the very period that fascinated his mentors. What he completed of his first volume was published posthumously as *America in 1750: A Social Portrait* (New York: Knopf, 1971).
9. Among the best of these was Dixon Ryan Fox, *The Decline of Aristocracy in the Politics of New York* (New York: Columbia University Press and Longmans, Green and Co., 1919).
10. For a summary of this anti-Progressive literature, see Bernard Bailyn, "Political Experience and Enlightenment Ideas in Eighteenth-Century America," *American Historical Review*, LXVII (1962), 339–351.
11. Edward Pessen, *Most Uncommon Jacksonians: The Radical Leaders of the Early Labor Movement* (Albany: State University of New York Press, 1967); Douglas T. Miller, *Jacksonian Aristocracy: Class and Democracy in New York, 1830–1860* (New York: Oxford University Press, 1967).
12. Richard Hofstadter, *The American Political Tradition and the Men Who Make It* (New York: Knopf, 1951), esp. 44–66; Bray Hammond, *Banks and Politics in America: From the Revolution to the Civil War* (Princeton: Princeton University Press, 1957).
13. Louis Hartz, *The Liberal Tradition in America* (New York: Harcourt, Brace, 1955).
14. Richard D. Brown, *Modernization: The Transformation of American Life, 1600–1865* (New York: Hill and Wang, 1976).
15. It was these headline events of politics and diplomacy that Henry Adams concentrated on in his classic account of the period. Henry Adams, *History of the United States of America During the*

Administrations of Thomas Jefferson and James Madison, 9 vols. (New York: Charles Scribner's Sons, 1889–1891).

16. See, for example, Mary Beth Norton, *Liberty's Daughters: The Revolutionary Experience of American Women, 1750–1800* (Boston: Little, Brown, 1980); Nancy F. Cott, *The Bonds of Womanhood: "Woman's Sphere" in New England, 1780–1835* (New Haven, CT: Yale University Press, 1977); Lee Chambers-Schiller, *Liberty, a Better Husband: Single Women in America: The Generations of 1780–1840* (New Haven, CT: Yale University Press, 1984); Joan M. Jensen, *Loosening the Bonds: Mid-Atlantic Farm Women, 1750–1850* (New Haven, CT: Yale University Press, 1986); Donald M. Scott, *From Office to Profession: The New England Ministry, 1750–1850* (Philadelphia: University of Pennsylvania Press, 1978); Gerard W. Gawalt, *The Promise of Power: The Emergence of the Legal Profession in Massachusetts, 1760–1840* (Westport, CT: Greenwood Press, 1979); W. J. Rorabaugh, *The Craft Apprentice: From Franklin to the Machine Age in America* (New York: Oxford University Press, 1986); Patricia Cline Cohen, *A Calculating People: The Spread of Numeracy in Early America* (Chicago: University of Chicago Press, 1982); Carl F. Kaestle, *Pillars of the Republic: Common Schools and American Society, 1780–1860* (New York: Hill and Wang, 1983); W. J. Rorabaugh, *The Alcoholic Republic: An American Tradition* (New York: Oxford University Press, 1979); Paul G. Faler, *Mechanics and Manufacturers in the Early Industrial Revolution: Lynn, Massachusetts, 1780–1860* (Albany: State University of New York Press, 1981); Sean Wilentz, *Chants Democratic: New York City and the Rise of the American Working Class, 1788–1850* (New York: Oxford University Press, 1984); Cynthia J. Shelton, *The Mills of Manayunk: Industrialization and Social Conflict in the Philadelphia Region, 1787–1837* (Baltimore: Johns Hopkins University Press, 1986); Paul Gilje, *The Road to Mobocracy: Popular Disorder in New York City, 1763–1834* (Chapel Hill: University of North Carolina Press, 1987); James H. Merrell, *The Indians' New World: Catawbas and Their Neighbors from European Contact Through the Era of Removal* (Chapel Hill: University of North Carolina Press, 1989); David Brion Davis, *The Problem of Slavery in the Age of Revolution, 1770–1823* (Ithaca, NY: Cornell University Press, 1975); Richard R. John, *Spreading the News: the American Postal System from Franklin to Morse* (Cambridge, MA: Harvard University Press, 1995); William E. Nelson, *Americanization of the Common Law: The Impact of Legal Change in Massachusetts Society, 1760–1830* (Cambridge, MA: Harvard University Press, 1975); Morton J. Horwitz, *The Transformation of American Law, 1780–1860* (Cambridge, MA: Harvard University Press, 1977); Donald A. Hutslar, *The Architecture of Migration: Log Construction in the Ohio Country, 1750–1850* (Athens, OH: Ohio University Press, 1986).

17. On the topics of research emerging in the historiography of the early Republic, see John Lauritz Larson and Michael A. Morrison, eds., *Whither the Early Republic: A Forum on the Future of the Field* (Philadelphia: University of Pennsylvania Press, 2005).

18. James Henretta, "Families and Farms: Mentalité in Pre-Industrial America," *William and Mary Quarterly*, 3rd ser., 35 (1978), 3–32; Christopher M. Jedrey, *The World of John Cleaveland: Family and Community in Eighteenth-Century New England* (New York: W. W. Norton, 1979); Allan Kulikoff, *The Agrarian Origins of American Capitalism* (Charlottesville: University Press of Virginia, 1992). Crucially important for dating the changes in the Northern economy is Winifred Barr Rothenberg, *From Market-Places to a Market Economy: The Transformation of Rural Massachusetts, 1750–1850* (Chicago: University of Chicago Press, 1992).

19. Daniel T. Rodgers, "Republicanism: The Career of a Concept," *Journal of American History*, LXXIX (1992), 25.

20. T. H. Breen, *American Insurgents, American Patriots: The Revolution of the People* (New York: Hill and Wang, 2010), 11.

21. Sir Lewis Namier, *Personalities and Powers* (London: Hamish Hamilton, 1955), 2.

22. For a fuller explanation of the view of the role of ideas in human experience, see Gordon S. Wood, "Intellectual History and the Social Sciences," in John Higham and Paul K. Conkin, eds., *New Directions in American Intellectual History* (Baltimore: Johns Hopkins University Press, 1979), 27. My approach to the role of ideas has been very much influenced by the work of Quentin Skinner. See James Tully, ed., *Meaning and Context: Quentin Skinner and His Critics* (Princeton: Princeton University Press, 1988). For concrete examples of Skinner's approach applied to history, see "The Principles and Practice of Opposition: The Case of Bolingbroke versus Walpole," in Neil

McKendrick, ed., *Historical Perspectives: Studies in English Thought and Society in Honour of J. H. Plumb* (London: Europa, 1974), 93–128, and John Brewer, *Party Ideology and Popular Politics at the Accession of George III* (Cambridge, UK: Cambridge University Press, 1976), 26–38.

23. Claude G. Bowers, *Jefferson and Hamilton: The Struggle for Democracy in America* (Boston: Houghton Mifflin, 1925), vi, 140.

24. For a major example, see Garry Wills, *"Negro President": Jefferson and the Slave Power* (Boston: Houghton Mifflin, 2003).

25. Doron Ben-Artar and Barbara B. Oberg, eds., *Federalists Reconsidered* (Charlottesville: University of Virginia Press, 1998), 10, 11. Of course, there were Southern Republicans who favored Jefferson's ideas of minimal government because they tended to lessen the threat to slavery, but to contend that the liberal late eighteenth-century Anglo-American belief in minimal government was fed by that concern alone is to grossly misunderstand the period. Radicals like Thomas Paine and William Godwin believed deeply in minimal government, and no one has accused them of being front men for slavery.

26. Gordon S. Wood, "The Creative Imagination of Bernard Bailyn," in James A. Henretta et al., eds., *The Transformation of Early American History: Society, Authority, and Ideology* (New York: Knopf, 1991), 38.

27. For examples of heavy-handed present-mindedness in histories of the early Republic, see Lawrence Goldstone, *Dark Bargain: Slavery, Profits, and the Struggle for the Constitution* (New York: Walker, 2005); and Robin L. Einhorn, *American Taxation, American Slavery* (Chicago: University of Chicago Press, 2006). For my review of these two works, see Gordon S. Wood, *The Purpose of the Past: Reflections on the Uses of History* (New York: Penguin, 2008), 293–308.

28. Thomas Jefferson to Benjamin Waterhouse, June 26, 1822, in Merrill D. Peterson, ed., *Thomas Jefferson: Writings* (New York: Library of America, 1984), 1459.

CHAPTER I, RHETORIC AND REALITY IN THE AMERICAN REVOLUTION

1. This is the title of a recent essay by Edmund S. Morgan in Arthur M. Schlesinger Jr. and Morton White, eds., *Paths of American Thought* (Boston: Houghton Mifflin, 1963), 11–33.

2. Samuel E. Morison, ed., "William Manning's *The Key of Libberty*," *William and Mary Quarterly*, 3rd ser., XIII (1956), 208.

3. Edmund S. Morgan, "The American Revolution: Revisions in Need of Revising," *William and Mary Quarterly*, 3rd ser., XIV (1957), 14.

4. William Vans Murray, *Political Sketches, Inscribed to His Excellency John Adams* (London: C. Dilly, 1787), 21, 48.

5. Daniel Leonard, *The Origin of the American Contest with Great-Britain…[by] Massachusettensis…* (New York: James Rivington, 1775), 40; Douglass Adair and John A. Schutz, eds., *Peter Oliver's Origin and Progress of the American Rebellion: A Tory View* (San Marino: Huntington Library, 1961), 159.

6. Simeon Baldwin, *An Oration Pronounced Before the Citizens of New-Haven, July 4th, 1788…* (New Haven, CT: J. Meigs, 1788), 10; [Murray], *Political Sketches*, 48; David Ramsay, *The History of the American Revolution* (Philadelphia: R. Aitken & Son, 1789), I, 350.

7. Thomas Paine, *Letter to the Abbé Raynal…* (1782), in Philip S. Foner, ed., *The Complete Writings of Thomas Paine* (New York: Citadel Press, 1945), II, 243; John Adams to H. Niles, February 13, 1818, in Charles Francis Adams, ed., *The Works of John Adams* (Boston: Little, Brown, 1850–1856), X, 282.

8. William Pierce, *An Oration, Delivered at Christ Church, Savanah, on the 4th of July, 1788…* (Savannah, GA: James Johnston, [1788]), 6; Enos Hitchcock, *An Oration; Delivered July 4th, 1788…* (Providence, RI: Bennett Wheeler, [1788]), 11.

9. Petition to the King, October 1774, in Worthington C. Ford, ed., *Journals of the Continental Congress, 1774–1789* (Washington, DC: U.S. Government Printing Office, 1904–1937), I, 118.

10. Samuel Williams, *The Natural and Civil History of Vermont…* (Walpole, NH: Isaiah Thomas and David Carlisle Jr., 1794), vii, 372–373; Pierce, *Oration…4th July, 1788*, 8.

11. Moses Coit Tyler, *The Literary History of the American Revolution, 1763–1783* (New York: G. P. Putnam's Sons, 1897), I, 8–9.

12. For a bald description of the assumptions with which this generation of historians worked, see Graham Wallas, *Human Nature in Politics*, 3rd ed. (New York: Knopf, 1921), 5, 45, 48–49, 83, 94, 96, 118, 122, 156.

13. Charles A. Beard, *An Economic Interpretation of the Constitution* (New York: Macmillan, 1935), x, viii.

14. While the Progressive historians were attempting to absorb and use the latest scientific techniques of the day, nonbehaviorists in government departments and others with a traditional approach to political theory—men like Andrew C. McLaughlin, Edwin S. Corwin, William S. Carpenter, Charles M. McIwain, and Benjamin F. Wright—were writing during this same period some of the best work that has ever been done on Revolutionary constitutional and political thought. However, because most of them were not, strictly speaking, historians, they never sought to explain the causes of the Revolution in terms of ideas.

15. Carl L. Becker, *The Declaration of Independence: A Study in the History of Political Ideas* (New York: Harcourt, Brace, 1922), 133, 203, 207.

16. Quoted in Philip Davidson, *Propaganda and the American Revolution, 1763–1783* (Chapel Hill: University of North Carolina Press, 1941), 141, 150, 373.

17. Arthur M. Schlesinger Jr., *Prelude to Independence: The Newspaper War on Britain, 1764–1776* (New York: Knopf, 1958), 34. For examples of the scientific work on which the propagandist studies drew, see note 1 in Sidney I. Pomerantz, "The Patriot Newspaper and the American Revolution," in Richard B. Morris, ed., *The Era of the American Revolution* (New York: Columbia University Press, 1939), 305.

18. Davidson, *Propaganda*, 59; Schlesinger, *Prelude to Independence*, 20.

19. Davidson, *Propaganda*, xiv, 46.

20. Schlesinger, *Prelude to Independence*, 44; Arthur M. Schlesinger Jr., *New Viewpoints in American History* (New York: Macmillan, 1922), 179.

21. Edmund S. Morgan, "Colonial Ideas of Parliamentary Power, 1764–1766," *William and Mary Quarterly*, 3rd ser., V (1948), 311, 341; Edmund S. Morgan and Helen M. Morgan, *The Stamp Act Crisis: Prologue to Revolution*, rev. ed. (New York: Collier Books, 1963), 306–307; Page Smith, "David Ramsay and the Causes of the American Revolution," *William and Mary Quarterly*, 3rd ser., XVII (1960), 70–71.

22. Jack P. Greene, "The Flight from Determinism: A Review of Recent Literature on the Coming of the American Revolution," *South Atlantic Quarterly*, LXI (1962), 257.

23. This revisionist literature of the 1950s is well known. See the listings in Bernard Bailyn, "Political Experience and Enlightenment Ideas in Eighteenth-Century America," *American Historical Review*, LXVII (1961–1962), 341n; and in Greene, "Flight from Determinism," 235–259.

24. Greene, "Flight from Determinism," 237, 257; Thad W. Tate, "The Coming of the Revolution in Virginia: Britain's Challenge to Virginia's Ruling Class, 1763–1776," *William and Mary Quarterly*, 3rd ser., XIX (1962), 323–343, esp. 340.

25. Bailyn, "Political Experience and Enlightenment Ideas," 339–351.

26. Bernard Bailyn, ed., assisted by Jane N. Garrett, *Pamphlets of the American Revolution, 1750–1776* (Cambridge, MA: Belknap Press of Harvard University Press, 1965–), I, viii, 60, x, 20. The 200-page general introduction is entitled "The Transforming Radicalism of the American Revolution."

27. This is not to say, however, that work on the Revolutionary ideas is in any way finished. For examples of the reexamination of traditional problems in Revolutionary political theory, see Richard Buel Jr., "Democracy and the American Revolution: A Frame of Reference," *William and Mary Quarterly*, 3rd ser., XXI (1964), 165–190; and Bailyn's resolution of James Otis's apparent inconsistency in *Revolutionary Pamphlets*, I, 100–103, 106–107, 121–123, 409–417, 546–552.

28. Smith, "Ramsay and the American Revolution," 72.

29. Morgan, "Revisions in Need of Revising," 13.

30. Adair and Schutz, eds., *Peter Oliver's Origin*, ix. In the present neo-Whig context, Sidney S. Fisher, "The Legendary and Myth-Making Process in Histories of the American Revolution," in American Philosophical Society, *Proceedings*, LI (Philadelphia: American Philosophical Society, 1912), 53–75, takes on a renewed relevance.

31. Bailyn, *Revolutionary Pamphlets*, I, 87, ix.

32. [Moses Mather], *America's Appeal to the Impartial World…* (Hartford, CT: Ebenezer Watson, 1775), 59; [John Dickinson], *Letters from a Farmer in Pennsylvania to the Inhabitants of the British Colonies* (Philadelphia: William and Thomas Bradford, 1768), in Paul L. Ford, ed., *The Writings of John*

Dickinson (Historical Society of Pennsylvania, *Memoirs*, XIV [Philadelphia: Historical Society of Pennsylvania, 1895]), II, 348. Dickinson hinged his entire argument on the ability of the Americans to decipher the "intention" of parliamentary legislation, whether for revenue or for commercial regulation. Ibid., 348, 364.

33. See Herbert Davis, "The Augustan Conception of History," in J. A. Mazzeo, ed., *Reason and the Imagination: Studies in the History of Ideas, 1600–1800* (New York: Columbia University Press, 1962), 226–228; W. H. Greenleaf, *Order, Empiricism and Politics: Two Traditions of English Political Thought, 1500–1700* (New York: University of Hull/Oxford University Press, 1964), 166; R. N. Stromberg, "History in the Eighteenth Century," *Journal of the History of Ideas*, XII (1951), 300. It was against this "dominant characteristic of the historical thought of the age," this "tendency to explain events in terms of conscious action by individuals," that the brilliant group of Scottish social scientists writing at the end of the eighteenth century directed much of their work. See Duncan Forbes, "'Scientific' Whiggism: Adam Smith and John Millar," *Cambridge Journal*, VII (1954), 651, 653–654. While we have had recently several good studies of historical thinking in seventeenth-century England, virtually nothing has been done on the eighteenth century. See, however, J. G. A. Pocock, "Burke and the Ancient Constitution—A Problem in the History of Ideas," *Historical Journal*, III (1960), 125–143; and Stow Persons, "The Cyclical Theory of History in Eighteenth Century America," *American Quarterly*, VI (1954), 147–163.

34. [Dickinson], *Letters from a Farmer*, in Ford, ed., *Writings of Dickinson*, 388.

35. Bailyn has noted that Oliver M. Dickerson, in chapter 7 of his *The Navigation Acts and the American Revolution* (Philadelphia: University of Pennsylvania Press, 1951), "adopts wholesale the contemporary Whig interpretation of the Revolution as the result of a conspiracy of 'King's Friends.'" Bailyn, *Revolutionary Pamphlets*, I, 724.

36. Morgan, "Revisions in Need of Revising," 7, 13, 8; Greene, "Flight from Determinism," 237.

37. Edmund S. Morgan, *The Birth of the Republic, 1763–89* (Chicago: University of Chicago Press, 1956), 51.

38. Greene, "Flight from Determinism," 258; Morgan, *Birth of the Republic*, 3.

39. Bailyn, *Revolutionary Pamphlets*, I, vii, ix.

40. Ibid., vii, viii, 17.

41. J. G. A. Pocock, "Machiavelli, Harrington, and English Political Ideologies in the Eighteenth Century," *William and Mary Quarterly*, 3rd ser., XXII (1965), 550.

42. Sir Lewis Namier, *England in the Age of the American Revolution*, 2nd ed. (London: Macmillan, 1961), 131.

43. Ibid., 129.

44. Bailyn, *Revolutionary Pamphlets*, I, 90, x, 169, 140. See Hannah Arendt, *On Revolution* (New York: Viking, 1963), 173: "American experience had taught the men of the Revolution that action, though it may be started in isolation and decided upon by single individuals for very different motives, can be accomplished only by some joint effort in which the motivation of single individuals…no longer counts…."

45. See Sir Lewis Namier, *The Structure of Politics at the Accession of George III*, 2nd ed. (London: Macmillan, 1961), 16; Sir Lewis Namier, "Human Nature in Politics," in *Personalities and Power: Selected Essays* (New York: Harper & Row, 1965), 5–6.

46. Bailyn, *Revolutionary Pamphlets*, I, 22. The French Revolutionaries were using the same group of classical writings to express their estrangement from the ancien régime and their hope for the new order. Harold T. Parker, *The Cult of Antiquity and the French Revolutionaries: A Study in the Development of the Revolutionary Spirit* (Chicago: University of Chicago Press, 1937), 22–23.

47. The relation of ideas to social structure is one of the most perplexing and intriguing in the social sciences. For an extensive bibliography on the subject, see Norman Birnbaum, "The Sociological Study of Ideology (1940–60)," *Current Sociology*, IX (1960).

48. Jacob Duché, *The American Vine, A Sermon, Preached… Before the Honourable Continental Congress, July 20th, 1775…* (Philadelphia: James Humphreys, 1775), 29.

49. For recent discussions of French and Puritan Revolutionary rhetoric, see Peter Gay, "Rhetoric and Politics in the French Revolution," *American Historical Review*, LXVI (1960–1961), 664–676; Michael Walzer, "Puritanism as a Revolutionary Ideology," *History and Theory*, III (1963), 59–90. This entire

issue of *History and Theory* is devoted to a symposium on the uses of theory in the study of history. In addition to the Walzer article, I have found the papers by Samuel H. Beer, "Causal Explanation and Imaginative Re-enactment," and Charles Tilly, "The Analysis of a Counter-Revolution," very stimulating and helpful.

50. Bryan A. Wilson, "Millennialism in Comparative Perspective," *Comparative Studies in Society and History*, VI (1963–1964), 108. See also Neil J. Smelser, *Theory of Collective Behaviour* (London: Routledge and Kegan Paul, 1962), 83, 120, 383.

51. Tate, "Coming of the Revolution in Virginia," 324–343.

52. Robert E. Brown and B. Katherine Brown, *Virginia, 1705–1786: Democracy or Aristocracy?* (East Lansing: Michigan State University Press, 1964), 236; Alexander White to Richard Henry Lee, 1758, quoted in J. R. Pole, "Representation and Authority in Virginia from the Revolution to Reform," *Journal of Southern History*, XXIV (1958), 23.

53. Purdie and Dixon's *Virginia Gazette* (Williamsburg), April 11, 1771; Rind's *Virginia Gazette*, October 31, 1771. See Lester J. Cappon and Stella F. Duff, eds., *Virginia Gazette Index, 1736–1780* (Williamsburg, VA: Institute of Early American History and Culture, 1950), I, 351, for entries on the astounding increase in essays on corruption and cost of elections in the late 1760s and early 1770s.

54. *The Defence of Injur'd Merit Unmasked; or, the Scurrilous Piece of Philander Dissected and Exposed to Public View. By a Friend to Merit, wherever found* (n.p., 1771), 10. Robert Carter chose to retire to private life in the early 1770s rather than adjust to the "new system of politicks" that had begun "to prevail generally." Quoted in Louis Morton, *Robert Carter of Nomini Hall: A Virginia Tobacco Planter of the Eighteenth Century* (Williamsburg: Colonial Williamsburg Inc., 1941), 52.

55. Jay B. Hubbell and Douglass Adair, "Robert Munford's *The Candidates*," *William and Mary Quarterly*, 3rd ser., V (1948), 238, 246. The ambivalence in Munford's attitude toward the representative process is reflected in the different way historians have interpreted his play. Cf. ibid., 223–225, with Brown, *Virginia*, 236–237. Munford's fear of "men who aim at power without merit" was more fully expressed in his later play, *The Patriots*, written in 1775 or 1776. Courtlandt Canby, "Robert Munford's *The Patriots*," *William and Mary Quarterly*, 3rd ser., VI (1949), 437–503, quotation from 450.

56. [John Randolph], *Considerations on the Present State of Virginia* ([Williamsburg], 1774), in Earl G. Swem, ed., *Virginia and the Revolution: Two Pamphlets, 1774* (New York, 1919), 16; Purdie and Dixon's *Virginia Gazette*, November 25, 1773.

57. Rind's *Virginia Gazette*, September 8, 1774; Brown, *Virginia*, 252–254; Morton, *Robert Carter*, 231–250.

58. See George Washington to George Mason, April 5, 1769, in John C. Fitzpatrick, ed., *The Writings of George Washington* (Washington, DC: U.S. Government Printing Office, 1931–1944). II, 502; Carl Bridenbaugh, *Myths and Realities: Societies of the Colonial South* (New York: Atheneum, 1963), 5, 10, 14, 16; Emory G. Evans, "Planter Indebtedness and the Coming of the Revolution in Virginia," *William and Mary Quarterly*, 3rd ser., XIX (1962), 518–519.

59. Rind's *Virginia Gazette*, August 15, 1766. See Carl Bridenbaugh, "Violence and Virtue in Virginia, 1766: or The Importance of the Trivial," Massachusetts Historical Society, *Proceedings*, LXXVI (1964), 3–29.

60. Quoted in Bridenbaugh, *Myths and Realities*, 27. See also Morton, *Robert Carter*, 223–225.

61. John A. Washington to R. H. Lee, June 20, 1778, quoted in Pole, "Representation and Authority in Virginia," 28.

62. Evans, "Planter Indebtedness," 526–527.

63. Julian P. Boyd et al., eds., *The Papers of Thomas Jefferson* (Princeton: Princeton University Press, 1950–), I, 560. Most of our knowledge of entail and primogeniture in Virginia stems from an unpublished doctoral dissertation, Clarence R. Keim, "Influence of Primogeniture and Entail in the Development of Virginia" (University of Chicago, 1926). Keim's is a very careful and qualified study and conclusions from his evidence—other than the obvious fact that much land was held in fee simple—are by no means easy to make. See particularly pp. 56, 60–62, 110–114, 122, 195–196.

64. Emory S. Evans, "The Rise and Decline of the Virginia Aristocracy in the Eighteenth Century: The Nelsons," in Darrett B. Rutman, ed., *The Old Dominion: Essays for Thomas Perkins Abernethy* (Charlottesville: University Press of Virginia, 1964), 73–74.

65. Max Farrand, ed., *The Records of the Federal Convention of 1787* (New Haven, CT: Yale University Press, 1911), I, 56; Bridenbaugh, *Myths and Realities*, 14, 16.

66. John Adams, "Novanglus," in Charles Francis Adams, ed., *The Works of John Adams* (Boston: Little, Brown, 1850–1856), IV, 14.

67. Arthur F. Bentley, *The Process of Government: A Study of Social Pressures* (Chicago: University of Chicago Press, 1908), 152.

AFTERWORD TO CHAPTER 1

1. Rhys Isaac, *The Transformation of Virginia, 1740–1790* (Chapel Hill: University of North Carolina Press, 1982); T. H. Breen, *Tobacco Culture: The Mentality of the Great Tidewater Planters on the Eve of the Revolution* (Princeton: Princeton University Press, 1985); Richard R. Beeman, *The Evolution of the Southern Backcountry: A Case Study of Lunenburg County, Virginia, 1746–1832* (Philadelphia: University of Pennsylvania Press, 1984); Jack P. Greene, "Society, Ideology, and Politics: An Analysis of the Political Culture of Mid-Eighteenth Century Virginia," in Richard M. Jellison, ed., *Society, Freedom, and Conscience: The Coming of the Revolution in Virginia, Massachusetts, and New York* (New York: W. W. Norton, 1976), 14–57; Jack P. Greene, *"Virtus et Libertas'*: Political Culture, Social Change, and the Origins of the American Revolution in Virginia, 1763–1766," in Jeffery J. Crow and Larry E. Tise, eds., *The Southern Experience in the American Revolution* (Chapel Hill: University of North Carolina Press, 1978), 55–65; Jack P. Greene, "Character, Persona, and Authority: A Study of Alternative Styles of Political Leadership in Revolutionary Virginia," in W. Robert Higgins, ed., *The Revolutionary War in the South: Power, Conflict, and Leadership* (Durham, NC: Duke University Press, 1979), 3–42.

CHAPTER 2, THE LEGACY OF ROME IN THE AMERICAN REVOLUTION

1. R. R. Palmer, *The Age of the Democratic Revolution: A Political History of Europe and America, 1760–1800*, 2 vols. (Princeton: Princeton University Press, 1959, 1964); Franco Venturi, *Utopia and Reform in the Enlightenment* (Cambridge, UK: Cambridge University Press, 1971), 90.

2. 1 Samuel 8:19–20.

3. John Adams to Richard Cranch, August 2, 1776, in L. H. Butterfield et al., eds., *Adams Family Correspondence* (Cambridge, MA: Harvard University Press), II, 74; see also Gordon S. Wood, *The Creation of the American Republic, 1776–1787* (Chapel Hill: University of North Carolina Press, 1969), 49–51; John Adams to Mercy Otis Warren, July 20, 1807, Massachusetts Historical Society, *Collections*, 5th ser., IV (1878), 353; Adams to J. H. Tiffany, April 30, 1819, Charles Francis Adams, ed., *Works of John Adams*, X, 378.

4. Montesquieu, *The Spirit of the Laws*, Franz Neumann, ed., pt. I, bk. ix, ch. 13 (New York: Hafner Press, 1949), 167; James William Johnson, *The Formation of English Neo-Classical Thought* (Princeton: Princeton University Press, 1967), 91–105; Richard Jenkyns, ed., *The Legacy of Rome: A New Appraisal* (Oxford: Oxford University Press, 1992), 26.

5. Peter Gay, *The Enlightenment: An Interpretation—The Rise of Modern Paganism* (New York: Knopf, 1966).

6. Wood, *The Creation of the American Republic*, 52, 414; Johnson, *Formation of English Neo-Classical Thought*, 239–240.

7. Johnson, *Formation of English Neo-Classical Thought*, 93, 246; Gay, *Enlightenment: Rise of Paganism*, 109; Bernard Bailyn, *The Ideological Origins of the American Revolution* (Cambridge, MA: Harvard University Press, 1967), 25.

8. J. G. A. Pocock, *The Machiavellian Moment: Florentine Political Thought and the Atlantic Republican Tradition* (Princeton: Princeton University Press, 1975); Johnson, *Formation of English Neo-Classical Thought*, 222–224; Meyer Reinhold, *Classica Americana: The Greek and Roman Heritage in the United States* (Detroit: Wayne State University Press, 1984), 30–31.

9. David Hume, "The British Government," in Eugene Miller, ed., *Essays: Moral, Political, and Literary* (Indianapolis: Liberty Classics, 1985), 51; Linda Colley, "The Apotheosis of George III: Loyalty, Royalty and the British Nation, 1760–1820," *Past and Present*, 102 (1984), 94–129; Jeffrey Merrick, *The Desacralization of the French Monarchy in the Eighteenth Century* (Baton Rouge: Louisiana State University Press, 1990)

10. Harold T. Parker, *The Cult of Antiquity and the French Revolutionaries* (Chicago: University of Chicago Press, 1937), 35, 39.

11. *South Carolina Gazette*, July 29, 1749, quoted in Hennig Cohen, *The South Carolina Gazette, 1732–1775* (Columbia: University of South Carolina Press, 1953), 218.

12. James Thomson, "Liberty," v, in *The Poetical Works of James Thomson* (Edinburgh: J. Nichol, 1863), 369.

13. Adams to Warren, July 20, 1807, 353; Adams to J. H. Tiffany, April 30, 1819, 378; Venturi, *Utopia and Reform in the Enlightenment*, 71.

14. Simon Schama, *Citizens: A Chronicle of the French Revolution* (New York: Knopf, 1989), 172; William L. Vance, *America's Rome*, 2 vols. (New Haven, CT: Yale University Press, 1989), I, 17, 15; John Barrell, *The Dark Side of the Landscape: The Rural Poor in English Painting, 1730–1840* (Cambridge, UK: Cambridge University Press, 1980), 7; Conyers Middleton, *The History of the Life of Marcus Tullius Cicero*, 2 vols. (London: James Bettenham, 1741), I, ix.

15. Caroline Robbins, *The Eighteenth-Century Commonwealthman: Studies in the Transmission, Development, and Circumstance of English Liberal Thought from the Restoration of Charles II Until the War with the Thirteen Colonies* (Cambridge, MA: Harvard University Press, 1959); Issac F. Kramnick, *Bolingbroke and His Circle: The Politics of Nostalgia in the Age of Walpole* (Cambridge, MA: Harvard University Press, 1968).

16. Edward Gibbon, *The Decline and Fall of the Roman Empire* (New York: Modern Library, 1931), I, 164–165; W. Jackson Bate, *Samuel Johnson* (New York: Harcourt Brace Jovanovich, 1975), 171–172.

17. William L. Grant, *Neo-Latin Literature and the Pastoral* (Chapel Hill: University of North Carolina Press, 1965), 255; Howard D. Weinbrot, *Augustus Caesar in "Augustan" England: The Decline of a Classical Norm* (Princeton: Princeton University Press, 1978), 47–48, 53, 62, 64; Howard Erskine-Hill, *The Augustan Idea in English Literature* (London: Edward Arnold, 1983), 249–266; Carl J. Richard, "A Dialogue with the Ancients: Thomas Jefferson and Classical Philosophy and History," *Journal of the Early Republic*, IX (1989), 445; Meyer Reinhold, ed., *The Classick Pages: Classical Readings of Eighteenth-Century Americans* (University Park, PA: American Philological Association, 1975), 100; Johnson, *Formation of English Neo-Classical Thought*, 226, 297, Hume, "Of the Parties of Great Britain," *Essays*, Miller, ed., 72.

18. Alexander Pope, "An Essay on Criticism," in Aubrey Williams, ed., *Poetry and Prose of Alexander Pope* (Boston: Houghton Mifflin, 1969), 41, lines 118–121.

19. Bertrand A. Goldar, *Walpole and the Wits: The Relation of Politics to Literature, 1722–1742* (Lincoln: University of Nebraska Press, 1976), 3, 22–23, 26, 135, 147–148, 158–159; Johnson, *The Formation of English Neo-Classical Thought*, 95–105; Reed Browning, *Political and Constitutional Ideas of the Court Whigs* (Baton Rouge: Louisiana State University Press, 1982), 5.

20. Johnson, *Formation of English Neo-Classical Thought*, 168.

21. Quentin Skinner, "The Idea of Negative Liberty: Philosophical and Historical Perspectives," Richard Rorty, et al., eds., *Philosophy in History* (Cambridge, UK: Cambridge University Press, 1984), 193–221; Michael Ignatieff, "John Millar and Individualism," in Istvan Hont and Michael Ignatieff, eds., *Wealth and Virtue: The Shaping of Political Economy in the Scottish Enlightenment* (Cambridge, UK: Cambridge University Press, 1983), 329–330.

22. David Hume, *A Treatise on Human Nature*, L. A. Selby-Bigge and P. N. Nidditch, eds. (Oxford: Clarendon Press, 1978), 587; Benjamin Franklin to Cadwallader Colden, October 11, 1750, Labaree, et al., eds., *Papers of Franklin*, IV, 68.

23. Gregory H. Nobles, *Divisions Throughout the Whole: Politics and Society in Hampshire County, Massachusetts, 1740–1775* (Cambridge, UK: Cambridge University Press, 1983), 182.

24. Thomas Jefferson, *Notes on the State of Virginia*, William Peden, ed. (Chapel Hill: University of North Carolina Press, 1954), 165.

25. Wood, *Radicalism of the American Revolution*, 240; Cicero, *Selected Works*, Michael Grant, ed. (Harmondsworth, UK: Penguin, 1960), 188.

26. Robert R. Livingston, quoted in Bernard Friedman, "The Shaping of the Radical Consciousness in Provincial New York," *Journal of American History*, LVI (1970), 786. For a discussion of Cicero's distinction between gentlemanly and vulgar callings, see Neal Wood, *Cicero's Social and Political Thought* (Berkeley: University of California Press, 1988), 95–100.

27. Adam Smith, *An Inquiry into the Nature and Causes of the Wealth of Nations*, ed., R. H. Campbell and A. S. Skinner (Oxford: Oxford University Press, 1976), I, 50–51; II, 781–783; Francis Hutcheson, *A System of Moral Philosophy in Three Books* . . . (London: R. and A. Foulis, 1755), II, 113.

28. Wood, *Radicalism of the American Revolution*, 83, 287–88, 290–92.
29. James Wilson, "On the History of Property," in McCloskey, ed., *Works of James Wilson*, II, 716; James Thompson, *The Seasons and the Castle of Indolence*, James Sambrook, ed. (Oxford: Oxford University Press, 1972), x; Virginia C. Kenny, *The Country-House Ethos in English Literature, 1688–1750: Themes of Personal Retreat and National Expansion* (New York: St. Martin's Press, 1984), 8–9; Jack P. Greene, *Landon Carter: An Inquiry into the Personal Values and Social Imperatives of the Eighteenth-Century Virginia Gentry* (Charlottesville: University Press of Virginia, 1965), 86–87.
30. William C. Dowling, *Poetry and Ideology in Revolutionary Connecticut* (Athens: University of Georgia Press, 1990).
31. John Dickinson, "Letters of a Farmer in Pennsylvania" (1768), in Paul L. Ford, ed., *The Writings of John Dickinson: I, Political Writings, 1764–1774* (Pennsylvania Historical Society, Memoirs, XIV [Philadelphia: Pennsylvania Historical Society, 1895]), 307.
32. Andrew R. L. Cayton, *The Frontier Republic: Ideology and Politics in the Ohio Country, 1780–1825* (Kent, OH: Kent State University Press, 1986), 12–32; Gibbon, *Decline and Fall of the Roman Empire*, I, 32; Tamara Platkins Thornton, *Cultivating Gentlemen: The Meaning of Country Life Among the Boston Elite, 1785–1860* (New Haven, CT: Yale University Press, 1989), 31.
33. Reinhold, *Classica Americana*, 98.
34. David Humphreys, "A Poem on the Industry of the United States of America," in Vernon L. Parrington, ed., *The Connecticut Wits* (New York: Thomas Y. Crowell, 1954), 401.
35. Ronald Paulson, *Representations of Revolution (1789–1820)* (New Haven, CT: Yale University Press, 1983), 12; Stephen Botein, "Cicero as Role Model for Early American Lawyers: A Case Study in Classical Influence," *The Classical Journal*, LXXIII (1977–1978), 313–321; Pauline Maier, *The Old Revolutionaries: Political Lives in the Age of Samuel Adams* (New York: Knopf, 1980), 33, 34, 47; Garry Wills, *Cincinnatus: George Washington and the Enlightenment* (New York: Doubleday, 1984).
36. Ezra Stiles, *Election Sermon* (1783), in John Wingate Thornton, ed., *The Pulpit of the American Revolution* (Boston: D. Lothrop, 1876), 460; John Adams to Abigail Adams, April 25, 1778, in L. H. Butterfield et al., eds., *The Book of Abigail and John: Selected Letters of the Adams Family* (Cambridge, MA: Harvard University Press, 1975), 210; Benjamin Rush to ———, April 16, 1790, in L. H. Butterfield, ed., *Letters of Benjamin Rush* (Princeton: Princeton University Press, 1951), I, 550.
37. Neil Harris, *The Artist in American Society: The Formative Years, 1790–1860* (New York: George Braziller, 1966), 42.
38. Eleanor Davidson Berman, *Thomas Jefferson Among the Arts: An Essay in Early American Esthetics* (New York: Philosophical Library, 1947), 84; Jefferson, *Notes on the State of Virginia*, 153; Jefferson to Madison, Sept. 20, 1785, in Julian P. Boyd et al., eds., *Papers of Thomas Jefferson* (Princeton: Princeton University Press, 1950–); VIII, 535; Jefferson to William Buchanan and James Hay, Jan. 26, 1786, in *Papers of Jefferson*, IX, 221.
39. Reinhold, *Classica Americana*, 129; Benjamin Rush to James Hamilton, June 27, 1810, in Butterfield, ed., *Letters of Benjamin Rush*, II, 1053.
40. Edward Everett, "An Oration Pronounced at Cambridge . . . 1824," in Joseph L. Blau, ed., *American Philosophic Addresses, 1700–1900* (New York: Columbia University Press, 1946), 77.

AFTERWORD TO CHAPTER 2

1. Bernard Bailyn, *The Ideological Origins of the American Revolution* (Cambridge, MA: Harvard University Press, 1967), 23–26.

CHAPTER 3, CONSPIRACY AND THE PARANOID STYLE

1. Jack P. Greene, "Search for Identity: An Interpretation of the Meaning of Selected Patterns of Social Response in Eighteenth-Century America," *Journal of Social History*, III (1970), 189–220.
2. Kenneth S. Lynn, *A Divided People* (Westport, CT: Greenwood Press, 1977), 105. Cf. Philip Greven, *The Protestant Temperament: Patterns of Child-Rearing, Religious Experience, and the Self in Early America* (New York: Knopf, 1977).
3. The best and most restrained of these efforts is Edwin G. Burrows and Michael Wallace, "The American Revolution: The Ideology and Psychology of National Liberation," *Perspectives in*

American History, VI (1972), 167–306. See also Winthrop D. Jordan, "Familial Politics: Thomas Paine and the Killing of the King, 1776," *Journal of American History*, LX (1973), 294–308.

4. Fawn M. Brodie, *Thomas Jefferson: An Intimate History* (New York: W. W. Norton, 1974); Peter Shaw, *The Character of John Adams* (Chapel Hill: University of North Carolina Press, 1976), and *American Patriots and the Rituals of Revolution* (Cambridge, MA: Harvard University Press, 1981); John J. Waters, "James Otis, Jr.: An Ambivalent Revolutionary," *History of Childhood Quarterly*, I (1973), 142–150; Bruce Mazlish, "Leadership in the American Revolution: The Psychological Dimension," in *Leadership in the American Revolution*, Library of Congress Symposia on the American Revolution (Washington, DC: Library of Congress, 1974), 113–133.

5. Jack P. Greene, "An Uneasy Connection: An Analysis of the Preconditions of the American Revolution," in Stephen G. Kurtz and James H. Hutson, eds., *Essays on the American Revolution* (Chapel Hill: University of North Carolina Press, 1973), 60; Greven, *Protestant Temperament*, 351.

6. Jack P. Greene, "Search for Identity," *Journal of Social History*, III (1970), 219; James H. Hutson, "The American Revolution: The Triumph of a Delusion?" in Erich Angermann et al., eds., *New Wine in Old Skins: A Comparative View of Socio-Political Structures and Values Affecting the American Revolution* (Stuttgart, Germany: Klett, 1976), 179–194.

7. Bailyn's introduction was entitled "The Transforming Radicalism of the American Revolution," in *Pamphlets of the American Revolution*, I (Cambridge, MA: Belknap Press of Harvard University Press, 1965), 3–202; Richard Hofstadter, *The Paranoid Style in American Politics and Other Essays* (New York: Vintage, 1965).

8. Bernard Bailyn, *The Origins of American Politics* (New York: Knopf, 1968), 13, and *The Ideological Origins of the American Revolution* (Cambridge, MA: Harvard University Press, 1967), 94–95.

9. For a typical example of the sociological studies of the early 1950s, see Daniel Bell, ed., *The New American Right* (New York: Criterion, 1955).

10. Hofstadter, *Paranoid Style*, 7.

11. Ibid., ix, 4, 6.

12. Ibid., ix.

13. Richard O. Curry and Thomas M. Brown, eds., *Conspiracy: The Fear of Subversion in American History* (New York: Holt, Rinehart & Winston, 1972), ix, x; David Brion Davis, ed., *The Fear of Conspiracy: Images of Un-American Subversion from the Revolution to the Present* (Ithaca, NY: Cornell University Press, 1971), xiv.

14. David Brion Davis, *The Slave Power Conspiracy and the Paranoid Style* (Baton Rouge: Louisiana State University Press, 1909), 29; Davis, ed., *Fear of Conspiracy*, 23.

15. James Kirby Martin, *Men in Rebellion: Higher Governmental Leaders and the Coming of the American Revolution* (New Brunswick, NJ: Rutgers University Press, 1973), 34; Daniel Sisson, *The American Revolution of 1800* (New York: Knopf, 1974), 130, 131, 132; Hutson, "American Revolution," in Angermann et al., eds., *New Wine in Old Skins*, 179, 180.

16. Lance Banning, "Republican Ideology and the Triumph of the Constitution, 1789 to 1793," *William and Mary Quarterly*, 3rd ser., XXXI (1974), 171.

17. Greven, *Protestant Temperament*, 349, 352.

18. Hutson, "American Revolution," in Angermann et al., eds., *New Wine in Old Skins*, 177, 180, 181, 182. In a more recent unpublished essay, "The Origins of 'the Paranoid Style in American Politics': Public Jealousy from the Age of Walpole to the Age of Jackson," Hutson has virtually repudiated his earlier psychological interpretation. He now suggests that "the special position the Revolution occupies in our national life" has inhibited historians from following him in making the Revolution "the first link on Hofstadter's paranoid chain." Perhaps other historians were quietly filling in behind him more than he realized. At any rate, he has retreated from his exposed position and returned to one not very different from Bailyn's. In this paper he describes the Americans' "paranoid style" as a product of their long tradition of jealousy and suspicion of governmental power. Such fears of abused political power, Hutson now concedes, made American conspiratorial views "altogether credible," at least up to 1830 or so. Only after that date, when American suspicions and jealousy were transferred from the government to nongovernmental agencies and groups, such as the Masons and the Roman Catholic Church, for which there was no tradition of past abuse, is it "possible," says Hutson, "to speak of these fears veering off towards pathology."

19. "The British ministers of the Revolutionary Era," writes Hutson, "were shifting coalitions whose principal discernible goal was the preservation of power. How could reasonable people believe them capable of fiendish malevolence, cunningly concerted and sustained, year in, year out?" ("American Revolution," in Angermann et al., eds., *New Wine in Old Skins*, 177.) Although not as boldly as Hutson, other historians trying to explain the Revolutionaries' conspiratorial beliefs in effect seem to be asking the same question.

20. Daniel Defoe, quoted in Maximillian E. Novak, ed., *English Literature in the Age of Disguise* (Berkeley: University of California Press, 1977), 2; George Farquhar, *The Beaux' Stratagem*, Charles N. Fifer, ed. (Lincoln: University of Nebraska Press, 1977), act 4, sc. 1; Swift, *Gulliver's Travels*, pt. III, chap. 6, in *The Writings of Jonathan Swift*, Robert A. Greenberg and William Bowman Piper, eds. (New York: W. W. Norton, 1973), 162–163.

21. Bailyn, *Ideological Origins*, 144–159, quotation on p. 153; Ira D. Gruber, "The American Revolution as a Conspiracy: The British View," *William and Mary Quarterly*, 3rd ser., XXVI (1969), 360–372; David T. Morgan, "'The Dupes of Designing Men': John Wesley and the American Revolution," *Historical Magazine of the Protestant Episcopal Church*, XLIV (1975), 121–131; J. M. Roberts, *The Mythology of the Secret Societies* (London: Secker and Warburg, 1972), 24; Georges Lefebvre, *The Great Fear of 1789: Rural Panic in Revolutionary France*, Joan White, trans. (New York: Pantheon Books, 1973), 60–62, 210; Jack Richard Censer, *Prelude to Power: The Parisian Radical Press, 1789–1791* (Baltimore: Johns Hopkins University Press, 1976), 99.

22. Johnson, *A Dictionary of the English Language . . .* , 12th ed. (Edinburgh: A. M. Knapton, 1802); Hofstadter, *Paranoid Style*, 36, 32, 27.

23. Erich Auerbach, *Mimesis: The Representation of Reality in Western Literature*, Willard Trask, trans. (Princeton: Princeton University Press, 1953), 463.

24. Niccolo Machiavelli, "Discourses on the First Decade of Titus Livius, Book 3," in *The Chief Works and Others*, Allan Gilbert, trans., 3 vols. (Durham, NC: Duke University Press, 1965), I, 428. See also letter CII in Montesquieu's *The Persian Letters*, George R. Healy, trans. (Indianapolis: Bobbs-Merrill, 1964), 170.

25. *American Museum, or, Universal Magazine*, XII (1792), 172; Samuel Kinser, ed., *The Memoirs of Philippe de Commynes*, Isabelle Cazeaux, trans., I (Columbia: University of South Carolina Press, 1969), 361.

26. Thomas Preston Peardon, *The Transition in English Historical Writing, 1760–1830* (New York: Columbia University Press, 1933), 35. See also Peter Burke, *Popular Culture in Early Modern Europe* (New York: Harper & Row, 1978), 173.

27. Myron P. Gilmore, *Humanists and Jurists: Six Studies in the Renaissance* (Cambridge, MA: Belknap Press of Harvard University Press, 1963), 59–60.

28. Keith Thomas, *Religion and the Decline of Magic* (New York: Charles Scribner's Sons, 1971), 78–112.

29. Increase Mather, *The Doctrine of Divine Providence Opened and Applyed* (Boston: Richard Pierce, 1684), quoted in Lester H. Cohen, *The Revolutionary Histories: Contemporary Narratives of the American Revolution* (Ithaca, NY: Cornell University Press, 1980), 27–29. Cohen's book is richly imaginative and by far the best work we have on early American historical thinking.

30. Halifax, quoted in Thomas, *Religion and the Decline of Magic*, 109. On the scientific revolution, see Herbert Butterfield, *The Origins of Modern Science, 1300–1800* (London, 1949), and J. Bronowski, *The Common Sense of Science* (Cambridge, MA: Harvard University Press 1953).

31. Bronowski, *Common Sense of Science*, 40; Smith, *The Lectures . . . on the Subjects of Moral and Political Philosophy* (Trenton, NJ: Daniel Fenton, 1812), I, 9, 122.

32. Steven Shapin, "Of Gods and Kings: Natural Philosophy and Politics in the Leibniz-Clarke Disputes," *Isis*, LXXII (1981), 192; M. B. Foster, "The Christian Doctrine of Creation and the Rise of Modern Natural Science," in Daniel O'Connor and Francis Oakley, eds., *Creation: The Impact of an Idea* (New York: Charles Scribner's Sons, 1969), 29–53; Francis Oakley, "Christian Theology and the Newtonian Science: The Rise of the Concept of the Laws of Nature," ibid., 54–83; P. M. Heimann, "Voluntarism and Immanence: Conceptions of Nature in Eighteenth-Century Thought," *Journal of the History of Ideas*, XXXIX (1978), 271–292; Roy N. Lokken, "Cadwallader Colden's Attempt to Advance Natural Philosophy Beyond the Eighteenth-Century Mechanistic Paradigm," American Philosophical Society, *Proceedings*, CXXII (1978), 365–376; Margaret C. Jacob, *The Newtonians and the English Revolution, 1689–1720* (Ithaca, NY: Cornell University Press, 1976).

33. The best brief discussion of the search for a science of human behavior in the eighteenth century is Gladys Bryson, *Man and Society: The Scottish Inquiry of the Eighteenth Century* (Princeton: Princeton University Press, 1945).

34. Smith, *Lectures*, II, 22; Warburton and Volney are quoted in R. N. Stromberg, "History in the Eighteenth Century," *Journal of the History of Ideas*, XII (1951), 300; Richard H. Popkin, "Hume: Philosophical Versus Prophetic Historian," in Kenneth R. Merrill and Robert W. Shahan, eds., *David Hume: Many-Sided Genius* (Norman: University of Oklahoma Press, 1976), 83–95.

35. On the effects of the new causal thinking on the development of the novel see Edward M. Jennings, "The Consequences of Prediction," in Theodore Besterman, ed., *Studies on Voltaire and the Eighteenth Century* (Oxford: Oxford University Press, 1976), CLIII, 1148–1149, and Martin C. Battestin, "'Tom Jones': The Argument of Design," in Henry Knight Miller et al., eds., *The Augustan Milieu: Essays Presented to Louis A. Landa* (Oxford: Oxford University Press, 1970), 289–319.

36. Bolingbroke, *Historical Writings*, Isaac Kramnick, ed. (Chicago: University of Chicago Press, 1972), 18, 21, 22; Gibbon, "Essai sur L'Etude de la Litterature," in *Miscellaneous Works of Edward Gibbon . . .*, John, Lord Sheffield, ed. (London, 1796), II, 477. These enlightened assumptions about man's responsibility for what happened led naturally to historical explanations that R. G. Collingwood thought were "superficial to absurdity." It was the Enlightenment historians, wrote Collingwood, "who invented the grotesque idea that the Renaissance in Europe was due to the fall of Constantinople and the consequent expulsion of scholars in search of new homes." For Collingwood, who usually had so much sympathy for the peculiar beliefs of the past, such personal sorts of causal attribution were "typical . . . of a bankruptcy of historical method which in despair of genuine explanation acquiesces in the most trivial causes for the vastest effects" (*The Idea of History* [Oxford: Oxford University Press, 1946], 80–81). Elsewhere, Collingwood of course recognized the historical differentness of the eighteenth century (ibid., 224).

37. David Kubrin, "Newton and the Cyclical Cosmos: Providence and the Mechanical Philosophy," *Journal of the History of Ideas*, XXVIII (1967), 325–346; P. M. Heimann and J. E. McGuire, "Newtonian Forces and Lockean Powers: Concepts of Matter in Eighteenth-Century Thought," *Historical Studies in the Physical Sciences*, III (1971), 233–306.

38. Arthur O. Lovejoy, *Reflections on Human Nature* (Baltimore: Johns Hopkins Press, 1961), 153; [John Trenchard and Thomas Gordon], *Cato's Letters: Or Essays on Liberty, Civil and Religious, and Other Important Subjects*, 5th ed. (London, 1748), IV, 86; Hans Kelsen, *Society and Nature: A Sociological Inquiry* (London: Kegan Paul, 1946), 42. On the ways in which Arminian-minded Protestants reconciled individual responsibility with God's sovereignty, see Greven, *Protestant Temperament*, 217–243.

39. Lokken, "Cadwallader Colden," American Philosophical Society, *Proceedings*, CXXII (1978), 370; Heimann, "Voluntarism and Immanence," *Journal of the History of Ideas*, XXXIX (1978), 273, 378–379.

40. David Hume, "An Enquiry Concerning Human Understanding," sec. VIII, pt. I, in *Essays, Moral, Political, and Literary*, T. H. Green and T. H. Grose, eds. (New York: Longmans, Green, 1912), II, 72, 77; Reid, quoted in S. A. Grave, *The Scottish Philosophy of Common Sense* (Oxford: Clarendon Press, 1960), 216.

41. [James Dana], *An Examination of the Late Reverend President Edwards's "Enquiry on Freedom of Will,". . .* (Boston: Daniel Kneeland, 1770), 81, 89; Stephen West, *An Essay on Moral Agency . . .*, 2nd ed. (Salem, MA: Thomas C. Cushing, 1794), 73–74.

42. George L. Dillon, "Complexity and Change of Character in Neo-Classical Criticism," *Journal of the History of Ideas*, XXXV (1974), 51–61; Warren, quoted in Cohen, *Revolutionary Histories*, 193–194; Bryson, *Man and Society*, 109.

43. [Dana], *Examination*, xi, 50, 62, 66. See Jonathan Edwards, *Freedom of the Will*, Paul Ramsey, ed. (New Haven, CT: Yale University Press, 1957), 156–162.

44. Merle Curti and William Tillman, eds., "Philosophical Lectures by Samuel Williams, LL. D., on the Constitution, Duty, and Religion of Man," American Philosophical Society, *Transactions*, N.S., LX, pt. 3 (1970), 114. Since the moral effects of human behavior were determined by the causes or motives of the actors, James Wilson devoted a large section of his "Lectures on Law" to an attempt to demonstrate that "the common law measures crimes chiefly by the intention." Such intention, he said, presupposed the operation of both understanding and will. "If the operation of either is wanting," as in the case of lunatics, children, and other dependents, "no crime can exist" ("Of the

Persons Capable of Committing Crimes; and of the Different Degrees of Guilt Incurred in the Commission of the Same Crime," in Robert Green McCloskey, ed., *The Works of James Wilson*, II [Cambridge, MA: Harvard University Press, 1967], 677). "In every moral action," wrote Samuel Stanhope Smith, "the principal ground on which we form a judgment of its rectitude or pravity is the disposition or intention with which it is performed" (*Lectures*, I, 313).

45. [Dana], *Examination*, 50, 66, 96; Hume, "Concerning Human Understanding," sec. VIII, pt. I, in *Essays*, Green and Gross, eds., 74.

46. Bernard Mandeville, *Free Thoughts on Religion, the Church, and Natural Happiness* (1720), quoted in H. T. Dickinson, "Bernard Mandeville: An Independent Whig," in Besterman, ed., *Studies on Voltaire*, CLII, 562–563.

47. Curti and Tillman, eds., "Lectures by Williams," American Philosophical Society, *Transactions*, N.S., LX, pt. 3 (1970), 121.

48. Bernard Mandeville, *The Fable of the Bees: Or, Private Vices, Publick Benefits*, F. B. Kaye, ed. (Oxford: Clarendon Press, 1924), 239; J. A. W. Gunn, "Mandeville and Wither: Individualism and the Workings of Providence," in Irwin Primer, ed., *Mandeville Studies; New Explorations in the Art and Thought of Dr. Bernard Mandeville (1670–1733)* (The Hague: Martinus Nijhoff, 1975), 101.

49. John Adams to Ebenezer Thayer, September 24, 1765, in Robert J. Taylor et al., eds., *Papers of John Adams* (Cambridge, MA: Belknap Press of Harvard University Press, 1977), I, 135.

50. Jonathan Edwards, *The Mind: A Reconstructed Text*, Leon Howard, ed. (Berkeley: University of California Press, 1963), 76–78. The mind is "informed by means of observed motion, of design," wrote the British scientist James Hutton in 1792, "for when a regular order is observed in those changing things, whereby a certain end is always attained, there is necessarily inferred an operation somewhere, an operation similar to that of our mind, which often premeditates the exertion of a power and is conscious of design" (quoted in Heimann and McGuire, "Newtonian Forces and Lockean Powers," *Historical Studies in Physical Sciences*, III [1971], 283).

51. Samuel Sherwood, *The Church's Flight into the Wilderness: An Address on the Times* . . . (New York: S. Loudon, 1776), 9, 13, 26, 29, 30, 38, 40, and *A Sermon, Containing Scriptural Instructions to Civil Rulers and All Free-born Subjects* . . . (New Haven, CT: T. and S. Green, 1774), vi; Nathan O. Hatch, *The Sacred Cause of Liberty: Republican Thought and the Millennium in Revolutionary New England* (New Haven, CT: Yale University Press, 1977), 56; James West Davidson, *The Logic of Millennial Thought: Eighteenth-Century New England* (New Haven, CT: Yale University Press, 1977).

52. [Moses Mather], *America's Appeal to the Impartial World* . . . (Hartford, CT, 1775), 59; Izrahiah Wetmore, *A Sermon, Preached Before the Honorable General Assembly of the Colony of Connecticut* . . . (Norwich, CT: Judah P. Spooner, 1775), 4, 11; Henry C. Van Schaack, *The Life of Peter Van Schaack* . . . (New York: D. Appleton, 1842), 56; Thomas Jefferson, A *Summary View of the Rights of British America* . . . (Williamsburg, VA: Clementine Rind, 1774), in Julian P. Boyd et al., eds., *The Papers of Thomas Jefferson*, I (Princeton: Princeton University Press, 1950), 125.

53. [Dickinson], *Letters from a Farmer in Pennsylvania* . . . (Philadelphia: William and Thomas Bradford, 1768), in Paul Leicester Ford, ed., *The Writings of John Dickinson* (Historical Society of Pennsylvania, *Memoirs*, XIV [Philadelphia: Historical Society of Pennsylvania, 1895]), 349, hereafter cited as Ford, ed., *Writings of Dickinson*; Griffith J. McRee, ed., *Life and Correspondence of James Iredell* . . . , I (New York: D. Appleton, 1857), 312. "If the American public had not penetrated the intentions of the English government," noted Jefferson's Italian friend Philip Mazzei in 1788, "there would have been no revolution, or it would have been stillborn" (*Researches on the United States*, Constance D. Sherman, trans. and ed. [Charlottesville: University Press of Virginia, 1976], 125).

54. Adams, "Misanthrop, No. 2" (January 1767), in Taylor et al., eds., *Adams Papers*, I, 187. "There is not an emotion or thought which passes through the mind," wrote Smith, "that does not paint some image of itself on the fine and delicate lines of the countenance" (*Lectures*, I, 30). Beliefs such as this led to the faddish science of physiognomy promoted by the Swiss J. K. Lavater. See Samuel Miller, *A Brief Retrospect of the Eighteenth Century* . . . , I (New York: T. and J. Swords 1803), 433–434.

55. Richardson, *The History of Clarissa Harlowe*, William Lyon Phelps, ed., IV (New York: Croscup & Sterling, 1902), 112 (Letter XXVIII); Defoe, quoted in Novak, ed., *Age of Disguise*, 2; Dillon, "Complexity and Change," *Journal of the History of Ideas*, XXXV (1974), 51–61.

56. Lord Chesterfield to his son, August 21, 1749, in Bonamy Dobrée, ed., *The Letters of Philip Dormer Stanhope, 4th Earl of Chesterfield*, IV (London: Eyre and Spottiswoode, 1932), 1382–1383. On the issue of sincerity see the engaging and learned article by Judith Shklar, "Let Us Not Be Hypocritical," *Daedalus* (Summer 1979), 1–25.

57. John Adams, August 20, 1770, in L. H. Butterfield et al., eds., *Diary and Autobiography of John Adams*, I (Cambridge, MA: Belknap Press of Harvard University Press, 1961), 363; *Am. Museum*, XII (1792), 172; Warren, quoted in Cohen, *Revolutionary Histories*, 207, 208.

58. Henry Fielding, "An Essay on the Knowledge of the Characters of Men," in *The Works of Henry Fielding*, XI (New York: Charles Scriber's Sons, 1899), 190; William Henry Drayton, *The Letters of Freeman, Etc.: Essays on the Nonimportation Movement in South Carolina*, Robert M. Weir, ed. (Columbia: University of South Carolina Press, 1977), 34; David Hume, *The History of England . . .*, VI (New York: Harper & Brothers, 1879 [originally published Edinburgh: Hamilton, Balfour, and Neill, 1754–1762]), chap. 65, 16; Alan Heimert, *Religion and the American Mind: From the Great Awakening to the Revolution* (Cambridge, MA: Harvard University Press, 1966), 308; Ian Watt, *The Rise of the Novel* (London: Penguin, 1970), 283–287; Smith, *Lectures*, I, 10, 314. "In Truth," wrote Trenchard and Gordon, "every private Subject has a Right to watch the Steps of those who would betray their Country; nor is he to take their Word about the Motives of their Designs, but to judge of their Designs by the Event" (*Cato's Letters*, I, 86).

59. Adams, "A Dissertation on the Canon and the Feudal Law" (1765), in Taylor et al., eds., *Adams Papers*, I, 127; Cooke, *A Sermon Preached at Cambridge . . . May 30th, 1770* (Boston: Edes and Gill, 1770), in John Wingate Thornton, ed., *The Pulpit of the American Revolution. Or, the Political Sermons of the Period of 1776* (Boston: Gould and Lincoln; Sheldon, 1860), 167; [Dickinson], *Letters from a Farmer*, in Ford, ed., *Writings of Dickinson*, 348. The eighteenth-century fascination with power, both in physics and in politics, was enhanced by this need to infer causes from their effects. Power or causation, "which," said Joseph Priestley, "is only the same idea differently modified," was not found in our sensory experience. "We all see events one succeeding another," wrote Thomas Reid, "but we see not the power by which they are produced." Locke had called power a "mysterious quality," and it remained such for Americans well into the nineteenth century. Power was something observable only from its effects. Whether from a magnet attracting iron, from a charged electrical jar giving a shock, or from a series of tax levies, men got the idea that some sort of cause or agent was at work. Power, said James Hutton, was "a term implying an unknown thing in action" (Heimann and McGuire, "Newtonian Forces and Lockean Powers," *Historical Studies in Physical Sciences*, III [1971], 266, 280, 286; Thomas Brown, "Inquiry into the Relation of Cause and Effect," *North American Review*, XII [1821], 401).

60. Hume, "Concerning Human Understanding," sec. VIII, pt. I, in *Essays*, Green and Grose, eds., 71. See also ibid., sec. VI, 48–49.

61. Smith, *Lectures*, I, 254. The colonists, writes Bailyn, had "a general sense that they lived in a conspiratorial world in which what the highest officials professed was not what they in fact intended, and that their words masked a malevolent design" (*Ideological Origins*, 98).

62. Jay Fliegelman, *Prodigals and Pilgrims: The American Revolution Against Patriarchal Authority, 1750–1800* (Cambridge, UK: Cambridge University Press, 1982), chap. 1; [Trenchard and Gordon], *Cato's Letters*, III, 330, 334; Priestley, quoted in Robert Darnton, *Mesmerism and the End of the Enlightenment in France* (Cambridge, MA: Harvard University Press, 1968), 16.

63. William Livingston, *The Independent Reflector: Or Weekly Essays on . . . the Province of New-York*, Milton M. Klein, ed. (Cambridge, MA: Belknap Press of Harvard University Press, 1963), 218; Courtlandt Canby, ed., "Robert Munford's *The Patriots*," *William and Mary Quarterly*, 3rd ser., VI (1949), 492; Tillotson, quoted in Leon Guilhamet, *The Sincere Ideal: Studies on Sincerity in Eighteenth-Century English Literature* (Montreal: McGill-Queen's University Press, 1974), 16. American Protestantism was always preoccupied with the problem of deception and hypocrisy. While seventeenth-century New England Puritans had recognized man's ultimate inability to discover who was saved or not and had accepted the possibility of some hypocrites being within the visible church, early nineteenth-century Christian perfectionists were sure they could tell who the deceivers were, for those "who bear a bold and living testimony against all sin, and confirm the same by their works" could not feign; their behavior thus "puts a period eventually, to all the contentions and

debates, about Who is a christian and who is not" (Perry Miller, *The New England Mind: From Colony to Province* [Cambridge, MA: Harvard University Press, 1953], 68–81; John Dunlavy, *The Manifesto, or a Declaration of the Doctrines and Practice of the Church of Christ* [Pleasant Hill, KY: P. Bertrand, 1818], 268, 283, 284–285).

64. Henrick Hartog, "The Public Law of a County Court: Judicial Government in Eighteenth-Century Massachusetts," *American Journal of Legal History*, XX (1976), 321–322. For some even the administration of all criminal justice could be reduced to the unmasking of deception. James Wilson thought that the word "felony"—"the generical term employed by the common law to denote a crime"—was derived from both Latin and Greek meaning "to deceive." It was not an injurious action alone that causes a crime, said Wilson; instead, the action revealed that the actor had a dispostion unworthy of the confidence of the community, "that he is false, deceitful, and treacherous: the crime is now completed" ("Law Lectures," in McClosky, ed., *Works of Wilson*, II, 622).

65. P. K. Elkin, *The Augustan Defence of Satire* (Oxford: Clarendon Press, 1973); Maynard Mack, "The Muse of Satire," in Richard C. Boys, ed., *Studies in the Literature of the Augustan Age: Essays Collected in Honor of Arthur Ellicott Case* (New York: Gordian Press, 1966); Basil Willey, *The Eighteenth Century Background: Studies on the Idea of Nature in the Thought of the Period* (New York: Columbia University Press, 1940), 100, 106.

66. [Adams], "U" to the *Boston Gazette*, August 29, 1763, in Taylor et al., eds., *Adams Papers*, I, 78, 79.

67. So Eustache LeNoble wrote in the preface to his novel *Abra-Mule* (1696): "The actions of sovereigns always have two parts, one is the public element which everyone knows and which forms the material of gazettes and the greater part of histories; the other, which these sovereigns hide behind the veil of their policy, are the secret motives of intrigue which cause those events, and which are known or revealed only to those who have had some part in these intrigues, or who by the penetration of their genius know how the one part becomes the other" (quoted in Rene Godenne, *Historie de la Nouvelle Française aux XVIIe et XVIIIe Siècles* [Geneva: Droz, 1970], 96).

68. Hume, *History of England*, VI, 64–65. In the years between the Restoration and the era of George III, the modern English notion of the criminal law of conspiracy was essentially formed. Basic to this notion was the belief that the criminality of conspiracy lay in the intent, which was revealed by the acts done. A justice in *Rex v. Sterling* (1664) had suggested that "the particular facts" were "but evidence of the design charged." A century later Lord Mansfield in *Rex v. Parsons et al.* elaborated the point by instructing the jury "that there was no occasion to prove the actual fact of conspiring, but that it might be collected from collateral circumstances" (James Wallace Bryan, *The Development of the English Law of Conspiracy*, Johns Hopkins University Studies in Historical and Political Science, XXVII [Baltimore: Johns Hopkins Press, 1909], 77, 78–79, 81. I owe this reference to Stanley N. Katz).

69. Edmund Burke, "Thoughts on the Cause of the Present Discontents" (1770), in *The Works and Correspondence of . . . Edmund Burke*, Charles William and Richard Bourke, eds. (London: Francis and John Rivington, 1852), III, esp. 112–114, 130–131. For the prevalence of the belief in a "double cabinet" operating "behind the curtain" in the era of George III, see Ian R. Christie, *Myth and Reality in Late-Eighteenth-Century British Politics and Other Papers* (London: Macmillan, 1970), 27–54.

70. Henry Laurens to John Brown, October 28, 1765, in George C. Rogers Jr., et al., eds., *The Papers of Henry Laurens*, V (Columbia: University of South Carolina Press, 1976), 30; Staughton Lynd, ed., "Abraham Yates's History of the Movement for the United States Constitution," *William and Mary Quarterly*, 3rd ser., XX (1963), 231, 232.

71. Richard Henry Lee to ———, May 31, 1764, in James Curtis Ballagh, ed., *The Letters of Richard Henry Lee*, I (New York: Macmillan, 1911), 7; James Boswell, *Life of Samuel Johnson*, Modern Library ed. (New York, 1945), 532. Even someone as enlightened and prone to conspiratorial thinking as John Adams repeatedly fell back on the "inscrutable" designs of "providence" in order to account for strange turns of events. This providential tradition, associated especially with Protestantism, was the only means in the eighteenth century, other than conspiracies, to account for events that seemed inconsistent with their causes (Taylor et al., eds., *Adams Papers*, II, 84, 236).

72. Nathanael Emmons, *A Discourse, Delivered on the National Fast, April 25, 1799* (Wrentham, MA: Nathaniel and Benjamin Heaton, 1799), 23.

73. *Boston Evening-Post*, December 29, 1766. See Lovejoy, *Reflections on Human Nature*, 129–215, and Albert O. Hirschman, *The Passions and the Interests: Political Arguments for Capitalism Before Its Triumph* (Princeton: Princeton University Press, 1977).

74. Duncan Forbes, "'Scientific' Whiggism: Adam Smith and John Millar," *Cambridge Journal*, VII (1954), 651, 653–654; Adam Ferguson, *An Essay on the History of Civil Society* (1767), Duncan Forbes, ed. (Edinburgh: Edinburgh University Press, 1966), 122, 123.

75. M. H. Abrams, *Natural Supernaturalism: Tradition and Revolution in Romantic Literature* (New York: W. W. Norton, 1971), 328; William Wordsworth, "The Borderers," in William Knight, ed., *The Poetical Works of William Wordsworth*, I (Edinburgh: William Patterson, 1882), 109. François Furet notes the differing views of the two French Revolutionary leaders, Brissot de Warville and Robespierre, over what was happening. Brissot, writes Furet, argued publicly in 1792 that "it was impossible to foresee the turn of events and that human intentions and the course of history were two separate matters." This "kind of historical objectivity, which made it possible to disregard the possibility—indeed, in this case, the probability—that evil intentions were at work, was by definition totally alien to Robespierre's political universe, in which it was implicitly assumed that intentions are perfectly coherent with the actions they prompt and the effects they aim at. . . . In such a universe, action never had unforeseeable consequences, nor was power ever innocent." The difference that Furet finds between the thinking of Brissot and Robespierre is precisely the difference between our modern conception of reality and that of the American Revolutionaries (*Interpreting the French Revolution*, trans. Elborg Forster [Cambridge, UK: Cambridge University Press, 1981], 67–68).

76. See esp. Roberts, *Secret Societies*, 160–167. On April 17, 1798, the recent immigrant to America Benjamin Henry Latrobe wrote to his Italian friend Giambattista Scandalla of the unprecedented turmoil of the French Revolution. "At the present moment the great convulsions of empires and nations, are so violent, that they lay hold of, and move individuals with an effect unknown in the former wars of kings. The surface—the great men of every nation—were once the only part of the mass really interested. The present storm is so violent, that the ocean is moved to the very depth, and you and I who inhabit it, feel the commotion" (John C. Van Horne and Lee W. Formwalt, eds., *The Correspondence and Miscellaneous Papers of Benjamin Henry Latrobe*, I [New Haven, CT: Yale University Press, 1988]).

77. Gouverneur Morris, "Political Enquiries," in Willi Paul Adams, ed., "'The Spirit of Commerce Requires that Property Be Sacred': Gouverneur Morris and the American Revolution," *Amerikastudien/American Studies*, XXI (1976), 328. Adams dates Morris's unpublished essay at 1776, but the content suggests that it was more likely written a decade or so later.

78. The fullest account of the Illuminati scare is Vernon Stauffer, *New England and the Bavarian Illuminati* (New York, 1967 [originally published 1918]). On conspiratorial thinking in the early Republic, see J. Wendell Knox, *Conspiracy in American Politics, 1787–1815* (New York: Arno Press, 1972).

79. David Tappan, *A Discourse Delivered in the Chapel of Harvard College, June 19, 1798* (Boston: Manning & Loring, 1798), 13, 19–21.

80. Ibid., 6; Dwight, *The Duty of Americans, at the Present Crisis, Illustrated in a Discourse Preached, on the Fourth of July . . .* (New Haven, CT: Thomas and Samuel Green, 1798), 16. It was this traditional assumption about the cause-effect relationship between beliefs and behavior that lay behind the Federalists' enactment of the Sedition Act of 1798. They could scarcely appreciate the emerging notion set forth by some Republicans that Americans should be free to believe and express whatever opinions they pleased.

81. Abraham Bishop, *Connecticut Republicanism. An Oration on the Extent and Power of Political Delusion . . .* (Albany, NY: John Barber, 1801), 8, and *Oration Delivered in Wallingford on the 11th of March 1801 . . .* (New Haven, CT: William W. Morse, 1801), 24. I owe some of these citations relating to the Illuminati conspiracy to David C. Miller, "The Ideology of Conspiracy: An Examination of the *Illuminati* Incident in New England" (seminar paper, Brown University, 1977).

82. Bishop, *Proofs of a Conspiracy, Against Christianity, and the Government of the United States . . .* (Hartford, CT: John Babcock, 1802), 10–12, and *Oration Delivered in Wallingford*, 25, 26.

83. By avowing that "'holiness' is no 'guarantee for political rectitude,'" Bishop, wrote a stunned Federalist David Daggett, was undermining the moral order of society. "What security then," asked

Daggett, "have we for 'political rectitude'?" (*Three Letters to Abraham Bishop* ... [Hartford, CT: Hudson and Goodwin, 1800], 27).

84. *Monthly Magazine and American Review*, I (1799), 289; Charles Brockden Brown, "Walstein's School of History," in *The Rhapsodist and Other Uncollected Writings*, Harry R. Warfel, ed. (New York: Scholars Facsimiles and Reprints, 1943), 147. In discussing the conspiratorial interpretation that saw the Order of the Bavarian Illuminati bringing about the French Revolution, Hofstadter wrote that "what is missing [in it] is not veracious information about the organization, but sensible judgment about what can cause a revolution" (*Paranoid Style*, 37). The basic question is why we think one judgment "sensible" and another not.

85. Robert K. Merton, "The Unanticipated Consequences of Purposive Social Action," *American Sociological Review*, I (1936), 894–904. Fisher Ames, the most pessimistic of Federalists, was one of the few Americans of these years who came to think like a European about revolutions and the "stream" of history. "Events," he wrote, "proceed, not as they were expected or intended, but as they are impelled by the irresistible laws of our political existence. Things inevitable happen, and we are astonished, as if they were miracles, and the course of nature had been overpowered or suspended to produce them" ("The Dangers of American Liberty" [1805], in Seth Ames, ed., *Works of Fisher Ames* ... , II [Boston: Little, Brown, 1854], 345).

86. See W. B. Berthoff, " 'A Lesson on Concealment': Brockden Brown's Method in Fiction," *Philological Quarterly*, XXXVII (1958), 45–57; Michael Davitt Bell, " 'The Double-Tongued Deceiver': Sincerity and Duplicity in the Novels of Charles Brockden Brown," *Early American Literature*, IX (1974), 143–163; John Clemen, "Ambiguous Evil: A Study of Villains and Heroes in Charles Brockden Brown's Major Novels," ibid., X (1975), 190–219; Mark Seltzer, "Saying Makes It So: Language and Event in Brown's *Wieland*," ibid., XIII (1978), 81–91; and David H. Hirsch, *Reality and Idea in the Early American Novel* (The Hague: Mouton, 1971), 74–100.

87. Charles Brockden Brown, *Wieland; or, the Transformation* (Philadelphia: McKay, 1889 [originally published 1798]), 234, *Edgar Huntly, or Memoirs of a Sleep Walker* (Philadelphia: McKay, 1887 [originally published 1799]), 267, and "Walstein's School of History," in *Rhapsodist*, Warfel, ed. 152, 154.

88. Jeremy Bentham, *An Introduction to the Principles of Morals and Legislation* (Oxford: University of London, 1907 [originally published London, 1789]), 102. Utilitarianism has often been used rather loosely by historians and equated simply with utility or happiness. Although late eighteenth- and early nineteenth-century Americans were centrally interested in the usefulness of behavior, most did not mean by it what Bentham did: the abandonment of a concern with motives in favor of consequences. This sort of Benthamite utilitarianism had very little influence in America. See Paul A. Palmer, "Benthamism in England and America," *American Political Science Review*, XXXV (1941), 855–871; Morton White, *The Philosophy of the American Revolution* (New York: Oxford University Press, 1978), 230–239; and Wilson Smith, "William Paley's Theological Utilitarianism in America," *William and Mary Quarterly*, 3rd ser., XI (1954), 402–424. Even in criminal legislation, where, through the influence of Beccaria, utilitarianism was rampant, an ultimate concern with motives insinuated itself. In designating punishments for various offenses, wrote New York penal reformer Thomas Eddy, modern legislators could scarcely take into account "the moral condition" of the criminals; they could "regard only the tendency of actions to injure society, and distribute those punishments according to the comparative degrees of harm such actions may produce." Yet this stark utilitarianism in criminal legislation was justified in Eddy's mind only because it gave the supervisors of the penitentiaries the opportunity of "distinguishing the shades of guilt in different offenders" and thus of effecting the moral reformation of the criminals (*An Account of the State Prison or Penitentiary House, in the City of New York* [New York: Isaac Collins and son, 1801], 51–52).

89. "Introduction," *United States Magazine and Democratic Review*, I (October 1837), in Joseph L. Blau, ed., *Social Theories of Jacksonian Democracy: Representative Writings of the Period 1825–1850* (New York: Bobbs Merrill, 1954 [originally published 1947]), 28.

90. George Washington (1788), quoted in Paul C. Nagel, *One Nation Indivisible: The Union in American Thought, 1776–1861* (New York: Oxford University Press, 1964), 149.

91. Jacob Viner, *The Role of Providence in the Social Order: An Essay in Intellectual History* (Philadelphia: American Philosophical Society, 1972), 111. "God governs the world by the laws of a general

providence," observed Peres Fobes in 1795. Things did not happen in violation of these laws, for "this would introduce such a train of miraculous events, as would subvert the whole constitution of nature, and destroy that established in connexion between cause and effect, which is now the principal source of human knowledge and foresight" (*A Sermon Preached before His Excellency Samuel Adams . . . Being the Day of General Election* [Boston: Young and Minns, 1795], 12).

92. Charles Stewart Davies, *An Address Delivered on the Commemoration at Fryeburg, May 19, 1825* (Portland, ME: J. Adams Jr., 1825), in Blau, ed., *Social Theories*, 40.

93. On the romantic historians' view of the progressive patterning of events that sometimes transcended individual motives see David Levin, *History as Romantic Art: Bancroft, Prescott, Motley and Parkman* (Stanford, CA: Stanford University Press, 1959), 40–43.

94. Timothy Dwight, quoted in Marie Caskey, *Chariot of Fire: Religion and the Beecher Family* (New Haven, CT: Yale University Press, 1978), 39; see also Lyman Beecher, *Sermons, Delivered on Various Occasions*, II (Boston: John P. Jewitt, 1852), 156–158. Although Beecher and the other New Haven theologians believed that people had free wills, they also believed that the law of cause and effect operated in the moral as in the natural world, "the laws of mind, and the operation of moral causes, being just as uniform as the laws of matter." This made revivalism a science like engineering (Conrad Cherry, "Nature and the Republic: The New Haven Theology," *New England Quarterly*, LI [1978], 518–520).

95. John Taylor, *An Inquiry into the Principle and Policy of the Government of the United States* (New Haven, CT: Yale University Press, 1950 [originally published 1814]), 96; Tocqueville, *Democracy in America*, Phillips Bradley, ed., II (New York: Knopf, 1945), 85. "It is evidently a general constitution of providence," wrote Nathaniel Chipman as late as 1833, "that the general tendency of *vice* is to produce misery to the agent, of *virtue*, to produce happiness, connected in both by the relation of cause and effect" (*Principle of Government; a Treatise on Free Institutions* . . . [Burlington, VT: Edward Smith, 1833], 22).

96. Everett, *An Oration Delivered at Concord, April the Nineteenth 1825* (Boston: Cummings, Hilliard, 1825), 3–4; Cohen, *Revolutionary Histories*, 86–127.

97. Haskell, *The Emergence of Professional Social Science: The American Social Science Association and the Nineteenth-Century Crisis of Authority* (Urbana: University of Illinois Press, 1977), 40.

CHAPTER 4, INTERESTS AND DISINTERESTEDNESS IN THE MAKING OF THE CONSTITUTION

1. Gladstone, quoted in Douglass Adair, "The Tenth Federalist Revisited," in Trevor Colbourn., ed., *Fame and the Founding Fathers* (New York: W. W. Norton, 1974), 81.

2. Henry Steele Commager, *Jefferson, Nationalism, and the Enlightenment* (New York: George Braziller, 1975), xix.

3. Charles Thomson to Thomas Jefferson, April 6, 1786, in Julian P. Boyd et al., eds., *The Papers of Thomas Jefferson* (Princeton: Princeton University Press, 1950–), IX, 380. On the demographic explosion of the 1780s, see J. Potter, "The Growth of Population in America, 1700–1860," in D. V. Glass and D. E. C. Eversley, eds., *Population in History: Essays in Historical Demography* (Chicago: Aldine, 1965), 640.

4. For examples of the various historians who have minimized the criticalness of the 1780s, see Charles A. Beard, *An Economic Interpretation of the Constitution of the United States* (New York: Free Press, 1913), 48; E. James Ferguson, *The Power of the Purse: A History of American Public Finance, 1776–1790* (Chapel Hill: University of North Carolina Press, 1961), 337; Merrill Jensen, *The New Nation: A History of the United States During the Confederation, 1781–1790* (New York: Harper and Brothers, 1950), 348–349; Bernard Bailyn, "The Central Themes of the American Revolution: An Interpretation," in Stephen G. Kurtz and James H. Hutson, eds., *Essays on the American Revolution* (Chapel Hill: University of North Carolina Press, 1973), 21.

5. "Amicus Republicae," *Address to the Public* . . . (Exeter, N.H., 1786), in Charles S. Hyneman and Donald S. Lutz, eds., *American Political Writing During the Founding Era, 1760–1805* (Indianapolis: Liberty Fund, 1983), 1, 644; Rush to David Ramsay, [March or April 1788], in L. H. Butterfield, ed., *Letters of Benjamin Rush* (Princeton: Princeton University Press, 1951), I, 454; Washington to John Jay, August 1, 1786, May 18, 1786, in John C. Fitzpatrick, ed., *The Writings of George Washington* . . . (Washington, DC: U.S. Government Printing Office, 1931–1944), XXVIII, 431–432, 503.

6. Jackson Turner Main, *The Antifederalists: Critics of the Constitution, 1781–1788* (Chapel Hill: University of North Carolina Press, 1961), 177–178.

7. William Findley to Gov. William Plumer of New Hampshire, "William Findley of Westmoreland, Pa.," *Pennsylvania Magazine of History and Biography*, V (1881), 444; Jerry Grundfest, *George Clymer: Philadelphia Revolutionary, 1739–1813* (New York: Arno Press, 1982), 293–294; John Bach McMaster and Frederick D. Stone, eds., *Pennsylvania and the Federal Constitution, 1787–1788* (Philadelphia: Pennsylvania Historical Society, 1888), 115.

8. On this point, see Robert A. Feer, "Shays's Rebellion and the Constitution: A Study in Causation," *New England Quarterly*, XLII (1969), 388–410.

9. George Washington to John Jay, May 18, 1786, in Fitzpatrick, ed., *Writings of Washington*, XVIII, 432; James Madison to Thomas Jefferson, October 24, 1787, in Boyd et al., eds., *Papers of Jefferson*, XII, 276.

10. Robert A. Rutland, editorial note to "Vices of the Political System of the United States," in William T. Hutchinson et al., eds., *The Papers of James Madison* (Chicago, Charlottesville: University of Chicago Press, University Press of Virginia, 1962–), IX, 346.

11. Thomas Jefferson quoted in Ralph Ketcham, *James Madison; A Biography* (New York: Macmillan 1971), 162; Drew R. McCoy, "The Virginia Port Bill of 1784," *Virginia Magazine of History and Biography*, LXXXIII (1975), 294; James Madison to Edmund Pendleton, January 9, 1787, to George Washington, December 24, 1786, in Hutchinson et al., eds., *Papers of Madison*, IX, 225, 244; A. G. Roeber, *Faithful Magistrates and Republican Lawyers: Creators of Virginia Legal Culture, 1680–1810* (Chapel Hill: University of North Carolina Press, 1981), 192–202.

12. McCoy, "Virginia Port Bill," 292; James Madison to George Washington, December 7, 1786, to Edmund Pendleton, January 9, 1787, to George Washington, December 24, 1786, to Thomas Jefferson, December 4, 1786, in Hutchinson et al., eds., *Papers of Madison*, IX, 200, 244, 225, 191; Ketcham, *Madison*, 172.

13. "Vices," in Hutchinson et al., eds., *Papers of Madison*, IX, 354, 355–356.

14. George Washington to Henry Lee, April 5, 1786, in Fitzpatrick, ed., *Writings of Washington*, XXVIII, 402; Grundfest, *Clymer*, 164, 165; E. Wayne Carp, *To Starve the Army at Pleasure: Continental Army Administration and American Political Culture, 1775–1783* (Chapel Hill: University of North Carolina Press, 1984), 209; Knox quoted in William Winslow Crosskey and William Jeffrey Jr., *Politics and the Constitution in the History of the United States* (Chicago: University of Chicago Press, 1980), III, 420, 421.

15. Benjamin Rush to Jeremy Belknap, May 6, 1788, in Butterfield, ed., *Letters of Rush*, I, 461; Elbridge Gerry, in Max Farrand, ed., *The Records of the Federal Convention of 1787* (New Haven, CT: Yale University Press, 1911, rev. ed., 1937), I, 48.

16. The best study of wartime mobilization in a single state is Richard Buel Jr., *Dear Liberty: Connecticut's Mobilization for the Revolutionary War* (Middletown, CT: Western University Press, 1980). For an insightful general assessment of the effects of mobilization, see Janet Ann Riesman, "The Origins of American Political Economy, 1690–1781" (Ph.D. diss., Brown University, 1983), 302–338.

17. Laurens quoted in Albert S. Bolles, *The Financial History of the United States from 1774 to 1789: Embracing the Period of the American Revolution*, 4th ed. (New York: D. Appleton, 1896), 61–62 (I owe this citation to Janet Riesman); Carp, *To Starve the Army*, 106.

18. Nathanael Greene to Jacob Greene, after May 24, 1778, in Richard K. Showman ed., *The Papers of General Nathanael Greene* (Chapel Hill: University of North Carolina Press, 1976–), II, 404; Richard Buel Jr., "Samson Shorn: The Impact of the Revolutionary War on Estimates of the Republic's Strength," in Ronald Hoffman and Peter J. Albert, eds., *Arms and Independence: The Military Character of the American Revolution* (Charlottesville: University Press of Virginia, 1984), 157–160. On the growth of commercial farming in the middle of the eighteenth century, see especially Joyce Appleby, "Commercial Farming and the 'Agrarian Myth' in the Early Republic," *Journal of American History*, LXVIII (1982), 833–849. There is nothing on eighteenth-century America's increased importation of "luxuries" and "comforts" resembling Neil McKendrick et al., *The Birth of a Consumer Society: The Commercialization of Eighteenth-Century England* (Bloomington: Indiana University Press, 1982). But see the articles of Carole Shammas, especially "The Domestic Environment in Early Modern England and America," *Journal of Social History*, XIV (1980), 3–24; Lois Green Carr and Lorena S. Walsh, "Inventories and the Analysis of Wealth and Consumption Patterns in St. Mary's County,

Maryland, 1658–1777," *Historical Methods*, XIII (1980), 81–104; and Gloria L. Main, *Tobacco Colony: Life in Early Maryland, 1650–1720* (Princeton: Princeton University Press, 1982).

19. For examples of the new thinking about luxury as an inducement to industry, see Drew R. McCoy, *The Elusive Republic: Political Economy in Jeffersonian America* (Chapel Hill: University of North Carolina Press, 1980), 97.

20. [William Barton], *The True Interest of the United States, and Particularly of Pennsylvania Considered ...* (Philadelphia: M. Carey, 1786), 12.

21. Ibid., 4, 25–26.

22. [William Smith], *The Independent Reflector ... by William Livingston and Others*, Milton M. Klein, ed. (Cambridge, MA: Belknap Press of Harvard University Press, 1963), 106. See J. E. Crowley, *This Sheba, Self: The Conceptualization of Economic Life in Eighteenth-Century America* (Baltimore: Johns Hopkins University Press, 1974), 38–39, 44, 49, 87, 97–99.

23. *Remarks on a Pamphlet, Entitled, "Considerations on the Bank of North-America"* (Philadelphia: John Steele, 1785), 14; James Madison to James Monroe, April 9, 1786, in Hutchinson et al., eds., *Papers of Madison*, IX, 26; [Barton], *True Interest*, 20; Pennsylvania Statute of 1785, cited in E. A. J. Johnson, *The Foundations of American Economic Freedom: Government and Enterprise in the Age of Washington* (Minneapolis: University of Minnesota Press, 1973), 43n.

24. Thomas Jefferson, *Notes on the State of Virginia*, William Peden, ed. (Chapel Hill: University of North Carolina Press, 1955), Query XXII, 175; Thomas Jefferson to G. K. van Hogendorp, October 13, 1785, in Boyd et al., eds., *Papers of Jefferson*, VIII, 633.

25. Madison to Monroe, October 5, 1786, in Hutchinson et al., eds., *Papers of Madison*, IX, 141; *Carlisle Gazette* (Pa.), October 24, 1787, quoted in Herbert J. Storing, ed., *The Complete Anti-Federalist* (Chicago: University of Chicago Press, 1981), II, 208; George Washington to James Warren, October 7, 1785, in Fitzpatrick, ed., *Writings of Washington*, XXVIII, 291; Hamilton, in Farrand, ed., *Records of the Federal Convention*, I, 378. On the nature and role of interests in eighteenth-century British politics, see Michael Kammen, *Empire and Interest: The American Colonies and the Politics of Mercantilism* (Philadelphia: J. B. Lippincott, 1970).

26. Pauline Maier, *The Old Revolutionaries: Political Lives in the Age of Samuel Adams* (New York: Knopf, 1980), 3–50, quotation at 47.

27. George Washington, quoted in Lester H. Cohen, *The Revolutionary Histories: Contemporary Narratives of the American Revolution* (Ithaca, NY: Cornell University Press, 1980), 273.

28. Joseph Lathrop (1786), in Hyneman and Lutz, eds., *American Political Writing*, I, 660; Wilson, in Farrand, ed., *Records of the Federal Convention*, I, 605; Thomas Jefferson to Edward Carrington, January 16, 1787, in Boyd et al., eds., *Papers of Jefferson*, XI, 49. See also Ralph Ketcham, *Presidents Above Party: The First American Presidency, 1789–1829* (Chapel Hill: University of North Carolina Press, 1984).

29. Jefferson, "Summary View of the Rights of British America" (1774), in Boyd et al., eds., *Papers of Jefferson*, I, 134.

30. Johnson, *A Dictionary of the English Language ...* (London: W. Strahan, 1755); Charles Royster, *A Revolutionary People at War: The Continental Army and American Character, 1775–1783* (Chapel Hill: University of North Carolina Press, 1979), 22–23.

31. John Brewer, *Party Ideology and Popular Politics at the Accession of George III* (Cambridge, UK: Cambridge University Press, 1976), 97.

32. George Washington to John Hancock, September 24, 1776, in Fitzpatrick, ed., *Writings of Washington*, VI, 107–108.

33. Adam Smith, *An Inquiry into the Nature and Causes of the Wealth of Nations*, R. H. Campbell and A. S. Skinner, eds. (Oxford: Oxford University Press, 1976) (V.i.f. 50–51), II, 781–783; [John Trenchard and Thomas Gordon], *Cato's Letters; or, Essays on Liberty, Civil and Religious, and Other Important Subjects*, 5th ed. (London: T. Woodward et al., 1748), III, 193; Phillips Payson, "A Sermon Preached before the Honorable Council ... at Boston, May 27, 1778," in John Wingate Thornton, ed., *The Pulpit of the American Revolution ...* (Boston, New York: Gould and Lincoln, Sheldon and Co., 1860), 337; Jefferson, "A Bill for the More General Diffusion of Education" (1779), in Boyd et al., eds., *Papers of Jefferson*, II, 527. On the eighteenth-century British developments out of which "Cato," Smith, and others wrote, see the illuminating discussion in John Barrell, *English Literature in History, 1730–80: An Equal Wide Survey* (London: Hutchinson, 1983), 17–50.

34. The best discussion of the distinctiveness of the gentry in colonial America is Rhys Isaac, *The Transformation of Virginia, 1740–1790* (Chapel Hill: University, of North Carolina Press, 1982), esp. 131–132.

35. Royster, *Revolutionary People at War*, 86–95; John B. B. Trussell Jr., *Birthplace of an Army: A Study of the Valley Forge Encampment* (Harrisburg: Pennsylvania Historical and Museum Commission, 1976), 86.

36. Francis Hutcheson, *A System of Moral Philosophy in Three Books* . . . (London: R. and A. Foulis 1755), II, 113. "Let not your Love of Philosophical Amusements have more than its due Weight with you," Benjamin Franklin admonished Cadwallader Colden at midcentury. Public service was far more important. In fact, said Franklin, even "the finest" of Newton's "Discoveries" could not have excused his neglect of serving the commonwealth if the public had needed him (Franklin to Colden, October 11, 1750, in Leonard W. Labaree et al., eds., *The Papers of Benjamin Franklin* [New Haven, CT: Yale University Press, 1959–], IV, 68).

37. Jack N. Rakove, *The Beginnings of National Politics: An Interpretative. History of the Continental Congress* (New York: Knopf, 1979), 216–239, quotation by William Fleming to Jefferson, May 10, 1779, at 237; George Athan Billias, *Elbridge Gerry, Founding Father and Republican Statesman* (New York: McGraw-Hill, 1976), 138–139.

38. See William R. Taylor, *Cavalier and Yankee: The Old South and American National Character* (New York: George Braziller, 1961).

39. Wilson, "On the History of Property," in Robert Green McCloskey, ed., *The Works of James Wilson* (Cambridge, MA: Harvard University Press, 1967), II, 716; Dickinson, "Letters of a Farmer in Pennsylvania" (1768), in Paul Leicester Ford, ed., *The Writings of John Dickinson*, vol. I, *Political Writings, 1764–1774* (Pennsylvania Historical Society, *Memoirs*, XIV [Philadelphia: Pennsylvania Historical Society, 1895]), 307 (hereafter cited as Ford, ed., *Writings of Dickinson*).

40. "We have found by experience, that no dependence can be had upon *merchants*, either at *home*, or in *America*," Charles Chauncy told Richard Price in 1774, "so many of them are so mercenary as to find within themselves a readiness to become slaves themselves, as well as to be accessory to the slavery of others, if they imagine they may, by this means, serve their own private separate interest" (D. C. Thomas and Bernard Peach, eds., *The Correspondence of Richard Price* [Durham, NC: Duke University Press, 1983], I, 170). For Adam Smith's view that the interest of merchants and indeed of all who lived by profit was "always in some respects different from, and even opposite to, that of the publick," see Smith, *Wealth of Nations*, Campbell and Skinner, ed. (I.xi.p.10), I, 267.

41. Richard Jackson to Benjamin Franklin, June 17, 1755, in Labaree et al., eds., *Papers of Franklin*, VI, 82. On the colonial merchants' "detachment from political activity," see Thomas M. Doerflinger, "Philadelphia Merchants and the Logic of Moderation, 1760–1775," *William and Mary Quarterly*, 3rd ser., XL (1983), 212–213; and Edward Countryman, *A People in Revolution: The American Revolution and Political Society in New York, 1760–1790* (Baltimore: Johns Hopkins University Press, 1981), 113.

42. William M. Fowler Jr., *The Baron of Beacon Hill: A Biography of John Hancock* (Boston: Houghton Mifflin, 1980); Charles W. Akers, *The Divine Politician: Samuel Cooper and the American Revolution in Boston* (Boston: Northeastern University Press, 1982), 121, 128, 130, 141, 176, 311; Henry Laurens to Richard Oswald, July 7, 1764, in Philip M. Hamer et al., eds., *The Papers of Henry Laurens* (Columbia: University of South Carolina Press, 1968–), IV, 338 (see also Rachel N. Klein, "Ordering the Backcountry: The South Carolina Regulation," *William and Mary Quarterly*, 3rd ser., XXXVIII [1981], 667); David Duncan Wallace, *The Life of Henry Laurens* . . . (New York: Russell and Russell, 1915), 69–70, quotation at 335. In the 1780s Elbridge Gerry likewise retired from mercantile business and "set himself up as a country squire" (Billias, *Gerry*, 135–136).

43. Leonard W. Labaree et al., eds., *The Autobiography of Benjamin Franklin* (New Haven, CT: Yale University Press, 1964), 196; Christopher, Collier, *Roger Sherman's Connecticut: Yankee Politics and the American Revolution* (Middletown, CT: Wesleyan University Press, 1971), 14, 21–22.

44. Jacob E. Cooke, ed., *The Federalist* No. 35 (Middletown, CT, 1961) [Barton], *True Interest*, 27. For arguments in pre-Revolutionary Virginia whether lawyers were practicing "a grovelling, mercenary trade" or not, see Roeber, *Faithful Magistrates and Republican Lawyers*, 156–157. Some conceded that lawyers were members of one of the "three genteel Professions," but that they were guilty of more "petit Larceny" than doctors and clergymen. Madison was not convinced of the disinterestedness of lawyers (ibid., 157, 147, Ketcham, *Madison*, 145). On the efforts of some nineteenth-century thinkers

to make professional communities the repositories of disinterestedness against the selfishness and interestedness of businessmen, see Thomas L. Haskell, "Professionalism *versus* Capitalism: R. H. Tawney, Emile Durkheim, and C. S. Peirce on the Disinterestedness of Professional Communities," in Thomas L. Haskell, ed., *The Authority of Experts: Studies in History and Theory* (Bloomington: Indiana University Press, 1984), 180–225.

45. Morris, "Political Enquiries," in Willi Paul Adams, ed., "'The Spirit of Commerce, Requires that Property Be Sacred': Gouverneur Morris and the American Revolution," *Amerikastudien/American Studies*, XXI (1976), 329; Alexander Hamilton to Robert Troup, April 13, 1795, in Harold C. Syrett, et al., eds., *The Papers of Alexander Hamilton* (New York: Columbia University Press, 1961–1979), XVII, 329.

46. George Washington to Benjamin Harrison, January 22, 1785, to George William Fairfax, February 27, 1785, in Fitzpatrick, ed., *Writings of Washington*, XXVIII, 36, 85.

47. George Washington to Benjamin Harrison, January 22, 1785, to William Grayson, January 22, 1785, to Lafayette, February 15, 1785, to Thomas Jefferson, February 25, 1785, to George William Fairfax, February 27, 1785, to Governor Patrick Henry, February 27, 1785, to Henry Knox, February 28, 1785, June 18, 1785, to Nathanael Greene, May 20, 1785, in Fitzpatrick, ed., *Writings of Washington*, XXVIII, 36, 37, 72, 80–81, 85, 89–91, 92–93, 146, 167. The only friend whose advice on the disposition of the canal shares Washington did not solicit was Robert Morris, perhaps because he feared that Morris might tell him to keep them. Instead he confined his letter to Morris to describing the commercial opportunities of the canals. To Morris, February 1, 1785, ibid., 48–55.

48. Cooke, ed., *The Federalist* No. 10; Gordon S. Wood, "Democracy and the Constitution," in Robert A, Goldwin and William A. Schambra, eds., *How Democratic Is the Constitution?* (Washington, DC: American Enterprise Institute, 1980), 11–12. On the tendency to misread Madison, see Robert J. Morgan, "Madison's Theory of Representation in the Tenth Federalist," *Journal of Politics*, XXXVI (1974), 852–885; and Paul F. Bourke, "The Pluralist Reading of James Madison's Tenth *Federalist*," *Perspectives in American History*, IX (1975), 271–295.

49. James Madison to George Washington April 16, 1787, to Edmund Randolph, April 8, 1787, in Hutchinson et al., eds., *Papers of Madison*, IX, 370, 384; John Zvesper, "The Madisonian Systems," *Western Political Quarterly*, XXXVII (1984), 244–247.

50. Jerome J. Nadelhaft, "'The Snarls of Invidious Animals': The Democratization of Revolutionary South Carolina," in Ronald Hoffman and Peter J. Albert, eds., *Sovereign States in an Age of Uncertainty* (Charlottesville: University Press of Virginia 1981), 77.

51. On Findley, see his letter to Governor William Plumer of New Hampshire, February 27, 1812, "William Findley of Westmoreland, Pa.," *Pennsylvania Magazine of History and Biography*, V (1881), 440–50; and Russell J. Ferguson, *Early Western Pennsylvania Politics* (Pittsburgh: University of Pittsburgh Press, 1938), 39–40.

52. Grundfest, *Clymer*, 141.

53. Claude Milton Newlin, *The Life and Writings of Hugh Henry Brackenridge* (Princeton: Princeton University Press, 1932), 71.

54. Ibid., 78, 80–81; Ferguson, *Early Western Pennsylvania*, 66–69.

55. Newlin, *Brackenridge*, 79–80, 83–84; Ferguson, *Early Western Pennsylvania*, 70–72.

56. Mathew Carey, ed., *Debates and Proceedings of the General Assembly of Pennsylvania on the Memorials Praying a Repeal or Suspension of the Law Annulling the Charter of the Bank* (Philadelphia: Carey and Co., Seddon and Pritchard, 1786), 19, 64, 10, 30.

57. Robert Morris to George Washington, May 29, 1781, E. James Ferguson et al., eds., *The Papers of Robert Morris, 1781–1784* (Pittsburgh: University of Pittsburgh Press, 1973–), I, 96; Ellis Paxson Oberholtzer, *Robert Morris, Patriot and Financier* (New York: Macmillan, 1903), 52–56, 70–71.

58. Carey, ed., *Debates*, 33, 79–80, 98 (quotations on 80, 98).

59. Ibid., 81; Oberholtzer, *Morris*, 285–286, 297–299, 301–303; Eleanor Young, *Forgotten Patriot: Robert Morris* (New York: Macmillan, 1950–), 170; Barbara Ann Chernow, *Robert Morris, Land Speculator, 1790–1801* (New York: Arno Press, 1978); H. E. Scudder, ed., *Recollections of Samuel Breck . . .* (Philadelphia: Porter & Coates, 1877), 203: *The Journal of William Maclay* (New York: Albert & Charles Boni, 1927 [orig. pub, 1890]), 132.

60. Carey, ed., *Debates*, 66, 87, 128, 21, 130, 38, 15, 72–73.

61. Cooke, ed., *The Federalist* No. 10; [William Findley], *A Review of the Revenue System Adopted at the First Congress under the Federal Constitution* . . . (Philadelphia: Bailey, 1794), 117.

62. Jonathan Elliot, ed., *The Debates in the Several State Conventions on the Adoption of the Federal Constitution* . . . (Philadelphia: J. B. Lippincott, 1896), II, 13, 260; [Findley], "Letter by an Officer of the Late Continental Army," *Independent Gazette* (Philadelphia), November 6, 1787, in Storing, ed., *Complete Anti-Federalist*, III, 95; Ruth Bogin, *Abraham Clark and the Quest for Equality in the Revolutionary Era, 1774–1794* (East Brunswick, NJ: Fairleigh Dickinson University Press, 1982), 32.

63. Philip A. Crowl, "Anti-Federalism in Maryland, 1787–88," *William and Mary Quarterly*, 3rd ser., IV (1947), 464; Richard Walsh, *Charleston's Sons of Liberty: A Study of the Artisans, 1763–1789* (Columbia: University of South Carolina Press, 1959), 132; [James Winthrop] "Letters of Agrippa," *Massachusetts Gazette*, December 14, 1787, in Storing, ed., *Complete Anti-Federalist*, IV, 80; "Essentials of a Free Government," in Walter Hartwell Bennett, ed., *Letters from the Federal Farmer to the Republican* (Tuscaloosa: University of Alabama Press, 1978), 10.

64. Benjamin Latrobe to Philip Mazzei, December 19, 1806, in Margherita Marchione et al., eds., *Philip Mazzei: Selected Writings and Correspondence* (Prato, Italy: Cassa di Risparmi e Depositi di Prato, 1983), III, 439 (I owe this reference to Stanley J. Idzerda).

65. Ibid.

66. James T. Schleifer, *The Making of Tocqueville's "Democracy in America"* (Chapel Hill: University of North Carolina Press, 1980), 242, 243; Tocqueville to Ernest de Chabrol, June 9, 1831, in Roger Boesch, ed., *Alexis de Tocqueville: Selected Letters on Politics and Society* (Berkeley: University of California Press, 1985), 38; Tocqueville, *Democracy in America*, ed. Phillips Bradley (New York: Vintage Books, 1954), I, 243. It was not, of course, as simple as Tocqueville made it out to be. The ideal of disinterested politics did not disappear in the nineteenth century, and even today it lingers on here and there. It formed the basis for all the antiparty and mugwump reform movements and colored the thinking of many of the Progressives. For Theodore Roosevelt in 1894, "the first requisite in the citizen who wishes to share the work of our public life . . . is that he shall act disinterestedly and with a sincere purpose to serve the whole commonwealth" (Roosevelt, *American Ideals and Other Essays, Social and Political* [New York: G.P. Putnam's Sons, 1897], 34 [I owe this reference to John Patrick Diggins]). Of course, at almost the same time, John Dewey was telling Americans that it was psychologically impossible for anyone to act disinterestedly. See John Patrick Diggins, *The Lost Soul of American Politics: Virtue, Self-Interest, and the Foundations of Liberalism* (New York: Oxford University Press, 1984), 341–343. See also Stephen Miller, *Special Interest Groups in American Politics* (New Brunswick, NJ: Transaction Books, 1983).

67. Wilson, in Farrand, ed., *Records of the Federal Convention*, I, 154; Cooke, ed., *The Federalist* No. 10. Vernon Parrington asked the same questions. If ordinary men were motivated by self-interest, as the Federalists believed, why would "this sovereign motive" abdicate "its rule among the rich and well born? . . . Do the wealthy betray no desire for greater power? Do the strong and powerful care more for good government than for class interests?" (*Main Currents in American Thought: An Interpretation of American Literature from the Beginnings to 1920* [New York: Harcourt, Brace, 1927], I, 302).

68. John Witherspoon, "Speech in Congress on Finances," *The Works of John Witherspoon* . . . (Edinburgh: John Turnbull, 1805), IX, 133–134.

69. Robert J. Taylor, *Western Massachusetts in the Revolution* (Providence, RI: Brown University Press, 1954), 20; Robert A. East, *Business Enterprise in the American Revolutionary Era* (New York: Columbia University Press, 1938), 20–22; Dickinson, "Letters of a Farmer," in Ford, ed., *Writings of Dickinson*, 307; Fowler, *Baron of Beacon Hill*, 251; Margaret E. Martin, *Merchants and Trade of the Connecticut River Valley, 1750–1820* (*Smith College Studies in History*, XXIV [Northampton, MA: Smith College, 1938–1939]), 159. See also Alice Hanson Jones, *Wealth of a Nation to Be: The American Colonies on the Eve of the Revolution* (New York: Columbia University Press, 1980), 145–153.

70. Carey, ed., *Debates*, 96; Aubrey C. Land, "Economic Base and Social Structure: The Northern Chesapeake in the Eighteenth Century," *Journal of Economic History*, XXV (1965), 650; Isaac, *Transformation of Virginia*, 133; East, *Business Enterprise*, 19; Robert D. Mitchell, *Commercialism and Frontier: Perspectives on the Early Shenandoah Valley* (Charlottesville: University Press of Virginia, 1977), 116, 123.

71. John Adams to James Warren, February 12, 1777, in Robert J. Taylor et al., eds., *Papers of John Adams* (Cambridge, MA: Belknap Press of Harvard University Press, 1983), V, 83; Riesman, "Origins of American Political Economy," 135–136, 144; Norman K. Risjord, *Chesapeake Politics, 1781–1800* (New York: Columbia University Press, 1978), 124; George Washington to Governor George Clinton, April 20, 1785, to Battaile Muse, December 4, 1785, in Fitzpatrick, ed., *Writings of Washington*, XXVIII, 134, 341; Carey, ed., *Debates*, 96.

72. Roy A. Foulke, *The Sinews of American Commerce* (New York: Dun & Bradstreet, 1941), 66–68, 74–75, 89; William E. Nelson, *Americanization of the Common Law: The Impact of Legal Change on Massachusetts Society, 1760–1830* (Cambridge, MA: Harvard University Press, 1975), 44–45. For a sensitive analysis of the Virginia planters' etiquette of debt, see T. H. Breen, *Tobacco Culture: The Mentality of the Great Tidewater Planters on the Eve of the Revolution* (Princeton: Princeton University Press, 1985), esp. 93–106.

73. Grundfest, *Clymer*, 177; *Providence Gazette*, August 5, 1786, quoted in David P. Szatmary, *Shays' Rebellion: The Making of an Agrarian Insurrection* (Amherst: University of Massachusetts Press, 1980), 51; Madison, "Notes for Speech Opposing Paper Money" [November 1, 1786], in Hutchinson et al., eds., *Papers of Madison*, IX, 158–159; Taylor, *Western Massachusetts*, 166.

74. Farrand, ed., *Records of the Federal Convention*, II, 310, III, 350.

75. Ruth Bogin, "New Jersey's True Policy: The Radical Republican Vision of Abraham Clark," *William and Mary Quarterly*, 3rd ser., XXXV (1978), 105.

76. David Ramsay, "An Address to the Freemen of South Carolina on the Subject of the Federal Constitution" (1787), in Paul Leicester Ford, ed., *Pamphlets on the Constitution of the United States* (Brooklyn, NY: Historical Printing Club, 1888), 379–380. Madison thought that the Anti-Federalist pamphlets omitted "many of the true grounds of opposition" to the Constitution. "The articles relating to Treaties, to paper money, and to contracts, created more enemies than all the errors in the System positive and negative put together" (James Madison to Thomas Jefferson, October 17, 1788, in Boyd et al., eds., *Papers of Jefferson*, XIV, 18).

77. Benjamin Rush to Jeremy Belknap, February 28, 1788, quoted in John P. Kaminski, "Democracy Run Rampant: Rhode Island in the Confederation," in James Kirby Martin, ed., *The Human Dimensions of Nation Making: Essays on Colonial and Revolutionary History* (Madison: State Historical Society of Wisconsin, 1976), 267; Rush to Elias Boudinot, July 9, 1788, in Butterfield, ed., *Letters of Rush*, I, 471.

CHAPTER 6, THE MAKING OF AMERICAN DEMOCRACY

1. R. R. Palmer, *The Age of the Democratic Revolution: A Political History of Europe and America, 1760–1800*, 2 vols. (Princeton: Princeton University Press, 1959, 1964).

2. Gabriel A. Almond and Sidney Verba, *The Civic Culture: Political Attitudes and Democracy in Five Nations* (Boston: Little, Brown, 1965), 2.

3. James Otis, *Right of the British Colonies Asserted and Proved* (Boston: Edes and Gill, 1764), in Bernard Bailyn, ed., *Pamphlet of the American Revolution, 1750–1776* (Cambridge, MA: Harvard University Press, 1965), 427.

4. Philadelphia *Pennsylvania Gazette*, April 24, 1776.

5. Edward Countryman, *A People in Revolution: The American Revolution and Political Society in New York, 1760–1790* (Baltimore: John Hopkins University Press, 1981), 33.

6. Clifford K. Shipton, "Jonathan Trumbull," in *Sibley's Harvard Graduates: Biographies of Those Who Attended Harvard College* (Boston: Massachusetts Historical Society, 1951), 8: 269.

7. Bernard Bailyn, *The Origins of American Politics* (New York: Knopf, 1968).

8. On the politics of the imperial relationship, see the works by Alison Gilbert Olson, *Anglo-American Politics, 1660–1775: The Relationship Between Parties in England and Colonial America* (New York: Oxford University Press, 1973), and Olson, *Making the Empire Work: London and American Interest Groups, 1690–1790* (Cambridge, MA: Harvard University Press, 1992).

9. On the increasing difficulties of colonial communication in the empire on the eve of the Revolution, see Michael Kammen, *A Rope of Sand: The Colonial Agents, British Politics, and the American Revolution* (Ithaca, NY: Cornell University Press, 1968).

10. Gary B. Nash, "The Transformation of Urban Politics, 1700–1764," *Journal of American History*, LX (1973), 605–632.

11. J. R. Pole, *The Gift of Government: Political Responsibility from the English Restoration to American Independence* (Athens, GA: University of Georgia Press, 1983).

12. *Acts and Resolves, Public and Private, of the Province of Massachusetts Bay* (Boston: Secretary of the Commonwealth, 1878), III, 70.

13. *South Carolina Gazette* (Charleston), May 13, April 29, 1784.

14. Philadelphia *Pennsylvania Evening Post*, July 30, 1776, quoted in David Hawke, *In the Midst of Revolution* (Philadelphia: University of Pennsylvania Press, 1961), 187.

15. Alfred Young, "The Mechanics and the Jeffersonians: New York, 1789–1801," *Labor History*, 5 (1964), 274; Donald H. Stewart, *The Opposition Press of the Federalist Period* (Albany: State University of New York Press, 1969), 389; Richard E. Ellis, *The Jeffersonian Crisis: Courts and Politics in the Young Republic* (New York: Oxford University Press, 1971), 173.

16. Philip Lampi's *Collection of American Election Data, 1787–1825,* for presidential, congressional, gubernatorial, and state legislative elections shows how popular and competitive American politics became during the first two decades of the nineteenth century. In other words, America did not have to wait for Andrew Jackson in order to become democratic. Lampi's *Collection* is available online via the American Antiquarian Society's Web page "A New Nation Votes: American Election Returns, 1787–1825."

17. Harvey Strum, "Property Qualifications and the Voting Behavior in New York, 1807–1816," *Journal of the Early Republic*, I (1981), 359.

18. Chilton Williamson, *American Suffrage: From Property to Democracy, 1760–1860* (Princeton: Princeton University Press, 1960); and Alexander Keyssar, *The Right to Vote: The Contested History of Democracy in the United States* (New York: Basic Books, 2000). Many states continued to maintain taxpaying requirements for voting.

19. James Madison to George Washington, April 16, 1787, in Jack N. Rakove, ed., *James Madison: Writings* (New York: Library of America, 1999), 81.

20. Walter R. Fee, *The Transition from Aristocracy to Democracy in New Jersey, 1789–1829* (Somerville, NJ: Somerset Press, 1933), 146; Joseph S. Davis, *Essays in the Earlier History of American Corporations, IV, Eighteenth-Century Business Corporations in the United States* (Cambridge, MA: Harvard University Press, 1917), 321; P. H. Woodward, *One Hundred Years of the Hartford Bank* ... (Hartford: CT: Case, Lockwood & Brainard, 1892), 50.

21. Jeffrey L. Pasley, "Private Access and Public Power: Gentility and Lobbying in the Early Congress," in Kenneth R. Bowling and Donald R. Kennon, eds., *The House and Senate in the 1790s: Petitioning, Lobbying, and the Institutional Development* (Athens: Ohio University Press, 2002), 74–76; Donald J. Ratcliffe, *Party Spirit in a Frontier Republic: Democratic Politics in Ohio, 1793–1821* (Columbus: Ohio State University Press, 1998), 79; Donald Hickey, *The War of 1812* (Urbana: University of Illinois Press, 1980), 122.

22. Strum, "Property Qualifications and the Voting Behavior in New York, 1807–1816," *Journal of the Early Republic*, I (1981), 350, 369.

23. Samuel Shapiro, " 'Aristocracy, Mud, and Vituperation': The Butler-Dana Campaign," *New England Quarterly*, XXXI (1958), 340–360.

24. Arthur Zilversmit, *The First Emancipation: The Abolition of Slavery in the North* (Chicago: University of Chicago Press, 1967), 222.

25. Leon F. Litwack, *North of Slavery: The Negro in the Free States, 1790–1860* (Chicago: University of Chicago Press, 1961), 75.

26. James M. McPherson, "The Ballot and Land for the Freedman, 1861–1865," in Kenneth M, Stampp and Leon F. Litwack, eds., *Reconstruction: An Anthology of Revisionist Writings* (Baton Rouge: Louisiana State University Press, 1969), 138.

27. *New York Times*, September 8, 2010.

28. Chilton Williamson, *American Suffrage from Property to Democracy, 1760–1860* (Princeton: Princeton University Press, 1960), 279.

CHAPTER 7, THE RADICALISM OF THOMAS JEFFERSON AND THOMAS PAINE CONSIDERED

1. Thomas Paine, *The Rights of Man: Part the Second* (1792), in Philip S. Foner, ed., *The Complete Writings of Thomas Paine* (New York: Citadel, 1969), I, 405–406; Thomas Jefferson to Thomas Paine,

March 18, 1801, in Barbara Oberg et al., eds., *The Papers of Thomas Jefferson* (Princeton: Princeton University Press, 2006), 33, 359.

2. Marquis de Chastellux, *Travels in North America in the Years 1780, 1781 and 1782*, Howard C. Rice, ed. (Chapel Hill: University of North Carolina Press, 1963), 2, 391.

3. John Keane, *Tom Paine: A Political Life* (Boston: Little, Brown, 1995), 211.

4. S. W. Jackman, "A Young Englishman Reports on the New Nation: Edward Thornton, to James Bland Burges, 1791–1893," *William and Mary Quarterly*, XVIII (1961), 110.

5. Thomas Jefferson, "A Summary View of the Rights of British Colonists (1774)," in Julian P. Boyd et al., eds., *The Papers of Thomas Jefferson* (Princeton: Princeton University Press, 1950–), I, 134.

6. Thomas Paine, *Common Sense* (1776), in Foner, ed., *Complete Writings of Thomas Paine*, I, 23.

7. Thomas Paine, "The Crisis Extraordinary," October 4, 1780, in Foner, ed., *Complete Writings*, I, 182.

8. Thomas Paine, *The Rights of Man: Part the Second* (1792), in Foner, ed., *Complete Writings*, I, 363; Thomas Jefferson to T. Law, June 13, 1814, in A. A. Lipscomb and Albert Ellery Bergh, eds., *The Writings of Thomas Jefferson* (Washington, DC: Thomas Jefferson Memorial Association, 1903), XIV, 141–142; Thomas Jefferson to Peter Carr, August 12, 1787, in Boyd et al., eds., *Papers of Jefferson*, XII, 15.

9. Thomas Paine, *Common Sense*, in Foner, ed., *Complete Writings*, I, 4.

10. Jonathan Mayhew, *Seven Sermons upon the Following Subjects . . .* (Boston: Alden Bradford, 1749), 126.

11. Thomas Paine, *The Rights of Man: Part the Second* (1792), in Foner, ed., *Complete Writings*, I, 357.

12. Ibid., 359.

13. Ibid., 355.

14. Ibid., 373; Thomas Jefferson to Governor John Langdon, March 5, 1810, in Merrill D. Peterson, ed., *Thomas Jefferson: Writings* (New York: Library of America, 1984), 1221.

15. Thomas Paine, *The Rights of Man: Part the Second*, in Foner, ed., *Complete Writings*, I, 355–356.

16. [Benjamin Lincoln Jr.], "The Free Republican No. III," Boston *Independent Chronicle*, December 8, 1785.

17. Thomas Paine, *The Rights of Man: Part the Second*, in Foner, ed., *Complete Writings*, I, 400.

18. Thomas Jefferson to Joseph Fey, March 18, 1793, in Boyd et al., eds., *Papers of Jefferson*, XXV, 402; Thomas Jefferson to William Short, January 3, 1793, in Peterson, ed., *Jefferson: Writings*, 1004; Thomas Jefferson to Tench Coxe, May 1, 1794, in Boyd et al., eds., *Papers of Jefferson*, XXVIII, 67.

19. Alexander Hamilton to Rufus King, June 3, 1802, in Joanne B. Freeman, ed., *Alexander Hamilton: Writings* (New York: Library of America, 2001), 993; Alexander Hamilton, "Views on the French Revolution (1794)," Harold C. Syrett et al., eds., *The Papers of Alexander Hamilton* (New York: Columbia University Press, 1962–), XXVI, 739–740.

20. Alexander Hamilton, "Views on the French Revolution (1794)," Syrett et al., eds., *Papers of Alexander Hamilton*, 739–740; Alexander Hamilton to Rufus King, June 3, 1802, in Freeman, ed., *Hamilton: Writings*, 993.

21. Thomas Paine, *The Rights of Man: Part the Second*, in Foner, ed., *Complete Writings*, I, 408.

22. Thomas Jefferson to William Plumer, July 21, 1816, in Lipscomb and Bergh, eds., *Writings of Jefferson*, XV, 46–47.

23. Thomas Paine, *The Age of Reason* (1794), in Eric Foner, ed., *Thomas Paine: Collected Writings* (New York: Library of America, 1995), 825; Thomas Jefferson to Horatio Spafford, March 17, 1814, Thomas Jefferson to James Smith, December 8, 1822, in James H. Hutson, ed., *The Founders on Religion: A Book of Quotations* (Princeton: Princeton University Press, 2005), 68, 218; Thomas Jefferson to Charles Clay, January 29, 1815, in Lipscomb and Bergh, eds., *Writings of Jefferson*, XIV, 233.

24. Thomas Paine to Henry Laurens, September 14, 1779, in Foner, ed., *Complete Writings of Paine*, II, 1178.

25. Ibid.; Thomas Paine to Robert Livingston, May 19, 1783, quoted in Keane, *Paine*, 242.

26. Thomas Jefferson to James Madison, October 18, 1785, in Peterson, ed., *Jefferson: Writings*, 841–842.

27. Thomas Jefferson to Thomas Paine, March 18, 1801, in Boyd et al., eds., *Papers of Jefferson*, XXXIII, 359.

CHAPTER 8, MONARCHISM AND REPUBLICANISM IN EARLY AMERICA

1. Patrick Henry, in Bernard Bailyn, ed., *The Debate on the Constitution* (New York: Library of America, 1993), II, 629, 675.

2. Patrick Henry, in Jonathan Elliot, ed., *The Debates in the Several State Conventions on the Adoption of the Federal Constitution* (Washington, 1854), III, 58, 491.

3. Benjamin Tappan to Henry Knox, April 1787, Henry Knox Papers, Massachusetts Historical Society. (I owe this citation to Brendan McConville.)

4. James Madison, cited in Gordon S. Wood, *The Creation of the American Republic, 1776–1787* (Chapel Hill: University of North Carolina Press, 1969), 410.

5. James Madison to Thomas Jefferson, October 24, 1787, in Julian P. Boyd et al., eds., *The Papers of Thomas Jefferson* (Princeton: Princeton University Press, 1950–), XII, 276.

6. Benjamin Rush, "To ———: Information to Europeans Who Are Disposed to Migrate to the United States," April 16, 1790, L. H. Butterfield, ed., *Letters of Benjamin Rush* (Princeton: Princeton University Press, 1951), II, 556.

7. James Madison, "Vices of the System of the United States," in Hutchinson et al., eds., *Papers of Madison*, IX, 352, 357.

8. Max Farrand, ed., *The Records of the Federal Convention* (New Haven, CT: Yale University Press, 1937), I, 65, 119; II, 513.

9. Thomas Jefferson to David Humphreys, March 18, 1789, in Boyd et al., eds., *Papers of Jefferson*, XIV, 679.

10. Louise B. Dunbar, *A Study of "Monarchical" Tendencies in the United States, from 1776 to 1801* (Urbana: University of Illinois Press, 1923), 99–100.

11. James McHenry to George Washington, March 29, 1789, in W. W. Abbot et al., eds., *Papers of Washington: Presidential Series* (Charlottesville: University Press of Virginia, 1983–), I, 461.

12. Winifred E. A. Bernard, *Fisher Ames: Federalist and Statesman, 1758–1808* (Chapel Hill: University of North Carolina Press, 1965), 92.

13. David W. Robson, *Educating Republicans: The College in the Era of the American Revolution, 1758–1800* (Westport, CT: Greenwood Press, 1985), 149; Thomas E. V. Smith, *The City of New York in the Year of Washington's Inauguration, 1789* (New York: Anson D. F. Randolph, 1889, reprint ed., Riverside, CT, 1972), 217–219; Barry Schwartz, *George Washington: The Making of an American Symbol* (New York: Free Press, 1987).

14. William B. Allen, ed., *George Washington: A Collection* (Indianapolis: Liberty Classics, 1988), 446.

15. Alexander Hamilton to George Washington, May 5, 1789, in Syrett et al., eds., *Papers of Alexander Hamilton*, V, 335–337.

16. John Adams to George Washington, May 17, 1789, in Abbot et al., eds., *Papers of Washington: Presidential Series*, II, 312.

17. James Thomas Flexner, *George Washington and the New Nation (1783–1793)* (Boston: Little, Brown, 1970), 195.

18. Leonard D. White, *The Federalists: A Study in Administrative History* (New York: Greenwood, 1948), 108.

19. David Waldstreicher, *In the Midst of Perpetual Fetes: The Making of American Nationalism, 1776–1820* (Chapel Hill: University of North Carolina Press, 1997), 120–122.

20. George Washington to James Madison, March 30, 1789, in John Rhodehamel, ed., *George Washington: Writings* (New York: Library of America, 1997), 723; John Adams to Benjamin Rush, June 21, 1811, in John A. Schutz and Douglass Adair, eds., *The Spur of Fame: Dialogues of John Adams and Benjamin Rush, 1805–1813* (San Marino, CA: Huntington Library, 1966), 181.

21. Kenneth R. Bowling and Helen E. Veit, eds., *The Diary of William Maclay and Other Notes on Senate Debates: Documentary History of the First Federal Congress of the United States of America, 4 March 1789–3 March 1791* (Baltimore: Johns Hopkins University Press, 1988), IX, 21; Schwartz, *Washington*, 62.

22. Bowling and Veit, eds., *Diary of Maclay*, 21.

23. Page Smith, *John Adams* (New York: Doubleday, 1962), II, 755.

24. Thomas Jefferson to James Madison, July 29, 1789, in Boyd et al., eds., *Papers of Jefferson*, XV, 316.

25. White, *Federalists*, 108.

26. Thomas Jefferson to Spencer Roane, September 6, 1819, in Paul L. Ford, ed., *The Writings of Thomas Jefferson* (New York: G. P. Putnam's Sons, 1899), X, 140.

27. Jefferson, First Annual Message, December 8, 1801, in Merrill Peterson, ed., *Thomas Jefferson: Writings* (New York: Library of America, 1984), 504.

CHAPTER 9, ILLUSIONS OF POWER IN THE AWKWARD ERA OF FEDERALISM

1. Linda K. Kerber, *Federalists in Dissent: Imagery and Ideology in Jeffersonian America* (Ithaca, NY: Cornell University Press, 1970), 1–22.

2. Manning J. Dauer, *The Adams Federalists* (Baltimore: Johns Hopkins University Press, 1953), 241.

3. Alexander Hamilton to Gouverneur Morris, February 29, 1802, Harold C. Syrett and Jacob E. Cooke, eds., *The Papers of Alexander Hamilton* (New York: Columbia University Press, 1961–1967), XXV, 544.

4. James Sterling Young, *The Washington Community, 1800–1828* (New York: Columbia University Press, 1966), 41.

5. The talk of the United States becoming more monarchical in these years was much more prevalent than we have generally admitted. The only significant study we have is Louise Burnham Dunbar, *A Study of "Monarchical" Tendencies in the United States from 1776 to 1801* (New York: Da Capo Press, 1970, [originally published 1922]).

6. Hamilton, Speech at New York Ratifying Convention, June 28, 1788, Syrett et al., eds., *Papers of Hamilton*, V, 118.

7. Alexander Hamilton, quoted in Thomas K. McCraw, "The Strategic Vision of Alexander Hamilton," *American Scholar* (Winter 1994), 40; George Washington to Henry Knox, February 28, 1785, in John C. Fitzpatrick, ed., *The Writings of George Washington* (Washington, DC: U.S. Government Printing Office, 1938), XXVIII, 93.

8. John Brewer, *The Sinews of Power: War, Money and the English State, 1688–1783* (New York: Routledge, 1989).

9. Hamilton, Speech at the New York Ratifying Convention, June 27, 1788, and in *The Continentalist*, no. V, April 18, 1782, in Syrett et al., eds., *Papers of Hamilton*, V, 96; III, 76.

10. Alexander Hamilton to Robert Troup, April 13, 1795, Syrett et al., eds., *Papers of Hamilton*, XVIII, 329; Sir James Steuart (1767), quoted in Stephen Copley, *Literature and the Social Order in Eighteenth-Century England* (London and Dover, NH: Croom Helm, 1984), 120; Alexander Hamilton, "The Defence of the Funding System, July 1795," Syrett et al., eds., *Papers of Hamilton*, XIII, 349.

11. Alexander Hamilton, "Conjectures about the New Constitution," Syrett et al., eds., *Papers of Hamilton*, IV, 276.

12. George Washington, quoted in Leonard D. White, *The Federalists: A Study in Administrative History* (New York: Greenwood, 1948), 404n; Alexander Hamilton, quoted in Richard H. Kohn, *Eagle and Sword: The Federalists and the Creation of the Military Establishment in America, 1783–1802* (New York: Free Press, 1975), 171.

13. Thomas Jefferson to Edmund Pendleton, August 26, 1776, in Julian Boyd et al., eds., *The Papers of Thomas Jefferson* (Princeton: Princeton University Press, 1950–), I, 505.

14. For two revisionist interpretations of the origins of judicial review, see J. M. Sosin, *The Aristocracy of the Long Robe: The Origins of Judicial Review in America* (New York: Greenwood Press, 1989); and Robert L. Clinton, *Marbury v. Madison and Judicial Review* (Lawrence: University Press of Kansas, 1989). For attempts to describe the judicial and legal climates out of which judicial review arose, see Gordon S. Wood, "The Origins of Judicial Review," *Suffolk Law Review*, XXII (1988), 1293–1307; and Wood, "Judicial Review in the Era of the Founding," in Robert Licht, ed., *Is the Supreme Court the Guardian of the Constitution?* (Washington, DC: AEI Press, 1993), 153–166.

15. This is the gist of Lance Banning's book *The Sacred Fire of Liberty: James Madison and the Founding of the Federal Republic* (Ithaca, NY: Cornell University Press, 1995).

16. *The Federalist* No. 10.

17. White, *The Federalists*, 301.

18. George V. Taylor, "Noncapitalist Wealth and the Origins of the French Revolution," *American Historical Review*, LXII (1967), 469–496; William Doyle, *Origins of the French Revolution* (Oxford: Oxford University Press, 1980), 17–18.

19. George Washington to Thomas Johnson, July 20, 1770, Fitzpatrick, ed., *Writings of Washington*, 3:18. On the efforts of some Boston gentry to set themselves up as country farmers, georgic style, see Tamara Platkins Thornton, *Cultivating Gentlemen: The Meaning of Country Life Among the Boston Elite, 1785–1860* (New Haven, CT: Yale University Press, 1989).

20. Samuel Eliot Morison, ed., "William Manning's *The Key of Liberty*," *William and Mary Quarterly*, 3rd ser., XIII (1956), 202–254.

21. Merrill Peterson, ed., *Democracy, Liberty, and Property: The State Constitutional Conventions of the 1820s* (Indianapolis: Bobbs-Merrill, 1966), 79–82. On the new democratic understanding of property as the product of labor, see Alan Taylor, *Liberty Men and Great Proprietors: The Revolutionary Settlement on the Maine Frontier, 1760–1820* (Chapel Hill: University of North Carolina Press, 1990), 25, 28.

22. Although Michael Merrill and Sean Wilentz have recently tried to portray Manning as someone opposed to capitalism, they admit that he was no "injured little yeoman" uninvolved in a commercial economy. He was more than a farmer in his little developing town of Billerica; he was as well an improver and a small-time entrepreneurial hustler. He ran a tavern off and on, erected a saltpeter works making gunpowder during the Revolutionary War, helped build a canal, bought and sold land, constantly borrowed money, and urged the printing of money by state-chartered banks, seeking (not very successfully, it seems) every which way to better his and his family's condition. By themselves Manning's commercial activities may not have been much, but multiply them many thousandfold throughout the society and we have the makings of an expanding capitalist economy. Michael Merrill and Sean Wilentz, eds., *The Key of Liberty: The Life and Democratic Writings of William Manning, "A Laborer," 1747–1814* (Cambridge, MA: Harvard University Press, 1993), 31–32.

23. Cathy Matson and Peter Onuf, "Toward a Republican Empire: Interest and Ideology in Revolutionary America," *American Quarterly*, XXXVII (1985), 496–531. Fanny Wright, in her *Views of Society and Manners in America*, Paul R. Baker, ed. (Cambridge, MA: Harvard University Press, 1963), 208, used the same phrase to describe American society a generation later. Although Hamilton's "Report on Manufactures" suggests that he understood the importance of domestic trade, in fact, as John R. Nelson has argued, he never fully appreciated nor supported the interests of manufacturers and those involved in domestic commerce. Insofar as he supported manufacturing, it was the manufacturing of goods for export. John R. Nelson Jr., *Liberty and Property: Political Economy and Policymaking in the New Nation, 1789–1812* (Baltimore: John Hopkins University Press, 1987), 37–51.

24. As John E. Crowley has shown, Americans were not very good students of Adam Smith: they tended to ignore his support for domestic trade over foreign trade and remained mercantilists a lot longer than the British; that is to say, they "slight[ed] or countermand[ed] the imperatives of market relations in the name of political imperatives." John E. Crowley, *The Privileges of Independence: Neomercantilism and the American Revolution* (Baltimore: Johns Hopkins University Press, 1993), xii–xiii, 133, 207.

25. Bray Hammond, *Banks and Politics in America from the Revolution to the Civil War* (Princeton: Princeton University Press, 1957), 126–127.

26. Joyce Appleby, *Capitalism and a New Social Order: The Republican Vision of the 1790s* (New York: New York University Press, 1984).

27. John R. Nelson, "Alexander Hamilton and American Manufacturing: A Reexamination," *Journal of American History*, LXV (1979), 971–995.

28. Jack P. Greene, *The Intellectual Construction of America: Exceptionalism and Identity from 1492 to 1800* (Chapel Hill: University of North Carolina Press, 1993), 189.

29. E. H. Smith, *A Discourse Delivered April 11, 1798 . . .* , quoted in Duncan J. MacLeod, *Slavery, Race and the American Revolution* (Cambridge, UK: Cambridge University Press, 1974), 29.

30. On "garrison governments," see the work of Stephen Saunders Webb (who coined the term) especially *The Governors-General: The English Army and the Definition of Empire, 1569–1681* (Chapell Hill: University of North Carolina Press, 1979).

31. Eugene Perry Link, *Democratic-Republican Societies, 1790–1800* (New York: Columbia University Press, 1942), 136–137. Jefferson had a very relaxed idea of the modern state and was never worried about Americans leaving the territorial boundaries of the United States. He always conceived of his "empire of liberty" as one of like principles, not like boundaries—similar to the way some eighteenth-century German and Italian intellectuals conceived of their nations. As long as Americans believed certain things, they remained Americans, regardless of the territorial boundaries of the government they happened to be in. At times he was remarkably indifferent to the possibility that a western confederacy might break away from the eastern United States. What did it matter? he asked in 1804. "Those of the western confederacy will be as much our children and descendents as those of

the eastern." Thomas Jefferson to Dr. Joseph Priestley, January 29, 1804, *Thomas Jefferson: Writings*, Merrill Peterson, ed. (New York: Library of America, 1984), 1142.

32. For some of these illusions about the West, see Andrew R. L. Cayton, *The Frontier Republic: Ideology and Politics in the Ohio Country, 1780–1825* (Kent, OH: Kent State University Press, 1986). "Neither the Federalist not the Republican vision of the future of the Ohio Valley was foolish or naive. The problem with both was that they were inappropriate for the kind of society emerging in Ohio." Ibid., 153.

CHAPTER 10, THE AMERICAN ENLIGHTENMENT

1. Benjamin Rush to Elias Boudinot?, "Observations on the Federal Procession in Philadelphia," July 9, 1788, in L. H. Butterfield, ed., *Letters of Benjamin Rush* (Princeton: American Philosophical Society, 1951), I, 470–475.
2. John Adams, "Dissertation on the Feudal and Canon Law" (1765), in Gordon S. Wood, ed., *The Rising Glory of America, 1760–1820* (New York: George Braziller, 1971), 29.
3. Charles S. Hyneman and George W. Carey, eds., *A Second Federalist: Congress Creates a Government* (New York: Appleton-Century-Crofts, 1967), 24.
4. "Centinel" [Samuel Bryan], in Bernard Bailyn, ed., *The Debate on the Constitution* (New York: Library of America, 1993), I, 686.
5. Allen R. Pred, *Urban Growth and the Circulation of Information: The United States System of Cities, 1790–1840* (Cambridge, MA: Harvard University Press, 1973), 26.
6. Evarts B. Greene, *The Revolutionary Generation, 1763–1790* (New York: Macmillan, 1943), 418; Colin Bonwick, *English Radicals and the American Revolution* (Chapel Hill: University of North Carolina Press, 1977), 13–14; Alan D. McKillop, "Local Attachment and Cosmopolitanism: The Eighteenth-Century Pattern," in Frederick W. Hilles and Harold Bloom, eds., *From Sensibility to Romanticism: Essays Presented to Frederick A. Pottle* (New York: Oxford University Press, 1965), 197; David Ramsay to John Eliot, August 11, 1792, in Robert L. Brunhouse, ed., *David Ramsay . . . Selections from His Writings* (Philadelphia: American Philosophical Society, 1965), 133.
7. Richard Price to Benjamin Franklin, September 17, 1787, Papers of Benjamin Franklin (unpublished).
8. Franco Venturi, *Utopia and Reform in the Enlightenment* (Cambridge, UK: Cambridge University Press, 1971), 133.
9. Julie Richter, "The Impact of the Death of Governor France Fauquier on His Slaves and Their Families," *Colonial Williamsburg Interpreter*, XVIII, no. 3 (Fall 1997), 2.
10. Joel Barlow, *Advice to the Privileged Orders in the Several States of Europe* (1792; repub. Ithaca, NY: Cornell University Press, 1956), 17; Harry C. Payne, *The Philosophes and the People* (New Haven, CT: Yale University, Press, 1976), 7–17.
11. Virginia Ratifying Convention, in John P. Kaminski and Gaspare J. Saladino, eds., *The Documentary History of the Ratification of the Constitution* (Madison: State Historical Society of Wisconsin, 1999), IX, 1044–1045.
12. Hector St. John de Crèvecoeur, *Letters from an American Farmer*, Letter III (New York: Penguin, 1981), 67.
13. Thomas Jefferson to Martha Jefferson, March 28, 1787, in Julian P. Boyd et al., eds., *The Papers of Thomas Jefferson* (Princeton: Princeton University Press, 1950–), XI, 251.
14. Thomas Jefferson to Lafayette, April 11, 1787, in Boyd et al., eds., *Papers of Jefferson*, XI, 285.
15. David Ramsay, *The History of the American Revolution*, Lester H. Cohen, ed. (1789; repub. Indianapolis: Liberty Press, 1989), II, 630.
16. Edwin T. Martin, *Thomas Jefferson: Scientist* (New York: Henry Schuman, 1952), 54.
17. Benjamin Rush, "Of the Mode of Education Proper in a Republic," in Dagobert D. Runes, ed., *The Selected Writings of Benjamin Rush* (New York: Philosophical Library, 1947), 88, 90.
18. Frank L. Mott, *A History of American Journalism in the United States . . . 1690–1940* (New York: Macmillan, 1941), 159, 167; Merle Curti, *The Growth of American Thought*, 3rd ed. (New York: Harper & Row, 1964), 209; Donald H. Stewart, *The Opposition Press of the Federalist Period* (Albany: State University of New York Press, 1969), 15, 624.
19. Thomas Jefferson to Maria Cosway, October 12, 1786, in Boyd et al., eds., *Papers of Jefferson*, X, 447–448.

20. Thomas Paine, *The Rights of Man* (1791), in Philip S. Foner, ed., *The Complete Writings of Thomas Paine* (New York: Citadel, 1969), I, 265–266.

21. Louis P. Masur, *Rites of Execution: Capital Punishment and the Transformation of American Culture, 1776–1865* (New York: Oxford University Press, 1989), 37.

22. Ibid., 77; *American Museum* (March 1970), 137.

23. Masur, *Rites of Execution*, 82.

24. Michael Meranze, *Laboratories of Virtue: Punishment, Revolution, and Authority in Philadelphia, 1760–1835* (Chapel Hill: University of North Carolina Press, 1996), 71; Masur, *Rites of Execution*, 65, 71, 80–82, 87, 88; Adam J. Hirsch, "From Pillory to Penitentiary: The Rise of the Criminal Incarceration in Early Massachusetts," *Michigan Law Review*, LXXX (1982), 1179–1269; Linda Kealey, "Patterns of Punishment: Massachusetts in the Eighteenth Century," *American Journal of Legal History*, XXX (1986), 163–176; Michael Meranze, "The Penitential Ideal in Late Eighteenth-Century Philadelphia," *Pennsylvania Magazine of History and Biography*, 108 (1984), 419–450; Bradley Chapin, "Felony Law Reform in the Early Republic," *Pennsylvania Magazine of History and Biography*, 113 (1989), 163–83.

25. Greene, *Revolutionary Generation*, 80.

26. Rush to Elisabeth Graeme Ferguson, July 16, 1782, in *Letters of Benjamin Rush*, L. H. Butterfield, ed., 280.

27. John Jay, *The Federalist* No. 2.

28. Richard L. Bushman, "American High Style," in Jack P. Greene and J. R. Pole, eds., *Colonial British America: Essays in the New History of the Early Modern Era* (Baltimore: Johns Hopkins University Press, 1984), 371–372.

29. John Witherspoon, "The Druid, No. V," in *The Works of the Rev. John Witherspoon*, 2nd ed. (Philadelphia: W. W. Woodward, 1802), IV, 417.

30. Noah Webster, *Dissertations on the English Language* (Boston: Isaiah Thomas, 1789), 36, 288. See Michael P. Kramer, *Imagining Language in America: From the Revolution to the Civil War* (Princeton: Princeton University Press, 1992).

31. Andrew Burstein, *Sentimental Democracy: The Evolution of America's Romantic Self-Image* (New York: Hill and Wang, 1999), 152.

32. Crèvecoeur, *Letters from an American Farmer*, Letter III, 80.

33. David Ramsay to Benjamin Rush, April 8, 1777, Brunhouse, ed., *Ramsay . . . Selections from His Writings*, 54; Arthur L. Ford, *Joel Barlow* (New York: Twaine, 1971), 31; Paine, *Common Sense*, in Foner, ed., *Writings of Paine*, I, 20.

CHAPTER II, A HISTORY OF RIGHTS IN EARLY AMERICA

1. John Phillip Reid, *Constitutional History of the American Revolution: The Authority of Rights* (Madison: University of Wisconsin Press, 1986), 3.

2. Lois G. Schwoerer, *The Declaration of Rights, 1689* (Baltimore: Johns Hopkins University Press, 1981).

3. Leonard Levy, *Legacy of Suppression: Freedom of Speech and Press in Early American History* (Cambridge, MA: Belknap Press of Harvard University Press, 1960).

4. William Penn, *England's Present Interest Considered* (1675), in Philip B. Kurland and Ralph Lerner, eds., *The Founders' Constitution* (Chicago: University of Chicago Press, 1987), I, 429.

5. Lee, quoted in Bernard Bailyn, *The Ideological Origins of the American Revolution* (Cambridge, MA: Harvard University Press, 1967), 189.

6. Reid, *Constitutional History: Authority of Rights*.

7. Gordon S. Wood, *The Creation of the American Republic, 1776–1787* (Chapel Hill: University of North Carolina Press, 1969), 268–269.

8. James Wilson, *Considerations on the Authority of Parliament* (1774), in Robert G. McCloskey, ed., *Works of James Wilson* (Cambridge, MA: Harvard University Press, 1967), II, 736–737.

9. Gordon S. Wood, *The Radicalism of the American Revolution* (New York: Knopf, 1992), 81.

10. William E. Nelson, *Americanization of the Common Law: The Impact of Legal Change on Massachusetts Society, 1760–1830* (Cambridge, MA: Harvard University Press, 1975), 37–38, 14.

11. William Douglass, *A Summary, Historical and Political, of the First Planting, Progressive Improvements, and Present State of the British Settlements in North America* (Boston London: R. Baldwin, 1749), I, 507.

12. Hendrik Hartog, *Public Property and Private Power: The Corporation of the City of New York in American Law, 1730–1870* (Chapel Hill: University of North Carolina Press, 1983), 62–68.
13. Ronald E. Seavoy, "The Public Service Origins of the American Business Corporation," *Business History Review*, LII (1978), 30–36.
14. Quentin Skinner, *Liberty Before Liberalism* (Cambridge, UK: Cambridge University Press, 1998).
15. John Adams, quoted in Wood, *Creation of the American Republic*, 62–63.
16. Wood, *Radicalism of the American Revolution*, 188.
17. Hartog, *Public Property and Private Power*, 155; Harry N. Scheiber, "The Road to Munn: Eminent Domain and the Concept of Public Purpose in the State Courts," *Perspectives in American History*, V (1971), 363; Horst Dippel, "Human Rights: From Societal Rights to Individual Rights," *Boletim Da Faculdade de Direito*, LXXXIV (Coimbra: Universidade de Coimbra, 2008), 343–348.
18. J. A. C. Grant, "The 'Higher Law' Background of the Law of Eminent Domain," *Wisconsin Law Review*, VI (1930–31), 70; William Michael Treanor, "The Origins and Original Significance of the Just Compensation Clause of the Fifth Amendment," *Yale Law Journal*, XCIV (1985), 694–716.
19. Wood, *Creation of the American Republic*, 410.
20. James Madison, "Vices of the Political System of the United States," April 1787, in Jack N. Rakove, ed., *James Madison: Writings* (New York: Library of America, 1999), 71; James Madison to Thomas Jefferson, October 17, 1788, in Rakove, ed., *Madison: Writings*, 421.
21. Thomas Jefferson, *Notes on the State of Virginia*, William Peden, ed. (Chapel Hill: University of North Carolina Press, 1955), 120.
22. Drew R. McCoy, *The Last of the Fathers: James Madison and the Republican Legacy* (Cambridge, UK: Cambridge University Press, 1989), 115.
23. Jefferson, *Notes on Virginia*, Peden, ed., 121.
24. *The Federalist* No. 71, No. 78, Jacob E. Cooke, ed. (Middletown, CT: Wesleyan University Press, 1961).
25. Lynn W. Turner, *William Plumer of New Hampshire, 1759–1850* (Chapel Hill: University of North Carolina Press, 1962), 34–35.
26. Alexander Hamilton, "Remarks in New York Assembly," February 6, 1787, in Harold C. Syrett et al., eds., *The Papers of Alexander Hamilton* (New York: Columbia University Press, 1961–1967), IV, 35.
27. Edward S. Corwin, "The Doctrine of Due Process of Law Before the Civil War," *Harvard Law Review*, XXIV (1911), 371–372.
28. Edward S. Corwin, "The Basic Doctrine of American Constitutional Law," *Michigan Law Review*, XII (1914), 254.
29. William E. Nelson, "Changing Conceptions of Judicial Review," *University of Pennsylvania Law Review*, CXX (1972), 1176.
30. Philadelphia *Pennsylvania Packet*, September 2, 1786.
31. On this point, see Barry Shain, *Myth of American Individualism: The Protestant Origins of American Political Thought* (Princeton: Princeton University Press, 1994); and Johann N. Neem, "Politics and the Origins of the Nonprofit Corporation in Massachusetts and New Hampshire, 1780–1820," *Nonprofit and Voluntary Sector Quarterly*, XXXII (2003), 344–365.
32. Louis Hartz, *Economic Policy and Democratic Thought: Pennsylvania, 1776–1860* (Cambridge, MA: Harvard University Press, 1948), 292.
33. Pauline Maier, "Revolutionary Origins of the American Corporation," *William and Mary Quarterly*, L (1993), 68–70.
34. Mathew Carey, ed., *Debates and Proceedings of the General Assembly of Pennsylvania . . .* (Philadelphia: Seddon and Pritchard, 1786), 11–12.
35. Hamilton, "The Examination," February 23, 1802, in Syrett et al., eds., *Papers of Hamilton*, XXV, 533.
36. Corwin, "The Basic Doctrine of American Constitutional Law."
37. Debates in the Senate of the United States on the Judiciary During the First Session of the Seventh Congress (Philadelphia: Thomas Smith, 1802), 39. (I owe this citation to Kurt Graham.)
38. R. Kent Newmyer, *Supreme Court Justice Joseph Story: Statesman of the Old Republic* (Chapel Hill: University of North Carolina Press, 1985), 132; Harry N. Scheiber, "Public Rights and the Rule of Law in American Legal History," *California Law Review*, LXXII (1984), 217–251.
39. Neem, "Politics and the Origins of the Nonprofit Corporation in Massachusetts and New Hampshire, 1780–1820," *Nonprofit and Voluntary Sector Quarterly*, XXXII (2003), 358.

40. L. Ray Gunn, *The Decline of Authority: Public Economic Policy and Political Development in New York, 1800–1860* (Ithaca, NY: Cornell University Press, 1988).

41. William J. Novak, *People's Welfare: Law and Regulation in Nineteenth-Century America* (Chapel Hill: University of North Carolina Press, 1996), 15, 88.

42. David Lieberman, *Province of Legislation Determined: Legal Theory in Eighteenth-Century Britain* (Cambridge, UK: Cambridge University Press, 1989).

43. Nelson, *Americanization of the Common Law*, 171–172.

44. *Marbury v. Madison* (1803), William Cranch, ed., *U.S. Supreme Court Reports . . .* (Washington, DC, 1804), 165, 177.

45. George L. Haskins, "Law Versus Politics in the Early Years of the Marshall Court," *University of Pennsylvania Law Review*, CXXX (1981), 19–20.

46. James Madison to George Washington, April 16, 1787, in Robert Rutland et al., eds., *Papers of James Madison* (Chicago: University of Chicago Press, 1975), IX, 384.

INDEX

CREDITS

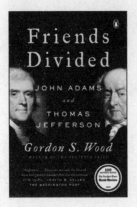  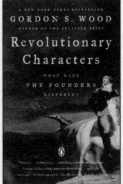
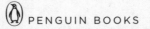